The Interregnum
Controversies In World Politics 1989–1999

CAMBRIDGE
UNIVERSITY PRESS

PUBLISHED BY THE PRESS SYNDICATE OF THE UNIVERSITY OF CAMBRIDGE
The Pitt Building, Trumpington Street, Cambridge, United Kingdom

CAMBRIDGE UNIVERSITY PRESS
The Edinburgh Building, Cambridge CB2 2RU, UK   www.cup.cam.ac.uk
40 West 20th Street, New York, NY 10011-4211, USA   www.cup.org
10 Stamford Road, Oakleigh, Melbourne 3166, Australia
Ruiz de Alarcón 13, 28104 Madrid, Spain

First published 1999

Printed in the United Kingdom by Henry Ling Ltd at the
Dorset Press, Dorchester, Dorset

A catalogue record for this book is available from the British Library

Library of Congress Cataloguing in Publication data applied for

ISBN 0 521 78509 X paperback

The Interregnum: Controversies in World Politics 1989–1999

CONTENTS

Acknowledgements   v

Foreword   vii
CHRISTOPHER J. HILL

Notes on contributors   1

Introduction   3
MICHAEL COX, KEN BOOTH and TIM DUNN

Historical Perspectives
1. The Rise and Fall of the Cold War in Comparative Perspective   21
    RICHARD NED LEBOW
2. History Ends, World Collide   41
    CHRIS BROWN
3. Globalization and National Governance: Antinomies or Interdependence?   59
    LINDA WEISS
4. Beyond Westphalia?: Capitalism after the 'Fall'   89
    BARRY BUZAN and RICHARD LITTLE

Contending Visions
5. The Potentials of Enlightenment   105
    FRED HALLIDAY
6. Marxism after Communism   127
    ANDREW GAMBLE
7. Liberalism Since the Cold War: An Enemy to Itself?   145
    GEOFFREY HAWTHORN
8. Clausewitz Rules, OK? The Future is the Past—with GPS   161
    COLIN GRAY

Geopolitical Landscapes
9. Mission Impossible? The IMF and the Failure of the Market Transition
    in Russia   183
    PETER RUTLAND

10. Europe after the Cold War: Interstate Order or post-Sovereign Regional System?   201
    WILLIAM WALLACE
11. Where is the Third World Now?   225
    CAROLINE THOMAS
12. Whatever Happened to the Pacific Century?   245
    ROSEMARY FOOT and ANDREW WALTER
13. Still the American Century   271
    BRUCE CUMINGS

    Index   301

ACKNOWLEDGEMENTS

This is the second Special Issue of the *Review of International Studies* that is appearing as a book in its own right. Our first venture in this field—'The Eighty Years Crisis: International Relations, 1919–1999'—has done very well indeed and has expanded the range of our readers well beyond those subscribing to the Journal. The experiment therefore has been a success and hopefully with the appearance of 'The Interregnum: Controversies in World Politics, 1989–1999' we will achieve our objective once more of bringing the work of serious scholars engaged in the analysis of international politics to a much wider audience. All collective intellectual efforts accumulate a series of individual debts and this one is no exception. First, the editors would want to extend their very great thanks to all their friends and colleagues at Cambridge University Press, in particular to Sue Belo, Michael Cook, Gwenda Edwards, John Haslam, Patrick McCartan and Kate Wain. Without their support, encouragement and expertise this particular experiment in publishing might never have left the 'lab'. Gratitude too is extended to Christopher Hill, current Chair of the British International Studies Association, not only for writing a very generous foreword to this volume but for his wise counsel and advice. A great debt is also owed to Steve Smith of the Department of International Politics at Aberystwyth for continuing to provide the editorial team with all the resources they needed, and more. Thanks must be extended as well to those various scholars—Robert Keohane, Fritz Kratwochwil, Mike Mastanduno, Craig Murphy, Jim Rosenau, Joel Rosenthal, Georg Sorensen and Ole Waever—who read the manuscript before it went to press. Finally, a very special word of tribute to Fiona Stephen, the editorial assistant of the Review, for all her hard work and dedicated commitment over the past year.

Michael Cox, Ken Booth and Tim Dunne

November 19th, 1999,
Aberystwyth,
Wales.

FOREWORD

Good journals attract good contributors. They also come up with good ideas for special issues, and thereby help to lead debate as well as reflect it. *The Review of International Studies* has now consolidated the breakthrough made by last year's special issue on 'the Eighty Years Crisis' of International Relations, by producing another collection of essays around a big theme which transcends the various specialisms and sub-divisions of the profession.

Here the big theme is the nature of the international system after the end of the Cold War. Historians might say that it is too early to tell what structural changes (if any) might have been brought about by the dramatic events of 1989–91, but other social scientists will not be discouraged from analytical speculation, bearing in mind that if Chou En Lai was right about even 200 years being insufficient to judge the impact of the French Revolution, we may as well chance our arm right from the start. A diverse and distinguished group of contributors has been brought together by the editors—themselves noted authorities on the Cold War and its aftermath—to deal with all the major aspects of the problem, geographical and thematic.

A particularly interesting strand running through all the articles in this collection is the way in which the end of the Cold War raises issues at all levels: for the state system, for world society, for the international political economy/global capitalism, and for the domestic affairs of particular countries. Yet this sense of inter-connectedness does not impose either a rigid notion of system-dominance, whereby change is seen to flow mainly from upheavals in big power relations, or a fuzzy holism in which the distinctions between structures and agents, states and system, domestic and international become lost. Conversely, the 'open' nature of the approach means that the future of liberal or Marxist ideas can be discussed in relation both to the global *geist* and to particular states like Russia. There is no sense of intellectual incarceration in the useful but ultimately academic distinctions between subjects like International Relations, comparative politics or political theory.

In this, the current collection lives up to the traditions and the title of the Journal, which reviews international studies from an eclectic and interdisciplinary standpoint. There can be no doubt that anyone with 'international' interests, whether historian, theorist, strategist, economist or regional specialist, will find something to compel their interest here. We may be disoriented by the end of the Cold War, even after ten years, but there is every chance of finding some marker-posts, both practical and conceptual, in this splendid special issue which marks the turn of our millennia.

Christopher J. Hill
Chair, British International Studies Association
September, 1999

NOTES ON CONTRIBUTORS

Chris Brown is Professor of International Relations at the London School of Economics and Political Science.

Ken Booth is E.H. Carr Professor of International Politics at the University of Wales, Aberystwyth.

Barry Buzan is Research Professor of International Studies at the University of Westminster.

Michael Cox is Professor of International Politics at the University of Wales, Aberystwyth.

Bruce Cumings is Norman and Edna Freehling Professor of History at the University of Chicago.

Tim Dunne is Senior Lecturer in International Politics at the University of Wales, Aberystwyth.

Rosemary Foot is Professor of International Relations at Oxford University.

Andrew Gamble is Professor of Politics at the University of Sheffield.

Colin Gray is Professor of International Politics at the University of Hull.

Fred Halliday is Professor of International Relations at the London School of Economics and Political Science.

Geoffrey Hawthorn is Professor of International Politics at Cambridge University.

Richard Ned Lebow is Director of the Mershon Center, Ohio State University.

Richard Little is Professor of International Politics at the University of Bristol.

Peter Rutland is Professor in the Department of Government, Wesleyan University, USA.

Caroline Thomas is Professor of Global Politics at the University of Southampton.

1

William Wallace (Lord Wallace of Saltaire) is Professor of International Relations at the London School of Economics and Political Science.

Andrew Walter is Reader in International Relations at the London School of Economics and Political Science.

Linda Weiss is Associate Professor in Comparative Politics at the University of Sydney.

Introduction:
The Interregnum: controversies in world politics, 1989–99

MICHAEL COX, KEN BOOTH AND TIM DUNNE

The shock waves of what happened in 1989 and after helped make the 1990s a peculiarly interesting decade, and while all periods in history are by definition special, there was something very special indeed about the years following the collapse of the socialist project in the former USSR and Eastern Europe. Unfortunately, this has not been reflected in the theoretical literature. Thus although there have been many books on the end of the Cold War,[1] even more on the 'new' history of the Cold War itself,[2] and several on the current state of international relations after the 'fall',[3] there has been relatively little work done so far on the landscape of the new international system in formation. Moreover, while there have been several post-Cold War controversies and debates—we think here of Fukuyama's attempt to theorize the end of history,[4] Mearsheimer's realist reflections on the coming disorder in Europe,[5] the various attempts to define the American mission without a Soviet enemy,[6] and Huntington's prediction about a coming clash of civilizations[7]—not much serious effort has been made to bring these various discussions together in one single volume. This is precisely what we set out to do here in the thirteen assembled essays, written by a variety of international experts. The editors have not attempted to impose a common conceptual framework, let alone suggest there is a single way of thinking about the years after 1989; and this is reflected in our choice of a suitably 'transitional' term designed to try and encap-

---

[1] Studies in this genre have assumed one of two forms: either detailed reconstructions of what happened in 1989 and after, or more analytical work on the implications of the end of the Cold War for international relations theory. The end of the Cold War has also generated a good amount of memoir writing, most of it useful enough but all designed to serve the purposes of the individual in question. Even spies and members of the intelligence services have felt the need (financial or otherwise) to rewrite history and tell it how 'it really was'. For an example see Markus Wolf, *Man Without A Face: The Autobiography of Communism's Greatest Spymaster* (London: Jonathan Cape, 1997) and Robert Gates, *From the Shadows: the Ultimate Insider's Story of Five Presidents and How They Won the Cold War* (New York: Touchstone Books, 1997).

[2] See the publications of *The Cold War International History Project* produced by the Woodrow Wilson International Centre for Scholars, Washington DC.

[3] One example amongst many is Michael W. Doyle and G. John Ikenberry (eds.), *New Thinking in International Relations Theory* (Boulder CO: Westview Press, 1997).

[4] See Francis Fukuyama, 'The End Of History?', *The National Interest*, 16 (Summer 1989), pp. 3–18.

[5] See John Mearsheimer, 'Back to the Future: Instability in Europe after the Cold War', *International Security*, 15:1 (1990), pp. 5–56.

[6] For one of the latest efforts see Richard N. Haass, *The Reluctant Sheriff: The United States After the Cold War* (New York: A Council On Foreign Relations Book, 1997).

[7] Samuel Huntington, 'The Clash of Civilizations?' *Foreign Affairs*, 72:3 (Summer 1993), pp. 22–49. Huntington later dropped the question-mark. See his *The Clash of Civilizations and the Remaking of World Order* (New York: Simon & Schuster, 1996).

sulate the character of the decade: the 'interregnum'.[8] We might have employed a different word or none at all.[9] But in the end, it was felt that the idea of an interregnum as a space between one era and another at least captured something about the ill-defined and almost impossible-to-define character of the last ten years. As we noted in a previous volume, while we might know what our modern era is not—it is not a Cold War—we are not at all sure what it is, or where it might be leading to.[10]

That said, there are a number of themes that deserve special mention here. One is the extent to which world politics has actually changed since the great crashes of 1989 and 1991. While most of the contributors agree that the world will never be the same again—that we now live for the first time since 1917 in a more open international system dominated by market relations—there is also a recognition that many things might not have altered at all. Thus, while sovereignty is under challenge (especially in Western Europe) the institution of the state remains more or less intact, in spite of various predictions about its decline and imminent demise in a world without major wars or borders.[11] There is also continued inequality and vast disparities of wealth; if anything the gap between the 'haves' and the 'have nots' is getting wider. The United States moreover remains the dominant power,[12] more so than ever since the fall of the USSR, the economic crisis in Asia Pacific and the perceived failure by the European Union to intervene with any degree of credibility in former Yugoslavia. Finally, states continue to act in ways which assume the possibility (no more) of future conflict. The landscape in 1999 may look very different to 1989, but there are still some very familiar landmarks.

A second set of issues revolves around the dynamics of globalization. Not all analysts subscribe to the notion. Indeed, there has been something of an intellectual backlash against the idea of late.[13] But it is difficult to avoid: in some respects, it has almost become the common sense of our time, provoking a series of critically important debates about the degree to which it has made national politics irrelevant,[14] the extent to which it has altered international relations as a discipline,[15] and whether or not it has benefited the larger cause of humanity. There are no neat formulaic answers provided to any of these problems in these essays. Overall,

---

[8] The dictionary definition of an 'interregnum' is a 'period of temporary authority exercised during a vacancy of the throne or a suspension of the usual government; the interval between the close of a king's reign and the accession of a successor; a cessation of or suspension of the usual ruling power'. See *The Shorter Oxford English Dictionary* (Oxford: Clarendon Press, 1973), p. 1099.

[9] E. H. Carr used the idea of an 'interregnum' to describe the period of transition between one phase of the Soviet story shaped by Lenin, and the next that was to be dominated by Stalin. The interregnum was in his view 'a marking of time', during which where there was an 'uneasy balance' between contending forces, ideas and personalities. By definition, it could not last, and according to Carr, it did not outlive the summer of 1924 and Lenin's death. See his *A History of Soviet Russia: The Interregnum 1923–1924* (Harmonsworth: Penguin Books, 1954; 1969), esp. pp. 349–73.

[10] See Tim Dunne, Michael Cox and Ken Booth (eds.) *The Eighty Years' Crisis: International Relations, 1919–1939* (Cambridge: Cambridge University Press, 1998), p. xiii.

[11] See Martin van Creveld, *The Rise and Decline of the State* (Cambridge: Cambridge University Press, 1999).

[12] For one, among many, who predicted otherwise see Steven Schlosstein, *The End of the American Century* (Chicago: Congdon and Weed, 1989).

[13] See Paul Hirst and Grahame Thompson, *Globalization in Question* (Oxford: Oxford University Press, 1996).

[14] See David Armstrong, 'Globalization and the Social State', *Review of International Studies,* 24:4 (1998), pp. 461–78.

[15] See Ian Clark, 'Beyond the Great Divide: Globalization and the Theory of International Relations', *Review of International Studies,* 24:4 (October 1998), pp. 479–98.

however, the consensus seems to be that while certain parts of the world like Western Europe and the United States have done rather well out of globalization, others, like Russia and the less developed countries, have suffered badly. The IMF in particular emerges from the various narratives here as one of the more influential, but most criticized of post-Cold War institutions, primarily because it has rigidly attempted to impose a neoliberal agenda on countries that were not ready for it, and whose position therefore has been made worse as a result. And while hardly anybody can see an alternative to the so-called 'Washington consensus', there remains a great deal of generalized discontent with the way in which the world's economy is currently being managed.

This brings us to a third issue: the fate of liberalism. In 1989, it was the American policymaker *cum* political theorist Francis Fukuyama who noted that the great ideological battles of the past had come to an end, and that individualism had finally won the war against its collectivist enemies on both the left and the right.[16] History in this particular sense had turned an important corner, and while the future might not be quite so exciting or enervating, it would at least be liberal.[17] This is not a view shared by all the contributors. On the other hand, it is not one which some of them dismiss as lightly as Fukuyama's many early critics. Several of the authors in fact express more than a passing sympathy with his way of defining the problem, without necessarily agreeing with his philosophical method (based as it is on a combination of Hegel and Kojeve) or his triumphal conclusions. But even those who would accept his general thesis believe he leaves too much out: the propensity of certain states to go to war, the potent force of nationalism and identity,[18] and the darker, less humane side of the whole liberal economic project. Liberalism might have helped shape the last ten years in ways that would have once been thought unlikely; it remains to be seen how future generations will view its achievements.

This leads us logically to the fourth theme: the intellectual and political consequences flowing from the failure of 'actually existing socialism'. The collapse of Soviet power was not just of strategic significance: it was also one of the great ideological events of the twentieth century, even of the last two hundred years. The reasons for this are not difficult to fathom. As the most serious alternative to capitalism—its 'other' if you like—Soviet communism helped define what the 'West' was and who 'we' were as individuals. Hence, its implosion was bound to have massive consequences. Moreover, because the fate of Marxism and what some have termed the modernist project was bound up with the existence of the Soviet Union, when the latter fell apart it inevitably altered the way people viewed the world around them. To some it signalled the end of hope, for others the final denouement of all grand universal narratives, and for a few the belief that society was moving in a 'comprehensive rational direction'.[19] However we read it, the impact of what

---

[16] Fukuyama later clarified his argument by noting that he did not think that 'today's stable democracies' were 'without injustice or serious social problems' but rather that 'the *ideal* of liberal democracy could not be improved upon'. See his *The End of History and the Last Man* (New York: The Free Press, 1992), p. xi.

[17] For an extended discussion on the nature of liberalism see Andrew Moravcsik, 'A Liberal Theory of International Politics', *International Organization,* 51:4 (1997), pp. 513–53.

[18] For a realist look at ethnicity and war in the post-Cold War era see the essays grouped together under the collective heading ' Ethnic Nationalism, Conflict and War', *International Security,* 21:2 (1996), pp. 5–138.

[19] See Hermione Martins, 'Technology, Modernity, Politics', in James Good and Irving Velody (eds.), *The Politics of PostModernity* (Cambridge: Cambridge University Press, 1998), p. 173.

happened in the first workers' state—where planning rather than profit shaped choices and determined outcomes—could not be anything but profound. The future, it was argued, had been tried and failed, leaving the world (or so we were informed) without a serious systemic alternative to liberal capitalism.[20]

A final, more implicit, theme relates to the problem of uncertainty and the extent to which we can ever really know what lies round the corner. None but the most avid positivist would pretend to be able to predict in any exact fashion.[21] On the other hand, the extent to which the various experts failed to come close to anticipating some of the key events of the 1990s is a little worrying. Who, in 1991, for example, would have predicted that Saddam would still be in power eight years later? Who, in addition, foresaw the peace process in Northern Ireland? The financial crash in Russia? The longest boom in America's economic history? Nelson Mandela as President of South Africa? Ethnic cleansing in Europe? Japan's swift transformation from global economic superpower to financial cripple? And NATO being used as an instrument of military humanitarianism in a part of Yugoslavia? The list could go on, but the answer is obvious: no one—or at least hardly anybody of significance.[22] The point is not a rhetorical one, but a serious reminder that history has a rare knack of playing tricks on people, increasingly so in this age of the unexpected where the old rules of the game appear to have been torn up and the new ones are still being written. It is a reminder too that what today might seem obvious will tomorrow look foolish, and what yesterday seemed too fantastic could in a very short space of time become commonplace. If we learn no other 'lesson' from the last ten years of the twentieth century, it is that we rule out the unlikely at our peril. The past has been full of 'radical surprises'.[23] No doubt the future will be too.

The notion of uncertainty is one we need to keep in mind as we reflect upon the rise and fall of the Cold War, the subject of Ned Lebow's opening contribution. Born out of the debris left behind by the Second World War, the conflict by the 1980s had almost assumed an air of permanency. Indeed, while Ronald Reagan spoke the language of communist rollback and talked optimistically about consigning the USSR to the dustbin of history, historians like John Gaddis ruminated in true Waltzian fashion about the peaceful and presumably beneficent character of the Cold War as a bipolar system.[24] Imagine the consternation therefore when this carefully constructed, and now intellectually respectable edifice, began to show signs of wear and tear and finally came tumbling down in the latter half of the 1980s. Ten years on, one might be forgiven for thinking it was all but inevitable: that the attractive pull of capitalism on the one side and the decrepitude of Soviet planning on the other, made its collapse a foregone conclusion.[25] But that is not how it

---

[20] In 1990 the novelist Salman Rushdie noted that 'we may be heading towards a world in which there will be no alternative to the liberal-capitalist social model'. In Alex Callinicos, *The Revenge of History: Marxism and the East European Revolutions* (Cambridge: Polity Press, 1991), p. 11.

[21] For an illuminating discussion of this issue see Michael Nicholson, *Causes and Consequences in International Relations* (London: Pinter, 1996), pp. 30–53.

[22] See Moises Nam 'Editor's Note', *Foreign Policy*, 110 (Spring 1998), p. 9.

[23] See Ken Booth, 'International Relations Theory vs. The Future', in Ken Booth and Steve Smith (eds.), *International Relations Theory Today* (Pennsylvania: The Pennsylvania State University Press, 1995), p. 329.

[24] John L. Gaddis, 'The Long Peace: Elements of Stability in the Postwar International System', *International Security*, 10:4 (Spring 1986), pp. 99–142.

[25] For a discussion of why Soviet collapse was not economically inevitable, but the result of Gorbachev's failed attempts to reform the system, see Michael Ellman and Vladimir Kontorovich (eds.), *The Disintegration of the Soviet Economic System* (London: Routledge, 1992).

seemed at the time. Having got used to the Cold War most writers (and policy-makers) were intellectually incapable of seeing beyond it.[26]

Lebow, however, is less concerned with our failure to see the end of the Cold War coming and more about the way in which we think about the superpower competition in history. The Cold War, he notes, was not a fixed entity but an evolving relationship which led the US and the USSR from the deep freeze of the immediate postwar years to the era of superpower détente in the 1970s. To this extent at least the conflict was already in a state of metamorphosis, even before Gorbachev came to power.[27] It would be more useful therefore to see the changes after 1985 not as a sudden break in an otherwise unrelieved history of hostility but instead as the last stage in a long process of accommodation that had been underway, albeit with fits and starts, for several decades. Certainly, there is little evidence to suggest the Cold War came to a sudden end as a result of renewed US pressure.[28]

But what was the Cold War? What was it all about? Lebow compares and contrasts four of the contending explanations: a realist one that views it as another phase in an unending and unchanging history of state conflict; another that sees it in largely ideological terms;[29] yet a third 'internalist' account which regards the antagonism as the by-product of the domestic structures of the two rival superpowers; and a fourth that focuses on leaders' perceptions and preferences.[30] In Lebow's view none is entirely adequate: all four have to be married if we are to get a complete picture of what actually happened after the Second World War. By the same measure, none provides us with a ready-made answer as to why the Cold War came to an end, least of all realism which assumed, and continues to maintain, that competition rather than accommodation between great powers is the historical norm.[31] But criticizing others is easy: the more difficult task is to explain what happened, and in Lebow's view we still do not have a full explanation as to why the Cold War finally withered away. And while more work still needs to be done in the newly opened archives in Russia and Eastern Europe, the most fruitful avenue for historians he feels is to compare the rise and fall of the Cold War with other long-term militarized rivalries—some of which did not end quite so peacefully.

If the end of the Cold War represented the final point in the evolution of one particular epoch and the beginning of another, the issue remains as to how best to characterize the decade after 1989. One way, as we have suggested, is to think of the

---

[26] A good example of this attachment to Cold War structures in Europe at least can be found in the influential study by former State Department official, Anton W. DePorte, *Europe between the Superpowers* (New Haven, CT: Yale University Press, 1978).

[27] See also Allen Lynch, *The Cold War is Over—Again* (Boulder, CO: Westview Press, 1992) and Walter LaFeber, 'An End to *Which* Cold War?', Michael J. Hogan (ed.), *The End of the Cold War: Its Meaning and Implications* (New York: Cambridge University Press, 1992), pp. 13–19.

[28] See also Richard Ned Lebow and Janice Gross Stein, *We All Lost the Cold War* (Princeton, NJ: Princeton University Press, 1994).

[29] See Nigel Gould-Davies, 'Rethinking the Role of Ideology in International Politics During the Cold War', *Journal of Cold War Studies*, 1:1 (1999), pp. 90–109.

[30] For a useful guide to the different theories of the Cold War see the relevant sections in Fred Halliday, *The Making of the Second Cold War* (London: Verso, 1983).

[31] Randall Schweller thus suggests about the post-Cold War world that 'precisely because intentions can change, history is far from over, and bold predictions of Kantian peace are not only naively optimistic but dangerously foolish'. See his *Deadly Imbalances: Tripolarity and Hitler's Strategy of World Conquest* (New York. Columbia University Press, 1998), p. 201.

period as an 'interregnum'.[32] Like some other contributors to this collection, Chris Brown wonders about this and argues that we might perhaps think of the 1990s less as an interval between two international orders, but rather as the new order itself after a two century transition which opened in 1789 with the French revolution and concluded two centuries later with the demise of communism. Brown thus asks us to think about our present in a more historically long-term fashion. But the problem still remains: how is this putative new order, if that is what it is, to be understood?

Brown examines a number of different possible answers and in so doing discusses some of the dominating debates of the 1990s. These, he argues, have been unhelpfully posed in the form of an either/or: either the end of history or the end of stable bipolarity; universalism or particularism; liberal dominance or a clash of civilizations; Jihad or McWorld. Brown prefers a different approach which tries to understand the world in terms of complex combinations rather than simple opposites. To proceed otherwise, he argues, would be both analytically and normatively confusing.

An important part of Brown's argument revolves around a sympathetic, but not uncritical evaluation of Fukuyama and the various intellectual alternatives in the shape of Samuel Huntington and the less well known Japanese analyst, Eusuke Sakakiba. Huntington, we know, believes that the end of the old Cold War conflict will be replaced (or has already been superseded) by a new 'clash of civilizations' or cultures. Sakakiba on the other hand insists that the Cold War was basically a civil war within the Western ideology of progressivism. Thus its passing does not represent a victory for political liberalism and 'neoclassical capitalism', but instead poses a new challenge to progressivism itself. In this sense, the world at the end of the 1990s is not at the end of *history* pace Fukuyama, only at the end of *one particular* history.[33] But whatever happens, the next period in history will not just be determined by large structural forces according to Brown, but also by what happens inside different countries as well. Liberalism may well have triumphed as Fukuyama claims, but at the end of the day the decisions that count will be made in Washington and elsewhere; and these in the end are going to be shaped by political necessity as much as anything else. In this very important sense, the major questions about the future of world order will not be answered in their own terms; the contingencies of power may still have the last word, as so often in the past.

In her essay Linda Weiss focuses on one of the issues addressed by Brown: the relationship between globalization and national governance. According to Weiss, the most extreme proponents of globalization see the 'global and national' in terms of '*conflicting* principles of organization'. Hence they take it as read that 'global networks are advancing *at the expense of* national ones'. Weiss is not only sceptical about such claims, but offers a powerful set of counter-arguments. Even in the developed world, she notes, the overwhelming bulk of production (about 90 per cent) is still carried out and consumed locally. Most large companies also concentrate most of their production and strategic assets in one country. World equity markets also remain poorly integrated. And though international trade and investment are clearly on the rise, the bulk of this is concentrated in a relatively small

[32] Gramsci defines an 'interregnum' as a period in which the old form of rule was dying but a new one had not yet born. See Quintin Hoare and Geoffrey Nowell Smith (eds.), *Selections From The Prison Notebooks Of Antonio Gramsci* (London: Lawrence and Wishart, 1971), p. 276.

[33] For a critique of Fukuyama see also John Gray, 'Global Utopias and Clashing Civilizations: Misunderstanding the Present', *International Affairs*, 74:1 (January 1998), pp. 149–63.

geoeconomic zone. The one area in which there are genuinely global markets is in finance. Otherwise, there is no compelling case to think we are now living in a fully integrated global economy.[34]

Nor have present economic trends undermined the possibility of (or need for) national political practices. As Weiss points out, it is quite misleading to think that economic interdependence is either destroying the state or the state's capacity to act. It is also untrue to think that globalization has undermined the provision of comprehensive welfare provision. Again, the evidence points to a different set of conclusions. As Weiss indicates, far from going down, welfare expenditure has remained constant over the past ten years; and where it has come under pressure, it has not been because of trans-border flows but because of low rates of world growth and shifting demographic and household patterns that are poorly accommodated by a welfare structure designed for an earlier era.

The conclusions Weiss draws are therefore challenging ones. The world order is certainly changing and changing fast, but the notion that globalization is already here and is rapidly eroding state power is simply not true. Unfortunately, the presumption that it is, has led many commentators to misidentify globalization as the major source of policy constraints, to overstate its transformative impact and to minimize its diverse outcomes. To avoid such errors in the future, analysts should thus stop thinking of the global and the national as competitive concepts and start seeing them as complementary. Only then will they be able to grasp what is going on in the contemporary world.

If Weiss asks some difficult but necessary questions about one of the key concepts of our time, Buzan and Little ask some equally penetrating ones about the viability of the traditional state system in an era of high capitalism. Forced off the intellectual agenda during the Cold War, capitalism they argue has staged something of an academic comeback. Indeed, with the end of the Cold War being so closely linked with the triumph of the market, it is now impossible to discuss the world without some evaluation of the unfolding international role being played by capitalism as an economic order.[35]

At the centre of this ongoing debate about future of international relations lie competing evaluations of what has come to be known as the Westphalian system; and the key issue according to Buzan and Little is the degree to which this system can survive the enormous changes now taking place in the world. They are in little doubt that the system is under threat. Not only has the behaviour of states and the patterns of interaction in international society changed as a whole, so too have the priorities which states set for themselves in the post-Cold War epoch. But does this add up to a fundamental transformation? Is the modern world order of sovereign states established in 1648 and after, finally giving way to what they term a 'new postmodern capitalist world order'? Not just yet, they conclude. We still live in a world of states while the logic of 'uneven capitalist development' continues to pull

---

[34] The literature on globalization is by now vast. For a guide to the issues see the two volumes by Ian Clark, *Globalization and Fragmentation: International Relations in the Twentieth Century* (Oxford: Oxford University Press, 1997) and *Globalization and International Relations Theory* (Oxford: Oxford University Press, 1999).

[35] For a discussion of the complex relationship between economics and security before and after the end of the Cold War, see Michael Mastanduno, 'Economics and Security in Statecraft and Scholarship', *International Organization*, 52:4 (1998), pp. 825–54.

the world in two different directions, creating two different zones in the process: one they call a 'postmodern security community' composed of 'powerful advanced capitalist industrial democracies' no longer operating by the realist rules of the game, and the other comprised of a mixture of modern and premodern states where international relations continue to operate by the Westphalian norms of power politics that prevailed all over the world up to 1945.

Yet the conclusion cannot be avoided that some quite fundamental trans-formations are underway in the international system. The spread of democracy and the sustained operation of global markets have begun to reshape some of the most long-standing fundamentals of international relations that only a decade ago would have seemed impossible. Westphalian realism may not have been rendered entirely irrelevant in the last decade of the twentieth century. Nevertheless, its traditional claim to serve as the commanding heights of how international relations can and should be understood is rightly under serious challenge.

If the end of the Cold War has threatened the once solid bastions of realism, the associated collapse of state socialism has also given an intellectual boost to those who not only seem to deny that there is such a thing as truth but that the world is moving (or has ever been moving) in a progressive direction. This in turn has been accompanied by a fairly sustained attack on all notions of science and rationality, and in particular on the Enlightenment, regarded by many as the original source of these ideas—ideas whose dark side, according to one influential theorist, had appalling political consequences in the twentieth century in the form of the planned and efficiently executed extermination of six million Jews.[36]

Fred Halliday disputes any such connection and vigorously defends the Enlightenment by way of a discussion of one of its more influential thinkers: Immanuel Kant. Kant remains a controversial as well as an influential theorist whose views on the conditions of peace continue to provoke a good deal of hostile comment from realists.[37] But Halliday is less concerned to defend Kant from his realist critics than those who would reject Kant's faith in the possibility of human progress. In a powerful broadside against what Gellner once termed 'the cosmo-politan conceit of postmodernism', Halliday takes to task all those who would spurn the Enlightenment and its rationalist belief in the possibility of progressive change measured alongside a set of universal values. While accepting that the challenge of postmodernism is an understandable response to our uncertain era following the collapse of Communism—the most radical of all responses to the crisis of the twentieth century—he concludes that it promises more than it delivers. In fact, many of the things identified as being central to the postmodern agenda such culture, identity, changing values and the importance of language in constituting social power, are not particularly postmodern at all, but very much features of modernity itself and have been so for a century or more. In this sense postmodernism con-stitutes less a serious alternative to modernity and more a parasitic growth upon it.

Halliday's main concern, however, is not to puncture what he views as the overblown claims of postmodernism, but rather to respond positively to what he regards as our deeply unsettling times. Soviet-style planning he agrees was a failure.

---

[36] See Zygmunt Bauman, *Modernity and the Holocaust* (Cambridge: Polity Press, 1989).
[37] For a brief but useful guide to Kant's thinking on international relations see Georg Cavallar, *Kant and the Theory and Practice of International Right* (Cardiff: University of Wales Press, 1999).

But that does not mean we have to accept all the claims made by apologists for liberal democratic capitalism. Modern democracy after all contains serious political imperfections; and the market continues to foster enormous inequalities. And while there is no ready alternative to either, we should not conclude that the *status quo* is sacrosanct. As Halliday notes, though we may not yet live in an enlightened age, we do live in an era where enlightened change is still possible; and a combination of purposive state action supported by social movements, improved education and greater participation by an active citizenry point the way to a better world. Whether, how or when we can move forward to what Halliday terms the triumph of reason no-one can tell. It is, nonetheless, a fitting goal for political and academic work, 'not least on this eve of the third millenium'.

While Halliday declares what to some is bound to look like an unfashionable faith in the possibility of progress, Andrew Gamble asks and seeks to answer the question: what relevance if any does the most radical faith of all—Marxism—have in a post-communist era? Gamble agrees that Marxism is in crisis, though not for the first time in its history. On this occasion however the malaise is more profound. Marxism's unfortunate association with a failed Soviet project, and the simple fact that the market is so dominant in the world, would appear to have consigned historical materialism to the dustbin of history—where many think it always belonged.[38] Gamble seeks to retrieve what is left but calls for two major changes if Marxism is to go forward. First, Marxists themselves must abandon their earlier attachment to a form of realism that saw an almost natural fit between the nation-state as a territorial unit and capitalism as an economic system. Such an approach makes no sense in an age of globalization. They must also give up their historicist claim that socialism was, or remains, the next step in humanity's evolution. Historical materialism, according to Gamble, needs neither an outmoded view of the international order nor a utopian vision of the future, and can only be entirely credible when it abandons both.

But given these revisions, there is no reason why Marxism cannot be deployed, and deployed most effectively, to understand the world around us. In many ways, it is peculiarly well-suited to do so. Marx after all was one of the very first theorists of globalization: he also had some profound insights into the ways in which the capitalist system operated over time and through space. Furthermore, Marxism contains a powerful ethical message which critics of the market can hardly ignore. Of course, in the same way as there are different varieties of realism, feminism and constructivism, so too are there different forms of Marxism. Marxists, as Gamble reminds us, remain divided in their approach and in their prognoses. Some are pessimistic and some are optimistic about the fate of capitalism. But all are agreed that classical Marxist theory—not to be confused with the official and ossified state doctrine of the Soviet Union—has continuing power to inspire important insights into the shape of the modern international political economy.[39]

---

[38] According to Stephen M. Walt, constructivism has now replaced Marxism as the principle paradigmatic rival to liberalism and realism. See his 'International Relations: One World, Many Theories', *Foreign Policy*, 110 (1998), pp. 32, 34.

[39] A view also shared by Peter J. Katzenstein, Robert O. Keohane and Stephen D. Krasner, 'International Organization and the Study of World Politics', *International Organization*, 52:4 (1998), pp. 645–85.

If the oft-proclaimed death of Marxism is premature according to Gamble, how then has Marxism's intellectual *alter ego* fared over the past ten years?[40] Not as badly as some anticipated, but definitely not as well as most liberals predicted back in 1989. That at least is the central thesis advanced in Geoffrey Hawthorn's contribution. As he points out, what liberals envisioned, and what they got after a decade, were not the same thing. In fact, the contrast between the original vision and the way events in world politics actually unfolded is so marked that he wonders whether liberalism has proved to be an enemy to itself.

Hawthorn begins by describing the early post-Cold War, liberal ideal of a New World Order. This vision, he notes, looked towards a future in which there would be peace, stability, increasing prosperity based on expanding markets and the extension and eventual consolidation of civil and political rights. All alternative approaches seemed to be exhausted. Unfortunately, reality proved to be more complex, and the world less susceptible to liberal restructuring than had originally been expected. However, though the world that has emerged is not as liberal as some might have hoped, it is a good deal more liberal than it once was. Today, for instance, human rights are more prominent on the foreign policy agenda;[41] humanitarian intervention is now at least feasible;[42] and the international economy promises new levels of prosperity. The paradox however is that these new possibilities can subvert what they claim to secure. Thus the urge to humanitarianism has turned out to be more complex and problematic than liberals had once thought, as the events in Kosovo demonstrated only too clearly; and the logic of liberal economics has led to new polarities between the beneficiaries of globalization and the increasing number of losers.

Hawthorn further explores the paradoxes of liberalism through the work of Carl Schmitt, one of liberalism's more trenchant critics. Liberals, according to Schmitt, will always avoid talk of power. It was true in the 1930s: it remains true today. And what liberals find most difficult to resolve now is that their vision of a better world depends on the exercise of a great deal of power by the United States. But how and under what circumstances will the United States deploy its power? According to Schmitt at least, the United States has to imagine an 'enemy'. The difficulty in the modern world is that there are few obvious antagonists; therefore the US either has to invent one or insist on what Hawthorn calls its 'liberal rectitude'—and under a weakening liberal President, who like other liberal presidents before him, was inexperienced in world affairs, the temptation has proved irresistible. In acting this way, however, the United States also reveals its own weakness, to overcome which it is prompted to act in the same way again—and in so doing, trap itself. The paradox of liberal hegemony in the post-Cold War era is that it is weak because it cannot convincingly be demonstrated—and insofar as it can be, threatens to undermine the principles on which it is built.

---

[40] On liberalism see also Robert Latham, 'History, Theory, and International Order', *Review of International Studies*, 23:4 (1997), pp. 419–43, and Daniel Deudney and G. John Ikenberry, 'The Nature and Sources of Liberal International Order', *Review of International Studies*, 25:2 (1998), pp. 179–96.

[41] See Nicholas J. Wheeler and Tim Dunne (eds.) *Human Rights in World Politics* (Cambridge: Cambridge University Press, 1998).

[42] For a radical critique of the new interventionism see Richard Falk, ' Intervention Revisited: Hard Choices and Tragic Dilemmas', *The Nation*, December 20, 1993, pp. 755–64.

Colin Gray is less worried about the paradoxes of liberalism than he is concerned to defend what he regards as the truths of realism against liberal illusions, and in particular the illusion that there has been (or will ever be) a benign transformation in 'human security affairs'. Gray is in no doubt. We are not, in his opinion, in an 'interregnum' leading to something different. Nor are we in a transitional stage leading to something better. We are instead living at the end of a 'postwar decade' during which nothing has fundamentally changed in the timeless character of world politics. The 1990s, therefore, should not be regarded as the start of anything new.[43]

Defending his 'neoclassical realist' position, Gray argues that the texts of classical realism offer us superior explanatory power because they are better grounded empirically than alternative theories of world politics. Realism is 'right', he argues, because the game of politics does not change from age to age, and even less so from decade to decade; what this means is that the 'past is the future in the ways that matter most', namely in the human capacity for folly and violence. Gray then goes on to discuss what he identifies as a set of modern 'popular myths', 'probable myths' and 'half-truths' that have marked the security debate in the last decade of the twentieth century. These include: endist visions of benign historical transformation, the idea that democracies do not fight each other, and the belief of some globalization theories in a 'technologically-mandated peace'. For Gray, 'a proclivity to combat helps define the human condition', as a result of which he does not believe that humans will either learn the ways of peace or be forced to be peaceful as a result of awesome technologies. War and strategy, he argues, are 'eternal', though their forms change with circumstances. Change in form however (such as an alteration in the distribution of power or in technology) should not be misconstrued as implying a change in the nature of world politics or a challenge to classical realism. The latter might appear to some to be 'old fashioned', but that does not necessarily make it incorrect. Clausewitz speaks to today's security problems as vitally as he did to his own time.

Gray's defence of classical realism is followed by a detailed discussion of one of the great policy challenges that has faced the West since the end of the Cold War: how to manage the transition from bureaucratic planned economy to market democracy in post-communist Russia. Defined by policymakers as the number one security issue facing the West in the 1990s, the reasons for supporting Russian reform seemed fairly apparent. If the transition were successful, then, according to the common wisdom of the time, the international system as a whole could look forward to a level of security it had not enjoyed for generations; if it failed, then the world would face a very uncertain future with the strong possibility of a renewed nuclear threat, higher Western defence budgets, spreading instability, the loss of new markets and a devastating setback for the world-wide movement towards liberal capitalism. The stakes in Russia were clearly huge.[44]

As Peter Rutland shows, the early hope—expectation even—that Russia would make a rapid move towards a vibrant democracy based on steady market-based growth has not been fulfilled; and far from moving speedily and painlessly forward,

---

[43] For a comprehensive survey of realism in the twentieth century see Michael Joseph Smith, *Realist Thought from Weber to Kissinger* (Baton Rouge: Louisiana State University Press, 1986).

[44] On this see Michael Cox, 'The Necessary Partnership? The Clinton presidency and post-Soviet Russia', *International Affairs*, 70:4 (October 1994), pp. 635–58.

Russia has lurched from one crisis to another. Admittedly, none of these have so far proved fatal. Even the financial meltdown of August 1998 has not led to tanks in the street or popular uprisings. Nevertheless, the situation is extraordinarily bleak and shows little sign of getting much better in the future. Naturally enough, some have gained under what one seasoned commentator recently termed Russia's unique form of 'crony capitalism', especially the new oligarchs who have stood behind their sometimes sober, increasingly unpopular man in the Kremlin.[45] A few have actually made vast fortunes, notably key members of the old communist *nomenklatura* who have used privatization as a means to enrich themselves. But overall Russia, and the vast majority of Russians, are in a much worse position at the end of the decade than they were at the beginning.

But who is to blame? Rutland offers no simple answers, but is in no doubt that the West in general (and the IMF in particular) has to bear a good deal of the responsibility. Guided by the 'Washington consensus' which assumes that what is good for America is good for everyone else as well, American advisors attempted to foist an inappropriate model of neoliberal market economics onto a country that was clearly not prepared for it. To make matters even worse, the US also decided to back the highly authoritarian Yeltsin while at the same time imposing a particularly elitist or presidentialist concept of democracy on Russia. By supporting the former, however, the US made itself hostage to Yeltsin's political whims; and by endorsing the latter, it proved virtually impossible to get popular backing for painful reform. The resultant impasse was as inevitable as it has been tragic, and has sent out the clear message to Russians, and many others, that IMF reforms offer a good deal of pain but little prosperity in return.

Ironically, though, the international consequences of Russia's ongoing impasse need not necessarily be as dangerous as some have feared. At one level, the West obviously has to be concerned about the emergence of a potential zone of instability stretching from the centre of Europe to the Pacific, especially when the zone in question borders so many other countries and is the site of so many nuclear weapons. Russia on the other hand has diminishing international assets, its economy is in a mess, its military is in tatters and its new elite almost completely dependent on Western institutions—including the much-disliked IMF. To this extent, Russian weakness rather than reform now seems to hold the key to Russia's relations with the West. But this may be no bad thing. As Vaclav Havel once observed, a sick Russia might be less of a problem for the rest of the world than a vibrant Soviet Union. Whether the former USSR was ever particularly vibrant is open to conjecture. What is not in doubt is the seriousness of Russia's illness and thus its continued inability to play a decisive role in world politics.[46]

While Russia drifts, Western Europe thrives, and its greatest test now is not how to survive or feed its people but how to adjust to the dynamics of rapid economic integration. As William Wallace points out, the most distinctive characteristic of the new West European system is 'its intensive multilateralism'. There are few areas of

---

[45] See Jonathan Steele, 'Keeping it in the family', *The Guardian* (London), 13 August, 1999.

[46] As one observer noted (writing about the once much-vaunted Russian military) 'Only a small part of the armed forces . . . still has any military role. Most of the rest just hang on, often unpaid. Many moonlight as security guards or taxi drivers. Some of the more senior ones act as brokers for their juniors' forced labour on building sites or in the fields. "You think it's an army. In fact all you've got is people in uniform" says Dimiti Trenin, a retired colonel now with the Carnegie Endowment.' See 'A cold, hungry, pointless Russian army', *The Economist*, November 21, 1998, p. 46.

policy that are untouched by the European Union as an institution. Even its various civil servants and politicians are in almost daily contact with each other. Trans-border activity meanwhile grows apace; regional committees have been established to remove transport bottlenecks at border posts; and various bilateral and multi-lateral agreements mean that passports are no longer required when travelling between many EU states. But this is only one side of the story. Western Europe may be what Wallace terms a 'post-sovereign regional system', but the state is still the only accepted basis for legitimate representation. And while elites appear to float freely in the new European space, the identity, loyalty and culture of the mass of people remain firmly anchored in national symbols and institutions. Finally, the core issues of high politics—foreign and defence policies—continue to be determined by national politicians accountable to national parliaments. The EU may be in the process of becoming post-Westphalian, postmodern even. However, it has not got there yet. The realists still have something to cling on to.[47]

If in Western Europe the big issue is integration, in the East the key task is reform and membership of the rich man's club to the West. However, even though the two parts of Europe are growing closer, the contrast between them could not be more stark. In Western Europe sovereignty is under challenge: in Central Europe however the new states are seeking to reclaim sovereignty as a symbol of independence in the post-Soviet era. The former is economically advanced; the latter relatively backward. There are still two Europes, therefore, combined together in a totally uneven relationship. The obvious result, as Wallace shows, is that the new democracies in the East have very quickly become dependent on the West for trade and security. It could not be otherwise: Eastern Europe after all needs its new western friends much more than the West needs the East. Nonetheless, the West can hardly avoid its responsibilities and has no alternative but to continue the process of incorporating the countries of the old Soviet bloc.

But at the heart of the whole European project is a fundamental dilemma. Western Europe may be a major player in the world economy, but it remains what Wallace terms a 'civilian power', dependent for its security on a non-European state: the United States of America. Neither is entirely happy with the situation. Both have their complaints. But the dangers of changing the current arrangement seem too great and the advantages of keeping it, too many. The *status quo*, though, is by no means sacrosanct. One day, the Americans might decide that the costs of entangle-ment are too high. The Europeans might in the end baulk at being led by an increas-ingly unsympathetic ally across the Atlantic. Hence, for Western Europe the hardest test in the future might not be whether it can manage its relations with the East Europeans, but whether it will have to do so—with or without the cooperation and support of the United States.

If Wallace dissects some difficult problems facing Europe, Caroline Thomas explores an even tougher issue confronting students of the Third World: namely, whether or not the Third World even exists in the post-Cold War era? The thesis she challenges is now a popular one. The Third World, it is claimed, not only represented a distinct geographical space but a particular statist strategy designed to

[47] Robert Jervis not only maintains that 'the state has proven remarkably resilient in the face of multiple social forces and the insistence of scholars that its importance is rapidly waning', but that even if the European Union were to 'supplant its members' it would still go on 'to form a state of its own'. See his 'Realism in the Study of World Politics', *International Organization*, 52:4 (1998), pp. 971–91.

achieve rapid independent economic development in the era of the Cold War. This entity, it is maintained, collapsed in stages, beginning in Mexico in the early 1980s and concluding with the collapse of Indian 'socialism' a few years later. What was left was not 'three' separate worlds but instead one world economy operating by the same economic rules drawn up in Washington by the economic liberals who occupied key positions in the key institutions such as the IMF and the World Bank. By the 1990s it thus made no sense to talk of a separate Third World. The strategy associated with its name had been abandoned and along with it any hope of finding an alternative path to economic modernity.[48]

According to Thomas, this argument is not so much wrong but misses the main point. Far from disappearing in fact, the Third World—here understood to mean economic marginalization, grinding poverty and economic insecurity—has acquired a more general character as a result of the triumph of global capitalism. From this perspective, what was once associated with countries and continents in the 'South' has now become an international phenomenon. The Third World has not died; it has simply extended its location.

Thomas's argument proceeds in three stages. The first sets out the central thesis, discussing the Cold War origins of the term 'Third World' and how it evolved over time. The second offers an empirical account of the contemporary 'global architecture' (in which the IMF is the lynchpin) and the underlying 'Washington consensus' that shapes economic agendas, coordinates policies and determines the rules by which all now live. As Thomas shows, massive inequality in the new world economic order is no accident but the logical outcome of the neoliberal project. Finally, she looks at two sets of political responses to what she terms the current 'crisis of globalization'. One she defines as 'reformist', which she takes to mean all those who basically want to improve the system but not change it fundamentally: the other she terms 'transformists', who reject the norms of the global market-based system, and look towards national and local control over development policies. Not surprisingly, both have very different solutions to the problems now facing the Third World, and Thomas goes to some length to illustrate this point through an examination of debt, finance, trade and investment. But while opinions might differ, there is little disputing the facts: and the simple facts of the matter are that until there is an alteration in the structure of the world economy, some will remain rich and many, many more will continue to endure misery and hardship.

Significantly, the one region of the world which managed to break free from the chains of underdevelopment in the postwar period was Asia Pacific. Whether this was the consequence of an entrepreneurial culture, social discipline, autocratic political rule, sheer hard work or even the Cold War itself—think of all those billions pumped into the region during the Korean and Vietnam Wars—ultimately Asia Pacific did manage to take off in the 1960s, consolidate its gains in the 1970s, and become a major force in the world economy in the 1980s. So successful did it become, in fact, that many started to talk glowingly of a new Pacific era, and began to search high and low for the secret of its success. More than that: from the late 1980s onwards, it was quite commonplace for journalists, politicians and academics alike to speculate about the decline of the West and the dawn of a new Pacific Century. The region, it seemed, could do no economic wrong; and though a number

---

[48] See, for example, Nigel Harris, *The End of the Third World* (London: Penguin Books, 1990).

of realists were concerned that this new-found economic power would bring with it greater political clout and increased military prowess,[49] there seemed little disagreement that a great shift had occurred in the international system: away from Europe, away from the US even, and towards the Pacific Rim.

Rosemary Foot and Andrew Walter put much of what they see as the myth of the Pacific Century to the sword.[50] The idea in their view 'was always overstated in economic, but especially in political terms'. But how did it arise in the first place? What was its empirical basis? One key element was rapid Japanese growth before 1973, and the generalization of this thereafter to the other 'tiger' economies of East Asia. Economic power, in turn, triggered a variety of studies claiming that there was a distinctive Asian model of development, possibly superior in kind, and definitely a challenge to that which existed in the other core areas of the capitalist world. To this one has to add another key ingredient which made the myth of the Pacific Century so beguiling: the equally powerful counter-narrative of American decline. Odd though this particular thesis might sound now, in the second half of the 1980s it had become *de rigeur* to contrast a healthy, vibrant Asia with its strong sense of family and community with a moribund United States wracked by crime, weakened by moral decay and going the way of all previous empires. To many, though not all commentators at the time, it was not a question of if, but when, the American Century would finally come to an end.[51]

Mythological though the idea of the Pacific Century might have become, it was nonetheless a powerful myth; and as Foot and Walter show, it took an almighty economic shock to undermine it. Nonetheless, the unexpected financial crisis did indicate just how vulnerable the so-called tigers of East Asia were. But instead of producing panic and shock in the West it has generated what might best—and most generously—be described as barely concealed *schadenfreude*. In the US in particular there has been an air of quiet self-satisfaction: partly because the collapse in Asia has confirmed the American model, partly because it has strengthened America's leverage in Asia itself, and partly too because it has reaffirmed US hegemony. Not everybody it seems has been upset to see the back of the short-lived Pacific Century.

Foot and Walter conclude their essay with a simple but powerful statement 'that the American century that Henry Luce first pointed to in 1941 has not yet run its course'. This is an idea that Bruce Cumings builds upon in his contribution. Like Foot and Walter he is especially keen to debunk myths, and in particular the myth, as he sees it, of American decline. Cumings pulls few punches and in a detailed analysis sets about the declinists with gusto. In his view it is disconcerting—in some cases almost embarrassing—to recall what was once said about the decline of the United States by seasoned analysts. Even more worrying perhaps is the extent to which the argument was accepted by many, though by no means all, commentators at the time.[52]

---

[49] Especially the military prowess of China. On this see the opposing essays by Dennis Roy and Michael G. Gallagher collected together under 'Dangerous Dragon or Paper Tiger?', *International Security*, 19:1 (Summer 1994), pp. 149–94.

[50] For an equally cautious look at the 'miracle' see Grahame Thompson (ed.), *The Economic Dynamism in the Asia-Pacific* (London: Routledge, 1998).

[51] One commentator who was never convinced was Christopher Coker, see his 'The Pacific Century is a Myth', *Washington Quarterly*, 11:3 (1988), pp. 5–16.

[52] For a typically robust attack on the decline thesis see Susan Strange, 'The Persistent Myth of Lost Hegemony', *International Organization*, 41:4 (1987), pp. 551–74, and 'The Future of the American Empire', *Journal of International Affairs*, 42:1 (1998), p. 18.

Cumings though does not merely assert his case; he sets out to prove why this is 'Still the American Century'. And as he points out, a combination of market size, technological prowess, financial power and military capability will guarantee that dominance for many years to come. Some may resent this. Many would wish it were otherwise. A few might hope the dream will go sour, one day. But it is here to stay; this liberal titan which rarely says please and never has to say sorry—like the one before it. But if England's century began with the Congress of Vienna and ended in 1914, is there still not a chance that America might go the same way, as Paul Kennedy once said it would? Not according to Cumings. Instead of a premature end to the American Century or a coming clash of civilizations, today, and for the forseeable future, there is only one global actor worthy of the name. Nor is there any likely contender on the horizon. In this, as in nearly everything else, the United States has proved to be an exception to the historic rule.[53]

We thus seem to have come full circle. The postwar period was shaped in large part by American power, and it would appear that the post-Cold War era is going to be as well. How the US deploys this power, and how effective it will be as the only, lonely superpower is a matter of some conjecture and speculation, and Cumings leaves it up to the reader to draw his or her own conclusions. But the power of the argument is in the evidence and the evidence points to the inescapable conclusion that American hegemony remains alive and well as we move into the next millennium.

If Cumings helps us think about our more immediate past and our future in a fresh and uncluttered way, then so too—we hope—do the other contributors to this collection. Taken together we certainly feel the essays on display here offer a comprehensive and provocative picture of the history, controversies and geopolitical landscapes that emerged out of the unexpected collapse of Soviet power. We also think they help us engage in a more sophisticated way with the sorts of issues that ought to be concerning students of world politics today. The more recent debates around method and epistemology have without doubt been indispensable in making us all aware of our own presuppositions, blind-spots and 'silences'. In the end, however, the purpose of international relations is not only to determine whether we can know the world, but also to explain and understand how the world operates.[54] And as the most cursory glance through the current literature shows, the range of issues now being discussed is vast, from the more traditional focus on the nature of war,[55] the reasons for wars ending[56] and the impact of war on the so-called ordinary people,[57] through to the relationship between norms and peaceful change,[58] the way revolutions have refashioned the global system[59] and the future role of international

---

[53] See also Alfredo Valadao, *The Twenty First Century Will be American* (London: Verso, 1996).

[54] On this question see Martin Hollis and Steve Smith, *Explaining and Understanding International Relations* (Oxford: Clarendon Press, 1990).

[55] See Lawrence Freedman, 'Victims and Victors: Reflections on the Kosovo War', *Review of International Studies*, 26:2 (July 2000).

[56] See the Special Issue of *Millennium*, 'War Endings; Reasons, Strategies and Implications', 26:3 (1997).

[57] On this see Christopher Hill, '"Where Are We Going?" International Relations and the Voice from Below', *Review of International Studies*, 25:1 (1999), pp. 107–22.

[58] See Friedrich V. Kratowchil, 'Politics, Norms and Peaceful Change', in Tim Dunne, Michael Cox and Ken Booth (eds.), *The Eighty Years' Crisis: International Relations 1919–1999*, pp. 193–218.

[59] See for example, Stephen M. Walt, *Revolution and War* (Ithaca: Cornell University Press, 1996).

institutions in an interdependent world.[60] There are, it would seem, as many facets to the contemporary subject as there are scholars; and it should be added, as many answers as there are questions. Clearly, we cannot resolve all these issues in a single volume. But we have, we think, provided a few suggestions as to how we might find our way in a situation where most of the old familiar signposts are less reliable than they used to be. As we noted at the beginning of this Introduction, there are a number of themes that run throughout this collection. But perhaps the most important one of all is the enormous challenge we all face as we try to come to terms with a complex reality that requires creative ways of thinking about some rather old, but also some fairly novel issues confronting the international system at large. To this extent at least, the 1990s have been very familiar terrain for us all.

---

[60] In this context, see Robert O. Keohane, 'International Institutions: Can Interdependence Work? *Foreign Policy*, 110 (Spring 1998), pp. 82–96.

The rise and fall of the Cold War in comparative perspective

RICHARD NED LEBOW

Introduction

Much of the discussion of the end of the Cold War starts from the premise that Gorbachev's domestic reforms and foreign policy initiatives set in motion a process that radically transformed the nature of East-West relations. The emphasis on the Gorbachev period is natural enough given the consensus among Western and Russian scholars that Gorbachev's domestic and foreign policies were the proximate cause of the end of the Cold War. The near exclusive focus on the causes and consequences of Gorbachev's policies nevertheless frames the analytical puzzle too narrowly. The Cold War was not a static conflict that continued unchanged from its origins in the late 1940s to the advent of Gorbachev some forty years later. Gorbachev's initiatives ushered in the terminal stage of a process of accommodation that had been underway, albeit with fits and starts, for several decades. The Gorbachev foreign policy revolution needs to be put into broader historical context.

To understand why the Cold War ended peacefully, it also needs to be compared to other war-threatening rivalries. Some of these rivalries also ended in peaceful accommodations. What, if anything, does the Cold War share in common with these conflicts? Do they reveal patterns that could help us better understand the Cold War, its dénouement and its broader lessons for conflict prevention and management?

I begin by describing the four generic explanations—structure, ideas, domestic politics and leaders—that have been advanced for the end of the Cold War. I then compare them along several analytical dimensions to situate them in a broader temporal and conceptual context. I do the same for the Cold War as a whole, and examine some of the different ways it can be compared to other militarized disputes. I conclude with a discussion of the methodological challenges and possibilities for comparative analysis to help bridge the gap that has developed between neopositivist and interpretivist approaches to the study of politics.

Four theories in search of the Cold War

The controversy surrounding the end of the Cold War represents a continuation of a debate that began almost fifty years ago with the earliest attempts to explain the Cold War. Our four generic explanations are linked to four different conceptions about the nature of the Cold War, and through them to different explanations for the origins of that conflict.

Realism, the most prominent structural explanation, conceives of the Cold War as a power struggle and the almost inevitable consequence of the power vacuum created in Central Europe by the collapse of Germany at the end of World War II. Some realists contend that the conflict assumed an added dimension because of the bipolar structure of the postwar world which transformed a regional conflict into a global one. Realists are found on both sides of the definition divide. Those who embrace the wider definition argue that the Cold War ended when one of the poles (the Soviet Union) recognized that it was no longer able to compete. Gorbachev's foreign policy was an attempt to extricate the Soviet Union from its conflict with the West on the best possible terms. The root cause of the Cold War and its demise was the rise and fall of the Soviet Union as a global power.[1]

The ideas explanation conceives of the Cold War as primarily an ideological struggle. The Soviet Union and the United States represented incompatible social systems, and the clash between them was the continuation of a struggle between Leninist-style socialism and Western capitalism that began with the Bolshevik revolution in 1918. No doubt the ideology on both sides shifted and changed over time. Indeed, according to one view of Soviet history, the USSR under Stalin more or less abandoned the ideal of world revolution altogether. But, still, at the heart of the conflict—and this is what made it especially intense and enduring—were different conceptions of society. And this conflict could only reach a terminal point therefore when one of the sides—in this case the Soviet Union—renounced its ideology and professed adherence to the political and economic values of its former adversaries. From this perspective, learning by Soviet leaders was the underlying cause of the Cold War's end.[2]

---

[1] Hans Morgenthau, *Politics Among Nations*, 4th edn. (New York: Alfred Knopf, 1966), distinguishes between the onset of the Cold War in 1947 and bipolarity, which he does not believe was achieved until the mid-1950s at the earliest. Kenneth N. Waltz, *Theory of International Politics* (Reading, MA: Addison-Wesley, 1979), and 'The Emerging Structure of International Politics', *International Security* 18 (Fall 1993), pp. 5–43; John J. Mearsheimer, 'Back to the Future: Instability in Europe After the Cold War', *International Security*, 15 (Summer 1990), pp. 5–56; William C. Wohlforth, 'Realism and the End of the Cold War', *International Security*, 19 (Winter 1994–95), pp. 91–129; Kenneth A. Oye, 'Explaining the End of the Cold War: Morphological and Behavioral Adaptations to the Nuclear Peace?', in Richard Ned Lebow and Thomas Risse-Kappen, *International Relations Theory and the End of the Cold War* (New York: Columbia University Press, 1995), pp. 57–84, describe the Cold War and bipolarity as more or less coterminous. For a review of recent historical literature sympathetic to the realist conception of the Cold War, see Howard Jones and Randall B. Woods, 'The Origins of the Cold War in Europe and the Near East: Recent Historiography and the National Security Imperative', *Diplomatic History*, 17 (Spring 1993), pp. 251–76, and commentaries in the same issue by Emily S. Rosenberg, Anders Stephanson and Barton J. Bernstein. For an overview see Michael Cox, 'From the Truman Doctrine to the Second Superpower Détente: the Rise and Fall of the Cold War', *Journal of Peace Research*, 27:1, 1990, pp. 25–41.

[2] Morgenthau, *Politics Among Nations*; Fred Halliday, *Rethinking International Relations* (Vancouver: University of British Columbia Press, 1994); Michael W. Doyle, 'Liberalism and the End of the Cold War', in Lebow and Risse-Kappen, *International Relations Theory and the End of the Cold War*, pp. 85–108. Gaddis, *The Long Peace*, and Thomas Paterson, *On Every Front: The Making and Unmaking of the Cold War* (New York: W.W. Norton, 1992), offer compound explanations of which the clash of visions is part. For extreme statements of this position, see Adam Ulam, *Expansion and Coexistence: Soviet Foreign Policy, 1917–1973*, 2nd edn. (New York: Praeger, 1974); Francis Fukuyama, *The End of History and the Last Man* (New York: Free Press, 1992) and Douglas J. Macdonald, 'Communist Bloc Expansion in the Early Cold War: Challenging Realism, Refuting Revisionism', *International Security*, 20 (Winter 1995), pp. 152–88. For a Weberian analysis of the evolution of Marxism and its influence on Soviet foreign policy up through Gorbachev, see Stephen E. Hanson, 'Gorbachev: The Last True Leninist Believer', in Daniel Chirot (ed.), *The Crisis of Leninism and the Decline of the Left* (Seattle: University of Washington Press, 1991), pp. 74–99. The standard reference for the debate in

The domestic politics explanation comes in several flavours. Its core assertion is that Truman or Stalin—or both—provoked the Cold War to solidify their domestic authority.[3] Some variants stress the role played by domestic politics once the Cold War was underway. The 'military-industrial complexes' of both superpowers profited from the conflict and kept it alive for parochial economic and political reasons. Contenders for power in both superpowers (e.g. Khrushchev and Reagan), and allied leaders (e.g. Kim Il-sung, Ulbricht and Chiang Kai-chek) are also alleged to have provoked confrontations to advance their political interests.[4] The Cold War ended when Gorbachev shifted the basis of his domestic authority and needed to reward a different set of constituencies whose interests required shifting resources away from defence. At least some scholars contend that shifting domestic coalitions in both superpowers were the root causes of the Cold War and its demise.[5]

The leaders explanation also addresses the beginnings and end of the Cold War. Scholars who emphasize the independent role of leaders invoke their goals and subjective understandings of their environments to explain their foreign policies. Individual level explanations tend toward constructivism: the Cold War was (is) what leaders (and now, scholars) make of it. Some Russian and American historians attribute the Cold War to Stalin's expansionist goals, and others to his paranoia, which they contend he made self-fulfilling.[6] It has also been suggested that

---

the West on the role of ideology in Soviet foreign policy is R. N. Carew Hunt, Samuel L. Sharp and Richard Lowenthal, 'Ideology and Power Politics: A Symposium', *Problems of Communism*, 7 (May-June 1958); For an overview of the historical debate on the role of ideology in the Cold War, see Stephen White and Alex Pravda (eds.), *Ideology and Soviet Politics* (Basingstoke, UK: Macmillan, 1988). For recent takes on ideology, see Martin Malia, *The Soviet Tragedy: A History of Socialism in Russia, 1917–91* (New York: Free Press, 1991); Odd Arne Westad, 'Secrets of the Second World: The Russian Archives and the Reinterpretation of Cold War History', *Diplomatic History*, 21 (Spring 1997), pp. 259–72.

[3] John Lewis Gaddis, 'The Tragedy of Cold War History', *Diplomatic History* 17 (Winter 1993), pp. 1–16; Vladislav Zubok and Constantine Pleshakov, *Inside the Kremlin's Cold War: From Stalin to Khrushchev* (Cambridge: Harvard University Press, 1996), chs. 1–3, on Stalin. Frank Kofsky, *Harry S. Truman and the War Scare of 1948: A Successful Campaign to Deceive the Nation* (New York: St. Martin's Press, 1993), is the most extreme statement of this position for Truman.

[4] Vladislav Zubok and Constantine Pleshakov, *Inside the Kremlin's Cold War: From Stalin to Khrushchev* (Cambridge: Harvard University Press, 1996).

[5] Thomas Risse-Kappen, 'Ideas Do No Float Freely: Transnational Coalitions, Domestic Structures, and the End of the Cold War', in Lebow and Risse-Kappen, *International Relations Theory and the End of the Cold War*, pp. 187–222; Matthew Evangelista, 'Transnational Relations, Domestic Structures and Security Policy in the USSR and Russia', in Thomas Risse-Kappen (ed.), *Bringing Transnational Relations Back In: Non-State Actors, Domestic Structures and International Institutions* (Cambridge: Cambridge University Press, 1995), pp. 3–36; Robert G. Herman, 'Identity, Norms and National Security: The Soviet Foreign Policy Revolution and the End of the Cold War', in Peter J. Katzenstein (ed.), *The Culture of National Security: Norms and Identity in World Politics* (New York: Columbia University Press, 1996), pp. 271–316; Jeffrey T. Checkel, *Ideas and International Political Change: Soviet/Russian Behavior and the End of the Cold War* (New Haven, CT: Yale University Press, 1977).

[6] For example, J. Garry Clifford, 'Bureaucratic Politics', in Michael J. Hogan and Thomas G. Paterson (eds.), *Explaining the History of American Foreign Relations* (New York: Cambridge University Press, 1991), pp. 141–50. Standard works that argue for the economic roots of American foreign policy and the Cold War include Lloyd C. Gardner, *Architects of Illusion: Men and Ideas in American Foreign Policy, 1941–1949* (Chicago: Quadrangle Books, 1970); Gabriel and Joyce Kolko, *The Limits of Power: The World and United States Foreign Policy, 1945–1954* (New York: Harper & Row, 1972); Thomas J. Paterson, *On Every Front: The Making and Unmaking of the Cold War*, rev. edn. (New York: W. W. Norton, 1992), Thomas J. McCormick, *America's Half-Century: United States Foreign Policy in the Cold War*, 2nd edn. (Baltimore: Johns Hopkins University Press, 1995).

Gorbachev was equally successful in making his cooperative vision a reality.[7] If leaders' goals and understandings can influence and possibly transform international relations, the Cold War can be described as the emergence and ascendancy of different understandings of East-West relations.

Building bridges

All four explanations offer distinctive accounts of the origins, nature and end of the Cold War. They are nevertheless difficult to compartmentalize because with few exceptions they hold themselves out as only partial explanations for these developments and acknowledge—sometimes only tacitly—the need to rely on one or more of the other explanations to account for the remaining variance. The only exceptions are some of the power transition variants of the structural explanation.[8] They assume that changes in the distribution of power lead ineluctably to predictable changes in behaviour. This relationship is independent of historical epoch, the nature of state or the quality of its leadership. Leaders are assumed to understand the balance of power and its trends, and to respond appropriately. Leaders, like electrons, are interchangeable conveyers of forces who exercise no independent influence on events.

More sophisticated realists have proposed weaker formulations that give primacy to structure but do not succumb to the 'sin' of determinism. Hans Morgenthau, the father of modern realism, always espoused such a variant. He maintained that nuclear bipolarity could promote peace or lead to war; the outcome would depend on the moral qualities of leaders.[9] More recently, both Kenneth Oye and William Wohlforth have treated leaders' perceptions of the balance of power and its future trends as an important intervening variable.[10] Weak structural explanations build bridges to ideas, domestic structures and politics, and leaders, and indeed depend on them to impart subjective meaning to the balance of power and to explain variance under similar structural conditions.

The ideas explanation also bridges to the other explanations.[11] Ideas are prompted by experience and environmental challenges, and in this way are related to structure. *Perestroika* and *Glasnost* were a response to the economic stagnation of

---

[7] Richard Ned Lebow and Janice Gross Stein, *We All Lost the Cold War* (Princeton, NJ: Princeton University Press, 1994), postscript.

[8] Dimitri Volkogonov, *Stalin: Triumph and Tragedy* (New York: Grove, Weidenfeld, 1988), ch. 54; Zubok and Pleshakov, *Inside the Kremlin's Cold War*, pp. 47–53; David Holloway, *Stalin and the Bomb* (New Haven, CT: Yale University Press, 1994), pp. 253–72; On the military lessons of World War II, see Raymond L. Garthoff, *The Soviet Image of Future War* (Washington, DC: Public Affairs Press, 1959).

[9] Morgenthau, *Politics Among Nations*, pp. 347–49.

[10] Kenneth A. Oye, 'Explaining the End of the Cold War: Morphological and Behavioral Adaptations to the Nuclear Peace', in Lebow and Risse-Kappen, *International Relations and the End of the Cold War*, pp. 57–84; William C. Wohlforth, 'Realism and the End of the Cold War', *International Security*, 19 (Winter 1994–95), pp. 91–129.

[11] The need to link ideas to other explanations is specifically acknowledged by Douglas W. Blum, 'The Soviet Foreign Policy Belief System: Beliefs, Politics and Foreign Policy Outcomes', *International Studies Quarterly*, 37 (December 1993), pp. 373–94, and Jacques Lévesque, *The Enigma of 1989: The USSR and the Liberation of Eastern Europe*, trans. Keith Martin (Berkeley: University of California Press, 1997).

the Soviet Union and the belief that this was due to the restraining hand of unimaginative, unresponsive party and governmental cadres. The equally important conception of common security was developed as an alternative to confrontational policies that were seen as dangerous, expensive and counter-productive.[12] In a more fundamental sense, the end of the Cold War and the subsequent collapse of the Soviet Union were due to widespread disenchantment with the Leninist model of society.[13] The ideas explanation relies on domestic politics and leaders to translate ideas into policies. Ideas need support in high places, and often among a wider public as well. Ideas depend on what John Kingdon has called 'policy entrepreneurs' to bring them to the attention of policymakers who in turn use them to shape and influence the policy agenda.[14] This process has been well-studied in the Soviet context in the domain of security policy and arms control, where scientific elites and *institutchiki* are said to have been an important conduit of ideas to Gorbachev and his immediate advisors who were attracted to them as solutions to policy or political problems.[15]

The domestic politics explanation recognizes the importance of ideas but reverses the arrow of causation. Ideas sell policies rather than motivate them. Politics is about power, but advocacy of appealing ideas helps office seekers gain power. Ideas are equally essential to coalitions. They form around interests, and, in all but the most corrupt political systems, interests need to be justified to leaders, legislators and other gatekeepers in terms of broader, shared interests or values. Ideas also help

[12] Eduard Shevardnadze, *The Future Belongs to Freedom* (New York: Free Press, 1991); Checkel, *Ideas and International Political Change*; Robert Herman, 'Ideas, Identity and the Redefinition of Interests: The Political and Intellectual Origins of the Soviet Foreign Policy Revolution', PhD dissertation, Cornell University, 1996; Coit D. Blacker, 'Learning in the Nuclear Age: Soviet Strategic Arms Control Policy, 1969–1989', in George Breslauer and Philip Tetlock (eds.), *Learning in US and Soviet Foreign Policy* (Boulder, CO: Westview, 1991); Sarah Mendelsohn, *Changing Course: Ideas, Politics and the Soviet Withdrawal from Afghanistan* (Princeton, NJ: Princeton University Press, 1998).

[13] Francis Fukuyama, *The End of History and the Last Man* (New York: Free Press, 1992); Fred Halliday, 'International Society as Homogeneity: Burke, Marx, Fukuyama', *Millennium: Journal of International Studies*, 21:3 (1992), pp. 435–61; Michael Doyle, 'Liberalism and the End of the Cold War', and Rey Koslowski and Friedrich V. Kratochwil, 'Understanding Change in International Politics: The Soviet Union's Demise and the International System', in Lebow and Risse-Kappen, *International Relations Theory and the End of the Cold War*, pp. 85–108 and 109–26; John Mueller, 'Realism and the End of the Cold War', in Mueller, *Quiet Cataclysm: Reflections on the Recent Transformation in World Politics* (New York: Harper-Collins, 1995), pp. 27–39; Charles W. Kegley, Jr, 'The Neo-Idealist Moment in International Studies? Realist Myths and the New International Realities', *International Studies Quarterly*, 27 (June 1993), pp. 131–47; Alexander Wendt, 'Collective Identity Formation and the International State', *American Political Science Review*, 88 (June 1994), pp. 1–13.

[14] Jack Walker, 'The Diffusion of Knowledge, Policy Communities and Agenda Setting', in John Tropman, Robert Lind and Milan Dluhy (eds.), *New Strategic Perspectives on Social Policy* (New York: Pergamon, 1981), pp. 89–91; John W. Kingdon, *Agendas, Alternatives, and Public Policies* (New York: Harper-Collins, 1984). See also, Giandomenico Majone, *Evidence, Argument and Persuasion in the Policy Process* (New Haven, CT: Yale University Press, 1989).

[15] Thomas Risse-Kappen, 'Ideas Do Not Float Freely: Transnational Coalitions, Domestic Structures, and the End of the Cold War', in Lebow and Risse-Kappen, *International Relations Theory and the End of the Cold War*, pp. 187–222; Jeffrey T. Checkel, *Ideas and International Political Change: Soviet/Russian Behavior and the End of the Cold War* (New Haven, CT: Yale University Press, 1997); Matthew A, Evangelista, 'Sources of Moderation in Soviet Security Policy', in Philip E. Tetlock, et al., *Behavior, Society and Nuclear War* (New York: Oxford University Press, 1991), vol. 2, pp. 254–354, and 'The Paradox of State Strength: Transnational Relations, Domestic Structures, and Security Policy in Russia and the Soviet Union', *International Organization*, 49 (Winter 1995), pp. 1–38; Lévesque, *The Enigma of 1989*, pp. 38–41, and passim.

provide general direction and incentive to bureaucracies charged with policy implementation.

Through ideas, domestic politics and leadership bridge to structural explanations. Only the 'great man in history' approach denies the importance of structure. None of the scholars who emphasize the importance of leaders in creating or ending the Cold War subscribe to this formulation. Even in the case of Stalin, whose idiosyncratic influence is widely recognized to have been extraordinary, the debate is between those who maintain the Soviet Union could have developed less violently and more democratically under a different leader, and their critics who contend that Stalin was the inevitable product of the terror-based political system created by Lenin. This political structure is the starting point for both sides.[16]

These four explanations do not constitute distinct alternatives as much as they do different points of entry into a problem that requires a complex and multi-layered explanation. The controversy about these explanations is really about the relevant point of entry into the problem. For scholars who believe that their preferred explanation accounts for much more of the variance than competitors, this is a significant decision. For those who see their explanation as essential but not necessarily privileged, the choice is one of intellectual appeal and convenience.

The initial task for scholars of either persuasion is to identify the most promising variants of their preferred explanation, specify them sufficiently to permit their evaluation, evaluate them on the basis of the available evidence, and note the kind of additional evidence that would aid in this task. The more important, follow-on task, will then be to build bridges across these variants to construct a more comprehensive explanation for the end of the Cold War.

Bringing in process

All four explanations posit motives for leaders to seek accommodation. Wishes do not always lead to deeds. Leaders who want accommodation must devise strategies to convince protagonists of their sincerity—and may need to convince these adversaries that accommodation is also in their interest. They must then negotiate terms, and mobilize allied and domestic support for them. Attempts at accommodation can fail, stall, or prove of limited duration if leaders fail in any of these tasks. However, many structural explanations ignore process; they assume that accommodations will take place when dictated by interests. Weak structural explanations speak only of the constraints and opportunities created by structures, and do not expect accommodations to occur every time the circumstances appear to be ripe. However, proponents of these explanations only occasionally offer *ex post facto* explanations of accommodations, or failed accommodations that invoke non-structural arguments.

---

[16] For recent works on Stalin that address this question, see Dimitri Volkogonov, *Stalin: Triumph and Tragedy* (New York: Grove, Weidenfeld, 1988); Robert C. Tucker, *Stalin in Power: The Revolution from Above, 1938–1941* (New York: Norton, 1990); Zubok and Pleshakov, *Inside the Kremlin's Cold War*, and Robert C. Tucker, 'Sovietology and Russian History', *Post-Soviet Affairs*, 8 (July–September 1992), pp. 175–96.

The ideas explanation does not address process, nor does it deny its importance. Ideas explanations, and many variants of domestic politics and leaders explanations, define their dependent variable as commitment to seek accommodation. They acknowledge that leaders' commitments are a necessary but insufficient condition for accommodation. Some domestic politics and leader explanations bridge into process to try to offer a fuller explanation. There is a growing literature on two-level games that links international negotiations with domestic politics.[17] Variants of leadership explanations sometimes address process by looking at the ways in which leaders' personalities or past experiences influence their strategies for dealing with allies and adversaries. A case in point is the work of James Goldgeier.[18] Goldgeier contends that Soviet leaders respond to their first major foreign policy crisis with the same strategy they used to win the leadership, whether or not this strategy is relevant to the crisis. Presumably, their past successes and failures would also influence how they pursue accommodation.

Most variants of our four explanations ignore process. However, the end of the Cold War cannot be understood without taking into account the interactions of leaders and bureaucracies within states, within alliances and between the super-powers and their respective blocs.

End games: path dependency

The years 1986–91 were the end game of the Cold War. In chess, an end game follows opening and middle games, but not every game reaches this stage. The structure, strategy and outcome of end games are determined by the number of pieces on the board, their location and who has tempo. End games are highly path dependent. What about the Cold War?

Path dependency is a concept developed in the physical sciences that has been most widely used in economics among the social sciences. Its strongest formulation, most appropriate to evolutionary biology, asserts that what happens at $T+3$ is entirely dependent on what happened at $T+2$, $T+1$ and T. If true, this would make meaningful cross-case comparison, the most common form of quantitative research in the social sciences, much more difficult. Comparisons could only be made among cases whose histories were similar in relevant dimensions. We use a more relaxed conception of path dependency here, which assumes only that the history of a conflict has a significant impact on its subsequent evolution, and that the evolution

[17] Robert Putnam, 'Diplomacy and Domestic Politics: The Logic of Two-Level Games, *International Organization*, 42 (Summer 1988), pp. 427–460; Peter B. Evans, Harold K. Jacobson and Robert D. Putnam (eds.), *Double-Edged Diplomacy: International Bargaining and Domestic Politics* (Berkeley, CA: University of California Press, 1993); David Carment and Patrick James, 'Two-Level Games and Third Party Intervention: Evidence from Ethnic Conflict in the Balkans and South Asia', *Canadian Journal of Political Science*, 29 (September 1996), pp. 521–54; Jeffrey Knopf, 'Beyond Two-Level Games: Domestic-International Interaction in the Intermediate-Range Nuclear Forces Negations', *International Organization*, 47 (Autumn 1993), pp. 599–628; Keisuke Iida, 'When and How Do Domestic Constraints Matter? Two-Level Games with Uncertainty', *Journal of Conflict Resolution*, 37 (September 1993), pp. 403–26; Michael McGinnis and John Williams, 'Policy Uncertainty in Two-Level Games: Examples of Correlated Equilibria', *International Studies Quarterly*, 37 (March 1993), pp. 29–54.
[18] Goldgeier, *Leadership Style and Soviet Foreign Policy*.

and outcome of the conflict cannot be understood without taking that history into account.[19]

Strong structural explanations deny dependency. When the power balance changes, leaders are expected to respond accordingly. Prior changes in the balance and past responses to them are irrelevant. Some realists acknowledge that actors do not always perceive power accurately, and weak structural explanations, as we have observed, emphasize the policy importance of perceptions. But they have made no attempt to explain perception with reference to the history of specific conflicts.

The ideas literature has long debated the relationship between ideas and the context in which they arise.[20] Structural explanations for ideas—Marxism is typical—consider them epiphenomena that have no independent existence apart from the structure that gives rise to them. Scholars who argue for the independent role of ideas in international relations acknowledge that they are to some extent context dependent. The environment provides stimuli to which people react, and also a social, political and intellectual setting that helps shape how they react. But there is ample room for individual, group and cultural variation.[21] Social concepts are generally unfalsifiable, and unlike concepts about the physical environment, can make themselves, at least in part, self-fulfilling. Leaders' beliefs that nuclear war should be avoided at almost any cost, and the recognition in the 1960s by each superpower that their adversary felt the same way, fundamentally transformed the character of the Cold War. So did Gorbachev's adoption of common security. To the extent that ideas and structures interact, any ideas-based explanation for the Cold War must to some extent be path dependent.

Domestic leadership explanations have not addressed the question of path dependency. They posit changes in leaders and coalitions that prompt changes in foreign policy, or changes in foreign policy by leaders anxious to maintain the support of coalitions and constituencies. But what produces coalitions and shifts in

---

[19] Stephen Jay Gould, *Wonderful Life: The Burgess Shale and the Nature of History* (New York: Norton, 1989). In economics, see Brian Arthur, 'Competing Technologies, Increasing Returns, and Lock-In by Historical Events', *Economic Journal*, 106 (March 1989), pp. 116–31, and *Increasing Returns and Path Dependence in the Economy* (Ann Arbor: University of Michigan Press, 1994); Robin Cowan and Philip Gunby, 'Sprayed to Death: Path Dependence, Lock-In and Pest Control Strategies', *Economic Journal*, 106 (May 1996), pp. 521–42; Thrainn Eggertsson, 'The Economic of Institutions: Avoiding the Open-Field Syndrome and the Perils of Path Dependence', *Acta Sociologica*, 36:3 (1993), pp. 223–37; Eban Goodstein, 'The Economic Roots of Environmental Decline: Property Rights or Path Dependence?', *Journal of Economic Issues*, 29 (December 1995), pp. 1029–43.

[20] See, Max Weber, 'The Social Psychology of World Religions', in Hans Gerth and C. Wright Mills (eds.), *Max Weber: Essays in Sociology* (New York: Oxford University Press, 1958); Quentin Skinner, 'Meaning and Understanding in the History of Ideas', *History and Theory*, 8 (1969), pp. 3–53, 'Conventions and the Understanding of Speech Acts', *Philosophical Quarterly*, 20 (1970), pp. 118–38, and 'Some Problems in the Analysis of Political Thought and Action', *Political Theory*, 2 (1974), pp. 227–303; Richard Rorty, *Contingency, Irony, Solidarity* (Cambridge: Cambridge University Press, 1989).

[21] See, Friedrich V. Kratochwil, *Rules, Norms, and Decisions: On the Conditions of Practical and Legal Reasoning in International Relations and Domestic Affairs* (Cambridge: Cambridge University Press, 1989); Nicholas Onuf, *World of Our Making* (Columbia: University of South Carolina Press, 1989); Alexander Wendt, 'Anarchy is What States Make of It: Social Construction of Power Politics', *International Organization*, 46 (Summer 1992), pp. 391–425; David Dessler, 'What's At Stake in the Agent-Structure Debate?', *International Organization*, 43 (Summer 1989), pp. 441–73. For a much narrower take on the role of ideas, see Judith Goldstein, *Ideas, Interests and American Trade Policy* (Ithaca, NY: Cornell University Press, 1993), and Judith Goldstein and Robert O. Keohane (eds.), *Ideas and Foreign Policy: Beliefs, Institutions and Political Change* (Ithaca, NY: Cornell University Press, 1993).

their membership or preferences? If these phenomena are random, we need not consider their origins, only their consequences. But to the extent that they are shaped by memories of prior leaders or coalitions, their politics and results, they are path dependent. The selection of Soviet leaders is a case in point. Khrushchev, a promoter of radical reform, was succeeded by Brezhnev, a defender of the *status quo*, who was followed by Gorbachev, another radical reformer. This progression was not fortuitous. Brezhnev garnered support for his coup against Khrushchev by warning that the latter's 'hare-brained schemes' threatened the survival of the communist system. Brezhnev's orthodoxy reflected his personal preferences and his political need to maintain the support of the coalition that kept him in power. The latter all but precluded the possibility of major reform even though there was growing recognition among the leadership that the Soviet economy was performing poorly. The *zasto'io* [stagnation] of the Brezhnev years and growing recognition within the elite that something had to be done about the economy paved the way for another reformer. By his own admission, Gorbachev's reforms were based on a careful reading of where and why Khrushchev had failed.[22] One of the challenges to domestic politics and leadership explanations is to root them in context to try to discover patterns associated with shifts in coalitions and leaders and the kinds of policies they espoused.

In a broader sense, the entire Cold War could be said to have been path dependent. American efforts to deter the Soviet Union through alliances, military buildups, forward deployments and threatening rhetoric, represented the 'lesson of Munich' and were implemented by leaders who had witnessed the failure of appeasement in the 1930s. Appeasement was a reaction to the horrors of World War I and the revisionist belief, that gained wide credence in the 1930s, that Wilhelminian Germany might have been restrained more effectively by a policy of reassurance.[23] From Moscow's perspective, attempts to extend Soviet control as far West as possible were motivated in part by the expectation that World War III would have the same cause as World War II: a crisis of capitalism that would prompt a restored Germany, backed by the Anglo-Americans, to attack the Soviet Union.[24]

The Cold War in comparative perspective

The Cold War and its dénouement need to be compared to other militarized rivalries and their outcomes. Comparison will help us to discover what is idiosyncratic about the Cold War and what it shares in common with other militarized disputes. It is

---

[22] Author interviews with Georgyi Shakhnazarov, Vadim Zagladin, Mikhail Gorbachev, Moscow, May 1989.

[23] On the Munich lesson, see Ernest R. May, *'Lessons' of the Past: The Use and Misuse of History in American Foreign Policy* (New York: Oxford University Press, 1973); Richard Ned Lebow, 'Generational Learning and Conflict Management', *International Journal*, 40 (Autumn 1985), pp. 555–85; Yuen Foong Khong, Analogies at War: *Korea, Munich, Dien Bien Phu, and the Vietnam Decisions of 1965* (Princeton, NJ: Princeton University Press, 1992).

[24] Volkogonov, *Stalin*, ch. 54; Zubok and Pleshakov, *Inside the Kremlin's Cold War*, pp. 47–53; David Holloway, *Stalin and the Bomb* (New Haven: Yale University Press, 1994), pp. 253–72; on the military lessons of World War II, see Raymond L. Garthoff, *The Soviet Image of Future War* (Washington, DC: Public Affairs Press, 1959).

also essential if we are to develop and evaluate explanations for the end of the Cold War based on more general theories or understandings of conflict.

So far there has been very little comparative analysis of the Cold War. Some realists have employed variants of power transition theories to explain Gorbachev's search for accommodation, and the author has compared Soviet-American rapprochement to that of Egypt-Israel and France-Britain to develop a set of propositions about at least one pathway to accommodation.[25] Several quantitatively oriented researchers have examined the Cold War in conjunction with other rivalries.[26] Working in the interpretivist tradition, Paul Schroeder employs the *Annaliste* concept of the *histoire de longue duré* to root the Cold War in a broader cycle of transformation of the international system.[27] These several efforts are described in the chapters that address structural, domestic politics and leader explanations for the end of the Cold War.

My goal in this section of the article is to encourage comparative study of the Cold War by proposing a framework that would be attractive to a wide range of scholars regardless of which of the four generic explanations they favour. This would require reasonable specification of the dependent variable(s), protocols for case identification and coding, and an appropriate data set of successful and unsuccessful attempts at accommodation. I will argue that such a framework would also be useful to interpretivist scholars.

Recent controversies in international relations scholarship—those surrounding deterrence and the democratic peace, for example—focus at least as much on the coding and interpretation of data as they do on research design or competing explanations for political phenomena. Indeed, the debate is often over whether or not there is any phenomenon to explain. Critics dispute the 'evidence' marshalled in support of immediate deterrence successes and the democratic peace. Such controversies are inevitable and constructive to the extent they draw attention to sloppy or inappropriate case selection and coding. But they are also frustrating when they render comparisons of research findings difficult or meaningless because the scholars involved are working with different dependent variables, data sets and case coding protocols.[28]

---

[25] Richard Ned Lebow, 'The Long Peace, the End of the Cold War, and the Failure of Realism', and Kenneth A. Oye, 'Explaining the End of the Cold War: Morphological and Behavioral Adaptations to the Nuclear Peace?', in Richard Ned Lebow and Thomas Risse-Kappen, *International Relations Theory and the End of the Cold War* (New York: Columbia University Press, 1995), pp. 23–56 and 57–84. Richard Ned Lebow, 'The Search for Accommodation: Gorbachev in Comparative Perspective', in Lebow and Risse-Kappen, *International Relations Theory and the End of the Cold War*, pp. 167–86, and 'Transitions and Transformations: Building International Cooperation', *Security Studies*, 6 (Spring 1997), pp. 154–79.

[26] Paul F. Diehl, *The Dynamic of Enduring Rivalries* (Urbana: University of Illinois Press, 1997); Gary Goertz and Paul F. Diehl, 'The Initiation and Termination of Enduring Rivalries: The Impact of Political Shocks', *American Journal of Political Science*, 39 (1995), pp. 291–308.

[27] Paul W. Schroeder, 'The End of the Cold War in the Light of History', unpublished paper, January 1997.

[28] Richard Ned Lebow and Janice Gross Stein, 'Deterrence: The Elusive Dependent Variable', *World Politics*, 42 (April 1990), pp. 336–69; Paul Huth and Bruce Russett, 'Testing Deterrence Theory: Rigor Makes a Difference', *World Politics*, 42 (July 1990), pp. 466–501, on deterrence. The literature on the democratic peace is vast. For a recent and thoughtful review of the controversy, see Steve Chan, 'In Search of Democratic Peace: Problems and Promise', *Mershon International Studies Review*, 41, Supplement 1 (May 1997), pp. 59–92.

It is naive to assume that the latter kind of conflicts can or should be avoided. It would nevertheless be an interesting exercise—and a highly productive one if it succeeded—to try to build a consensus around a research design among a diverse community of scholars. The goal of a common research design is not to preclude other approaches—fortunately, no attempt to impose orthodoxy is ever likely to succeed—but rather to encourage a corpus of research based on the same dependent variables and data that will facilitate meaningful comparisons. The only possible way to build a consensus around a research design is to bring scholars together *before* they have carried out major research projects and have become committed to particular ways of framing the problem or of identifying and coding cases. As so little comparative research has been conducted on the peaceful resolution of militarized rivalries, this might be an attractive problem in which to try such a cooperative strategy.

The starting point for any research design is the dependent variable. Just what is it that we want to explain? Peaceful accommodation is the greatest enigma associated with the Cold War. Even a cursory review of the literature on accommodation reveals that the concept is often left undefined or used differently by different researchers. I propose a three-stage conceptualization of accommodation based on the recognition that the first, and most essential, step toward any meaningful accommodation is reduction of the threat of war. Every accommodation must start with this goal, and some do not go beyond it. Egypt and Israel are currently stalled at this stage. Since the Camp David Accords and the peace treaty they signed in 1979, the threat of war between these former adversaries has significantly diminished. Both countries have redeployed their forces away from each other's borders, adhered to the terms of the political-military agreements to which they are signatories and have refrained from provocative military actions or manoeuvres directed against the other. Egyptian and Israeli analysts, and outside experts, judge the risk of war between them to be extremely low, and this despite acute tensions in the region that have led to deteriorating political relations.

Israeli-Egyptian rapprochement has not progressed beyond the stage of war reduction. There is a limited exchange of tourists, most of them Israelis who visit Cairo and Red Sea beach resorts, hardly any trade, and the Egyptian media remain staunchly anti-Israel in substance and tone. It is possible that in the aftermath of an Israeli-Palestinian accord, and an upturn in the Egyptian economy that reduced the influence of fundamentalists, the two countries might increase their trade and social contacts. Egypt under a different government—the worst case being a fundamentalist regime that encouraged similar movement elsewhere in the Middle East—and a failed peace process between Israel and the Palestinians could escalate tension to the point where another war would become conceivable.

More profound accommodations involve a broader range of positive political, military, economic and social interactions that build a trajectory of cooperation and goodwill between former adversaries. These interactions must involve peoples, businesses, educational and cultural organizations, local and regional authorities, not just national governments. They must become institutionalized at all levels, creating a common interest and mutual expectations of further cooperation and raising the costs of defection. Over time, cooperation must be seen by peoples and leaders alike as the 'natural' order of things, and war, not only unlikely, but almost unthinkable. Karl Deutsch called this stage of accommodation a 'security community'.[29] The United States and Britain, Britain and France, France and Germany, and the United States and Japan can all be said to have reached this stage of accommodation.

Other accommodations, like Russia and Germany, Russia and the United States, and China and the United States, are best classified as transitional. Foreign relations with former adversaries are focused on the resolution or diminution of political friction and the expansion of trade and other kinds of intercourse. These dyads have passed beyond the first stage of accommodation and their relations are characterized by some of the characteristics that promote security communities. In the American accommodation with Russia and China, intergovernmental tension remains muted to acute over a range of issues (e.g. human rights, nuclear weapons, NATO expansion, Taiwan). Only time will tell if cooperation between these former adversaries deepens, broadens and become more institutionalized, stalls, or slips back toward confrontation.

My threefold categorization attempts to capture distinctive stages of a process that is sequential but neither inevitable nor irreversible. It allows us to track and assess the progress of militarized rivalries toward accommodation, and to make appropriate comparisons across cases. As each stage of the process has different defining features, it is likely to be characterized by a distinct set of dynamics. The catalysts for each stage, and the conditions that facilitate and sustain it, are also likely to be different. For purposes of analysis, the *problematique* of accommodation is best studied in discrete, well-defined stages. This is the implicit assumption of this volume, whose chapters speak primarily to the attainment of stage one.

Judging when and where a particular stage begins or ends, or what stage of accommodation describes specific conflict, will always be a matter of interpretation. It could plausibly be argued that the Cold War moved toward the first stage of accommodation with the détente of the late 1960s, slipped back to confrontation in the middle 1970s, and moved more convincingly into the first stage in the late 1980s. In the early 1990s, following the unification of Germany, the dissolution of the Warsaw Pact and the breakup of the Soviet Union, Russia's relations with the countries of Western Europe and the United States moved into the transitional stage. The periodization of the Cold War, by this or any other scheme, encourages us to think conceptually about the broader context of Gorbachev's foreign policy revolution and the end of the Cold War it helped to bring about. The interpretation I offer above, for example, suggests the proposition that the accommodation initiated by Gorbachev was predicated upon earlier, if temporarily aborted, progress toward significantly reducing the threat of war. Does this hold true in other cases?

If the end of the Cold War represents the decisive attainment of stage one with subsequent progress toward stage two, we would want to compare it to other militarized rivalries that have also at least moved as far toward accommodation. For this, we need an appropriate data that could be used by quantitatively and qualitatively oriented researchers to develop and test a wide range of propositions

---

[29] According to Karl W. Deutsch, et al., *Political Community and the North Atlantic Area* (Princeton, NJ: Princeton University Press, 1957), pp. 5–6, a security community exists where 'there is a real assurance that members of that community will not fight each other physically, but will settle their disputes in some other way'. Deutsch distinguished between amalgamated security communities, where there has been a formal merger of two more previously independent units, and pluralistic communities in which separate governments retain legal independence.

about accommodation and its causes. Researchers interested in enduring rivalries and militarized rivalries have constructed data sets that could serve as useful starting points for our effort.[30] William Thompson and Paul Diehl and Gary Goertz are both assembling data sets of enduring rivalries. Diehl and Goertz expect to produce a comprehensive list of rivalries for a 175 year period ending in 1992. We could apply our criteria to decide which of these cases to include, and then proceed to identify all attempts at accommodation made by either protagonist, and determine their outcomes. We could also chart the progress any of these rivalries made through different stages of accommodation, and identify those that were resolved peacefully (reached the third stage of accommodation). Other questions could be posed to reflect the interests of participating international relations scholars.

A data set of this kind is a major undertaking that requires the assistance of historians with detailed knowledge of these rivalries. We would need to involve historians whose collective expertise covers the time period, regions and conflicts included in the data set. The political scientists involved in the project would have to provide the historians with appropriate conceptual tools including precise working definitions of attempts at accommodation, success and failure, and of the three stages of accommodation—or of any other typology about which we all concur. If possible, we should ask more than one historian to search and evaluate each conflict, and send controversial cases to a panel of historians for assessment. The historians could also be asked to flag those cases, or aspects of them, they find difficult or problematic to code. In all cases, the historians should provide short written justifications of their judgments concerning attempts at accommodation, their outcomes and the stages these conflicts passed through. If there is considerable variation in judgment across historians concerning particular cases, we could produce more than one version of our data set to allow researchers to see how robust their findings are across these several sets.

The resulting data set would provide the empirical basis for a major collaborative project by a diverse group of international relations scholars. Participants could formulate individual research designs and propositions and use the data set to test them. Quantitatively oriented scholars could do cross-case comparisons, and qualitatively disposed scholars could study a sample of cases in detail. Individual scholars from the two groups should be encouraged to cooperate; scholars with quantitative interests and skills could help their qualitative colleagues test propositions they have developed from cases in larger samples. Scholars with case study skills could help their quantitative colleagues try to establish causation through process tracing in selected cases. Both groups might profit from the deductive theories and insights of formal or computational modellers.

---

[30] Charles. S. Gochman and Zeev Maoz, 'Militarized Interstate Disputes, 1816–1976', *Journal of Conflict Resolution*, 28 (December 1984), pp. 585–615; Gary Goertz and Paul F. Diehl, 'The Empirical Importance of Enduring Rivalries', *International Interactions*, 18:2 (1992), pp. 151–63, and 'The Initiation and Termination of Enduring Rivalries: The Impact of Political Shocks', *American Journal of Political Science*, 39 (February 1995), pp. 30–52, and 'Enduring Rivalries: Theoretical Constructs and Empirical Patterns', *International Studies Quarterly*, 37 (June 1993), pp. 147–71; William R. Thompson, 'Principal Rivalries', *Journal of Conflict Resolution*, 39 (1995), pp. 195–223; John A. Vasquez, 'Distinguishing Rivals That Go to War from Those That Do Not: A Quantitative Comparative Case Study of the Two Paths to War', *International Studies Quarterly*, 40 (December 1996), pp. 531–58.

We would need the further assistance from the historians after the initial stage of quantitative and case study research. Propositions that appear robust in explaining attempts at accommodation need to be tested against a sample that allows variation on the dependent variable. This should be relatively straightforward for efforts to explain the success and failure of attempts at accommodation because our data set is almost certain to include both outcomes. It is more difficult for explanations of attempts at accommodation because the data set would be composed entirely of such events. I hypothesize that one of the situations in which leaders seek accommodation is when (1) they are committed to domestic reforms that they believe require accommodation with a foreign adversary for strategic and tactical reasons; (2) are convinced that confrontation has failed in the past and will fail again in the future; and (3) expect their conciliatory overtures to be reciprocated. To test the null hypothesis, I would have to go back and search the conflicts for the presence of these conditions on occasions other than those where leaders made or even seriously considered attempts at accommodation. I would have to reconsider my explanation if I find such examples. The help of historians would be essential in testing this and other explanations for attempts at accommodation.

I have described a standard cross-case research design. This research strategy can be problematic in international relations. Cross-case comparison requires independence among cases; the outcome of one cannot be influenced by the outcome of another. It seems self-evident that this condition does not hold in many attempts at accommodation. Successful accommodations can become catalysts for other accommodations because they encourage trust or optimism or because of the strategic dilemmas they create for third parties. The Anglo-French Entente made Anglo-Russian rapprochement possible, and France played an important role behind the scenes in bringing it about. The Israeli-Palestinian breakthrough in Oslo promptly led to an Israeli-Jordanian rapprochement. The end of the Cold War has had global reverberations, and to varying degrees and for different reasons, has been a catalyst for accommodation in interstate and internal conflicts in Northeast and South Asia, the Middle East and Southern Africa.

The end of the Cold War in turn might be understood as the result of a deeper transformation. Some liberals might contend that it was due to the spread of democratic ideas and widespread desires for a market economy, and that this also accounts for recent progress toward accommodation elsewhere in the world. According to Paul Schroeder, the Cold War was a struggle to work out a new, practical definition of peace that could become the basis for legitimate international order. The end of the Cold War, and progress toward accommodations elsewhere, reflect the emergence and wide acceptance of such a definition. Cross-case comparisons that studied conflicts without taking such underlying, contextual features into account could fail to capture the most essential features of the phenomenon under study.

Cross-case comparison can also be insensitive to the internal history of the conflicts. As noted earlier, at least some scholars believe that the kind of accommodation set in motion by Gorbachev's foreign policy revolution would have been difficult to achieve at an earlier stage of the East-West conflict. No Soviet leader would have had the incentive or latitude to make the kinds of unilateral concessions that Gorbachev did or to expect a conciliatory and self-restrained response on the part of the West. Sino-American accommodation is similarly difficult to imagine in the 1950s or 1960s, given the still-fresh memories of war, unresolved and potentially explosive conflicts concerning Taiwan and the political future of Indochina, and the domestic constraints operating in Peking and Washington. To understand accommodation, conflicts need to be put into historical context in a triple sense. They are dependent on the prior course and evolution of the conflict; developments in other conflicts, especially those to which they are in some way connected; and more general shifts in power capabilities and ideas in the international system or community. Adequate conceptual tools to relate individual conflicts to these contextual influences have yet to be developed.

Quantitative research on accommodation can incorporate contextual features by relying on typologies of conflict that capture salient features of context, and limit comparisons to cases in the same cells. Can such typologies be developed? Neopositivists are likely to be more optimistic than interpretivists, who tend to stress the idiosyncratic features of individual conflicts and the importance of path dependency. Here too, some kind of collaboration could be fruitful. Quantitative and case study researchers, the latter drawn from both neopositivist and more interpretivist perspectives, might work together to understand the different ways in which features of context help and hinder accommodation, and to debate their implications for individual cases and cross-case comparisons.

Test—Evaluate—Verify

The need to develop compound explanations for the end of the Cold War should be recognized by scholars regardless of their point of entry into the analytical puzzle. The starting point of such a venture is identification, specification and evaluation of the most promising variants of our four generic explanations. None of these variants in and of itself can provide a compelling explanation for the end of the Cold War. But they are the building blocks for compound explanations that may succeed in this task and, by doing so, direct our attention to building theories that combine explanations across levels of analysis.

An enterprise of this kind requires agreed-upon protocols to test or evaluate variants of the four generic explanations for the end of the Cold War. I use both the verbs test and evaluate because the proposed enterprise should be open to participants from both the neopositivist and interpretivist traditions.

Testing is relevant to cause-and-effect propositions rooted in the nomothetic idea that recurrent law-like processes exist. Testing takes two forms: prediction and explanation. Prediction attempts to establish association between the expectations of a theory or proposition and real-world behaviour, past, present or future. The data set used for testing must be different from the one from which the theory or propositions may have been derived. Explanation identifies the causal mechanisms responsible for the predicted outcome. In social science, explanation—as distinct from association—is most frequently established by process tracing, where researchers use case studies to document the links between the causal mechanisms that are posited and the behaviour in question.

Evaluation is appropriate to the interpretivist perspective, where understanding (*verstehen*) is the goal, and is rooted in the assumptions that reason and irrationality are constitutive of actors and the societies in which they are embedded. Interpretivists deny the feasibility of objective theories of social behaviour. The purpose of social science is to help us understand our own lives, individually and collectively. History is a repository of human experience that each generation examines anew from the perspective of its own experience and concerns. There is no one correct way of framing or analysing a problem, but multiple interpretations that generate different and valuable insights. Interpretivist scholarship also aspires to high professional standards. It can be evaluated by the quality of its narrative. Does it provide a coherent explanation that makes sense of the empirical evidence in terms of the subjective understandings relevant actors have of this evidence, themselves and the social context in which they operate? Other accounts may also 'fit' the evidence, and competing accounts ought to be further evaluated on the basis of their 'generative' properties. Do they highlight and draw attention to hitherto unknown or neglected processes, turning points and collective understandings that raise interesting questions and prompt research into them? Such a research agenda may succeed in redefining in fundamental ways our conception of the Cold War. Some interpretivists contend that research can also be evaluated in terms of the insights it offers into contemporary life and its problems.

The two traditions are generally thought of as antithetical, or at least orthogonal, but they intersect in interesting ways. Both base their legitimacy on compelling interpretation of empirical evidence. For many interpretivists case analysis is the ultimate goal, while for positivists it is only a means to the end of theory building and testing. Positivistic approaches to international relations have traditionally placed more emphasis on deductive theory building and statistical techniques of testing than they have on the interpretative problems involved in data set construction and the coding of cases. In recent years, quantitative researchers have become more sensitive to these problems and more open to dialogue with qualitative researchers, some of whom work in the interpretivist tradition. A recent, prominent study of research methods in international relations contends that qualitative researchers should emulate the methodological rigour of their quantitative colleagues.[31] But many quantitative researchers recognize that they can also profit from the methods and experience of qualitative researchers.

Large *n* studies depend on typologies to provide relevant categories of analysis and to code cases either on the dependent or independent variables. In international relations, most typologies are based on structural characteristics (e.g. polarity) of the environment or behaviour (e.g. deterrence) of actors. Case selection is based on the fit of cases with these structural or behavioural criteria, and cases are then selected to provide variation on dependent and independent variables. Typologies, case selection and coding are often treated as unproblematic, or merely technical questions. Interpretivist case research, which emphasizes the intersubjective understandings actors have of themselves, other actors, their relationships with these actors, and the environment, suggests that categories of analysis used by international relations scholars often bear little relationship to the categories and case interpretations actors use to frame problems, evaluate their interests, make policy

---

[31] Gary King, Robert O. Keohane and Sidney Verba, *Social Inquiry: Scientific Inference in Quantitative Research* (Princeton, NJ: Princeton University Press, 1994). See also the critical review symposium in *American Political Science Review*, 89 (June 1995), pp. 454–82.

and draw lessons. Interpretivist scholarship suggests that it is necessary to work with the subjective understandings of actors to understand or predict their behaviour.

Theories of unit level behaviour with categories of analysis irrelevant to or different from those of actors are not likely to model their behaviour well. Theories with more appropriate categories, but which rely on observers rather than actors to apply these categories to specific cases, are likely to fail for the same reason. The deterrence literature illustrates both problems. Neopositivist analyses of immediate deterrence have assumed that the military balance and reputation are the decisive categories of analysis for challengers and defenders. Interpretivist case studies indicate otherwise. They also reveal that the roles of challenger and defender—the categories on which the theory and strategy of deterrence are premised—are rarely shared understandings; both sides in so-called immediate deterrence encounters are likely to see themselves as the defender and the other side as the challenger. Interpretivists contend that statistical findings based on the codings of scholar-observers at variance with those of actors are meaningless.[32]

Some neopositivist scholars have rejected this critique out of hand.[33] A more responsive approach would be to construct typologies and other categories of analysis on the basis of actors' subjective understandings of themselves, other actors and their environment. Theories of this kind would be more rigorous in the proper sense of the term and likely to have a better fit with the empirical reality they purport to explain and predict. Such an approach would require a greatly expanded dialogue between large n and case researchers, and greater investment in case and data interpretation by quantitative researchers, but the payoff might be commensurate with the effort.

And back to the empirical

Good social science requires explanation as well as prediction. Theories are incomplete if they do not specify the reasons why the outcomes they predict occur. They remain unsubstantiated even if the predicted outcome occurs because it could be the result of co-variation and explained better by some other theory. Case studies are an ideal vehicle for the kind of process that helps to show causation by documenting the links between independent and dependent variables. The nature of these links will vary as a function of the *explanans*. For structural theories that expect actors to react to the constraints and opportunities of the international or domestic environment, it is necessary to show that policymakers understood these constraints and opportunities and formulated the initiatives in response to them. For idea-based explanations, researchers must establish that policymakers were motivated by goals associated with these ideas, or framed the policy problem and their interests in terms

---

[32] Robert Jervis, Richard Ned Lebow and Janice Gross Stein, *Psychology and Deterrence* (Baltimore, MD: Johns Hopkins University Press, 1985); Beyond Deterrence, George Levinger (ed.), *Journal of Social Issues*, 43:4 (1987); Paul C. Stern, Robert Axelrod, Robert Jervis, Roy Radner (eds.), *Perspectives on Deterrence* (New York: Oxford University Press, 1989); The Rational Deterrence Debate: A Symposium, *World Politics*, 41 (January 1989), pp. 143–266.

[33] Huth and Russett, 'Testing Deterrence Theory', and Lebow and Stein, 'Deterrence: The Elusive Dependent Variable'.

of them. Leader-based explanations must demonstrate the connections between leaders' decisions and their goals, personalities and subjective understanding of their environment.

Process tracing makes heavy requirements on data, and even in data-rich situations it is often difficult to document the motives and calculations of key actors. In the Soviet Union, access to key archives is still restricted and uncertain, and pessimists in this field worry that the window of opportunity we have been exploiting may close in post-Yeltsin Russia. We have also benefited from interviews with former Soviet, American and European officials who were key participants in the decisions that ended the Cold War. Most of these officials are still alive and retain vivid, if not always accurate, memories of these events. Documents are essential for process tracing, but recent studies of Cold War crises indicate that they can be incomplete and sometimes misleading. The Soviet decision to deploy missiles in Cuba in May 1962 was shrouded in secrecy, and very few written records were kept by the handful of officials involved in its planning and initial execution. On the American side, President Kennedy deliberately avoided leaving any paper trail of his agreement to withdraw the Jupiter missiles from Turkey in return for withdrawal of the Soviet missiles from Cuba. In October 1973, Leonid Brezhnev made all the important decisions concerning Soviet Middle East policy in consultation with a small circle of advisors, and few records were kept of their deliberations. Process tracing of the decisions that led to the end of the Cold War must rely on oral as well as written evidence.[34]

The Soviet Union was one of the most secret societies the world has known, and it was not until the era of *glasnost* that Russian or Western scholars could gather the kind of evidence necessary to conduct meaningful case studies. The recent flow of evidence has encouraged high expectations about resolving some of the mysteries of the Soviet system and its leaders, and much of interest has come to light. New evidence from archives, interviews and conferences will never produce a definitive 'answer' to the question of what brought the Cold War to an end.[35] Nor is it likely that a consensus will form around any variant explanation, or combination of variants. An analogy to 1914 is relevant. The outpouring of documents and memoirs on the origins of World War I fuelled, rather than resolved, controversy. But it also encouraged a more sophisticated debate by discrediting early, simplistic explanations (e.g. the Kaiser planned a war of aggression), and elicited more complex and nuanced explanations that built on evidence and insights from social science. By compelling scholars to specify different pathways to war, the *Kriegschuldfrage* also provided conceptual lenses and analogies that proved useful in understanding the Cold War and other conflicts. In sum, the decades-long debate over the origins of World War I, while still unresolved, was an important catalyst for the development both of international relations theory and foreign policy thinking. President Kennedy's reluctance to carry out an air strike in the Cuban missile crisis derived in large part from his earlier reading of Barbara Tuchman's *The Guns of August*, and its portrayal of World War I as a case of runaway, mutual escalation. There is every reason to expect that rigorous study of the end of the Cold War, based on new

---

[34] Lebow and Stein, *We All Lost the Cold War*, pp. 9–14, for a fuller discussion of this problem.
[35] This point is also made by William Wohlforth, 'New Evidence on Moscow's Cold War: Ambiguity in Search of Theory', *Diplomatic History*, 21 (Spring 1997), pp. 229–42.

empirical evidence, better specification, and even reformulation of existing explanations, their evaluation by means of an in-depth case study, and subsequently, by comparative analysis, will generate the same kinds of theoretical and policy insights into the process of accommodation.

History ends, worlds collide

CHRIS BROWN

Introduction

The end of the Cold War was an event of great significance in human history, the consequences of which demand to be glossed in broad terms rather than reduced to a meaningless series of events. Neorealist writers on international relations would disagree; most such see the end of the Cold War in terms of the collapse of a bipolar balance of power system and its (temporary) replacement by the hegemony of the winning state, which in turn will be replaced by a new balance. There is obviously a story to be told here, they would argue, but not a new kind of story, nor a particularly momentous one. Such shifts in the distribution of power are a matter of business as usual for the international system.[1] The end of the Cold War was a blip on the chart of modern history and analysts of international politics (educated in the latest techniques of quantitative and qualitative analysis in the social sciences) ought, from this perspective, to be unwilling to draw general conclusions on the basis of a few, albeit quite unusual, events. Such modesty is, as a rule, wise, but on this occasion it is misplaced. The Cold War was not simply a convenient shorthand for conflict between two superpowers, as the neorealists would have it. Rather it encompassed deep-seated divisions about the organization and content of political, economic and social life at all levels.

An interregnum?

The sense that something important happened in 1989 is conveyed by the general theme of this collection, although it should be noted that the Gramscian notion of an 'Interregnum' is, in one important respect, question-begging. If the Cold War is taken to begin not with conflicts over the post-1945 future of Eastern Europe, but with the ideological clash between Woodrow Wilson and Lenin in 1917, or perhaps

---

[1] Key writings expressing this perspective are helpfully collected in Michael E. Brown, Sean M. Lynne Jones and Steven Miller (eds.), *The Perils of Anarchy: Contemporary Realism and International Security* (Cambridge MA: MIT Press, 1995). This *International Security* Reader contains the most influential post-Cold War realist theoretical manifestos, John Mearsheimer 'Back to the Future: Instability in Europe after the Cold War', *International Security*, 15 (1990), pp. 5–56 and Kenneth Waltz 'The Emerging Structure of International Security', *International Security*, 18 (1993), pp. 44–79. William Wohlforth 'Realism and the End of the Cold War', *International Security*, 19 (1994/5) and in the same collection, argues that the Cold War was not a balanced system, and its ending simply confirmed US hegemony.

much earlier, with the failed liberal revolutions of 1848 or even the French Revolution of 1789, then what we have seen in the 1990s may not have been part of an interregnum, an interval between two different international orders: this may actually *be* the new order. It is not impossible, although perhaps a little improbable, that the period from 1789–1989 may come to be seen as the real interregnum, a two-century long transition period during which the implications of the fall of the *Ancien Régime* worked their way through domestic and international political, economic and social systems. On the other hand, as Chou En Lai is alleged to have remarked when questioned on the significance of the French Revolution, it may be too soon to say.

How is this putative new order to be understood? A bewildering number of different approaches to this issue have circulated over the last decade. Some of the most famous have been based on positively apocalyptic predictions such as 'the end of history' or the 'clash of civilizations'.[2] Such formulations certainly take seriously the scale of the change taking place, and the debates they have stimulated have performed a valuable service in bringing this issue of scale to the forefront. Nonetheless, it may be premature to attempt to capture the nature of our time with such broad brush-strokes. Equally valuable may be the many less grandiloquent, more empirical, attempts to work out what is going on. Labourers in the 'democratic peace' vineyard, theorists of liberal hegemony, writers on modernization and globalization, students of cultural diversity, cosmopolitan democrats—the list of those who have tried to put things together but who have resisted the lure of overgeneralization is long.

In what follows, an attempt will be made to bring together these different bodies of work. It will be seen that two quite different stories about the post-Cold War world emerge. In one, the end of the Cold War is seen as ushering in an (indefinite) period of world dominance by forces which, using the term very broadly, could be seen as 'liberal'. One version of this story stresses the hegemony of the United States, the liberal-democratic, 'constitutional' empire; another—but at the same level of analysis—looks to the democratic peace and the realization of Kant's vision of a pacific union of republican states; and yet another emphasizes the ideological dimension of 1989, the sense that market economies are somehow 'natural' and liberal democratic politics 'normal', both terms being much used in East Central Europe and the Soviet Union in the late 1980s. Fukuyama writes of 'the total exhaustion of viable systemic alternatives to Western liberalism' as a precondition for his end of history.[3] The dystopic consequences of this ideological dimension are stressed by those who fear the adverse effect of neoliberal economics on the poor, and the homogenization brought about by a 'McWorld' version of globalization. All these approaches agree that, for better or for worse, the essentially liberal combination of a market economy with a system of representative democracy has seen off all its deadliest enemies—the immediate future may involve a number of 'mopping-up' operations (ideological and military) in which pockets of resistance are overcome, but the real campaign is over.

---

[2] Francis Fukuyama 'The End of History?', *The National Interest*, 16 (1989), pp. 3–16, and *The End of History and the Last Man* (New York: Free Press, 1992): Samuel Huntington 'The Clash of Civilizations', *Foreign Affairs*, 72 (1993) and *The Clash of Civilizations and the Remaking of World Order* (New York: Simon and Schuster, 1996).
[3] 'The End of History', p. 3.

The alternative vision of the future cannot be summarized so easily, because its very essence is to predict difference and diversity. From this perspective the contending parties in the Cold War had more in common than they were prepared to admit; liberalism and communism are but different versions of Western post-Enlightenment universalism, and the victory of liberalism over communism does no more than end a civil war within the West. The real divisions in the world lie elsewhere, between civilizations, or religions or ethno-national groupings, and the ending of the Cold War simply allows this real agenda to become visible once again (or, perhaps, for the first time). Modernity is not something that comes with a Western trademark—the 'Jihad' that Barber opposes to 'McWorld' can be fought with the Internet and the fax machine as well as more traditional methods of self-sacrifice and terror.[4] There are alternatives to neoliberal economic doctrines and liberal democratic politics, and the environmental degradation which the former causes and the latter is unable to prevent provides a strong reason for thinking that these alternatives will prevail in some parts of the world. Civilizations may clash or they may coexist but either way they will remain plural. The victory of the West has been much exaggerated.

These two different visions of the future will be examined below, but, as will gradually become apparent, the terms of this binary opposition are highly suspect. Although there has been a tendency in the literature to organize discussion around a debate between Western liberalism and its critics (even the West versus the Rest) this may be both analytically and normatively confusing—the future may well be more a case of but/and rather than either/or.[5] However, before this conclusion can be reached a number of earlier stages of the argument must be rehearsed, beginning with an account of liberalism triumphant.

Liberalism triumphs

Of all the post-communist national leaders in Eastern Europe and the former Soviet Union, none can claim greater moral or intellectual authority than Václav Havel, the former dissident, political prisoner, playwright and Velvet Underground fan who became President of Czechoslovakia after 1989, and is now President of the Czech Republic. His reflections on our era are worthy of respect; naturally enough he is a democrat and a political liberal, but slightly less predictable are his thoughts on economic organisation:

Though my heart may be left of centre, I have always known that the only economic system that works is a market economy, in which everything belongs to somebody—which means that somebody is responsible for everything. . . . This is the only natural economy, the only kind that makes sense, the only one that can lead to prosperity because it is the only one that reflects the nature of life itself. The essence of life is infinitely and mysteriously multiform, and therefore it cannot be contained or planned for, in its fullness and variability, by any central intelligence.[6]

---

[4] Benjamin Barber, *Jihad vs. McWorld* (New York: Ballantine Books, 1996).
[5] Kishore Mahbubani, 'The West and The Rest', *The National Interest*, 28 (1992), pp. 3–13.
[6] Václav Havel, 'What I Believe', in *Summer Meditations on Politics, Morality and Civility in a Time of Transition* [Tr. Paul Wilson] (London: Faber and Faber, 1992), p. 62.

His first point—that under a market system somebody is responsible for everything—may seem overoptimistic to those more familiar with the ability of capitalist enterprises to dodge this responsibility, but makes sense coming from someone who was only too well aware of the environmental degradation inflicted on the industrial areas of Czechoslovakia, Poland and the German Democratic Republic by communist industrial policy. His second point repays closer examination.

Arguments for the naturalness of markets—even, or perhaps especially, when buttressed by meditations about the essence of life—are not usually taken seriously. Most social scientists learn early on in their education that the historical record undermines any idea that markets are the only way of organizing economic activity, and that the ideas of the political economists of the eighteenth and nineteenth centuries were products of their age and not, as they believed, for all time; Havel's remarks are unlikely to shake our faith in the fundamental truth of these positions. However, add two qualifications taken for granted by Havel, and a different, more plausible picture emerges. First, restrict consideration to complex industrial and post-industrial societies and the inevitability of a market economy becomes apparent. If there is one clear lesson to be learnt from the Soviet experiment it is that once the early stages of industrialization have been gone through, the command economy cannot be made to work. The range of variables which need to be kept in play to ensure that, for a very simple example, the right number of size nine boots are available in Kiev when people need them is simply too large to be modelled even using the most advanced computers—and this is without taking into consideration issues such as consumer choice, style and fashion.[7]

Of course, the command economy can be made to work after a fashion if it is combined with political repression, but Havel's second unspoken assumption—unspoken on this occasion at least—is that this is unacceptable. Some form of representative democracy is the only legitimate form of government, not because it is the most efficient, or because it can be relied upon to make the 'best' decisions from some external viewpoint, but because it is the only form of government consistent with the assumption of natural human equality.[8] Alternative modes of legitimation such as the authority of the party crumbled in the face of this fact in the 1980s. There is a real irony here. The 'legitimation crisis' predicted for post-1945 welfare capitalism by Habermas, O'Connor and others in the 1970s did not occur; wholesale disruptions to pre-established social patterns took place in many of these societies, Britain in particular, in the 1980s but de-legitimation did not take place because no acceptable alternative to representative democracy was available.[9] Far lower levels of disruption led to the de-legitimation of the Soviet regime precisely because its rulers were unelected and were unwilling to replace the mild repression of the Brezhnev years with a return to Stalinism.

If these points are right, then something very important has been demonstrated over the last decades. The combination of some kind of market economy with repre-

---

[7] Alec Nove, *The Economics of Feasible Socialism* (London: Allen and Unwin, 1983) and *The Economics of Feasible Socialism Revisited* (London: Unwin Hyman, 1991), provides the demonstration of this point.

[8] See Brian Barry, 'Is Democracy Special?', in *Democracy, Power and Justice: Essays in Political Theory* (Oxford: Clarendon Press, 1989), p. 56.

[9] Jürgen Habermas, *Legitimation Crisis* (London: Heinemann Educational books, 1976); James O'Connor, *The Fiscal Crisis of the State* (New York: St. Martins Press, 1971).

sentative democracy does seem to be the only effective way of running complex industrial and postindustrial societies. This should not be read as an endorsement of Thatcherism or Reagonomics (which, unfortunately, is how the lessons of 1989 have been misunderstood in parts of East-Central Europe); rather, this combination leaves room for a great deal of variation in types of regime and in the level of planning that accompanies markets, from neoliberal systems, to welfare capitalism, traditional social democracy, the 'Third Way' and so on. But it does rule out some possibilities that have been taken very seriously in the past. Since the emergence of industrial society, the most persistent opponents of liberal capitalism from right and left have argued that it is both possible and desirable to replace the impersonal forces of the market by conscious human control. Even those who were repelled by the politics of the Soviet Union and the stupidities of Soviet central planning assumed that a better way of reaching the same goal could be devised. Part of this process would be the simultaneous replacement of 'bourgeois' democracy with a genuine people's democracy (as opposed to the fake version offered by 'really-existing socialism'). Recent experiences make it difficult to take either of these ideas seriously. Richard Rorty captures the significance of this very crisply when he remarks that '[if] you still long for total revolution, for the Radical Other on a world historical scale, the events of 1989 show that you are out of luck'.[10]

There obviously remain many serious problems with liberalism/capitalism. The transition to liberal political and economic forms has not gone smoothly in many areas of Eastern Europe, partly because of the misunderstanding noted above; broadly speaking, those countries where some kind of civil society survived under communism have done best, in some cases very well indeed, while those (including the Russian Republic) where civil society and an effective state-apparatus had to be created simultaneously have done much less well, in some cases very badly. Some kind of authoritarian rule may emerge in these latter countries but no-one, including the reformed communist parties of the region, anticipates the re-establishment of old-style command economies. In this sense, the absence of a viable systematic alternative form of rule, liberalism has triumphed. The next step is to examine whether, as Fukuyama and others have suggested, this triumph applies equally to those parts of the world which were not directly involved in the great contest between liberalism and socialism of the past century and a half. But before moving in this direction a digression on the international relations of triumphant liberalism is in order.

Liberal empire, democratic peace?

'Liberal internationalism' is what one might term the 'default' liberal theory of international relations. Given its clearest expression in 1917–19 by Woodrow Wilson, Leonard Woolf, Robert Cecil and other advocates of international organization in

---

[10] Richard Rorty, 'The End of Leninism, Havel, and Social Hope', in *Truth and Progress: Philosophical Papers*, vol. 3 (Cambridge: Cambridge University Press, 1998), p. 229. This essay, originally written in 1991, is one of the best reflections on the implications for the democratic Left of the end of the Cold War.

the post-World War I era, it envisages a world of democratic states committed to the principles of national self determination and free trade between nations, the rule of law internationally and membership of global institutions. It draws upon Kantian notions of a federation of republican states dedicated to the abolition of war, and Manchester School doctrines stressing the importance of non-intervention and the peace-generating qualities of trade. It finds contemporary expression in the United Nations system (and in particular in the cluster of specialized agencies that have grown up to manage, or oversee, the global economy), in regional bodies such as the European Union (although the latter may have ambitions to outgrow the pluralism of liberal internationalism), and in the international human rights regime. President Bush's 'New World Order' of 1990 was a marginally modified version of the doctrine; as is Prime Minister Tony Blair's 'Doctrine of the International Community'.[11] Many contemporary theorists of international relations, impressed with the difficulty of managing cooperation among egoistic states, now think in terms of neoliberalism rather than liberal thought unqualified, nevertheless, liberal internationalism in the full sense still has its supporters.[12]

Perhaps the strongest contemporary support for the underlying theoretical assumptions of liberal internationalism comes from the literature on the 'democratic peace'. Nearly twenty years ago, the basic proposition of this body of work was given its clearest expression by Michael Doyle: constitutionally stable democracies do not fight each other, he noted.[13] Doyle based this proposition on some simple statistics and an argument drawn from Kant (although his equation of modern liberal-democracies with Kantian republics can be questioned). However, a great many writers after Doyle, driven partly no doubt by the changing circumstances of the 1980s and 1990s (and in particular by the growth in the number of liberal democracies), have carried out very sophisticated statistical analyses, and found it to be highly robust, that is to say not dependent on particular definitions of either war or democracy.[14] In spite of this, the democratic peace hypothesis has attracted a great deal of hostile commentary: in part from neorealists for whom model regime-type is, by definition, irrelevant; but also from liberals who, for reasons that are not entirely clear, find the proposition unconvincing if not positively offensive.[15] Possibly the latter have not grasped the nature of the argument, thinking, wrongly, that the proposition asserts a general peacefulness on the part of liberal states, or believing

---

[11] Tony Blair, 'Doctrine of the International Community', speech in Chicago, 22 April, 1999.

[12] Robert O. Keohane, *International Institutions and State Power* (Boulder, CO: Westview Press, 1989) is a standard reference point for neoliberalism, along with the essays collected in David A. Baldwin (ed.), *Neorealism and Neoliberalism The Contemporary Debate* (New York: Columbia University Press, 1993). An interesting recent contribution, difficult to classify is Andrew Moravcsik 'Taking Preferences Seriously: The Liberal Theory of International Politics', *International Organisation*, 51 (1997), pp. 513–53.

[13] Michael Doyle, 'Kant, Liberal Legacies and Foreign Policy', parts 1 & 2, *Philosophy and Public Affairs*, 12, (1983), pp. 205–35, 323–53; see also Doyle 'Liberalism and World Politics', *American Political Science Review*, 80 (1986), pp. 1151–70.

[14] Particularly useful collections are Bruce Russett, *Grasping the Democratic Peace: Principles for a Post Cold War World* (Princeton, NJ: Princeton University Press, 1993) and Nils P. Gleditsch and Thomas Risse-Kappen (eds.), 'Democracy and Peace', Special Issue *European Journal of International Relations*, 1 (1995), pp. 429–574.

[15] See, e.g. John Macmillan, 'Democracies Don't Fight: A Case of the Wrong Research Agenda', *Review of International Studies*, 22 (1996), pp. 275–99, Raymond Cohen 'Pacific Unions: A Reappraisal of the Theory (sic) that "Democracies Do Not Go to War with Each Other"', *Review of International Studies*, 20 (1994), pp. 207–23.

that it is possible to refute a statistical generalization by anecdote. More charitably, critics of all types point out rightly that the 'democratic peace' is not a theory of international relations, but simply an empirical observation. What they perhaps fail to see is that this observation provides quite important support to liberal inter-nationalist accounts of international relations. When in 1919 liberals argued that liberal-democratic states would not go to war with each other, they had very little empirical support for this generalization, there having been too few liberal-democratic regimes at the time to provide a suitable data-base. Nowadays this proposition is very well supported, and writers such as Russett have begun the task of identifying the mechanisms by which democracy, selectively, hinders war-making.[16]

Part of the reason for scepticism about the 'democratic peace' perhaps derives from the current distribution of world power, that is from the status of the US as the only surviving superpower. In any event, American predominance certainly does have considerable significance for any current assessment of liberal internationalism; in 1919 it was assumed that in the emerging order the US would be one of the most powerful liberal states, and perhaps the most powerful, but no-one at that point envisaged the kind of concentration of power that emerged immediately after 1945, and has emerged again with the ending of the Cold War and the rapid decline of Soviet and Russian power. One result of this predominance is that it becomes simultaneously both very important and very difficult to distinguish between the impact on the world system of a victorious liberal internationalism and that of hegemonic America—to distinguish between the New World Order and the New World giving the Orders, as the saying goes. Characterizing the contemporary inter-national order becomes, in important respects, a matter of characterizing America's role in world affairs, forming a view about the way in which the United States exercises, and has exercised, its power.

One very instructive account of the exercise of American power is that given in a recent series of articles by G. John Ikenberry.[17] His thesis is that in the post-1945 world the US employed its power to create institutions which were designed to act in such a way as to bind the United States itself as well as its competitors. In so doing, the US in effect traded some of the potential short-term gains from its pre-dominance in exchange for a greater flow of benefits over the longer term. Thus, initially, a system of international rules and regulations would constrain US policy more than that of other states, because the US had the power to act on its own and they did not, but, in the longer run, in so far as other states found themselves increasingly able to develop independent positions but were constrained from so doing, the system would benefit the US. The US effectively foreswore direct use of its hegemony in order to create a 'constitutional' basis for world politics, thereby

---

[16] Russett *Grasping the Democratic Peace*, refers to 'cultural-normative' and 'structural-institutional' explanations for the democratic peace; David Lake presents a compelling argument in terms of democratic elites resisting rent-seeking militarists both at home and abroad in 'Powerful Pacifists: Democratic States and War', *American Political Science Review*, 86 (1992), pp. 24–37.

[17] G. John Ikenberry, 'Constitutional Politics in International Relations', *European Journal of International Relations*, 4 (1998), pp. 147–177, 'Institutions, Strategic Restraint, and the Persistence of American Post-War Order', *International Security*, 23 (1998/9), pp. 43–78. See also *After Victory: Institutions, Strategic Restraint, and the Rebuilding of Order after Major Wars* (forthcoming).

regulating the terms of interstate competition to its long-run advantage.[18] On Ikenberry's account, the US will continue to reap the benefits of this policy so long as it does not turn its back on constitutional international politics by reneging on its international obligations, and undermining the organisations it created, by looking for short-term gains—a serious possibility given the populist streak always present in US politics, but one that he believes can be resisted. What is striking about this perspective is the way in which it can be aligned with what, on the face of it, seems to be the very different angle on American power developed by Susan Strange.[19] Strange's analysis of the continuing structural power of the US parallels Ikenberry's account of the benefits to be gained by 'constitutionalizing' world politics; her realist insistence that international regimes mask power is recognized by his model—the point at which they part company is over whether or not international relations are generally to be characterized as norm-governed. Strange argued that they are not, while Ikenberry's account assumes that norms can be made to stick.

The liberal approach to international relations rests very heavily upon the ability of international institutions to promote cooperation and collectively manage conflict; given America's central role in the international economy, and its undoubted military predominance, international institutions are unlikely to work effectively unless it is US policy that they should do so. Similarly, if the promotion of liberal values in the world, the protection of human rights (or at least the prevention of wholesale 'human wrongs') is part of the liberal approach to international relations, then, in the last resort, this will only happen if the US is prepared to make it happen; economic pressures only work when the world's largest economy is behind them, and only the US possesses the logistic capacity, military infrastructure and hardware to engage in humanitarian interventions on any serious scale.

In effect, this means that the liberal nature of contemporary international relations is at the mercy of the contingencies of US policies and politics. This is an uncomfortable situation; at best the American political system is vulnerable to pressures from special interests (the various groups which have consistently distorted US policy towards the Middle East in favour of Israeli interests are an obvious example) while at worst, a President and Congress obsessed with the most recent opinion poll are incapable of developing a consistent attitude towards the rest of the world. The various US foreign policy failures of the last decade nearly all relate to the unwillingness or inability of her leaders to persuade the American people to take a long view of their interests. Such short-termism, unless checked, will eventually undermine Ikenberry's 'constitutional' world politics. Moreover, the unwillingness on the part of American Presidents to place US soldiers 'in harm's way' places a serious constraint on the use of force whether in defence of the national interest or in situations where threats to liberal values would seem to demand a military response. The liberal world is curiously vulnerable to threats which ought, in principle, to be easy to deal with. The world's only superpower possesses military might that far surpasses that of its potential enemies, but is prepared to use only those dimensions of this force that do not put more than a few of its soldiers' lives at risk,

---

[18] This is a more fruitful use of notion of hegemony than in the standard 'hegemonic stability' debate— e.g. Robert O. Keohane, 'The Theory of Hegemonic Stability and Changes in International Economic Regimes 1967–77, in *International Institutions and State Power* (Boulder, CO: Westview Press, 1989).

[19] See e.g. Susan Strange, 'The Persistent Myth of Lost Hegemony', *International Organisation*, 41 (1987), pp. 551–74 and S*tates and Markets* (London: Pinter Publishers, 1988).

which means, in practice, cruise missiles and air-power. A state with a military establishment which, while prepared to kill, is not prepared to risk the lives of its soldiers is morally compromised and highly vulnerable to political leaders who are not so constrained.

The unfolding events in the Balkans in the Spring and Summer of 1999 put these points into perspective. Far more than the Gulf War of 1990–91, does it seem likely that NATO's war with Yugoslavia over the fate of Kosovo will be seen as a defining event of the post-Cold War era. NATO, here, has been fighting a liberal's war; that is to say, a war fought predominantly in response to gross human rights violations and threats of genocide, although it is fair to say that, as the conflict has progressed, NATO's own credibility as an organization also became an issue. The war was opposed in the United States and Western Europe by those who believe that foreign policy decisions should be made on the basis of a narrow definition of the national interest, and supported by those who believe that the Western alliance has a duty to prevent wholesale breaches of humanitarian law, most notably the New Labour government in Britain, the Social Democrat/Green coalition in Germany and most democratic shades of opinion in France.[20] It would seem that NATO's campaign was a qualified success, although exactly why Milosevic agreed to withdraw his troops is likely to be debated by future historians and our evaluation of the war will have to await the test of time. In any event, some general points about the conflict can be still be made.

First, the crisis underlined the extent to which the fate of liberal internationalism is tied up with American domestic politics. President Clinton's capacity to ask for the kind of sacrifices from the American people that it seemed a successful prosecution of the war would probably require was seriously compromised by his recent political troubles, and it is noticeable that all of the main contenders to succeed him in office were rather more circumspect about the aims of the campaign than the main NATO leaders in Britain, France and Germany.

Second, the war emphasized the surreally inappropriate understanding of the nature of warfare, whether modern or postmodern, by most contemporary liberals on both sides of the Atlantic.[21] This is not simply a matter of expecting to fight a war without sustaining casualties; equally striking is the apparent belief that *inflicting* casualties is, in almost all circumstances, morally unacceptable, irrespective of the overall justice of the action or the intentions of the participants. Judging by the reactions of the media, the liberal expectation is that it is possible to fight a war without accidents, errors or misjudgments and while preserving at all times the reality of non-combatant immunity; the Yugoslav ability to manipulate that media, especially television, by providing ample access to NATO 'atrocities' while ensuring that there were no photo-opportunities of the crimes committed by its own police and paramilitaries, fed off and reinforced this absurd expectation and might well have undermined the campaign as a whole—in which case the killing fields of Kosovo would have remained forever closed to prying eyes.

---

[20] Of course, some who share the liberal aspirations of the latter have, not unreasonably, questioned NATO's strategy and tactics in this particular case (albeit usually without suggesting plausible alternative ways in which liberal values could be defended), and those who oppose American policies as a matter of course, more or less irrespective of content, have found ways of describing NATO policies as yet one more example of US imperialism.

[21] See, for a diagnosis and corrective, Christopher Coker, *War and the Illiberal Conscience* (Boulder, CO: Westview Press, 1998).

Third, and most significant, if, as at one time seemed likely, NATO had failed to achieve its prime objective (that is, the reversal of the deportation of the population of Kosovo by the Yugoslav government) the institutional structure upon which liberal internationalism has been based would have been placed under extreme pressure, the post-Cold War expansion of NATO halted or reversed, EU expansion put on hold and, *in extremis*, the link between US and Western European security forged over the last half century broken. Had that happened the development of a European defence identity would not have been impossible, but John Mearsheimer's prediction of a return to the traditional, pre-1914 pattern of international politics would have been a more likely outcome—that is to say, although we may have had a world predominantly composed of 'liberal' states, these states would conduct their international relations not in accordance with the principles of liberal inter-nationalism, but by responding to the alleged imperatives of national interests shaped by international anarchy. This fate has probably been avoided (or at least deferred) by NATO's victory.

The end of history, or the end of *a* history?

After this digression on the fate of liberal internationalism, it is now appropriate to return to the main narrative of this essay, and consider Fukuyama's account of liberalism's triumph. So far, this discussion of the consequences of the end of the Cold War has addressed mainly the question of how things stand between the two ideological parties which fought out that conflict. This parochialism must now be overcome, and the wider question asked—what is the significance of the ending of the Cold War, and particularly of the terms under which the Cold War ended, for the rest of the world, for those countries who were touched by the great conflict but did not consider themselves to be directly involved, for those cultures whose underlying principles differ radically from those of either liberalism or communism? One answer to this question was given quite early on, in 1989, by Francis Fukuyama in his 'End of History' article.

So much has been written about Fukuyama's thesis—much of it on the false, and rather silly, assumption that the 'end of history' means that there will be no more events and that in the future nothing will happen—that the core of the argument has, effectively, been lost sight of; Fukuyama aided this process by expanding the article into a book in which his original Hegelian thesis was swamped by what was originally no more than a sub-text, namely a Nietzschean fear that the era of the 'last men' was about to be established.[22] Once this diversion is removed, what remains is a thesis of considerable strength and subtlety. Fukuyama argues that recent events have demonstrated yet again that the basic liberal model—the rule of law, political equality, representative democracy, the market economy—is, appar-ently, neither capable of being improved upon, nor vulnerable to external attack. The elements of this package have been around for approximately two centuries (Hegel first declared a kind of end to history in 1806) and have developed consider-ably since first formulated—thus, equality is now seen to encompass women as well

---

[22] For the 'last men' see the Prologue to Friedrich Nietzsche, *Thus Spake Zarathustra*.

as men, the working class and non-whites are no longer excluded and so on—but they have not been superseded. Attempts to transcend the limits of representative democracy, and critiques of the rule of law in terms of its bourgeois origins, whether launched from left or right, communism or fascism, have simply paved the way for tyranny. There is no viable form of emancipatory politics except that which takes place within the basic liberal model. Perhaps equally significant, is the fact that liberal states have proved more than capable of defeating tyrannies even on the grounds that the latter have chosen as consonant with their values; liberal states have been as effective in war as in peace—the martial spirit associated with autocracy and fascism has been unable to overcome the material and organisational superiority of states organised on liberal principles.[23]

In short, the big political questions have all been decided, and the age of romantic political heroism is over. Politics in the sense of struggles over who gets what, when and where remain and there is no reason to think that the international politics of the future will be characterized by the kind of cooperation that is envisaged by liberal internationalists; the point is that this kind of politics, unlike the heroic struggles of the past, is devoid of any kind of deep meaning. It is in this sense that history 'ends', and it is for this reason that the tone of Fukuyama's work is wistful rather than, as so many have assumed, triumphalist. Much of this is no more than a reworking in Hegelian language, modified by Alexandre Kojève, Allan Bloom, and Leo Strauss, of ideas that writers such as Havel have expressed in somewhat less flamboyant terms.[24] However, what does come through very clearly in Fukuyama's formulation is the strong universalist spin given to the triumph of liberalism. It is not simply that liberalism has outlived authoritarianism, fascism and communism: rather there is now no systematic alternative to liberalism in any part of the globe. Authoritarian ideas may persist, nationalism is still a potent force, religious 'fundamentalism' of one kind or another is not going away, but, Fukuyama argues, none of these forces provides the kind of package for handling modernity that liberalism provides. Globalization means the global spread of western liberalism, albeit not in any overt sense, and neither immediately nor without provoking often quite strong reactions; still, over the longer-run, it is only the liberal package that can provide other cultures with the resources to cope with the problems of legitimacy and effectiveness that globalization brings in its wake.

One response to this thesis—to be discussed in the next section of this article—puts a different spin on globalization altogether, arguing that far from creating uniformity, globalization encourages the expression of difference. Huntington's 'clash of civilizations' is one of the best known Western reference points for this position. However, as interesting, and perhaps more to the point, is a rather less well known text produced by a bureaucrat in the Japanese Ministry of Finance, Eisuke Sakakiba, whose article 'The End of Progressivism' was published in *Foreign Affairs* in 1995.[25] Progressivism, for Sakakiba is the belief that there is only one ideal end, a unique path for all human beings; both socialism and neoclassical capitalism are

---

[23] Always assuming, of course, that the liberal states in question are truly committed to the struggle and prepared to make the kind of sacrifices needed for victory; it is this commitment which appeared at one stage to be lacking in Kosovo.

[24] The source for many of Fukuyama's ideas on Hegel is Alexandre Kojève, *Introduction to the Reading of Hegel Lectures on the Phenomenology of Spirit*, ed. Allan Bloom (New York: Basic Books, 1969).

[25] 'The End of Progressivism: A Search for New Goals', *Foreign Affairs*, 74 (1995), pp. 8–15.

progressivist ideologies, and the former Soviet Union and the United States, experimental progressivist states. *Pace* Fukuyama, the demise of socialism—the ending of the Cold War which was a civil war within the Western ideology of progressivism—has not produced a victory for political liberalism and 'neoclassical capitalism'; instead it is progressivism as such that is under threat, made outdated by more fundamental issues, the need to control environmental pollution and establish the peaceful coexistence of civilizations.

As to the first of these points—the dream of neoclassical capitalism that the problems of consumption could be solved on a long term basis, and that the appeal of progress and the spread of mass consumption would perpetuate the domination of one kind of civilization on a long-term basis—this has proved an illusion in the face of problems of economic management, experienced in different ways by all the advanced industrial societies, and the emergence of environmental constraints to continued growth. What is required today is an ending of the belief that there can be a technological fix for these problems, the development of a less anthropocentric approach to nature, and, most of all, the recognition of the worth of different civilizations. The West must abandon sectarian progressivism in favour of respect for the environment and tolerance for other civilisations. Coexistence of civilizations is possible and existed in premodern times—'the clash of civilizations is not the unavoidable result of coexisting civilizations, but rather the result of contact with Western progressivism'—a point directed, of course, as much at Huntington as at Fukuyama, as is the thesis as a whole.[26]

Sakakiba's renaming of liberalism as one variant of Western sectarian progressivism constitutes a rather more basic challenge to Fukuyama's position than is customary. On this account it is not simply the case that liberalism fails to provide a universal model for the rest of the world—rather it is the very idea that there could be such a model that is under attack; the suggestion is that not only is liberalism not a suitable model for the rest of the world, it is not in fact a suitable model for the West itself. The problems of environmental degradation to which Sakakiba refers are taken to provide a general challenge to contemporary capitalism, not simply a comment on the future of capitalism in the non-western world.

On Sakakiba's account, Fukuyama has traced not the end of history, but the end of one particular history. Although Sakakiba does not use these terms, both liberalism and Soviet communism, in their different ways, were ideologies of the Enlightenment, and the victory of the first is a victory for the Enlightenment over itself rather than over some external enemy. On a wider stage the issue remains open. Sakabira's use of the term 'progressivism' seems somewhat reductionist—both liberalism and communism mean rather more than simply the assertion of one unique path for humanity—and a critic willing to use *ad hominem* arguments might well point out that the Director General of the Japanese International Finance Bureau is actually rather well placed to see exactly how far the liberal package of ideas had penetrated Japan and how attractive those ideas have been to the Japanese people. The real issue is whether the universal message Sakakiba deplores is inextricably built into this liberal package.

---

[26] Sakakiba, 'End of Progressivism', p. 13.

Globalization and the clash of civilizations

The relationship between globalization, westernization and universalism is complex and difficult to visualize, largely because each of these terms can be defined in a number of different ways, and the relationship is highly sensitive to which definitions are chosen. If we think of globalization in terms of the existence of a world economy in which production and finance are integrated by the new information technologies, and accompanied by common consumption patterns and socio-cultural trends spread by the 'infotainment' industry those technologies have spawned, then it would indeed be possible to assert that globalization goes together with westernization and universalism. A world in which everyone watches MTV or CNN while eating a Big Mac and wearing Nike trainers may not be a particularly attractive result of westernization but it can hardly be seen as the product of any other culture. However, as has often been pointed out, this is a picture of the emerging world that, precisely because it is so unattractive and devoid of food for the human spirit, stimulates powerful antibodies. Often these antibodies take the form of the kind of cultural and political movements that, because they frequently draw upon religious roots no longer taken seriously in most of the West, are termed by the latter 'fundamentalist', although other 'anti-systemic' movements take a different and less regressive form.[27]

The broad idea that the great world civilizations will be able to cope with globalization without becoming westernized is given one expression in Samuel Huntington's influential account of the 'clash of civilizations'. The burden of Huntington's thesis is that, with the end of the Cold War, a new basis of division has emerged in the world; the ideological conflicts of the past will be replaced by conflicts between 'cultures' or civilizations. Huntington identifies as the major contemporary civilizations the Sinic, Japanese, Hindu, Islamic and Western, with Orthodox and Latin American civilizations as possible derivations of Western civilization with identities of their own, and Africa (perhaps) making up the list. There is, to put it mildly, a certain element of the *ad hoc* about this, as Huntington concedes. In any event, on his account, there are three civilizations which are likely to generate serious potential problems in the near future—the declining West, the rising Sinic, and the unstable Islamic.

As this formulation might suggest, the first two components go together—economically, demographically and, ultimately, militarily, the West is losing power to the Asian civilizations and in particular to China (Huntington anticipates that China will come to dominate Japan and that the Japanese are likely to accept, tacitly, a subordinate status). This was, of course, written before the recent collapse of the Asian economic boom, but it is a moot point whether this would change the basic argument here. An increasingly successful and powerful China will not accept a world in which its values are regarded as inferior to those of the West and will not accept global socioeconomic institutions which limit its possibilities—and Huntington acknowledges that the existing structure of international institutions is indeed a product of Western/American hegemony and reflects Western values. Only by the West adopting a policy of coexistence and recognising the legitimacy of the

---

[27] See Giovanni Arrighi, Terence Hopkins and Immanuel Wallerstein, *Antisystemic Movements* (London: Verso, 1989).

Confucian way will violent conflict be avoided between these two civilizations. Chinese civilization will pose, indeed is posing, problems (particularly for the West but also for Japan) because of its success; the world of Islam will pose, indeed is posing, problems for all its neighbours because of its failure. Demographic pressures in Islam and the lack of any core Islamic state with the potential of China, or even the 'baby tigers' of south-east Asia, will lead to frustrations; moreover, Islam is a proselytising religion and Islamic civilization has borders with most of the other world civilizations. These borders ('fault-lines') will be, indeed already are, the site of many cross-civilizational conflicts, from Bosnia and Chechnya to Kashmir and the Sudan. Ending such conflicts may be virtually impossible, and certainly is far more difficult that the daunting enough task of promoting coexistence between Chinese and Western civilizations.

It is easy to pick holes in Huntington's work, especially the book-length version of his argument, which, precisely becomes it contains so much more detail is much more open to criticism—broad generalizations which pass muster in the enclosed context of a short article are less tolerable when more space is available.[28] Right from the outset his account of 'civilization' is *ad hoc* and muddled; civilizations are systems of ideas, and, as such, it is difficult to see how they could clash, although individuals and groups claiming to represent these ideas certainly can. Moreover, these systems of ideas are not now, nor have they ever been, self-contained or impermeable, a fact that Huntington acknowledges, but the significance of which he, perhaps, underplays. On the other hand, he deserves considerable credit for attempting to break up what was becoming in the early 1990s a rather sterile debate about the post-Cold War world. In his response to critics 'If not Civilizations, What?', Huntington suggests that the only alternative models for what he is interested in are the old statist paradigm and a new 'un-real' vision of one world united by globalization; this is to put the matter rather starkly, but there is some justice to this claim.[29] In effect, Huntington is providing a non-statist, but nonetheless realist, account of the world, which is an interesting addition to the conceptual toolkit of contemporary international relations theory. Part of the problem with Huntington's analysis, though, is that, although not statist, it remains spatial/territorial.

The prevailing metaphor in that book is that there are physical 'fault-lines' between civilizations. There are two problems with this notion; first, the analysis underplays the extent to which key dividing lines are man-made and recent—in former Yugoslavia, for example, the recurrent crises of the 1990s owe more to the success of Milosevic in mobilizing political support behind the nationalist cause of Greater Serbia than they do to largely spurious ethnic and religious differences, much less historical divides that go back to the Middle Ages or earlier. Such differences and divides certainly exist and have always existed, but their current political significance is the result of contingency rather than some inevitable process. Second, and rather more important, the 'tectonic' notion of civilizations does not recognise sufficiently the extent to which civilizations are already interpenetrated. The clash of civilizations, in so far as it exists at all, is more likely to take the form of the politics of multiculturalism and recognition in the major cities of the world than

---

[28] Much the same could be said of the relationship between Fukuyama's article and book, although, unlike Huntington, Fukuyama does actually develop a somewhat different line of argument in his longer work.

[29] Huntington, 'Response: If not Civilizations, What?', *Foreign Affairs*, 72 (1993).

violent clashes on the so-called 'fault-lines'; policing problems in London are, thankfully, more characteristic of this politics than ethnic cleansing in Kosovo, horrifying though the latter may be.

Bearing this latter point in mind, it may be worth examining another, more culturally oriented, notion of globalization, that offered by Arjun Appadurai, an Indian critic domiciled in the United States.[30] Appadurai suggests that the key features of globalization are the combination of mass migration and mass mediation. The large scale movement of peoples whether as refugees, migrants or guest workers, which is not in itself unique, creates a situation which is genuinely new when it is combined with revolutions in information technology and the mass media. Large-scale diasporic communities have formed throughout the world, no longer isolated from their homelands and destined to merge with the majority population, but now directly connected to these homelands by satellite television (both the globally owned networks and local stations), fax machines, cheap telephone calls, imported video-tapes and, most recently, the Internet. Using these resources diasporic communities are able to participate in homeland politics, and indeed, may, on occasion offer a political lead ; the role of the Sikh diaspora in Canada, the US and the UK in creating the Khalistan movement is a case in point. However, the change in sensibilities that globalization has brought about is not necessarily characterized by such dramatic doings; more significant in the longer run is that, for the first time in history, virtually everyone in the world is capable of imagining that they might *be* somewhere else, indeed might almost become *someone* else. So-called fundamentalists (religious and political) may not wish to admit this latter point, but the very violence with which contemporary fanatics express their viewpoints is an indicator of the extent to which they are aware that there are alternatives.[31]

This potential for mobility does not, Appadurai suggests, open the way to homogenization, but neither does it leave things as they are. Diasporic communities now have the ability to be as closely in touch with their places of origin as they wish to be, but neither community is unchanged by this intercourse. And, of course, host communities are changed by the presence of diaspora communities in their midst, and change those communities in turn. There is always a potential conflict between the images conveyed by local community-controlled media and the world of Baywatch, MTV and McDonald's, and Appadurai is sensitive to the ways in which various homogenizing images and practices become dispersed throughout the globe; his point is that these images and practices change in the process. One of his most interesting extended analyses of this process concerns the 'decolonization of Indian cricket', the ways in which a game introduced to India as a way of conveying British

[30] Arjun Appadurai, *Modernity at Large: Cultural Dimensions of Globalization* (Minneapolis, MN: Minnesota University Press, 1996).
[31] A remark made by an Islamic radical during a television debate on the Rushdie affair, to the effect that the Enlightenment had destroyed Christian belief and he and his followers were not going to allow it to destroy Islam, sticks in the mind (although, unfortunately, the exact reference does not). The point is that this remark indicates that the battle is already lost; clearly the speaker could envisage an alternative to his religion in a way that his forefathers could not, and traditional belief was, thus, no longer open to him. Once religion becomes something that one has chosen, its nature changes irretrievably.

imperial values has become an expression of Indian nationalism.[32] It is difficult to believe that anything remotely similar will happen to cultural practices such as looking at television pictures of scantily clad Californian life-guards, but the general point holds—it is a big mistake to think that the forces of globalization are unambiguous in their effects, or that different people in radically different environments read the same images in the same way. Equally it is a mistake to think of the effects of globalization in either/or terms—either McWorld or Jihad, universalism or particularism; the actual politics of globalization may involve both or neither.

Conclusion

Throughout this article—and following most of its sources—the issue of the nature of the post-Cold War international order has been posed in terms of oppositions: the end of history or the end of progressivism, liberal dominance or a clash of civilizations, Jihad or McWorld. This set of choices does indeed convey some sense of what is going but on the whole it obscures more than it illuminates. What is particularly damaging about the way in which these oppositions are set up is that they tend to define the most important questions about the future in terms of a choice between universalism and particularism, with the underlying assumption that the former is the progressive option, while the latter, though possibly unavoidable, is regressive and not to be desired. Even where universalism is given a somewhat sinister or troublesome connotation (McWorld or the 'End of History') the alternative is usually portrayed in even less favourable terms. Sakakiba and Appadurai are, of course, exceptions here, but it is noticeable that the discourse of contemporary international relations has made less of these figures than of their more Manichean counterparts.

This tendency to see things in either/or terms is particularly unfortunate because it misses some of the most important features of the actual debates on these issues. For example, in the field, as it were, it can be seen that some of the most effective moves made by critics of triumphalist (neo)liberalism actually draw on liberal and universalist thinking, most obviously the notions of global distributive justice and the idea of universal human rights. Such moves are not unproblematic; Immanuel Wallerstein catches the point nicely here in *Geopolitics and Geoculture*—universalism is 'a "gift" of the powerful to the weak' which places them in 'a double-bind: to refuse the gift is to lose; to accept the gift is to lose'.[33] The language of universal rights and justice is, on the one hand, a powerful resource in resisting the undesirable effects of globalization, but, on the other, is itself an agent of a particular kind of homogenization. To employ the language of global justice in order to deliver a

---

[32] *Modernity at Large*, ch. 5. 'Playing with Modernity: the Decolonization of Indian Cricket'; it is noteworthy that during the recent Cricket World Cup most of the television advertising on Sky Sports was oriented to British Asians, even when, in the best matches of the competition, South Africa played Australia. Cricket is now a Sub-Continental game with adherents in the rest of the Commonwealth rather than an English game with Sub-Continental followers.

[33] Immanuel Wallerstein, *Geopolitics and Geoculture: Essays on the Changing World-System* (Cambridge: Cambridge University Press, 1991), p. 199. Fred Dallmayr develops a similar line of argument (citing this passage), in *Alternative Visions: Paths in the Global Village* (Lanham, MD: Rowman and Littlefield, 1998).

critique of neoliberal economic policies in the South may involve accepting premises which entail agreeing that sometimes 'there is no alternative' to such policies. What possible response can there be to this dilemma? Wallerstein, and those who think with him on this, looks to the growth of antisystemic movements which will preserve difference but gradually grow into a global consciousness and, finally, restore the 'universal reality of liberty and equality'. Whether or not such a route to a new kind of liberal universalism is viable, this millenarian vision does at least have the merit of addressing the issues in terms which are frequently employed by the actual participants in contemporary political disputes, in a way that formulations such as the end of history or the clash of civilizations are not.

This latter point can be generalized, and in the process some notions that were set aside at the very beginning of this article can perhaps be partially rehabilitated. As noted then, realists are resistant to the idea that anything fundamental has changed over the last decade, and insist on our ability to understand the international system without reference to grand (or grandiloquent) formulations. As the rest of this article has attempted to show, this general approach is mistaken, but there are some elements of the realist package that it would be unwise to discount. The context under which state-power is exercised has changed dramatically in recent years, but states are still important entities in global politics, and political power has not been abolished, much less politics itself. One of the striking features of so many of the models for a new world order is the extent to which they are apolitical, to which they assume that the forces they identify will work themselves out in the world without reference to political power. It is not necessary to be a realist of any denomination to regard this as implausible. The future of America's liberal hegemony is not simply a function of the future of liberalism as a set of ideas; as suggested above, it is also, perhaps mainly, a function of political decisions made in Washington and elsewhere and made for contingent rather than principled reasons. Equally, whether 'civilizations' clash along particular fault-lines is going to depend on how the inhabitants of those key areas, and their neighbours, near and far, choose to define themselves or allow political entrepreneurs to define them, and this is a political process, not one that follows a cultural recipe book. More generally, the future of globalization will be a product of political practice rather than cultural or economic theory. In short, one way or another, the major questions about the future of world order which this article has addressed will be answered in the years to come, but they will not necessarily be answered in their own terms; the contingencies of political power may have the last word, as so often in the past.

Globalization and national governance: antinomy or interdependence?

LINDA WEISS

'Regardless of how you define or measure it, globalization is real and its impact on state power is significant', says the globalist. 'But how do you know?' replies the sceptic. In this opening interchange one sees the origin of a controversy that after almost a decade shows few signs of abating. Globalists continue to maintain that there are big, *fin-de-siècle* transformations under way in the world at large, which can be laid at the door of something called globalization. This new era—popularized as a 'world without borders' and symbolized by the dismantling of the Berlin Wall— ostensibly came into its own where the Cold War left off. Globalists of all shades see a new world order in the making, marked by the de-territorialization of economic and political affairs, the ascendance of highly mobile, transnational forms of capital, and the growth of global forms of governance. By the same token, globalization sceptics, scrutinizing very similar empirical terrain, continue to pose the same insistent question. The dispute between globalists and sceptics is *not* about the *reality* of change; it is about the nature and significance of the changes under way as well as the driving forces behind them. 'There is something out there', agree the sceptics, but it is not necessarily, or even primarily, responsible for what is going on 'in here'. The changes that fundamentally interest globalists are usually less economic than political. That is to say that their efforts to analyse or demonstrate economic change—the extent to which national economies have become more inter-connected through trade, production, finance, and the growing web of international rules and institutions—are often a prelude to the political project.

Whether that project seeks to promote economic liberalism, political cosmo-politanism, or global peace, it entails showing that the political geography of nation-states, and with it the territorial principle, is being outflanked by the economic geography of capital flows, that national forms of governance are thus swiftly becoming outdated or redundant, and that the task of intellectual analysis is to prepare the ground for political and policy transformation to better adapt to the new geoeconomic reality.[1] While the ultimate objectives of that project vary accord-ing to the broader interests and political orientations of the analyst,[2] most accounts

[1] Wolfgang H. Reinicke, *Global Public Policy: Governing Without Government?* (Washington, DC, 1998) offers an unusually rigorous and coherent statement of this position.

[2] For liberal internationalists the project of advancing economic interdependence is a means to a political end: de-territorializing/de-nationalizing politics and advancing new forms of democracy and governance. See for example the Brookings Institution's project on 'Integrating National Economies', which has published a series of 20 or so studies analysing governance issues on a wide range of topics. For some former Marxists as well, global economic integration is to be welcomed rather than opposed because it is the vehicle whereby the contradictions of capitalism are being intensified (as Marx noted in *The Communist Manifesto*), a key difference being that this time around the nation state will not be in a position to effect a rescue of the economic system. I thank Mhegnad Desai for this clarification.

59

nevertheless agree on one point: the state is no longer in command of its territory, governments have mostly lost control of the national economy, and their policies to promote wealth creation and social protection are destined to be ineffective. In various refinements of this idea, the nation-state is not necessarily displaced, but its powers are profoundly altered and in some fundamental respects superseded by new forms of governance above and below it.[3]

As far as globalists (and indeed many of their sceptic critics who devote much effort to measuring and refuting its importance) are concerned, then, global and national are *conflicting* principles of organization, and global networks are advancing *at the expense of* national ones. Most definitions presuppose this antinomy, and presumptions about globalization's policy impacts reinforce it.

This article argues that the juxtaposition of global and national is unfruitful. Its presumption of a zero-sum logic has led many commentators to mis-identify globalization as the major source of policy constraints, to overstate its 'transformative' (read 'weakening') impact, and to minimize its diverse outcomes. Globalization—as a real reflection of transborder flows rather than a jazzy metaphor for interconnectedness—is a highly circumscribed, partial process, and intrinsically limited by its dependence on (embeddedness in?) national and international rules and institutions. The world order has evolved in its present form not in opposition to the territorial principle, but rather on the basis of national *cum* institutional diversity (varieties of capitalism). To eliminate such diversity may also mean to destabilize rather than secure that order.

The article has four parts. The first outlines key points of agreement and disagreement between globalists and sceptics and notes considerable overlap in the way the meaning of globalization has often become confused with statements about its impact: i.e, as a process of state power erosion or transformation. The remaining sections show why this presumption of a zero-sum logic in the juxtaposition of global and national cannot be sustained. Part two contests the claim that increasing enmeshment in international regimes (political interdependence) marks the death of sovereignty and national policy autonomy, showing that international cooperation has been a pillar of so-called policy autonomy, and is increasingly the basis for capacity enhancement. Parts three and four appraise the proposition that transborder flows (economic integration) are eroding domestic capacities for economic governance and producing a new kind of (regulatory) state; these sections present a counterargument based on a range of comparative evidence—on social and industrial-techonology policies, as well as on approaches to financial liberalization—which point to the importance of domestic constraints, domestic orientations, and institutional capacities in understanding the global-national dynamic. A concluding section follows.

---

[3] For a clear statement of the globalization thesis and the way global flows are seen to impact on the state, see Jan Aart Scholte, 'Global Capitalism and the State', *International Affairs*, 73:3 (1997), pp. 427–52. See also, Susan Strange, *The Retreat of the State* (Cambridge, 1996); Philip G. Cerny, 'Globalization and Other Stories: The Search for a New Paradigm for International Relations', *International Journal*, 29: 1 (1996), pp. 617–37; Stephen J. Kobrin, 'The Architecture of Globalization: State Sovereignty in a Networked Global Economy', in J. H. Dunning (ed.), *Governments, Globalization, and International Business* (Oxford and New York, 1997); David Held, Anthony McGrew, Jonathon Perraton, and David Goldblatt, *Global Transformations* (Cambridge, 1999).

Why the fuss about globalization?

Ever since comparative historians and macrosociologists drew attention to the messiness that makes up a 'society', the idea of a nation-state as a self-contained entity, of a pure 'inside' set against an equally pure 'outside', has seemed little more than a convenient fiction.[4] Nation-states, like societies, have always been composed of multiple, conflicting, overlapping networks of interaction—social, cultural, economic, technical, even political. Some of those networks reach across to nearby borders, others to more far flung places; some networks are widely dispersed in space, others more narrowly based. Similarly, some of those far-flung networks may reach deeply into the nation-state, involving a significant share of its population (e.g. the market for tradeables), while others intersect more broadly though superficially (e.g. sports, arts, and media communities).

Nation-states, then, have always been enmeshed in multiple crossborder networks of interaction. So why the fuss about 'globalization'? The dispute between globalists and sceptics is not about whether nation-states are penetrated by crossborder networks of trade, finance and production, or enmeshed with other nation-states by virtue of these linkages, for in varying degrees this has long been the case. Rather, there are two major points of contention. The first is whether this enmeshment has led to the 'transcendence' of territory, that is, to the stage where 'cross-border' and 'open-border' relations—synonyms for internationalization and liberalization respectively—have been superseded by 'trans-border' relations.

While definitional disputes can slide into tedious concept chopping, the globalization debate has suffered less from the phenomenon of competing definitions than from the tendency to avoid any precision or consistency of useage. The use of precise terminology is however important if one is to understand what is really going on and how social and political actors may deal with it. If territorial transcendence has not occurred, then the concept of globalization is redundant.[5] In order to avoid redundance, globalists must therefore provide clear criteria for distinguishing *cross-border* flows (between entities operating in different countries) from *trans-border* ones (between entities operating without regard to territory).

But as soon as we ask the meaning of the phrase 'without regard to country/ territory/national boundary', it becomes clear that it cannot mean 'without regard to *any and every* territory'. In this sense, there can be no 'transcendence' of territorial space: for beyond the high seas and the high skies, every relationship and transaction (even those using electronic means, in so-called cyberspace) takes place within nationally defined borders—and is thereby subject, *in principle*, to the rules and laws of the nation-state in which it transpires (including intrafirm trade which is often misleadingly cited as evidence of 'trans-border'activity).[6] Thus the phrase 'without

---

[4] See, in particular, Michael Mann, *The Sources of Social Power*, vol. 1 (Cambridge, MA: 1986).

[5] Scholte, 'Gobal Capitalism and the State'.

[6] The important exception appears to be derivatives trading. See in particular, William D. Coleman , Private Governance and Democracy in International Finance', *Institute on Globalization and the Human Condition*, Working Paper Series, February (1999), pp. 14–15, who carefully dissects the domestic, international, and global aspects of financial systems and their governance. One could argue that the evolution of offshore debt or credit markets, designated as 'Euromarkets' to distinguish them from national financial systems, are a further important exception. These banking and securities markets, the basis for much of the global capital market development over the past 25 years, remove

regard to territory' can only mean 'without regard to *any particular* territory'—in the sense that, let us say for illustrative purposes, I am a trans-territorial global citizen to the extent that I call no place 'home' and have no legal, financial, political, professional or other attachment to any particular country. Of course I must live somewhere and work from some base (however impermanently), and while doing so I must observe the regulations of the country in which I reside; while in principle I can 'easily' change my base by moving to another country, my choice of country is not likely to be completely open-ended or arbitrary, but shaped by considerations of language, culture, professional appeal and other 'national' differentials.

Thus, one may operate in a transborder or global capacity, but this does not create a transcendent reality. It is more appropriately a 'globalization with borders'.[7] Indeed, non-empirical terms like transcendence—which evoke that other 'G' word—are perhaps best left to metaphysics. Similarly, just as borders are not being transcended, so they are not, in a literal sense, 'dissolving' or 'breaking down'. In some ways the existence of borders is being strengthened and affirmed so that the passage of goods and people is made more costly or difficult, in other ways the reality of borders has become less important (i.e., less constraining). Thus the statement, 'MNCs are less constrained by *particular* borders' seems more accurate than 'MNCs are unconstrained' (capital mobility is relative, not absolute); just as the statement, 'the state is more constrained by certain forms of mobile capital' (namely, by the bond and foreign exchange markets) is more accurate than 'the state is eroded by capital mobility'.[8] I shall not deal with the normative question of whether borders are a 'good' thing.[9] But as to whether they are the source of the world's most divisive struggles, historians of nationalism find no evidence that the Enlightenment ideal of a borderless world would bring an end to ethnic tribalism.[10]

A key question then, for both rigorous globalists and their sceptic critics, is whether the weight of transborder/global networks is increasing relative to national and international ones. Sceptics, necessarily rigorous in their measurement of global flows, have arrived at the conclusion that globalization is fundamentally a financial phenomenon, limited to certain capital markets.[11]

From this literature we can extract a number of stylized facts which contradict the globalist claim that the national economy is increasingly irrelevant: (1) in most

borrowing and lending from the jurisdiction and regulatory influence of national authorities. Thus, for example, the markets for dollar-denominated loans, deposits, and bonds in Asia or Europe are not subject to US banking or securities regulations. The differences in interest rates and other conditions that exist beween domestic and external markets stem mainly from the extent to which national regulatory constraints can be avoided. Yet even in offshore debt markets, where the role of territorially-based domestic institutions is marginal, at least on a day-to-day basis, 'every international bank is ultimately accountable to a single national regulator' (Kapstein, 1994).

[7] The phrase is from Michael Borrus and John Zysman, 'Globalization with Borders: the Rise of Wintelism as the Future of Global Competition', *Industry and Innovation*, 4: 2 (1997), pp. 141–66.

[8] On the overstatement and underevidencing of 'capital mobility', see the thought-provoking comments in M. Pollin (ed.), *Globalization and Progressive Economic Policy* (Cambridge, MA: 1998).

[9] On the post-Cold War sentiment that borders are inimical to peace, see Barry S. Strauss, 'A Truly Crucial Chapter In the History of Borders', *International Herald Tribune*, 30 April (1999), p. 9, Director of the Peace Studies programme at Cornell University.

[10] See, in particular, Anthony D. Smith, *Nations and Nationalism in a Global Age* (Cambridge, 1995).

[11] See Robert Wade, 'Globalization and Its Limits: Reports of the Death of the National Economy Are Greatly Exaggerated', in S. Berger and R. Dore (eds.), *National Diversity and Global Capitalism* (Ithaca, NY, 1996); Paul Hirst and Graham Thompson, *Globalization in Question* (Cambridge, 1999); Andrew Glyn, 'Internal and External Constraints on Egalitarian Policies', in D. Baker, G. Epstein, and R. Pollin (eds.), *Globalization and Progressive Economic Policy* (Cambridge, MA: 1999).

developed economies, about 90 per cent of production is still carried out for the domestic market and about 90 per cent of consumption is locally produced; (2) domestic investment by domestic capital is financed mostly by domestic savings and far exceeds the size of FDI flows in all major markets; (3) FDI inflows into OECD countries are predominantly (i.e., more than 50 per cent) for mergers and acquisitions which typically resemble portfolio investments, hence 'involving a change in ownership but with relatively little [international] impact on industry behavior'[12]; (4) world equity markets remain poorly integrated; all the major stock exchanges are primarily local markets deriving the bulk of their turnover from intracountry trading, not simply because most firms have an insufficiently strong global reputation to be traded actively on foreign markets, or because traders prefer to trade without exchange risk, but also because international issues of stocks must carry the same rights as, and be fungible with, domestic stock; as such, they tend to find their way back to the home market. Moreover, unlike the Euro- (read 'global') bond markets, international trading in stocks goes on in the same manner as domestic trading: e.g., a German mutual fund buys and sells IBM stock on the New York Stock Exchange just as an American fund would do; (5) companies remain mostly multinational rather than transnational, concentrating most of their production, assets, and strategic decision-making in their home country (and trade in their 'home' region); while MNCs produced some 40 per cent of world output in 1990, the share of their overseas subsidiaries and affiliates was only seven per cent, confirming the dominance of the home base; thus most R&D is still undertaken at home rather than spread across the globe; (6) trade and investment patterns indicate strong regional concentration rather than world-wide or even north-south integration; finally, however (7) finance remains the one area where genuinely global markets have evolved, most notably in foreign exchange which accounts for the majority of financial transactions conducted globally on a daily basis, but also to some degree in bank lending (through syndicated 'offshore' loans), and certain securities (mainly bonds and derivatives).

So as far as sceptics are concerned, then, outside of finance a compelling case for a globalization tendency has not been established. Sceptics would agree that national economies are today closely interconnected (whether more or less than in some previous era is an interesting issue but irrelevant to an understanding of how that interconnectedness may presently constrain national economic management).[13] But the degree and nature of those changes are often highly exaggerated: economies are still primarily national in scope; their enmeshment through trade, investment, and finance has not displaced the preponderance of 'national' networks of interaction. If anything, it has produced a more complex system in which international and transnational have developed in parallel with and complementary to national systems of production and finance.[14] If this conclusion has made little impression on globalists,

---

[12] Glyn, 'Internal and External', p. 402.

[13] For a balanced account of trends in international production and finance before 1914, see Paul Bairoch and Richard Kozul-Wright, 'Globalization Myths: Some Historical Reflections on Integration, Industrialization and Growth in the World Economy', UNCTAD discussion papers, 113:March (1996).

[14] Coleman observes that in the most 'globalized' sector, that of finance, the emergence of global markets in most areas of financial services has run in parallel and complemented processes of internationalization based on distinct national financial systems; see 'Private Governance and Democracy in International Finance', p. 5; On the rejection of the global-national dualism in international production, see Borrus and Zysman, 'Globalization with Borders'.

however, it is because most analysts assume that however limited globalization may presently seem in some respects, its further advancement is only a matter of time.[15]

From global flows to power shift?

But even if we were to assume further such advancement, in what way would it matter? Just how much is at stake in resolving the 'measurement' issue? Would it matter much whether countries and firms were trading more of their domestic output, or investing more of their capital abroad, or producing more of their goods offshore, or forming more alliances and entering agreements with other international actors? As far as most participants in the debate are concerned, it appears to matter a great deal, for one simple reason. *Both globalists and many of their sceptic critics have assumed that a globalized world involves a dramatic power shift*: one that restricts the scope for national institutions, actors, and policies while elevating the interests and preferences of non-national actors in a zero-sum form of logic. (Hence the widespread view that many political and policy changes among OECD governments, ranging from financial and welfare reforms to intergovernmental agreements, represent the response of besieged or hapless governments to transborder flows.)

In short, built into the very concept of globalization itself is a presumption about its win-lose impact on particular power actors. Definitions of globalization are often impossible to disentangle from causal statements about globalization's alleged effects (mainly on the state). Indeed, many definitions and recent accounts of globalization presuppose the very causal linkages which need to be demonstrated: if there is a globalization tendency, it is widely anticipated that this must entail less autonomy, capacity, or effectiveness for national decision-making *vis-à-vis* the domestic economy.[16] Thus, if global networks exist, it must be at the expense of national ones; and if national networks are under strain, it must be due to the impact of global ones. In short, globalization has by and large become synonymous with *state power erosion*. This zero-sum logic drives the reasoning process to the irresistible conclusion that global and national are antinomies rather than interdependent, competing rather than complementary.[17]

---

[15] A noteworthy exception is Reinicke, *Global Public Policy*, who draws attention to the sectoral, historical and geographical limits of globalization (while nevertheless being a strong advocate for a 'global' public policy).

[16] As Bairoch and Kozul-Wright observe, 'behind the basic disagreement as to whether globalization will lead to immizeration and economic crisis or to faster economic growth and convergence, there is a widely shared assumption that the role of the State in managing economic activity has already diminished under globalization pressures and will become irrelevant in the truly global economy', 'Globalization Myths', p. 4.

[17] There are several noteworthy exceptions to this negative-sum reasoning, among them those deriving from close analysis of international finance, production, and public policy, such as William D. Coleman, Financial Services, *Globalization and Domestic Policy Change: A Comparison of North America and the European Union* (Basingstoke, 1996); Reinicke, *Global Public Policy;* and Borrus and Zysman , 'Globalization with Borders'. For an argument that globalization has at times increased state sovereignty in the Southeast Asian growth economies, see Richard Stubbs, 'States, Sovereignty and the Response of Southeast Asia's "Miracle" Economies to Globalization', in D. Smith, D. J. Solinger and S. Topic (eds.), *State and Sovereignty in the World Economy* (London, forthcoming). Questioning of the global-national dualism is also a feature of recent conceptual analyses, in particular, Michael Mann, 'Has Globalization Ended the Rise and Rise of the Nation-State? *Review*

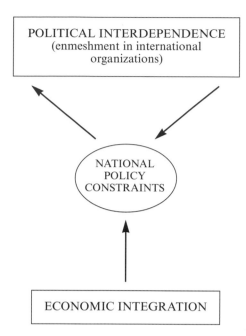

Figure 1. *The globalization hypothesis.*

Thus globalization has come to mean two quite different things: first, that trans-border networks are becoming more important than national and international ones; and second, that this process of economic enmeshment is eroding the basis of the state's authority and capacity to protect the social and economic well-being of its citizenry. In the language of globalism, state powers are being diminished, challenged, compromised, severely constrained, and ultimately transformed. And this is allegedly because of the advance of global and transnational networks, ostensibly exerting pressure both from below, in the form of mobile capital, and from above, in the form of a growing web of international rules and economic institutions.[18]

of International Political Economy, 4:3 (1997), pp. 472–96; and Ian Clark, 'Beyond the Great Divide: Globalization and the Theory of International Relations', *Review of International Studies*, 24 (1998), pp. 479ff. For many such writers a legitimate concern is that the regulatory bodies emerging out of intergovernmental cooperation to oversee global flows are not subject to democratic control—a sentiment neatly encapsulated in Scholte's statement that 'contemporary globalizing capital presents a challenge not to the survival of states, but to the realization of democracy', 'Global Capitalism and the State', p. 452. That may nonetheless downplay a more serious possibility. For if we turn our focus to 'threats' rather than 'challenges', we would have to conclude that some aspects of contemporary globalizing capital present a major threat not to the system of nation-states as such, but to the stability of the world economic order. Indeed, in the most globalized, risk-intense markets of all—derivatives—it is not even the absence of democracy, but the absence of any form of public governance that appears truly threatening. See Coleman, 'Private Governance and Democracy in International Finance'.

[18] Treaties relating to trade, tax and investment policies, as well as banking regulation, currency convertibility and so forth, tie countries together through multilateral agencies like the WTO, the G-7, and so forth.

But the question of whether or not there is a globalization tendency may ultimately prove less important than hitherto supposed. For the existence of globalization may be a poor predictor of its impact on state power. Figure 1 outlines the causal relationships implied in the globalist proposition that *economic integration creates national policy constraints, which together drive political interdependence (international cooperation), which in turn further reduces the scope for national governance.*

If we adopt this view, then state powers (specifically the capacity to pursue 'national policy preferences') are being forced to stand aside by two forces of globalization: on one hand the growth of economic integration, on the other, the increase in political interdependence. Regarding the first of these, the impact of economic integration on state power, it is important to emphasise that the policy constraints so often assumed to issue from global forces, in reality have quite complex sources—often of a predominantly domestic or structural character, as we shall see. In particular, I shall argue against globalism's central postulate that capital mobility has not only tied the hands of the social-protection state (social policy), but also proven the futility of its production-enhancing strategies (technology-industry policy). A related point is that some constraints are global only in an 'additional' sense—meaning that the constraints would exist *even in the absence of* international openness (as indicated below concerning the reaction of developed financial markets to deficit spending).

With regard to the second change in the environment of nation-states, the issue has to do with the alleged impact of international cooperation on national decision-making. To the extent that one can talk of a growing international political society—an expanding web of international norms, treaties, and institutions giving rise to sustained cooperation and higher levels of governance above the nation-state—this is indeed a major development. An unprecedented widening and deepening of international cooperation has led some to maintain that the nature of the state and of world politics are being fundamentally transformed. If this is simply taken to mean that states now cooperate over many more areas than in the past (hence by definition not monopolizing jurisdiction over 'internal' matters whenever these have 'external' consequences), then there is little to disagree with. Experts on jurisprudence may wish to cross swords on whether or not the state's sovereignty (a legal concept) is thereby affected, and whether it is properly 'internal' or 'external' sovereignty that is most implicated.[19] But for the purposes of appraising the capacity for national governance, we can safely leave such matters to one side.

If, however, political transformation is taken to mean that states have been compelled into cooperation by economic integration, or that international regimes displace fundamental national orientations and institutions, then there is much to disagree with concerning both the sources and consequences of cooperation, which are discussed in the following section.

---

[19] Among the many authors discussing this topic, see Robert O. Keohane, 'Sovereignty, Interdependence, and International Institutions', in L.B. Miller and M.J. Smith (eds.), *Ideas and Ideals* (Boulder, CO: 1993); Stephen D. Krasner, 'Westphalia and All That', in J. Goldstein and R.O. Keohane (eds.), *Ideas and Foreign Policy* (Ithaca, NY: 1993); Gianfranco Poggi, *The State: Its Nature, Development and Prospects* (Stanford, CA: 1990).

Does political interdependence curtail national policy autonomy?

On the sources of international cooperation, the main point to emphasize is that the foundations for international collaboration were laid long ago in the postwar settlement. That settlement called for a liberal regime of economic openness and international cooperation to sustain it. From this perspective, international political cooperation (systematized through the institutions of Bretton Woods) paved the way for economic integration (mainly through trade) rather than *vice versa*. If this feature is given less attention than it deserves, it is thanks largely to the impact of the Cold War. For in magnifying the importance of the 'containment order', Cold War politics served to deflect attention from this evolving internationalist 'liberal democratic order'. Multilateralism thus advanced in the aftermath of World War II under the Bretton Woods system, deepening political reciprocity and economic ties above all through institutional support for an open trading system. In this light, the end of the Cold War appears less as a watershed than a marker in the rediscovery and retrieval of the liberal internationalist project that had all along been developing at its own pace. As John Ikenberry writes, in putting a destructive era of economic rivalry and political turmoil behind them,'The major industrial democracies took it upon themselves to 'domesticate' their dealings through a dense web of multilateral institutions, intergovernmental relations, and joint management of the Western and world political economies.'[20] Clearly, then, while the multilateral order has grown in recent years, globalization is not responsible for its emergence: the vision, the means, and the power sharing arrangements at international level all predate the boom in capital mobility and transborder flows that has so inspired the new globalism.

Integration and interdependence as pillars of, or threats to, policy autonomy?

In what way, if any, has state power declined, and to what extent can such decline be attributed to the rise of transborder power actors? According to current conviction, state power has declined in one fundamental respect, namely, in its 'policy autonomy'. It is claimed that national governments can no longer readily pursue their policy preferences, or if they do they will incur unacceptably high costs. A key stimulus for this assertion is the notion that governments have veered away from Keynesian solutions to the twin problems of the advanced democracies—slow growth and high unemployment. The economist Maynard Keynes proposed that governments could play a major role in increasing employment at times of economic downturn. He argued that unemployment was cyclical, arising from a shortfall in demand for goods and services, and advocated two policies, both monetary and fiscal, for demand stimulation. The orthodox monetary prescription of lower interest rates sought to induce employers to invest in capital goods; while the more radical fiscal strategem of deliberate budget deficits aimed to increase demand through

---

[20] G. John Ikenberry, 'The Myth of Post-Cold War Chaos', *Foreign Affairs*, 75: 3 (1996), pp. 79–91. On the role of the IMF in promoting the postwar vision of liberal internationalism, see Louis W. Pauly, 'Promoting a Global Economy: The Normative Role of the International Monetary Fund', in R. Stubbs and G. Underhill (eds.), *Political Economy and the Changing Global Order* (New York, 1994).

public spending. Keynes insisted that the control of aggregate demand required governments to pursue both measures. It is often argued that Keynesian policies in this sense are 'severely constrained' by 'globalization' and economic openness. One response then is to try to turn back globalization in order to eliminate constraints.

However, the important issue is not the existence of constraints but their sources. Constraints on deficit spending tend to apply *even in the absence of financial globalization*. The transnationalization of financial markets can certainly speed up the response to deficit spending, but there is no evidence that it is the cause of that response in the sense of being either necessary or sufficient. A more insightful understanding of the causal process can be gained by asking what it is that triggers the adverse response of financial markets to deficit spending. As economists remind us, deficit spending increases the likelihood and anticipation of faster inflation in the future. It is the prospect of this inflationary outcome which induces capital flight, which in turn pushes up interest rates as investors attempt to circumvent future losses on their financial assets. In this way, the actions of financial markets end up bringing about the very outcomes that they anticipate. The key point, however, is that '*This [anticipatory action] would occur in any developed financial market and is not dependent on international financial integration*'.[21]

Whether the disciplinary action of finance comes in the form of a run on the currency due to balance of payments crises (for example, Britain in the 1960s), or the removal of capital offshore due to anticipated changes in government (for instance, the rise of Italy's Communist Party in the 1970s), the fact is that capital has long demonstrated willingness and ability to react to what it perceives as unfavourable policies. Indeed, there is ample evidence that capital mobility has long exerted a constraining impact on domestic policy, certainly well before one could speak meaningfully of global finance. Thus, while it may be argued that the creation of global financial markets has reinforced domestic policy constraints (and especially heightened awareness of them), the key point is that such constraints would exist independently of globalization. The main independent effect of financial globalization would therefore appear to be rather less than conventionally claimed.

The received wisdom nonetheless holds that after the Keynesian era, the state is 'less autonomous' and has 'less exclusive control' over economic and social processes within its territory. It is of course much easier to make assertions about 'more' and 'less' than it is to give substance to these notions. The effect of such statements is to construct a mythical Keynesian-era state: one wielding absolute autonomy and exclusive control.[22] Booming economies and high rates of world growth in the two decades after World War II helped to nurse the myth along by planting the idea that states were, once upon a time, wholly in command of their economies. In one sense, of course, there was the appearance of 'greater' autonomy than today: governments could more freely control the internal price of money (interest rates) and thus count on a more stable environment in which to advance their policy preferences (which, as Germany showed, were not necessarily 'Keynesian'). But the point that needs to be

---

[21] See Glyn, 'Internal and External Constraints on Egalitarian Policies', p. 397. Emphasis added.

[22] The idea that national governments were in control of their economies, independently pursuing their preferences took hold in the three decades after 1945, when trade openness was still a highly managed affair, and financial liberalization had barely begun. See Meghnad Desai, 'Global Governance', in M. Desai and P. Redfern (eds.), *Global Governance: Ethics and Economics of the World Order* (London and New York, 1995).

emphasized is that the 'greater autonomy'of yesteryear was only possible because states adhered to an internationally agreed system of rules for controlling the external price of money (fixed exchange rates).

'National' autonomy was therefore highly dependent on 'international' cooperation—under the so-called Bretton Woods system of fixed exchange rates. That international regime itself was highly dependent on the actions of one particular nation-state. As soon as the US withdrew (following Nixon's closure of the gold window in 1971), the system of fixed exchange rates could no longer be sustained and the state of the so-called Keynesian era (which is what most English-speaking analysts seem to intend by 'national economic management'), entered a more constraining environment. When states stopped cooperating in this formal manner, they lost their policy autonomy. The main point however is that then, as now, *policy autonomy was only partial*, and its foundations lay beyond the territorial control of any single state. National (policy) networks of interaction were thus closely intertwined with international ones.

International cooperation and infrastructural power

The preceding discussion made the point that globalists have overstated changes in state power (policy autonomy) and misidentified its sources. Since the end of World War II, macroeconomic policy autonomy has always been partial, highly dependent on the international context, and constrained by the existence of financial markets. The emergence of global financial markets, especially over the 1980s and 1990s, has not removed policy autonomy so much as heightened awareness of its partial nature. Nonetheless, globalists have gone on to make more ambitious claims about the impact of international institutions on state behaviour. They are certainly not overstating one of the novel features of our times in pointing to the expanding web of international treaties and institutions, which has emerged to regulate and adjudicate on matters of interstate behaviour. The number of conventional intergovernmental organizations alone rose from 123 in 1951 to 337 by 1986. (If one adds 'nonconventional' organizations, the numbers would more than double.)[23] The issue, however, is whether all of this cooperative activity is the harbinger of a new world political order. For that is fundamentally what many globalists appear to claim.[24] Does the multilateral revolution and its expression in institutions like the World Trade Organization (WTO) imply a corresponding obsolescence in the functions and capacities of national governance? Are the substantive policymaking powers of national governments being displaced in favour of supranational authorities? In short, is it the case—as implied in Figure 1—that these more or less

---

[23] Mark W. Zacher, 'The Decaying Pillars of the Westphalian Temple: Implications for International Order and Governance', in J. N. Rosenau and E.-O. Czempiel (eds.), *Governance Without Government: Order and Change in World Politics* (Cambridge, MA: 1992).

[24] See, for instance, David Held and Anthony McGrew, 'The End of the Older Order? Globalization and the Prospects for World Order', *Review of International Studies*, 24 (1998), pp. 219–43.

permanent alliances of sovereign states extinguish sovereignty and foreclose key areas for policy discretion as so widely believed?[25]

Experts in international relations have long debated the impact of international regimes (norms, rules, and institutions) on state behaviour. However, they have been at loggerheads over a much more modest set of claims than those expressed by globalists. Specifically, analysts from the realist tradition contest the liberal institutionalist's claim that international regimes can mitigate the effects of anarchy (a state system in which there is no central authority to keep sovereign states in check), and thus modify state behaviour to forego short-term advantages in exchange for long-term gains. Prominent institutionalists like Robert Keohane claim that once established, multilateral institutions (e.g., the World Bank, the International Monetary Fund, the WTO, the Bank of International Settlements) take on a life of their own, even though a world power or hegemon—in this instance, the US—may have been necessary for their creation.[26] Moreover, because of the services provided by international institutions (in particular, reducing uncertainty and the costs of making and enforcing agreements), states have an interest in their preservation. Thus if, as realists claim, the world is dominated by sovereign states, the function of international institutions appears especially puzzling. Moreover, the puzzle must remain without solution, says Keohane, *as long as institutions are viewed as standing in opposition to, or above, the state*; the problem can be solved however if institutions are 'viewed as devices to help states accomplish their objectives'.[27]

Although the role and impact of international institutions are controversial, when viewed in this way, one is struck by the complementarity of realist and liberal institutionalist positions, not their antagonism. Political interdependence does not mean that states trade in their objectives, but that they advance them through power sharing. Whatever their points of disagreement, analysts from both traditions share the view that multilateral institutions cannot compel states to act in ways that are contrary to states' own selfish interests. It may be that as states have become more enmeshed in an expanding web of economic and political ties, the costs of disrupting those ties through unilateral actions have grown. But that is an empirical claim that needs to be tested against specific cases. One may well find that the cost deterrent applies more clearly to the use of military force than to the protection and/or promotion of national economic interests, and more readily to small states than to larger ones. Certainly the proliferation of trade disputes even under a strengthened WTO offers some support for the latter part of this proposition. (Even

---

[25] Many assess this development in normative terms: as 'a good thing', on the assumption that any process or institution which dilutes sovereignty must be good for world peace or world freedom. The Enlightenment thinkers thought along parallel lines, advocating commerce as an antidote to war. See Albert Hirschman, *The Passions and the Interests: Political Arguments for Capitalism Before Its Triumph* (Princeton, NJ: 1977). Such reasoning culminated in Adam Smith's celebrated study, *The Wealth of Nations,* in which he proposed that increasing international trade would eliminate war between nations.

[26] See Robert O. Keohane, *International Institutions and State Power* (Boulder, CO: 1989); for a recent contribution to, and defence of, the realist position, which examines the problem of relative gains, see Joseph Grieco, 'Anarchy and the Limits of Cooperation: A Realist Critique of the Newest Liberal Iinstitutionalism', in D. Baldwin (ed.), *Neorealism and Neoliberalism: the Contemporary Debates* (New York, 1993).

[27] 'International institutions: can interdependence work?', *Foreign Policy*, 110 (1998), p. 84.

as this article is being written, it is hard to ignore the preemptory unilateral measures taken by the United States in mid-1999 to protect both its lamb against imports and its genetically enhanced beef exports to the EU.) In sum, prominent institutionalists—like their realist counterparts—continue to stress the central role of the state and, while regarding the end of the Cold War as marking an important shift in the global balance of power, they do not see in the proliferation of international regimes a qualitative transformation in the nature of world politics.[28]

This conclusion is clearly at some remove from the globalist claim that national governments are no longer the locus of effective political power.[29] Our brief review of liberal institutionalism's stance on the matter indicates that it is both possible and necessary to go beyond this negative-sum way of understanding international cooperation. We can add to institutionalism's positive conclusion that states cooperate to achieve certain objectives by noting four limitations of the globalist view. First, it overestimates the 'encompassing' quality of international agreements, and underestimates the tenacity of national arrangements as well as the adaptivity of national actors. (Moreover, adaptivity is not one-way; like states, firms have also had to adjust to a more competitive environment as a result of changes in state policies.) To use a parallel from taxation rules, just as the existence of new tax rules does not thereby bring tax-minimising schemes to a standstill in the corporate sector, so there is no reason to assume that the emergence of international rules governing trade and investment will bring activist states and their production-enhancing schemes to a standstill. The WTO, for instance, may appear to be crowding out state activism in the domestic arena by seeking to exclude certain forms of government subsidy, but that is likely to have little impact on the new forms of industry promotion and more resonance in liberal market settings where states have traditionally applied themselves to regulatory rather than developmental policies (see the following section).

Second, the long-term survival of international regimes, especially in the economic sphere, appears contingent upon the continued welfare-increasing benefits of cooperation. This is not simply a theoretical postulate on which both neorealists and liberal institutionalists can agree. It is also the perception of leading decision-makers in the field. In discussing the key features of policies directed at promoting international integration, for example, Lawrence Summers, now Secretary of the United States Treasury, recently observed that one major feature 'has been the consistent desire to finesse sovereignty problems by highlighting the national benefits of internationally congenial behavior'. Thus, as Summers points out,

... there is the greatest willingness to cede power to international institutions where there is the greatest technical agreement on what needs to be done and where issues of values are less paramount. Thus, for example, there is more international agreement on questions like air safety standards and bank capital requirements than on questions like tax rules and labor standards .[30]

---

[28] See Stephen M. Walt, 'International Relations: One World, Many Theories', *Foreign Policy*, 110 (1998), p. 46.

[29] See, for example, David Held and Anthony McGrew, 'The End of the Old Order? Globalization and the Prospects for World Order', *Review of International Studies*, 24 (1998), p. 235.

[30] 'Reflections on Managing Global Integration', paper presented at the Annual Meeting of the Association of Government Economists, New York City, 4 January (1999), p. 10.

Third, it must be said that international rules and organizations do change the environment in which states must act and often redefine the instruments with which states can legitimately pursue their objectives. But international regimes do not *in themselves* change domestic goals and orientations, the commitment of state actors, or the institutional approach to achieving their goals. In the 1990s, scholars in comparative political economy still identify different configurations of national ideas, goals and institutions. Whether one distinguishes these domestic regimes as liberal, corporatist, and statist or some similar set of labels, it is clear that such regimes are not readily redefined by the advent of international organizations. This is not to deny that at critical moments state preferences, identity, and goals may be shaped and reshaped by the international context, as constructivists have argued.[31] Nor is it to deny that the spread of democratic norms, for example, has made it more difficult for modern states to act despotically by ignoring human rights issues. But these sorts of observations centre on changes in the legitimate purposes for which state power may be employed: in particular, by excluding the doing of physical harm to others. Yet this change appears to have less to do with the power of international regimes *per se* than with the 'liberal democratic' nature of inter-nationalism. Moreover, the disciplinary power of democratic norms (preventing states from harming their citizens) is of a different order from the power implied by the globalist's view of multilateralism (effecting state transformation). State trans-formation involves reconfiguring power, purpose and institutions. But, as com-parativists have shown, such configurations are path dependent; transforming domestic orientations and institutions will take much more than suprational rules and organizations. Moreover, in so far as diversity persists in domestic regimes, one can expect different outcomes in the way countries adapt to and implement inter-nationally agreed rules (as well as in the way they undertake common liberalising reforms, as we shall see in the East Asian case discussed later).[32]

Finally, by aligning with other state actors, a state does not necessarily give up powers (infrastructural reach) exercised within its own domain; it may actually extend its penetrative capacities via international reciprocity, negotiation, and power sharing. Thus in a wide range of areas—from drug trafficking and money laundering to illegal immigration and environmental pollution—states are gaining infra-structural reach by cooperating with other state actors in order to prevent harm to themselves. A similar principle of *enhancing capacity* applies when governments enter into domestic cooperative alliances with business to attain their goals. Depending on the state's internal characteristics, the reciprocity or power sharing involved does not necessarily compromise or weaken the state's powers, but instead may enhance them by increasing the effectiveness of state involvement and thus the

---

[31] Both Japan and Germany, for example, traded in their militarism after 1945 for a more pacific identity, concentrating on economic strength; but that transformation required the foundation of shattering defeat on which national shame could help reshape national purpose while admission to the international community could keep it on course. See Peter Katzenstein (ed.), *The Culture of National Security* (New York, 1996).

[32] On the persistence of capitalist diversity, in spite of liberalizing reforms, see in particular Steven Vogel, *Freer Markets, More Rules* (Ithaca, NY: 1996), and Vivien Schmidt, 'Still Three Models of Capitalism? National Adjustment to Globalization and Europeanization', unpublished paper, Boston University, 16 May (1999).

chances of achieving its goals.[33] States enter into international agreements with the anticipation of similar power-sharing outcomes. Such outcomes are of course much easier to discern where prevention of harm or risk is at stake (as in prosecuting international crime), and more open to question where prevention of economic advantage is at issue (as in implementing trade agreements).

Nonetheless, even with the more restrictive functions of a body like the WTO, it is possible to see cooperation as part of a new power infrastructure of states whereby they not only maintain control of territory (setting and monitoring rules 'within'), but also extend their infrastructural reach 'without' by aligning with other state actors. Such forms of cooperation mean that in principle there is no territorial space that is beyond the reach of any particular nation-state (that is, for the purposes of controlling activities outside its borders, which would impact on activities inside its borders). The historical dynamic suggests that the techniques and tools of state power are constantly spinning out of control and away from the state as society invents new means of organising its activities—means which cannot be monopolized by states[34] (e.g., formerly writing, now the Internet); but then states acquire new means of regaining control (e.g., by reorganizing, as they are now doing via cooperative arrangements).

Such adaptation to new challenges may not always be successful and can never be guaranteed in advance. The point however is that by taking the long view, it is easier to appreciate the significance of the contemporary dynamic: the process of states and societies gaining new organizational means has been going on over many centuries and viewing this in win-lose terms seems unfruitful. One can, for example, without too much effort envisage an environmental equivalent of the WTO which will impose new standards on the countries of the world; but rather than seeing an end to institutional and power diversity, such standards are just as likely to nurture it as industries in different countries invent new ways of being green and clean and as public purpose is marshalled to support them. Current Japanese and German initiatives in environmental technology at public and private levels offer interesting glimpses of such a future.[35] Moreover public-private innovation clusters, stretching from Taiwan to Saxony and Silicon Valley, are increasingly the preferred means of doing 'industrial policy' in the 1990s, not because the WTO has foreclosed other forms of economic promotion, but because supporting innovation and thus upgrading industry and skills is central to sustained national wealth creation.

Does economic globalization constrain national governance?

Having appraised the tranformative impact of political interdependence on national

---

[33] See Linda Weiss, *The Myth of The Powerless State* (Ithaca, NY and Cambridge, 1998), ch. 7. The important qualification is that if states enter such alliances from a position of structural and organizational weakness or ideational uncertainty, they are more prone to 'capture' by business and to exploitation by other states Hence the greater likelihood of a lopsided or hierarchical relationship emerging out of such power imbalances. See Peter Evans, *Embedded Autonomy* (Princeton, 1995) and Weiss, *The Myth of the Powerless State*, ch. 3.

[34] Mann develops this argument at length in Volume I of *The Sources of Social Power* (1996).

[35] Germany and Japan have made great strides in developing environmental technology as an industry of the future; these developments have gone hand-in-hand with some of the tightest environmental regulations in force in the world today.

governance, we turn now to a similar set of claims regarding the constraining consequences of economic integration. As we have seen, many commentators believe that states are no longer the primary decision-making authorities in matters governing their territory and many have chorused the 'erosion of national political autonomy'. But the criteria for assessing this erosion have been 'at best vague and tailored to meet the particular demands of the moment'.[36] Moreover, this way of looking at the matter may be somewhat arcane and abstract. The more fruitful question to pose is whether states can act to enhance wealth creation and social protection within their territorial domain. And if so, why policy preferences may or may not lean in that direction. Does globalization (transborder flows, capital mobility) either prevent or—to use the language of state power erosion—'seriously challenge and constrain' the national pursuit of these objectives? In short, what has economic globalization to do with the capacity of national governments to enhance or assist the processes of social protection and wealth creation? Let us examine each policy area in turn.

Globalization and welfare state erosion

Why do analysts link globalization with welfare state reforms and cutbacks? The answer, in a nutshell, has to do with fiscal policy—the purported decline of revenues essential to sustain social policy; a decline due to pressures placed on governments by mobile capital in order to reduce costs. An influential claim maintains that governments in the developed world are confronted with an eroding tax base; that this erosion has come about because of increased transborder capital mobility; and that this enhanced mobility impacts on fiscal policy in a number of ways, but most of all by inducing governments to lower corporate taxes in order to attract and retain capital. If we examine the evidence for this proposition, however, globalization has little if anything to do with the current challenges or changes to the welfare state.

Have the pressures of capital mobility (arising from financial deregulation and revolutionary changes in technology) induced governments unilaterally to reduce corporate tax rates in order to attract or retain capital, and thereby whittled away the revenue base for social protection programmes? The question needs to be posed because the claim is widely repeated as if it were an established fact. Yet recent research for the most part demolishes this conclusion. In the most rigorous comparison of corporate taxation to date, covering 17 OECD countries over the 1966–93 period, Swank evaluates the extent to which the globalization of capital markets has led to decreases in business social security, payroll and profit taxes. Since the findings overturn the common wisdom, they are worth reporting in some detail.

The most important finding is that, in contrast to expectations, the 'direct effects of globalization of capital markets are [if anything] associated with slightly higher business taxes and, to a degree, the diminution of tax policy responsiveness to the conditions that underpin investment'.[37] The explanation given for this is straight-

---

[36] Guy B. Peters, '"Shouldn't Row, Can't Steer": What's a Government to Do?', *Journal of Public Policy and Administration*, 12:2 (1997), p. 54.

[37] Duane Swank, 'Funding the Welfare State: Globalization and the Taxation of Business in Advanced Market Economies', *Political Studies*, 46:4 (1998), p. 691.

forward: as capital flows were liberalized, so business tax policies 'were stripped of their explicit market-regulating roles'. This meant that although policymakers viewed tax rate cuts as economically advantageous, they nevertheless insisted on the need to make overall changes revenue-neutral. Accordingly, to protect the state's revenue requirements, rate cuts came to be offset, in particular, by elimination of corporate tax and other benefits such as investment credits, allowances, and exemptions. Where tax rates were altered, these were not made to privilege business but to allow for greater market discipline. As Swank reasons, 'the emphasis in business income tax policy became the creation of a level playing field, where the market allocates investment and the revenue needs of the state are satisfied'.[38] Thus there have been no general reductions in corporate taxation; where specific rate cuts have been made, these have generally been offset by cuts to business benefits and investment incentives.

The conventional wisdom nonetheless receives confirmation in one respect: that is, with regard to the influence of trade liberalization (as distinct from the deregulation of financial markets or the rise in so-called 'capital mobility'). Rises in international trade openness have exerted some pressure on policymakers to lower business costs through tax reductions. Yet, even here, the pressures are found to be 'modest' rather than substantial and the driving forces behind them turn out to be more clearly connected with plain old 'international competition', than with the 'transborder' flows of globalization. Moreover, policymakers have introduced tax rate changes that might improve the international price competitiveness of firms regardless of their level of 'mobility'. Thus the targets of the lowered tax rates include both export firms competing in international markets and non-export firms exposed to import competition in the domestic market. Ultimately, however, even with regard to international trade pressure, it appears that its overall tax-reducing effects have been 'weak'. Rodrik, whose study is sometimes cited in support of the opposite conclusion, concurs.[39] He finds that trade openness is associated with higher taxation of labour and lower taxation of profits. Yet, his data, drawn from a group of OECD countries for the period 1965–92, show only a weak tendency for taxes on labour to rise faster than those on capital.

Finally, with regard to the impact of the globalization of capital markets on business tax and on the capacity of states to pursue social protection policies of their choosing, Swank's study concludes that

While tax policy has been market-conforming, there is little evidence that aggregate tax burdens themselves have been reduced. Indeed, there is an emphasis on 'defending the treasury' in the contemporary period. Thus, from the perspective of the taxation of business in the advanced democracies, there appears to be no dramatic, irresistible pressure to radically retrench social spending and eliminate public goods provision. Within relatively tight parameters, governments of all ideological and programmatic orientations appear to have room to pursue their preferred policy goals.[40]

This conclusion dovetails with that of recent studies of welfare state developments. Specialists in the field of social policy show three things: (1) The rhetoric of cuts is not matched by the reality which overall shows persistence of expenditure

---

[38] Ibid.
[39] Dani Rodrik, *Has Globalization Gone Too Far?* (Washington, DC: 1997), Table 4.5.
[40] Swank, 'Funding the Welfare State', p. 691.

levels rather than decline;[41] (2) changes have occurred at the margin rather than to the core programmes;[42] (3) the welfare state is certainly under pressure, but not from transborder flows; rather, the postwar welfare state is strained by more than two decades of low rates of world growth as well as shifting demographic and household patterns that are poorly accommodated by a welfare structure designed for an earlier era. Consequently, welfare states are in need of considerable revamping, not in response to pressures of internationalization, but in order to meet the new needs thrown up by structural and life-style changes.[43]

In sum, welfare provision *is* strained for revenue; but this would be the case in any low-growth environment. Pressures for change reside chiefly in demographic shifts (an ageing population requiring pension support in retirement); in household shifts (e.g., the rise of one-parent families and two-bread-winner families, the latter which tend to be relatively income rich, yet like the first type, time poor); and in low job creation necessary to absorb persistently high unemployment, largely of low-skilled labour. While the causes of high unemployment, especially in Europe, are in dispute, the low rate of job creation has largely domestic sources.[44] To a considerable degree therefore governments can, in principle, make a difference to the outcome.

Recent analyses indicate two different areas of the labour market are involved. The first concerns raising the supply of knowledge-intensive skills for growth sectors such as the ever-expanding information-technology market. The second concerns increasing the demand for time-intensive labour—specifically in those service areas largely sheltered from international competition. It is noteworthy that none of these job-creation strategies involve Keynesian demand management techniques. The first entails a continuous provisioning for (re-)training and education that equips people to work with the new information technology. As such it requires an *enhanced*, not reduced, role for government policy.[45] The second sphere of action involves changing the regulatory regime which, in several continental European countries, protects skilled labour at the expense of the jobless (since it appears that no amount of retraining provision will completely eliminate the demand for some low-skilled labour). As such, it would most fruitfully entail *sectoral* (rather than generalized) deregulation to enable the formation of a service sector capable of supplying moderately-priced personal services and thus job creation for the low-skilled; the

---

[41] For a state-of-the-art analysis on this whole topic, See Martin Rhodes, 'The Implications of Globalization and Liberalization for Income Security and Social Protection', Robert Schuman Centre, European University Institute, Florence (1999); See also OECD, *National Account Statistics*, vol. II, Country Tables (Paris, various years), which show almost universally that the trend is towards increasing welfare expenditure levels in the 1990s, compared with the 1980s.

[42] Paul Pierson, 'The New Politics of the Welfare State', *World Politics*, 48: 2 (1996), pp. 143–80.

[43] See Gosta Esping-Andersen (ed.), *Welfare States in Transition: National Adaptations in Global Economies* (London, 1996); and Martin Rhodes, 'The Implications of Globalization and Liberalization for Income Security and Social Protection'.

[44] Colin Crouch argues that decline in the demand for low-skilled labour is not due to increased international competition *per se*. It is because the welfare state had grown to its limits, especially with respect to its financing; increased pressures on the public purse have curtailed job creation schemes in the public sector, an important, widespread means of creating employment for relatively low-skilled workers in the 1970s and early 1980s. See Colin Crouch, E. Hernerijck, and David Finegold, 'The Skill Predicament in the Open Economy', Conference paper for 'Relations between Social Protection and Economic Performance', Florence, EUI, European Forum, Centre for Advanced Studies, May 6–7, (1999), p. 32.

[45] See Colin Crouch, David Finegold and Marie Sako (eds.), *Are Skills the Answer?: The Political Economy of Skill Creation in Advanced Industrial Economies* (Oxford, 1999).

effect of selective deregulation would be to shift services from the unpaid household sector into personal services provision, which is more sheltered from international competition.[46]

To conclude, there are pressures on contemporary welfare states, but one does not need to invoke 'transborder capital' to explain them. The generalized revenue constraints can be linked directly to the slowdown in world growth that has persisted since the end of the long boom (an unhappy coincidence with the growth of globalization over the same period?). Further pressures have come in part from demographic shifts (the ballooning claim on pension entitlements as the population ages) and partly from high rates of hard-to-shift unemployment of low-productivity, low-skill labour. Globalization may have contributed to the world-wide slowdown—though this is not what some globalists would wish to argue. On the other hand, globalization has nothing to do with the added claims on the public purse brought about by demographic change; and it may be only weakly related to unemployment in so far as trade can be shown to have some employment-displacing effects (the recent growth of unemployment in some countries, like Germany, having little to do with deindustrialization). The unemployment issue, however, can more fruitfully be understood as fundamentally a problem of job creation—and as European experts on labour markets point out, this is essentially a problem of public policy, hence involving national economic management and government-industry collaboration.

The futility of wealth creation strategies?

The claim that international flows render national governance ineffective takes many forms. The most recent in the globalist's armoury focuses on the importance of 'strategic alliances' between MNCs. The strategic alliance is widely perceived as the latest and most powerful threat to an active wealth creation strategy, driving the last nail in the coffin of the activist state: an end to technology policy.

Thus one of globalism's more recent assertions that has yet to attract close scrutiny is the claim that policies to improve domestic innovation capacity are futile because of the leakage that comes with crossborder (note, not 'transborder') alliances. By trying to improve the technological capabilities of 'its' firms, a government merely ends up helping others. While more systematic research is required here, at least three observations indicate that the leakage hypothesis—like many other aspects of the globalization argument—has inflated a small and partial (and not quite novel) truth into the status of a new and substantial constraint on national governance. Let me explain further.

First, if there is substance to the policy futility claim in the face of leakage, it should apply to any kind of crossborder (i.e. international) activity where resources can migrate or leak abroad. Thus, it should apply equally to education and training policies aimed at inculcating specialist knowledge and upgrading technological skills. Whether trained in the arts or sciences, in information technology or advanced engineering, the knowledge worker of today is no less (and indeed may be considerably more) mobile than the MNC. Indeed, in an expanding world market for

---

[46] Gosta Esping-Andersen, *Social Foundations of Postindustrial Economies* (Oxford, 1999).

specialist skills, the problem of how to prevent highly skilled labour from migrating to the highest bidder—the so-called 'brain drain'—has been documented at least since the nineteenth century. (The Taiwanese government successfully introduced 'reverse brain drain' policies in the 1980s and 1990s to lure Taiwanese nationals from Silicon Valley back to Taiwan in order to help implement the state's own high-technology strategy for industry.) Remarkably, however, such mobility has not led globalists to conclude that education and training policies are futile! Indeed, it usually leads to the opposite conclusion.[47] Why then should it be any different for innovation and technology (which are essentially the up-to-date version of industry) policies?

Second, open economies deal with the problem of leakage by inventing new ways of promoting 'their' industry. Nowadays, for example, such promotion relies much less on the use of the export 'subsidy' and the import tariff. This is only partly because subsidies are increasingly condemned by international trade agreements; it is also because they have diminishing relevance to the new technological conditions of competition. Increasingly, where governments can effectively enhance wealth creation through industry promotion, they act as catalysts for innovation—the development of high skill, high technology clusters—drawing on a range of resources and strategies according to the distinctive institutional features of their national context. The well-documented catalytic role of Taiwan's Industrial Technology Research Institute (ITRI) can also work in unexpected ways. For example, by merely initiating a consortium of Taiwanese firms to develop LCD technology (Japanese firms having continually rejected ITRI's overtures for techno-logy partnerships), this pushed the Japanese leader in LCD technology to offer the Taiwanese a joint venture.[48]

More generally, as technologies become more complex and the scope for inno-vation expands, governments play a catalytic role in sponsoring applied research and technology transfer institutes. This remains true for the countries of 'managed capitalism', whether one includes the newly developed economies of Taiwan and Singapore—where specialized institutes are the nodal points for high technology clusters, scanning, absorbing, sharing and diffusing technical know-how—or the more highly developed countries of Japan and Germany. But even in the more 'market capitalist' US, industry promotion through support for national technology networks has become a more prominent feature of policy. As competition intensified between Japanese and American high-technology industry in the late 1980s, cooperative mechanisms enabled government and firms to combine resources to relaunch the US semiconductor industry. The success of the socalled Sematech initiative has stimulated further public-private cooperative research programmes, for example, the recent launch of a ten-year, $600m programme between the US Department of Defence, leading chipmakers and 14 leading research universities to develop the next generation of semiconductor technology. As recent studies have documented, American technology policy has shifted since 1993 towards an expansion of public investments in partnerships with private industry.[49]

The leakage hypothesis clearly contains a kernel of truth, but its veracity does not depend on the existence of *strategic alliances*. Mergers and acquisitions (M&As) are

[47] See, for example, Robert Reich, *The Work of Nations* (New York, 1992).
[48] I owe this point to Tain-Jy Chen at the Chung-Hua Institution for Economic Research, Taipei..
[49] See, for example, L. Branscomb and J. Keller (eds.), *Investing in Innovation* (Cambridge, NY: 1998).

a much older version of the way in which 'national' and 'international have long intermeshed. M&As have frequently been carried out by foreign firms with a view to gaining entry to the insider government-business relationships reserved for national firms.[50] Just as these entry points have often been blocked to outsiders, so one must reserve judgment for the 'new' strategic alliances. When the US government was confronted with what to do about such alliances as Sematech, which was formed in 1987—the semiconductor technology consortium established with a 50–50 partnership between government and business, which lasted ten years—it resolved the matter straightforwardly. Foreign firms were simply excluded from the consortium, a situation which endured for the ten-year period of that partnership. Some might maintain that the remarkable turnaround of the US semiconductor industry owes little to this public-private partnership; but few commentators would seriously seek to argue that the policy was futile because it directly benefited the foreign partners of the US firms in the consortium.

Finally, though, there may be a more serious flaw in the leakage reasoning: it presumes that strategic alliances are between *similarly endowed entities* and that therefore as one gains from the insider relationship with government, so this gain will spill over to the foreign firm. But this may be true only in the most indirect sense, for the reasons why firms enter into strategic alliances have mostly to do with the quite *different specialisms* that each firm brings to bear on a common project. By combining their different knowledge resources, they can more quickly and economically acquire what is needed to be effective in different markets and technologies. Because the rationale for coming together turns on the possession of different not similar strengths, strategic alliances may in fact have quite marginal implications for national policy leakage.

We return then to our opening question. Can national governments act to enhance the wealth creation process? Comparative analysis indicates that in principle, there is considerable scope for such involvement, but that in practice there is significant diversity in the extent of such involvement. Such comparisons have been pursued in detail elsewhere.[51] They indicate that to the extent that policy is 'constrained', the sources of constraint are less external or global in origin that domestic-institutional. In short, the most important limitations on national governance are self-imposed rather than externally induced and stem from fundamental ideas and orientations about the scope of state involvement in the economy, and from institutional capabilities that have evolved around those orienting ideas. International flows and organizations can modify the options available to national governments—or more precisely, alter the means that states can deploy to further their preferences—*viz.* the restrictions imposed on the use of the subsidy by highly developed nations. But in contrast to 'market-led' capitalism, in settings where managed capitalism has prevailed, we should expect to find that this modification gives rise to a search for new means of achieving desired outcomes and preserving valued institutional arrangements.

---

[50] Yves Doz and Gary Hamel, *Alliance Advantage: The Art of Creating Value Through Partnering* (Harvard, MA: 1998).

[51] See, for example, Weiss, *The Myth of the Powerless State*.

A new kind of state?

As centralized governing bodies, states have traditionally exercized two sorts of powers: substantive and outcome-oriented decision-making powers, and formal-procedural powers involving the state as a regulatory authority. For a number of commentators, these two aspects are now pulling apart as economic management becomes increasingly futile, giving rise to a 'regulatory' state denuded of its substantive policymaking role. Even sceptics can be found to argue that the power of states as policymaking bodies has 'declined' and that the scope of national economic management has been restricted by economic integration.[52] From this perspective, the outcome-oriented (i.e., economic management) functions of national governance are declining while the procedural-regulatory functions are becoming more important.

Such a conclusion would sit just as easily with the more moderate globalists. For them too, the state is becoming more monofunctional—approximating more and more to a regulatory body, ceding substantive power to supra-state agencies. But moderate globalists would be quick to agree with their sceptic critics that 'nation states are still of central significance'. They are no longer central to substantive decision-making, for they apparently cede this to supra-state agencies. Rather they are central because they acquire new roles, in particular, legitimating and supporting the supranational authorities they have created by virtue of pooling sovereignty.[53] Thus *if states are still significant it is no longer as sources of substantive and outcome-oriented decisions or national economic management.* It is rather because they are the key sources of constitutional order and legal power distribution, giving shape and legitimacy to other authorities above and below.[54]

I do not wish to dispute this conclusion in its entirety. It may well be an accurate statement of tendency for some states in some settings (a specifically liberal pattern?). However, in this section I shall indicate two major limitations of a conceptual and empirical nature. Taken together, they considerably weaken the regulatory hypothesis as a general statement of tendency. Finally I shall draw on recent research on the Asian crisis by way of illustration.

State diversity and path dependence

One limitation of interpretive judgments of this kind, which are clearly unavoidable for some purposes, is that they offer no way of recognising, weighing or evaluating differences between states to begin with. The implication is that whatever differences there may have been to start with—between, say, Germany, France, and Japan on one hand and Britain, Canada, and the US on the other—they are of little con-

---

[52] See, for instance, Hirst and Thompson, *Globalization in Question*, ch. 9.
[53] Ibid.
[54] Globalists who reject the global-national dualism, however, do not necessarily accept this emasculated capacity interpretation (see, e.g., Scholte, 'Global Civil Society: Changing the World?', *CSGR Working Paper* no. 31 (1999), p. 23; see also Richard Higgott, 'Economics, Politics and (International) Political Economy: The Need for a Balanced Diet in an Era of Globalization', *New Political Economy*, 4:1 (1999).

sequence now since most if not all states are held to be moving more decisively towards a regulatory model, away from substantive outcome-oriented decision-making. But what if many states have not really moved very far at all—simply because *they were already there*? This at least is the conclusion one might reach on the basis of comparative political economy analyses. Conversely, what if those states which have most consistently deviated from the regulatory path are those most likely to continue along a different trajectory? Let me elaborate.

In 1982, Chalmers Johnson pioneered the fruitful distinction between two types of states associated with two different kinds of political economy: the 'regulatory' (procedurally oriented) state and the 'developmental' (outcome-oriented) state.[55] The first is typified by the liberal states of market capitalism, the US and the UK, primarily active in establishing the rules of competition and fair play rather than pursuing substantive outcomes. The second is more commonly associated with the state guidance of managed capitalism in Japan, Taiwan, Korea and Singapore (and one might include certain European states, such as Germany, Austria, and France).[56] In economic matters, it is no exaggeration to say that developmental states have been much more concerned with achieving substantive goals: for example, raising the level of savings and investment, acquiring particular technologies, upgrading the industrial portfolio, and so on. In elaborating the idea of the developmental state, Johnson was also drawing attention to the misleading nature of the Cold War polarity which described a world divided between command-led economies and market-led economies. Capitalism, in short, was not monolithic. It came in different varieties. Nowadays, however, the future of that variety is in doubt: pressured from below by capital mobility and from above by supranational forms of governance, it is most unlikely to endure, say the globalists.

But the most important implication of the Johnsonian conclusion for the present discussion is that whatever pressures are 'out there' (whether coming from above or below and whether we agree to label them internationalization or globalization), *states are responding from very different institutional and ideational bases* and are therefore most unlikely to be moving in a single (regulatory) direction. This is because, in an internationalized economy, path-dependency (historical linkages between institutions which create interlocked systems) still carries weight: the weight of both historically formed regime orientations (e.g., fundamental norms about the state's role in economic and social relations) and institutional configurations (e.g., the availability of cooperative mechanisms for public-private governance).[57]

Regulation as capacity enhancement

There is a further limitation to the regulatory state hypothesis. While there is some substance to the notion that states are becoming more active as regulators—how

---

[55] Chalmers Johnson, *MITI and the Japanese Miracle* (Berkeley, CA: 1982). We are of course talking in terms of broad 'ideal types'. All states in reality combine both features; the purpose of the ideal type is to highlight and magnify those features which tend to predominate.

[56] See Meredith Woo-Cumings (ed.), *The Developmental State* (Ithaca, NY: 1999).

[57] For the argument that there are still three models of capitalism in spite of international integration, see Vivien Schmidt, 'Still Three Models of Capitalism?'.

could it be otherwise when so much 'deregulation' calls for 'reregulation'?[58]—it does not follow that states generally are abandoning or sidelining substantive, outcome-oriented action.[59] As a small open economy, the experience of Taiwan in confronting financial liberalization is particularly noteworthy.

The case of Taiwan's monetary authority offers an instructive illustration of how, even when a state agency appears to be acting in a strictly 'regulatory' capacity, it can use the rules to achieve *substantive* outcomes—rather than simply focusing on procedural issues. Thus as Taiwan embarked on a further phase of financial deregulation in 1993, the Central Bank of China deployed new rules that would favour developmentalism while guarding against foreign exchange speculation.[60] The issue concerned liberalization of the market for corporate bonds. While the process was one of deregulation—allowing Taiwanese firms to remit the proceeds in NT dollars of their offshore bond issuances—there was accompanying reregulation: the stipulation that such domestic remittances could be invested *only* in plant expansion.[61] Thus central bankers have simultaneously guarded against sudden inflows disrupting money markets (in particular, the risk that inflows would be used to speculate against the currency) and enhanced developmental capacity. As this example shows, regulatory activity may also entail substantive outcomes, while at the same time enhancing rather than diminishing the state's powers of coordination. Whether states will seek to use regulatory controls in this way is likely to depend on the pre-existing constellation of institutions and orientations that give state capacities their shape and *raison d'être*. In view of their different legacies, it would therefore be most unwise to anticipate the end of national economic management in the developmental states of Europe and Asia.

We have, then, two major limitations of the regulatory state hypothesis. First, it understates institutional diversity and overlooks the impact of path dependence, the significance of institutional and ideational differences in filtering and shaping national responses and policy outcomes. Second, it ignores the way in which 'regulatory' activity may itself offer states new ways to achieve substantive outcomes, rather than simply to perfect new control procedures. If there is one major constraint preventing such an outcome, it is to be found in the underlying regime goals and orienting ideas of state actors themselves. When state actors, for whatever reason, begin to question their purpose, goals, or commitment, the unravelling of state capacity is not far away, as the case of Korea illustrates in the decade preceding its embroilment in the Asian financial crisis (see below). In this sense, state

---

[58] Steven Vogel, *Freer Markets, More Rules*.

[59] See, for example, Woo-Cumings, *The Developmental State*; Schmidt, 'Still Three Models of Capitalism?'; Lonny E. Carlile and Mark Tilton, *Is Japan Really Changing Its Ways?* (Washington, DC, 1998); Weiss, *The Myth of the Powerless State*; Linda Weiss, 'Developmental States in Transition: Adapting, Dismantling, Innovating, not "Normalizing"', *Pacific Review*, 13:1 (2000).

[60] Indeed, during our most recent round of interviews with the Central Bank of China, conducted in Taipei in June 1999, it became clear that developmentalism is not just the central defining feature of the Ministry of Economic Affairs or the Committee for Economic Planning and Development; it is a fundamental orienting quality of the central bank. The regional financial crisis has provided a critical if unexpected test of Taiwan's developmental commitment and the result has been a reaffirmation of the latter, accompanied by a sharpening of the state's monitoring and coordinating powers, especially where short-term capital flows are perceived to threaten Taiwan's industrial competitiveness. These ideas are developed in Wan-wen Chu and Linda Weiss, 'Has state capacity survived liberalization and democratization in Taiwan?' (forthcoming).

[61] For the detailed argument, see Linda Weiss, 'State Power and the Asian Crisis', *New Political Economy*, 4:3 (1999).

orientations matter and have consequences and in this light the argument that 'governments are most constrained when they believe themselves to be powerless, and least constrained when they do not', deserves to be taken seriously.[62]

To illustrate how changing orientations mattered to the use of state power and the differential capacity to withstand the regional financial crisis of 1997, consider the cases of Korea and Taiwan.

The critical role of state capacity in the Asian crisis: Korea and Taiwan

The Asian crisis is a powerful illustration of the new global orthodoxy that markets rule supreme. When the economies of East Asia went into a deflationary tailspin in late 1997, many commentators, including the IMF, argued that the 'Asian model' was unsustainable because it ignored the realities of globalization—i.e., the power of international markets to punish policies and arrangements that deviated too far from the neoliberal (Anglo-American) norm. But this tends to distort by over-generalizing (and under-conceptualizing) the so-called Asian model. Indeed the uneven impact of the Asian crisis offers support for two propositions at the centre of this article: (1) that the impact of 'global' flows is highly dependent upon the character of national purpose and institutions; and (2) that global networks depend on national networks of interaction in order to function. In this way, they emphasize the limits to liberalization. Let us take each point in turn.

National mediation of global impacts

The significance of the Asian crisis, for the purpose of this argument, is that it seems to many to signal the end of the developmental state's viability and its trans-formation into a different kind of beast. In that respect, the crisis is pivotal to the Western confidence that globalization curtails capitalist diversity (read divergence from the free market norm), and that state-guided capitalism has failed the survival test. There are, however, at least three problems with the view that the crisis was a byproduct of the developmental model of capitalism. First, none of the most troubled Southeast Asian economies—Thailand, Indonesia and Malaysia—could be seen as developmental states, let alone transformative states. If they fell victim to international financial markets, they did not do so from a position of robust institutional capacity. Second, Japan itself was not a victim of the financial meltdown. It certainly had a banking crisis of its own, but this was mainly self-induced and long predated the events of 1997. Thus the Japanese model is not directly implicated. Third, the one developmental state which did become a victim of the financial debacle—Korea—had undergone such a substantial institutional makeover by the time the crisis struck, that one might plausibly argue that it was Korea's emerging neoliberalism rather than the legacy of statism that made it more vulnerable to a financial shakedown. In fact, one can turn the IMF argument on its

---

[62] See Vogel, *Freer Markets, More Rules.*

head: Korea was pulled into the financial maelstrom not because it deviated too far from the free market but, as I have argued at length elsewhere, because it had abandoned too much of its transformative capacity.[63]

Dismantling of Korea's developmental arrangements began very gradually in the early 1980s. State actors began slowly to unravel the financial ties which bound the chaebol closely to the state. Multiple overlapping crises—political, financial, and social—forced a questioning of statist arrangements and propelled the authorities towards domestic reform. In particular, state actors perceived financial liberalization as a means of distancing the state from the chaebol's financial affairs by expanding their financing options. Liberalization was thus initially aimed at the domestic arena as the state gradually privatised state-owned banks, increased reliance on equity financing through the creation of a stock market, and reduced policy loans. Financial market opening gathered pace very quickly in the first half of the 1990s as firms and financial institutions were allowed to raise more and more funds on overseas markets, with little or no supervision of the level or composition of those funds. The result was a surge in the inflow of portfolio investment in the 1990s. During 1990–94 alone, the net inflow of foreign capital, reaching some $32 bn, was more than ten times the total for the 1980s. Most of this was short-term portfolio investment, exceeding $27 bn in the 1991–94 period alone. This massive influx of capital took place as the developmental state's key agency was being marginalized, culminating in the definitive dismantling of the EPB, the pilot agency which coordinated Korea's rapid industrial transformation. Without coordinating discipline, there was no corrective to the high-risk, expansionist, surplus capacity tendencies of the chaebol, a weakness which soon became manifest in the economic vulnerabilities that exposed Korea to financial crisis: declining export growth, soaring current account deficits and debt repayment difficulties.

The argument that Korea's malaise is due more to an abandonment of transformative capacity than deviation from free-market rules gains strength when we reflect on the differential involvement of Taiwan and Korea in the events of 1997. In Taiwan, state actors approached financial reform very differently from their Korean counterparts. The state centred on Taipei has held fast to a transformative orientation, reflected *inter alia* in one of the world's strongest national innovation and upgrading programmes. Developmentalism was further reinforced through the stance and policies of the Central Bank of China (CBC) whose unusual vigilance and conditionalities ensured that financial liberalization would mean keeping a tight rein on foreign exchange activity.

In short, Taiwan's regime goals and institutional arrangements were largely intact when it set about regulatory reform in the late 1980s and 1990s. While Korea set about liberalizing finance in a way that would complement the larger goal of dismantling the structures of credit activism and industrial policy, in Taiwan the process of liberalizing capital inflows involved re-regulation to enhance existing capabilities. Thus, in the political bargaining that preceded capital account opening in the early 1990s, the CBC held out for a safety blanket, insisting on guaranteed emergency powers should things go wrong. Under these powers, the central bank has kept strict control of the foreign currency market, intervening to discipline

---

[63] The points in this paragraph and the following are based on material drawn from Weiss 'State Power and the Asian Crisis', and 'Developmental States in Transition'.

international speculators in the wake of the Asian crisis. Thus, as indicated earlier, the very process of opening up Taiwan's capital markets in the 1990s has brought with it new regulatory controls which have preserved and at times strengthened coordination powers. Financial liberalization in the hands of the Taiwanese has thereby become much more an instrument for complementing and enhancing state capacities than for relinquishing them.

The key points then are twofold. First, in the Asian setting, developmental state weakness or dismantling paved the way for a particular approach to liberalization, one in which financial reform was perceived as a means of distancing the state from industrial governance (the Korean experience), rather than complementing its transformative capabilities. Thus, where coordinating powers were relatively weak to begin with (as in Southeast Asia), or had been partially dismantled in response to domestic crises (as in Korea), liberalization was undertaken in a way that would emphasize and reinforce institutional weakness rather than enhance capability. Second, where developmental state dismantling did not occur, liberalization was a more highly managed process (the Taiwan experience). In the Taiwanese setting, managed liberalization was undertaken in a manner that sought to complement and enhance developmental capacities, not to retreat from industrial governance.

(National) limits to liberalization

The idea that global finance needs strong national institutions would seem to be—paradoxically—one important lesson of the Asian financial crisis. For if the crisis has taught us anything about the power of globalization, surely it is that when left to their own devices, unregulated capital markets in the form of massive movements of short-term capital flows end up cannibalizing not just the national economy, but ultimately the very basis for the financial market's global operation. Global finance can act like a 'wrecking ball', to use the vivid imagery of George Soros, but the wreckage can undermine its own conditions for existence. Thus the more national economies are damaged, the less institutional and ideological support exists for strengthening interdependence in the form of open capital markets. Witness, for example, the renewed support for controls on short-term capital flows in the region and the mounting challenge to free-floating finance that has occurred more generally in the wake of the ruin created by global finance. While it is important not to overstate the significance of this movement, one of the main consequences of the crisis has been a worldwide questioning of the benefits of removing capital controls, and in the Asian region at least, a partial closure against global financial markets. Even policymakers in the United States now intellectually accept the case for limits on short-term capital flows, although the interests they serve may prevent explicit support for this agenda.[64] These wider consequences of the crisis do give some basis for the proposition that there are important national (institutional) limits to globalization.

More generally, the Asian crisis has left little doubt that exposure to volatile (short-term) capital flows is bad for growth, damaging even the most sound econo-

---

[64] I owe this point to Jeremy Heimans, reporting comments from an interview with Joseph Stiglitz.

mies. The conclusion to draw from this, however, is not that global financial markets have somehow disempowered the state or that national systems are converging on liberal economics. Any such triumph would be a phyrric victory for globalism for it would mean undercutting its very foundations of existence. If this reading is correct, then rather than a retreat or transformation of the state (developmental or otherwise), we are much more likely to see a retreat of untrammelled markets in favour of the prudential use of capital controls.

Conclusion

The general argument here has been that whether or not a globalization tendency exists may in the final analysis not be deeply important, at least not for the institutions of national governance and their capacity to improve wealth creation and social protection. The key proposition is that global and national are interdependent principles of organization rather than antinomies. Global networks have evolved and strengthened on the basis of national and international institutions; they are more likely to be sustained where they complement and coexist with such institutions, rather than by weakening or displacing them. In this sense, 'global' is no more a pure concept than 'national' or 'international'. I draw three main conclusions from the argument offered in this article.

First, globalization, itself a partial and limited process, has not so much undermined national capacity for wealth creation as increased the need for it, an argument which has been advanced in much greater detail elsewhere.[65] Just as some have argued that there can be no globalization without (national) social protection, so there can be no social protection without wealth creation, and ultimately no sustained wealth creation without national governance. National governments can act to improve social welfare (read 'social protection' and 'wealth creation'). But this must be taken as an 'in principle' statement. If in practice many governments do not act in this way, it is less because of pressures stemming from the global economy than because of constraints imposed by underlying regime orientations and institutional capacities.

Proposing that states act as mediators and midwives, rather than being mere victims of economic integration, does not mean that political choices are utterly open-ended. The big choices that state actors make—*vis-à-vis* regulatory reform, social protection, and wealth creation—are strongly informed by external-competitive pressures; but the way in which states tackle such issues as well as their outcomes are path dependent. This means that the choices actors make and their outcomes are to a large degree shaped by (domestic) regime characteristics rather than being imposed on them. There are still constraints, but the way states respond to them is much more regime dependent than externally determined. So in assessing the impacts of international integration, we need to distinguish between two different issues. The first is why states make certain choices, e.g., to alter social policy programmes, to deregulate a particular industry, and so forth (which may or may not have to do with 'external' structural changes and pressures and the costs and

---

[65] See Weiss, *The Myth of the Powerless State*.

benefits thereof). Second, even when those choices appear to stem from common sources, the issue is why apparently similar choices may produce distinctively different outcomes. One important implication of the preceding argument is that we can expect continuing diversity in national systems of political economy—in short, varieties of capitalism.

Second, growing political interdependence has not eliminated the territorial principle but rather organizationally 'tamed' it. In subdued form today, this 'neo-territoriality' continues to provide the foundation for enhanced cooperation.[66] Indeed without a territorial basis, it is hard to imagine why states would be disposed to engage in interstate cooperation. It is not hard to appreciate that economic integration has increased hand-in-hand with the strengthening of nationally distinct forms of economic management. Under the Cold War regime, countries and regions have become more diverse, not more homogeneous. And it has been on the basis of accepting and strengthening diversity—not imposing uniformity—that international cooperation has flourished. The combination of increasing interdependence (particularly in trade) and the consolidation of different national models of economic and political management defines a major and distinctive feature of the developed world's postwar 'golden age' period.[67] Variations on the free-market norm were once tolerated as part of the United States' strict-geopolitical—relaxed-economic stance, which encouraged and supported capitalist diversity as a means of strengthening capitalism against communism. Once the Cold War ended, however, tolerance for capitalist diversity rapidly declined (a trend especially evident in the United States' recent dealings with East Asia). But if that old adage of 'strength in diversity' remains valid in the world of international affairs, then current attempts to submerge the national with the global rather than to support and encourage their coexistence may prove the greater threat to world order in the long run. In sum, if the postwar pattern offers any guide to future stability, the persistence of national institutional diversity rather than its suppression would appear a more robust basis for the consolidation of international cooperation.

Finally, the big choices in international relations theory between anarchy and cooperation, realism and liberal institutionalism appear less clear cut. Realists will no doubt continue to insist on the enduring reality of the sovereignty principle, on the impossibility of changing the nature of states as a result of their cooperation. Institutionalists, on the other hand, will be more inclined to see in international forms of cooperation a newly emergent institutional reality, whereby the whole becomes more than the sum of its sovereign parts. But unlike individuals who eventually lose control over the institutions they have historically set in motion (control over the state itself being a primary example), states may not succumb to a similar institutional dialectic. For—however much they orient themselves to internationalism they remain anchored in a domestic constituency. Similarly, one may argue that, like cats, states can be 'domesticated' via international society; but for all their domestication, cats are still prone to hunt down their feathered friends when circumstances favour. Binding states into international organizations may be a bit

---

[66] John Hertz's term refers to 'a world in which sovereign states recognize their interests in mutual respect for each other's independence and in extensive cooperation', cited in Zacher, 'The Decaying Pillars of the Westphalian Temple', p. 100.

[67] Lars Mjoset, 'Atlantic, West-European and Nordic integration', Department of Sociology and Human Geography, University of Oslo (1999), p. 12.

like making the cat wear the proverbial bell: it's good for the society of wildlife and it does no harm to the cat. The lesson may be that states can be increasingly dual creatures: exercising their cooperative (international) aspect, as well as their more traditional self-interested side as circumstances require. That of course is the critical point. Over the long haul, much depends on the fruits of cooperation. States will cooperate as long as the welfare benefits of doing so outweigh the sovereignty costs. It would be unwise to expect states willy nilly to abandon self-interest or sacrifice national welfare on behalf of interdependence.

Beyond Westphalia? Capitalism after the 'Fall'

BARRY BUZAN AND RICHARD LITTLE

Capitalism and the meaning of Westphalia

When the Berlin Wall was breached in 1989 and the Cold War ended, specialists in the field of international relations (IR) readily acknowledged that it was necessary to take stock and assess the historical significance of these events. Unsurprisingly, no agreement has been reached. For most realists, the events reflect no more than an important shift in the power structure of the international system. But for liberals, the forty years of Cold War are now depicted not as a struggle for power, but as an ideological battle between capitalism and communism from which capitalism has emerged triumphant. The significance of this development for the future of international relations is difficult to gauge. As a key concept, 'capitalism' has largely been the preserve of the Marxian fringe in IR. It did not resonate amongst most mainstream theorists in the field, whether realist or liberal.[1] The concept was most familiar as a term of communist propaganda. It was avoided by many specialists during the Cold War era who failed to see how capitalism could promote an understanding of superpower relations. But with the end of the Cold War now linked to the triumph of capitalism, it is impossible for liberals, in particular, to discuss the future of the international system without some evaluation of the unfolding international role being played by capitalism.

At the centre of this ongoing debate about the future of international relations lie competing evaluations of what has come to be known as the Westphalian system. Westphalia has been accorded iconic status in IR. There is a near consensus in the field that the 1648 treaties represent the benchmark for the transformation of the international system, or at least the European international system, from medieval to modern form. Westphalia is associated with the formal emergence of a distinctive system of sovereign states. It is, of course, possible to debate whether the treaties deserve the stature they have,[2] and arguments can also be found for pushing the key date of transformation backwards or forwards by a century or so. But although the medieval to modern transformation is understood to have been a process taking place over some centuries, almost nobody in the field disputes that a major transformation of the international system did take place around this time, and that the treaties of Westphalia mark one of the key stages in this.

---

[1] It does not, for example, appear in the text to Robert O. Keohane and Joseph S. Nye, *Power and Interdependence: World Politics in Transition* (Boston: Little, Brown, 1977).

[2] Stephen, D. Krasner, 'Compromising Westphalia', *International Security*, 20 (1995/6), pp. 115–51; Stephen, D. Krasner, 'Westphalia and All That' in Judith Goldstein and Robert O. Keohane (eds.), *Ideas and Foreign Policy: Institutions and Political Change* (Ithaca, NY: Cornell University Press, 1993).

With the ending of the Cold War, only hardened realists in IR have not been tempted to ask 'are we moving into a new world order?' In other words, is the Westphalian international order coming to an end, and, if so, what is going to replace it? Are we facing another transformation of the international system equivalent in significance to that symbolised by 1648, or is the basic framework set by Westphalia still the most accurate way to characterize the international system? In order to look at this question, it helps to understand the type of change that Westphalia is generally understood to represent. Our key to grasping its significance for IR is the idea that Westphalia represents the arrival of a new type of dominant unit, the sovereign, territorial state, and a distinctive form of international society associated with that unit. The Westphalian state differed in two substantial ways from both the very diverse primary units of the medieval world (church, empire, religious orders, cities, city-leagues, guilds, aristocratic estates and suchlike), and also from the main units of the wider non-European ancient and classical world (empires, city states, barbarian tribes). First, the Westphalian state had hard and precisely defined boundaries, and second, it consolidated into a single centre all the powers of self-government. This arrangement was in sharp contrast to those which preceded it. In the ancient and classical, and medieval, worlds, boundaries were more often frontier zones where authority faded away, and sovereignty was often dispersed, with different aspects of governance located in different actors.

Along with this new dominant unit came a new type of international society. Westphalian states constructed a diplomacy based on mutual acceptance of each other as legal equals, a practice in sharp contrast to the norm of unequal relations that prevailed in both ancient and classical and medieval international systems. They took religion out of international politics, and generated a self-conscious principle of balance of power aimed at preventing any one state from taking over the system. The Westphalian international order was very much driven by military and political considerations. Given the obsession with exclusive sovereignty, the political structure of the system was necessarily anarchic, and its international politics dominated by self-help and military insecurity. States needed to pursue power if they were to survive, and their pursuit of power ensured that the system was marked by military competition and the security dilemma.

The Westphalian international order just described is the model for the realist (and neorealist) paradigm of how to understand and theorize about the international system. In a move of quite breathtaking Eurocentric audacity, realists assume that the Westphalian model is somehow able to embrace all of world politics since the rise of civilization. Realism stresses states, balance of power, insecurity and competition as the key features of the international system. It assumes that the high politics of war and military rivalry dominate the international agenda, and that states will subordinate other objectives to those priorities. During the Cold War, liberals also accepted an essentially realist orientation on international relations,[3] but unlike the realists, they insisted that the Westphalian order contained the potential for systemic transformation. In the post Cold War era, whereas realists continue to view international relations from a Westphalian perspective, liberals are paying increasing attention to the transformative consequences of the global expansion of liberal capitalism.

[3] Robert D.McKinlay and Richard Little, *Global Problems and World Order* (London: Francis Pinter, 1986).

In considering whether Westphalia/realism is still valid or not, one needs to look at three issues: is the dominance of traditional high politics—of military-political process—changing? Is the dominant unit changing? And is the nature of international society changing? As we will see, the answer to each of these questions is inextricably bound up with the future orientation of liberal capitalism.

Is the dominant process changing?

If military-political 'high' politics is no longer the dominant, system-shaping process, then both the Westphalian model and realism are in deep trouble. And a case can be made that some quite fundamental transformations are underway in the relative importance of military-political as opposed to economic interactions in the international system. This case rests on two stories that are now very prominent in discussions of international relations: 'democratic peace' and 'globalisation'.

Democratic peace is about the apparent end of Great Power war in the international system, and thus about the quality, political salience, and perhaps also the amount, of interaction within the military-political sector. Specifically, it is about the statistical observation that democracies (and particularly liberal democracies) very seldom if ever go to war with each other. Explanations for the apparent abandonment of war amongst a growing group of states that includes all of the most developed and powerful societies, vary from fear of nuclear weapons, through economic interdependence, to the spread of democracy (though for the purposes of the argument we want to make here, the causes matter less than the simple fact). If sustained, the cessation of Great Power war would dethrone military interaction from its millennia-long reign as the principal defining process of international systems. The shift from negative (balance of power, war) to positive (security regime, security community) security interdependence not only changes the dominant type of military-political interaction, but makes that type of interaction a less urgent and less prominent feature in the day to day life of states. Closely linked to this story is the assumption that as capitalism extends into non-democratic areas of the world liberal democracies will eventually form in its wake. From this perspective, the most effective way of promoting liberalism in countries such as China is to engage them in the capitalist world economy.

Globalization is about the truly enormous, and ongoing, rise of economic interaction in the system, and the effects of that on other sectors. It is the catch-phrase for the liberal interpretation of the way the world is going. Although it has taken some knocks from the financial crises starting in 1997, the liberal triumphalist view is still powerful. Since its victory in the Cold War, liberalism is without effective challengers as the organising ideology for an industrial (and post-industrial) capitalist world. Fukuyama's notion of 'the end of history' assumes that the triumph of the global capitalist market will endure despite its ups and downs.[4] The liberal vision rests on the sustained operation of global markets, and the social and political effects that are, and will be, generated by freer trade, easier movement of capital, and globalized production. In the liberal vision, the pursuit of economic

[4] Francis Fukuyama, *The End of History and the Last Man* (London: Penguin, 1992).

efficiency is not only good in itself (because it offers the best prospect of improving human welfare), but is also strongly connected to the development of individual rights, democracy, and peace. These connections may take several generations to reach full flower, but the argument is that market economies inevitably diffuse power widely into society. By this process totalitarianism and authoritarianism become increasingly difficult to sustain, and pluralism unfolds into democracy and individualism. These developments constrain war amongst liberal societies, and as such societies spread, war diminishes. Not only does the divorce of wealth from the control of territory reduce the traditional incentives for war, but democratic societies in an open international system become increasingly difficult to mobilize for conflict or for traditional imperial projects. The globalization story in many ways contains the one about democratic peace.

There is strong evidence that substantial parts of this vision are shaping the new world order in serious ways. Before the late 1990's downturn dented their claims, liberals could argue that much of Asia was firmly embarked on the climb out of poverty. To the extent that the current crisis can be interpreted as part of the normal ups and downs of capitalist development, and therefore intrinsically temporary, this claim still has great force. If the main countries of Asia, particularly China and India, can follow Japan, Singapore, Hong Kong, Taiwan and South Korea into modernization, then the majority of humankind will be on the right side of the development gap. The democratic peace has also reshaped world order. Great Power war and direct military-political imperialism by the strong against the weak have all but disappeared. New forms of collective intervention, whether by INGOs in Africa or by NATO and the EU in former Yugoslavia, are beginning to emerge, based much more on humanitarian than on either extractive or power rivalry motives. And these achievements look pretty durable. Local wars and great power interventions have of course not disappeared, but since liberal political practice is still far from universally applied, that does not discredit the underlying theory. The globalization logic is powerful even in realist terms because it concerns the most powerful and dominant units in the system.

Putting the stories of economic globalization and democratic peace together, one could argue that the liberal vision has begun to reshape some of the most longstanding fundamentals of international relations theory and practice. The Westphalian/realist understanding of international relations placed sovereign states at the centre, and concentrated on the high politics of politico-military relations amongst them. But if we take the 'democratic peace' and 'globalization' stories and consider them together, then a different understanding emerges. If both these stories are substantially true, then international relations cannot be operating according to Westphalian/realist principles. If democratic peace is true, then preparing for war is neither the principal responsibility of states, nor the main force shaping their development. The force of the globalization story is captured in the following statistics.[5] Since 1750, the world's population has grown about eight times, from around 770m to around 6 bn. The global GNP has increased by a multiple of 41, from $148 bn in 1750 to $6,080 bn in 1990. And the value of world trade between 1750 and 1994 has increased from $700m to $8,364,321m, a multiple of 11,506. This

[5] See Barry Buzan and Richard Little, *International Systems in World History: Remaking the Study of International Relations* (Oxford: Oxford University Press, 2000), ch. 14.

rather astonishing figure suggests that during the last 250 years, world trade has outperformed the growth in the human population by over 1,400 times and outperformed global GNP by 281 times. Taken together, these two stories suggest that international relations may well now be more shaped by economic interactions and structures than it is by military ones: 'geopolitics' to 'geoeconomics' as Luttwak puts it.[6] If such a shift has occurred, or is even clearly on the horizon, this would be a momentous and historic change in human affairs.

Is the dominant unit changing?

The globalization argument is not just that economic interaction is becoming more and more important in the day to day life of units, but also that it is transforming the units themselves. The pursuit of the liberal goals that are seen to be essential to the promotion of late twentieth century capitalism requires a big reduction in the state's control of the national economy, and a general opening of borders to economic transactions. It creates powerful roles for TNCs, some IGOs (WTO, IMF, IBRD), and a host of INGOs ranging from sports federations and governing bodies to Greenpeace and Amnesty International. Because of the knock-on effects of trying to separate economic from political life, many argue that the state itself is being hollowed out. At the same time, the traditional military role of the state, the foundation of its claim to political primacy, has shrunk to marginal status because the democratic peace has diminished the threat of invasion and war. If the military-political sector is losing dominance as the defining process of the system, and if globalization is pushing the state out of many aspects of the economy, can the traditional dominance of the Westphalian state as the defining unit of the international system be maintained?

When one looks at the leading contemporary states, there are quite strong grounds for thinking that the series of (r)evolutions which characterized their development throughout the modern era (from absolutist to nationalist to democratic, not to mention from agrarian to industrial to postindustrial) is still underway. The much commented upon 'hollowing out' of the state might be seen as a fourth round representing yet another shift in the empowerment of civil society, and particularly economic actors (firms, banks, IGOs, INGOs, regimes) and structures (markets), in relation to governments. Cerny labels this phase 'the competition state'[7], though others see it more as a regression to nineteenth century laissez-faire, before the state became so intrusive into economic and social life. But is this best understood as a fourth round of the modernist development, still within the Westphalian model, or as a transition to a different kind of dominant unit—the postmodern state?[8] If one accepts the idea that a sectoral transformation from military dominant to economic dominant is underway, then it becomes easier to argue that we are looking not just at a change *in* the dominant unit, but a change *of* it.

---

[6] Edward Luttwak, 'From Geopolitics to Geoeconomics', *The National Interest*, 20 (1990), pp. 17–24.

[7] Philip G. Cerny, 'Globalization and the Changing Logic of Collective Action', *International Organization*, 49 (1995), pp. 595–625.

[8] 'Postmodern' here meaning 'after the modern, or Westphalian state', and not referring to the cultural theory of postmodernism.

There are two steps to the argument that we may be witnessing a change *of* rather than *in* the dominant unit. First is the erosion of hard boundaries and strong sovereignty as the defining elements of national states and their relations, and their replacement by a much more complicated arrangement of permeable boundaries, layered sovereignty and common international and transnational 'spaces' (cyberspace, civic space, commercial space, legal space). For many purposes (trade and finance, communications and media, tourism, some aspects of law) state boundaries have become not just permeable, but shot through with large holes. If hard boundaries and hard sovereignty are being abandoned in enough important ways, then perhaps we are no longer looking at Westphalian states but at postmodern ones. This development is most obvious within the subsystem of the EU,[9] though it can also be seen more generally within and among the OECD states. With the EU, the question of unit transformation arises both in relation to the EU itself as a new type of entity with actor quality, and to its effect on its member states. The EU does not seem likely to become simply another large federal state. Instead it is experimenting with a new form of both unit and sub-system structure, where the sharp inside/outside features of the modernist era are blurring into a mixture of the domestic and the international. States still exist, but they are embedded in a layered sovereignty, and for many purposes their boundaries are highly porous.

The second step is to see that this change is not just about the state, but also about upgrading the relative autonomy of the economic and civic units that had until recently gestated within the modern state. Are we seeing a combined move away from the dominance of military-political units, and towards a situation in which there is variety of dominant units, analogous to the medieval system? The postmodern state has both dissolved its borders for many types of interaction and begun to disperse its sovereignty to other levels. Again, this is most obvious in the EU where layered governance is explicit, and the principle of subsidiarity is the guiding rule. But it is also apparent, though more weakly, in the international system at large, where a variety of regimes and institutions are providing elements of global governance in some specific areas of policy (think of the WTO, or the nuclear non-proliferation regime and its inspection arm, the IAEA). Non-state actors such as TNCs, banks, mafias, and INGOs (Amnesty International, the World Wildlife Fund, Greenpeace) are able to move with considerable autonomy in the transnational legal space created by open borders and layered governance. In a sense, part of the civic space that was opened up *within* the most advanced modern states as they moved towards democracy, is now being shifted into the system level, the space *between* states, especially democratic ones. In the process, the sharp inside/outside delineation of the Westphalian system, where the domestic and international political realms were strongly differentiated, is breaking down. If this development continues, it points towards an international system that has no single, clearly dominant, multipurpose, multi-sectoral type of unit, but instead has a variety of more sector-specialised units.

Unsurprisingly there is no consensus about this interpretation. While it is clear that something interesting is going on, it is not clear that the departure from the Westphalian model is as yet so deep or so widespread to count as a transformation of units. The state still retains its unique multisectoral role, and it still remains the

---

[9] Robert Cooper, *The Postmodern State and the World Order* (London: Demos, Paper no. 19, 1996).

primary source of political legitimacy. Its boundaries may have become more permeable, but as would-be migrants from poor countries can attest, boundaries remain
hard for some purposes. The main centres of supposedly postmodern evolution in
North America, Europe and Japan also remain remarkably parochial, culturally self-
centred, and politically inward looking. And while some IGOs and INGOs might
have achieved significant levels of relative autonomy, it is much less clear either that
they have escaped the dominion of the state, or that they are themselves plausible
candidates for status as new types of dominant unit.

There are many contending voices trying to capture current developments. Albert
and Brock put forward the idea that 'debordering' is effectively dismantling the
Westphalian system, making way for a non-territorial politics combining elements of
neomedievalism and world society.[10] Rosecrance also sees deterritorialisation, and
advocates surrender to economic forces in a mobile, meritocratic world.[11] McRae
tends to agree, arguing that we are at the beginning of 'reestablishing markets, as
opposed to state bureaucracy, as the main method of allocating resources', with the
state shifting from being a provider of services (failed model) to being a regulator,
and a new class of internationally mobile professionals emerging.[12] Watson sees all
this as good, making a sustained argument against the excesses of sovereignty and
non-intervention in international society, and in favour of more acceptance of
hegemonial authority. He sees the modernist European anarchic model as too prone
to excess, and not possible in a world with microstates and weak states. He wants to
see the system managed by a hegemonic coalition of great powers, and adopting a
value base wider than just Western.[13] McNeill like Watson, postulates a turn away
from the extreme of the nation-state towards more polyethnic political constructions
reminiscent of classical empires. He sees migration and ethnic loyalty creating
ghettos just as in the classical empires, and dismisses the nation state as a temporary
throwback to the simpler patterns of barbarian, and classical Greek times.[14] And yet
it is also possible to argue that territorial boundaries have become more stable than
ever before, in the sense that movement of boundaries is much less common than it
used to be until very recently and that for some purposes they remain hard.[15]

All of this suggests that the question of unit transformation is firmly, and rightly,
on the agenda of contemporary international systems analysis, but that the jury is
still out. Not the least of the problems involved is that there are no agreed criteria
for distinguishing when changes *in* the dominant unit add up to a change *of*
dominant unit.

[10] Mathias Albert and Lothar Brock, 'Debordering the World of States: New Spaces in IR' (Frankfurt,
  Working Paper 2, 1995).
[11] Richard Rosecrance, 'The Rise of the Virtual State' *Foreign Affairs*, 75 (1996), pp. 45–61.
[12] Hamish McRae, *The World in 2020* (London: Harper Collins,1994), pp. 21–3, 185–205.
[13] Adam Watson, *The Limits of Independence: Relations Between States in the Modern World* (London:
  Routledge, 1997).
[14] William H., McNeill, 'The Fall of Great Powers: An Historical Commentary', *Review*, 17 (1994),
  pp. 123–43.
[15] Robert H. Jackson and Mark W. Zacher, 'The Territorial Covenant: International Society and the
  Stabilization of Boundaries', (Paper presented to PIPES, University of Chicago, May 1997).

Is the nature of international society changing?

If the dominance of military-political interaction is being challenged by a capitalist mode of economic interaction, and if the leading states are beginning to assume a post-Westphalian form, is the basic nature of international society also changing away from Westphalian norms? There are many contending views on this question and little sense of emergent consensus.

Some analysts expect neorealist logic to soldier on more or less unaffected. They expect the US to become the target of balance of power behaviour, and the EU to break down into a balance of power subsystem.[16] Huntington's 'clash of civilisations' thesis implausibly tries to extend this hard realist structural logic from the state level up to the civilizational level.[17] But questions need to be asked about how the whole logic of neorealism functions in a strongly capitalized and marketized global system without Great Power war. Such a system can remain anarchic and stable both because a strong international society provides a framework of rules and principles that legitimizes the functional and sectoral differentiation amongst the units, and because of the different quality of the survival imperative in the economic realm as compared to the military one. As Waltz himself points out, firms die more naturally and frequently than do states.[18] The neorealist logic of like units might well survive, but only in relation to classes of units (all postmodern states become like, all TNCs become like, all INGOs become like, etc.) and not in the way that a single type of unit must become dominant. Thus, ironically, the neorealist conception of structure might get substantially shifted back to the economic domain from whence it came.

To the extent that conflict is replaced by mutual security (security regimes, security communities) the shoving and shaping forces of socialization and competition become less driven by military considerations, and more driven by economic and societal ones. This shift might well be the defining feature of the transformation from a modern, Westphalian international system to a postmodern one. The comparative advantage that enables some units to dominate others (or inspires some to emulate others) will shift away from military capability, and towards both economic prowess, societal dynamism, and the diplomatic skills necessary to build, and to expand, both strong systems, or subsystems, of international society, and the 'world society' patterns of shared identity at the individual level on which such liberal constructions will need to rest. Military skills will certainly not disappear in a postmodern international system. They will continue to be central in many relationships amongst states outside the core (e.g. India-Pakistan, Iran-Iraq, North and South Korea, China and Taiwan), and will also play a selectively important role in relations between core and periphery where periphery states get designated either as a local nuisance (Serbia, Iraq), or as threats to world order (e.g. Iran, Libya, North Korea, possibly China). But they will matter less than they did before in

[16] Kenneth N. Waltz, 'The New World Order', *Millennium*, 22 (1993), pp. 187–95. John J. Mearsheimer, 'Back to the Future: Instability in Europe after the Cold War', *International Security*, 15 (1990), pp. 5–56.

[17] Samuel P. Huntington, 'The Clash of Civilizations?', *Foreign Affairs*, 72 (1993), pp. 22–49; and Samuel P. Huntington, Samuel P., *The Clash of Civilizations and the Remaking of World Order* (New York: Simon & Schuster, 1996).

[18] Kenneth N. Waltz, *Theory of International Politics* (Reading, MA: Addison-Wesley, 1979), p. 95.

building comparative advantage at the commanding heights of global international society. Real comparative advantage will lie with those most able to sustain and expand zones of economic and political openness within which the threat and use of force between states is largely replaced by diplomacy and geoeconomics. The Cold War itself, and its outcome, might be taken as an illustration. Whereas the capitalist West was able to construct an expanding zone of security community and economic openness, the communist world remained economically primitive, and not only failed to establish a security community amongst its members but quite frequently resorted to military-political confrontation (China-USSR, USSR-Yugoslavia) or invasion and war (China-Vietnam, Vietnam-Cambodia, USSR-Hungary, USSR-Czechoslovakia).

The intensification of the capitalist and global market structure seems almost certain to continue, carrying with it an increasingly dense regulatory framework at all levels of governance. By the late twentieth century, the global market had reached sufficient strength that it could begin to change the political structure by unpacking the hard borders and centralized sovereignty of the modern state. This is the globalization story we have told above. But while there is little doubt that the global market structure is powerful while it operates, there is much argument about how stable it is.

The liberal self-understanding of globalization tends to see it as generally benign, with the various costs it imposes being discounted against the wider gains of peace, democracy and prosperity in the longer run. Liberal triumphalism is in fashion, and as Fukuyama's notion of 'the end of history' suggests, their assumption is that the victory of the capitalist global market will endure. But there are at least two big worms in the liberal apple. The first is an array of worries about both the stability and the impact of really existing liberalism, particularly the economic liberalism that is currently in the driving seat. Not all these have roots in Marxian thinking, but they paint plausible pictures of a rampant and self-destructive capitalism impoverishing the third world and undermining the social and political stability of even the advanced industrial states.[19] Chase-Dunn sees the victory of neoliberalism as having 'occurred within a context of a capitalist crisis of immense proportions' caused by irrationality, inequality, ecological damage, fiscal crises and racial antagonisms.[20] Some interpret this as a crisis not just of capitalism, but of modernism *per se:* Judt sees Europe as 'about to enter an era of turmoil, a time of troubles' because of the disarray in its enlightenment-ordering ideas.[21] Others have a less apocalyptic view, but still one that questions the stability of the liberal order. McRae sees the coming crisis in terms of demography, with a growing divide between a young, unstable, poor world and a rich, old, stable one, and in terms of declining US leadership, and withdrawal of American support from internationalism and liberalism.[22] Horsman and Marshall worry that the state is being dismantled by liberal capitalism, taking with it citizenship, accountability and the general framework of sociopolitical stabi-

[19] L. S. Stavrianos, *Lifelines from Our Past* (London: I. B. Tauris, 1990), pp. 139–87; Immanuel Wallerstein, 'The World System after the Cold War', *Journal of Peace Research*, 30 (1993), pp. 1–6.
[20] Christopher Chase Dunn, 'Technology and the Logic of World Systems', in Ronen P. Palan and Barry Gills (eds.), *Transcending the State-Global Divide: A Neostructuralist Agenda in International Relations* (Boulder, CO: Lynne Rienner, 1994), p. 102.
[21] Tony Judt, 'Nineteen Eighty-Nine: The End of *Which* European Era?', *Dædalus*, 123 (1994), pp. 1–19.
[22] McRae, *The World in 2020*, pp. 97–119, 209–24).

lity. They worry that 'the creation of risk has outpaced the creation of trust'. They hope for a more layered form of politics up and down from the state, but fear that the economic sector is outpacing the political framework, and that there is 'no global liberal consensus on how capitalism should operate'.[23] Buzan, Wæver and de Wilde focus on the operating instabilities of the global market in terms of credit bubbles and reactions to the political and social effects of intense competition.[24] But this sort of gloom about the fate of capitalism is of course perennial, and Wood is rightly sceptical about the easy calling of yet another terminal crisis of capitalism, noting that capitalism is 'the system that dies a thousand deaths'.[25]

The second worm is liberalism's failure to contain the security agenda.[26] In fairness, it has of course to be noted that liberalism is not a doctrine that stresses security. Its catch-phrase is freedom, and this includes the freedom to fail. Without that basic insecurity, capitalist market economies could not function. Liberals expect the application of their doctrine to reduce the role of war in international relations, and can claim some success on this front. But in many other ways, liberal practice has generated insecurity. This is most obvious in the economic realm itself, where intense competition and financial liberalizsation create fears both of individual impoverishment and instability in the world economy as a whole. Much of the environmental security agenda hangs on the contradiction between liberal commitments to growth and consumcrism and the finite carrying capacity of the planetary ecosystem. Insecurity about identity is strongly shaped by the homogenizing tendencies of globalization and the challenge of liberal ideas to many cultural traditions: commercialism is not culturally neutral. There is even room for fear that the hollowing out of the state contingent on globalization is threatening the foundations of democracy without putting anything in their place. Whatever the benefits it may have brought, 'real existing liberal capitalism' is also generating its own set of security problems, and to the extent that security issues become dominant, this reinforces the Westphalian character of the international system.

There are good reasons for thinking that the controversies about capitalism will continue: capitalism is seemingly in endless crisis, but also endlessly inventing new technologies, both physical and social, with which to keep itself in business. The crisis of capitalism is always in motion, and seems likely to remain so until some fundamental change, such as the final solving of the problem of production by technology, sweeps away the conditions on which it rests. Major crises over trade or money, such as that which hit much of East Asia during 1997–9, will doubtless remain a recurrent feature of the global market, but there is little sign that the market structure itself is under terminal threat, either from its own operation or from a reassertion of military primacy. Only the worst of the environmental scenarios could easily unseat the power of the global market.

Along with the intensification of the market comes a wider range of rules, norms and institutions, especially economic liberal ones. Again, there is no consensus on

---

[23] Matthew Horsman and Andrew Marshall, (1995), *After the Nation-State: Citizens, Tribalism and the New World Disorder* (London: Harper Collins, 1995), pp. 208 and 212.

[24] Barry Buzan, Ole Wæver and Jaap de Wilde, *Security: A New Framework for Analysis* (Boulder, CO: Lynne Rienner, 1998), ch. 5.

[25] Ellen Meiksins Wood, 'What is the "Postmodern" Agenda?', *Monthly Review*, 47 (1995), pp. 1–12.

[26] Barry Buzan, Barry and Ole Wæver, *Liberalism and Security: The Contradictions of the Liberal Leviathan* (Copenhagen: COPRI, Working Paper 23, 1998).

how to understand the current condition and prospects of international society. Both 'clash of civilisation' and 'decline of the US/West' views carry the implication that international society is not much more than a projection of Western power, and that as the West declines so inevitably will international society. Similar worries about the excessively Western character of international society can be found in the work of Watson and Cohen.[27] These concerns have to be set against the fact that both of their underlying assumptions are disputed. Not everyone thinks that the West/US is declining[28] and some argue that international society is not Western but Westernistic.[29] This latter view is based on the understanding that the originally Western ideas on which international society rests—the state, sovereignty, nationalism and diplomacy—have now become effectively universal—as, almost, has acceptance of the market. If this is accepted, then the foundations of international society no longer depend on Western power. What one sees through this lens is neither a subtle form of Western imperialism nor a new kind of sociopolitical universalism. It is in part, both. There is universalism in the general acceptance of sovereign equality and the framework of international law and diplomacy based on that. And there is Western imperialism both in the projection of some contested values (human rights, democracy), and in the fact that the Western core and its immediate circle of Westernistic associates have developed a much thicker version of international society amongst themselves than they share with the rest. International society may be unevenly developed, but it is not fragile.

Indeed, others note that international society is now sufficiently powerful and embedded that it is actually responsible for creating many of the states in the system, not just in Africa and parts of the Middle East, but also in Eastern Europe (after the First World War).[30] These states, and in some ways also several of the successor states to the Soviet Union, have been given 'juridical sovereignty' by international recognition, without having first established 'empirical sovereignty' in terms of effective government over their territories.[31] Alan James argues that international society, in the form of the doctrine of legal equality amongst states, has significantly constrained the exercise of power in the contemporary international system.[32] Hedley Bull goes even further, developing the view that the sovereign rights of states derive from the rules of international society and are limited by them.[33]

Bull's is a very advanced view of international society, placing rights in the system rather than in the units, and so raising fundamental questions about Wesphalian state-centrism. If correct, this view of a strengthening and universally rooted international society slots in nicely to the stories above about sectoral transformations and the possible emergence of a new type of postmodern dominant unit which shares international space with TNCs, INGOs and some IGOs whose legal status

---

[27] Watson, *Limits of Independence*; and Raymond Cohen, 'In the Beginning: Diplomatic Negotiation in the Ancient Near East' (Paper presented to the ECPR-SGIR Conference, Paris, 1995).

[28] Susan Strange, 'Defending Benign Mercantilism', *Journal of Peace Research*, 25 (1988), pp. 273–7.

[29] Barry Buzan and Gerald Segal, 'A Western Theme', *Prospect*, 27 (1998), pp. 18–23.

[30] Christopher Clapham, *Africa and the International System* (Cambridge: Cambridge University Press, 1996), pp. 15–16, 24.

[31] Robert H. Jackson, *Quasi-States: Sovereignty, International Relations and the Third World* (Cambridge: Cambridge University Press, 1990).

[32] Alan James, 'The Equality of States: Contemporary Manifestations of an Ancient Doctrine', *Review of International Studies*, 18 (1992) pp. 377–92.

[33] Hedley Bull, *Justice in International Relations* (Hagey Lectures, University of Waterloo, 1984).

gives them a quasi-autonomous status in the system. If this 'neomedieval' image of multiple types of units is where things are going, then the function of the strong international society will change. In Westphalian mode, international society has rested on reinforcing sovereign equality amongst states, excluding other units, and thus supporting a neorealist international system of like units. But as indicated in the discussion of units above, this Westphalian mode is already under question, and may be entering into a significant change. A postmodern, capitalist international society might well still rest on the state as the ultimate source of political authority, albeit moderated by some international legal bodies with independent power to generate some types of international law (e.g. ICJ, European Court of Human Rights, International Criminal Court). In this way, international society would retain a strong Westphalian foundation based on like units with equal legal and diplomatic rights. But it would have to add to this an agreed set of principles of differentiation, which set out the rights and obligations of different types of unit— states, TNCs, INGOs, IGOs—and how they relate to each other. The rationale for these principles of differentiation would have to rest on the liberal logic of division of labour. Firms and states would have to accept that neither should try to do the other's job, and that their legal rights and obligations need to be clearly demarcated. There are already signs of developments in this direction in the framework of laws about incorporation, finance, property rights and suchlike that define the relative autonomy of non-state units and how they relate to the postmodern state.

Two worlds: how will they relate?

Does this add up to a case for thinking that the world order set by Westphalia is now giving way to a new postmodern capitalist world order? Probably not yet, though it certainly provides evidence both to show that the question is worth asking, and perhaps to inspire the thought that the international system may be entering a process of transition. The case for thinking that we might be witnessing a process of system transformation rests mainly on the sectoral shift, and its unfolding effects on dominant units and international society. This is something new in human history. Of course one has always to be suspicious of those making claims for the dawn of a new era. Such claims often privilege present events. They structure perceptions of both the past and the future, and they are nearly always aimed at steering present behaviour in directions desired by the proclaimer.

In addition to doubts about the transformation of the state, perhaps the main objection to talking about a transformation to a postmodern capitalist world order is the widely held view that uneven capitalist development is pulling the international system into 'two worlds'.[34] This view supposes that a partial transformation of the

[34] Keohane and Nye, *Power and Interdependence*; Barry Buzan, 'New Patterns of Global Security in the Twenty-First Century', *International Affairs*, 67 (1991), pp. 431–51. Barry Buzan, 'Conclusions: System Versus Units in Theorizing About the Third World', in Stephanie Neuman (ed.), *International Relations Theory in the Third World* (New York: St. Martin's Press, 1998); Fukuyama, *The End of History*; James M. Goldgeier and Michael McFaul, 'A Tale of Two Worlds: Core and Periphery in the Post-Cold War Era', *International Organization*, 46 (1992), pp. 467–91; Max Singer and Aaron Wildavsky, *The Real World Order* (Chatham, NJ: Chatham House Publishers, 1993); Robert O.

international system has taken place. Rather than being a single politico-strategic space, with a single set of rules of the game, the international system has divided into two worlds. One world (call it the zone of peace or the post-historical world) is defined by a postmodern security community of powerful advanced capitalist industrial democracies, and international relations within this world no longer operate according to old Westphalian/realist rules. In the zone of peace, states do not expect or prepare for war against each other, and since this zone contains most of the great powers this is a very significant development for the whole of the international system. Reflecting the character of postmodern states, highly developed capitalist economies and societies are exceptionally open and interdependent, transnational players are numerous and strong, and international society is well developed.

The other world (call it the zone of conflict or the historical world) is comprised of a mixture of modern and premodern states. In relations amongst (and within) these states classical realist rules still obtain, and war is a useable and used instrument of policy. In this zone, international relations operate by the Westphalian/realist rules of power politics that prevailed all over the world up to 1945. States expect and prepare for the possibility of serious tension with their neighbours. Some restraint is provided by deterrence (in a few places nuclear deterrence) but economic interdependence between neighbours is generally low, and populations can often be easily mobilized for war. Especially within premodern, but also within some modern states, political power is frequently contested by force. Even in the capitalist and modernizing states of East Asia where economic interdependence between neighbours is growing, the states are still often fragile and highly protective of sovereignty, and use of force amongst some of them cannot be ruled out.

To divide the world in this way of course oversimplifies. Some places close to the core of the zone of peace behave like the zone of conflict (ex-Yugoslavia, Albania, Northern Ireland), and some ostensibly in the zone of conflict have managed to build substantial regional barriers against local wars (the Association of South-East Asian Nations—ASEAN, the Southern African Development Community—SADC, and possibly Mercosur in the Latin American southern cone). An alternative view is that these two worlds exist not as distinct and separate territorial spaces, but as interleaved modes of living. Thus parts of some cities in the West contain their own zones of conflict. Nevertheless the general distinction seems valid, even at the risk of creating an exaggerated sense of spatial separation, and the claim for two parallel modes of international relations seems plausible, even though there is significant overlap between them. There are fundamental qualitative differences in the way in which the states and societies of Europe, North America and Japan relate both to each other and to their populations on the one hand, and the way in which states in the Middle East, South Asia, and many other places do so. These differences are rooted deeply in the form and character, and therefore also the history, of the states and societies within the two zones.

A central issue in the two worlds formulation is how the zone of peace and the zone of conflict relate to each other, for that they do relate in many and significant

Keohane, 'Hobbes' Dilemma and Institutional Change in World Politics: Sovereignty in International Society', in Hans-Henrik Holm and Georg Sørensen (eds.), *Whose World Order?* (Boulder, CO. Westview Press, 1995); A. P. Rana, 'The New Northern Concert of Powers in a World of Multiple Independencies', in K Ajhua, H. Coppens and H. van der Wusten (eds.), *Regime Transformation in Global Realignments*, (London: Sage, 1993); Cooper, *The Postmodern State.*

ways is beyond question. At whatever point in history one looks at the international system, some strong pattern of uneven development and different forms of political economy will be present. The diffusion of goods, ideas, and people works continuously to erode uneven development, but never (yet) succeeds in doing so. Some cultures have great difficulty absorbing new goods and ideas without self-destructing. And the game is not static. The leading edge cultures are themselves continuously evolving (or in some cases declining), so opening up new space and new zones to maintain the pattern of unevenness.

In recent times, some attention has focused on the relationship between centre and periphery, and with the Cold War out of the way we can expect this to intensify. How the two zones will relate to each other is one of the great unanswered questions for the twenty-first century. Will the weaker, but perhaps more aggressive, zone of conflict begin to penetrate and impinge upon the zone of peace through threats of terrorism, long-range weapons of mass destruction, migration, disease, debt repudiation, and suchlike? Will the unquestionably more powerful zone of peace seek to penetrate and influence the zone of conflict, using the levers of geo-economics, and occasionally more robust forms of intervention, to manipulate state-making in the zone of conflict? Will the postmodern world try to insulate itself by constructing buffer zones in Mexico, Central Europe, Turkey and North Africa, and trying to stay out of the more chaotic parts of the zone of conflict? Or will it try to engage with the whole, pushing towards a new world order in its own image? We can only guess at the answers to these questions, but what is clear is that complete, or even substantial, separation of the two zones is highly unlikely.

One partial answer seems to be emerging in the former Yugoslavia in the practice of what might be labelled 'postmodern colonialism'. This stands in sharp contrast to more traditional forms of imperialism. In old style Western colonialism the idea of promulgating a 'standard of civilization' was part of the rhetoric for justifying territorial seizures, economic exploitation, imperial rivalry and racism. 'Lesser breeds' were either to be given the benefit of exposure to Western civilization, or else replaced by European migrants who carried that standard with them. While there was some real transfer of social and physical technologies across cultures, perhaps only some missionaries and a few idealistic administrators actually believed that colonialism was primarily a civilizing project. Conquest and accumulation of power were the main themes. Social Darwinist attitudes underpinned routine and potentially endless expansion and self-aggrandizement.

By contrast, postmodern colonialism puts the civilizing mission first and actually means it. Indeed, it is hard to think of what other justification it might have. At the dawn of the twenty-first century, nearly all of the traditional motivations for colonialism are either irrelevant or marginal. There are no longer any great national imperial projects to divide up the world into economically and culturally competing zones. Likewise, all of the great ideological rivalries that throughout the twentieth century spurred the powers to compete for control of global territory are now over, and all of humankind is tinkering with various mixtures of the same formula of states, nations, markets and international regimes. Global economic liberalization, though by no means perfectly in place, is sufficiently entrenched so that the pursuit of wealth is effectively divorced from the control of territory. Tiny Singapore and resource-poor Japan get rich, while big and resource-rich Russia stays poor. Advances in military technology, reductions in global military engagements, and the replacement of great Power rivalries with military integration and cooperation, all conspire to downgrade the need for overseas bases. And the official rejection of racism has delegitimized the idea that any people has the right to conquer another and treat it as inferior. Postmodern colonialism is therefore exceptional rather than routine, a last resort rather than a first one, to be undertaken reluctantly rather than with enthusiasm.

It is clear that none of the traditional motives apply to Western actions in the Balkans. Western engagement there is hesitant rather than crusading, and coordinated and collective, rather than fragmented and rival. Other than fulfilling a certain vision of 'Europe', and creating some minor (and regretted) frictions with Russia, there are no great geopolitical forces in play. Some construction and infrastructure companies might stand to make good profits, but the main military and economic prospect is of sustained costs. There is no desire to garrison the Balkans or to build military bases there, though there is acceptance of a probably long-term burden of peacekeeping. There is no inclination to construct the Balkan peoples as inferior, and no desire to bear the burden of managing their political life for any longer than is absolutely necessary. Despite the fact that wars have been fought, and substantial military forces have been inserted, conquest is not the objective.

Postmodern colonialism is almost entirely about enforcing a standard of civilization, and in particular a liberal vision of human rights. In that sense it has imperial qualities. Because it is primarily a cultural project it does not easily take on universalist pretensions. It is of great significance that the principle of human-rights-motivated military intervention is being practised strongly only in NATO's and Europe's backyard. Although human rights rhetoric is part of Western tensions with many countries in Asia and Africa, and clearly does represent a universal vision, there is little possibility of this being backed up further afield by the kind of intervention we are now witnessing in Southeast Europe. There is a significant difference of degree between postmodern colonialism, which is about taking direct responsibility for remaking political culture, and the more general attempt to persuade or cajole others into accepting Western standards of human rights. What is going on in the Balkans is primarily about, and more importantly within, European and Western civilization, and much less about a shift to a more militant pursuit of Western values around the world. In a Huntingtonian sense, the West has the right to intervene forcefully in the Balkans because the peoples there are culturally part of 'us'. Except for the more extreme form of universalist liberal, that right does not exist with anything like the same clarity across civilizational boundaries. Thus the West did not try to recolonize and remake Iraq, Rwanda or Liberia, and nor will it do so, though it will of course try to influence political developments in those places. It might intervene militarily, as in the case of Iraq, to defend crucial economic interests, but this is not postmodern colonialism.

There can be no doubt that the actors (states, TNCs, INGOs) in the zone of peace are largely responsible for creating and maintaining the international system and international society within which the actors in the zone of conflict have to operate. Everything from norms, rules and laws, through capital and information flows, to the structure of power is shaped by the zone of peace, and *strongly* shaped. The international system and society in which the zone of conflict is embedded is arguably the most powerful, comprehensive and pervasive ever seen on the planet.

So great is its impact that it is possible to ask whether (or to theorize that) the core in the zone of peace is in some ways responsible for the social, political and economic weakness in the periphery. Does economic, cultural, political and military pressure from the core actually destabilize the periphery and inhibit its development, or does it provide role models, resources and capital that should help the periphery to overcome obstacles to development that are rooted in its own cultures and history? The answer to that question is hotly contested and far from empirically clear, but it is not unreasonable to ask it. Neither is it unreasonable to ask whether the power differential between core and periphery is so great that it is only a matter of time before the core assimilates much of the periphery. The vast modernization process underway in much of East Asia, and possibly beginning in South Asia, will forever change the balance between wealth and poverty, and core and periphery, in the international system. If it succeeds, the core will no longer be rooted in just one civilization (the West), but will span several continents in a global network of power and prosperity.

There *are* two worlds whose political life is defined by differences in their level and type of political, social and economic development. But while these worlds may well be different, they are not separate. There is a strong, if lopsided, interaction between them, and whatever their differences, both worlds are firmly embedded in what might best be labelled the late modern international system. Westphalian/realist logic is clearly of diminishing importance in understanding the international relations of the zone of peace. But it remains substantially in force for thinking about much of the zone of conflict, albeit that some emergent zones of failed states in Africa and Asia have a distinctly pre-Westphalian quality. It also remains relevant for thinking about much of the relationship between the zone of peace and the zone of conflict.

Westphalian realism is still relevant. But its traditional claim to serve as the commanding heights of how international relations can and should be understood is rightly under serious challenge.[35]

---

[35] For further elaboration of points made here see Buzan and Little, *International Systems in World History*. An earlier version of the paper was presented to the Conference on '1648 and European Security', National Defence College, Stockholm, October 1998.

The potentials of Enlightenment

FRED HALLIDAY

'The radical critique of reason exacts a high price for taking leave of modernity', Jurgen Habermas, *The Philosophical Discourse of Modernity* (Cambridge: Polity, 1987), p. 336.

Introduction: the challenges of the 1990s

The greatest works of political and social theory are often the shortest, and none more so than the text of Immanuel Kant, *Idea for a Universal History*, written just over two hundred years ago in 1784: it is all of thirteen pages long, and advances a thesis that should concern us all. In essence, it argues that history can, and to some degree does, move in a progressive direction—one in which the domestic organisation of states on an increasingly legal, constitutional, basis will lead to greater cooperation between states and ultimately to some form of world government. Kant's hope was 'that after many reformative revolutions, a universal cosmopolitan condition, which Nature has as her ultimate purpose, will come into being as the womb wherein all the original capacities of the human race can develop'.[1] There are many readings of Professor Kant, not least when this text is combined with others.[2] Yet to put it in modern terms, not entirely traducing his meaning, his work can be read as envisaging a world of constitutional regimes and liberal democracies, one that will be without war. This is a bold thesis with many unproven assumptions: but it is not entirely implausible, on either theoretical or historical grounds. Abused as it may have been by the twin menaces of a modish post-1989 triumphalism, and a postmodernist pessimism, it nonetheless sets us a goal that can, and should, command attention. Two centuries later, the goals of Enlightenment, and a measured concept of progress, retain an, albeit chastened, validity in international as in domestic affairs.

There has been much creative discussion in recent times of the relationship between international relations and the Enlightenment. The Enlightenment, as a broad intellectual process, was not specifically concerned with international issues. Its relevance to the international is as much in the implications of general assumptions as in any particular 'international' arguments that its proponents may have made. Kant's formulation, in *Idea for a Universal History* as in his later *Perpetual*

---

[1] 'Idea for a Universal History from a Cosmopolitan Point of View', in Kant, *On History*, edited by Lewis White Beck (New York, Bobbs-Merrill, 1963), p. 23.
[2] For one astute adjudication see Andrew Hurrell, 'Kant and the Kantian Paradigm in International Relations', *Review of International Studies*, 16:3, (1990).

Peace has the benefit that, in conjunction with his other general philosophical works, he brings together, in respect of the field of international relations, several of the themes that are associated with the Enlightenment: progress, peace, internationalism, purposive human agency. As a current of thought that was itself transnational, the Enlightenment, in Kant as in his contemporaries, contained much that is of relevance to the international: above all, the belief in the ability of a new scientific outlook to master reality, and history, was reflected in the study of the international field. If the Enlightenment was primarily about human progress in general, its implications for IR are clear enough: universalism of values, peace, and cooperation linked to reason and compromise. In the face of all the urgent problems that we have, we need to recall Kant's argument, that humanity has the capacity to fashion a better, more stable, more democratic, more prosperous international order. We are a long way from it, but the very recognition of that distance should encourage us to face the world with a spirit at once more critical and more determined.

Here one may, in regard to IR, invoke the arguments of three prominent, contrasted, figures of late twentieth century thought, who have argued for a reappraisal but reaffirmation of Enlightenment thinking: from a more contented liberal perspective, Isaiah Berlin; from a Marxist standpoint, Jurgen Habermas; and from a discontented liberal standpoint, Ernest Gellner. All set themselves against the claims, narrative and analysis, of anti-Enlightenment fashion. Postmodernism here, as elsewhere, makes strange bedfellows. While Berlin has defended the 'intellectual power, honest, lucidity, courage and disinterested love' of Enlightenment thinkers,[3] Habermas has, while recognising the 'incomplete' character of modernity, asserted its benefits, as against the backwardness of the pre-Enlightenment, and the confusion of the postmodernist. Their arguments too can, with suitable adjustment, be applied to the international.[4] For his part Gellner is, as ever, brisk: 'What is to be done? *Shto dyelat*? We simply cannot return to the claustrophobic, isolationist relativism which our romantics recommend so blithely; each community back to its own totem pole!'[5]

We are not dealing here with a single univocal set of ideas. The Enlightenment, as much as any other body of thought, contains a plurality of possible interpretations, it allows of no single reading to which a retrospective responsibility can be ascribed; it is contradictory. In general political terms, it can be read as enjoining both the right of individuals, and the primacy of states or *raison d'état*. It can endorse both freedom of identity and expression and the power of collectivities. It can be read as favouring interaction of peoples but also autarchy. The scepticism of Hume runs together with the progressivist determinism of Condorcet. Voltaire made a fool of himself in his admiration of despots, Rousseau in his romanticization of the impoverished shepherds of Corsica. To ring the changes on themes central to IR: the

---

[3] 'The intellectual power, honesty, lucidity, courage and disinterested love of the most gifted thinkers of the eighteenth century remain to this day without parallel. Their age is one of the best and most hopeful episodes in the life of mankind', quoted in 'Crimes of Reason', *The Economist*, 16 March 1996.

[4] Jürgen Habermas, 'Modernity—An Incomplete Project', in Hal Foster (ed.), *Postmodern Culture* (London: Pluto, 1985). On Habermas and the international see Andrew Linklater, *The Transformation of Political Community* (Cambridge: Polity Press, 1998), together with the 'Forum' discussion of Linklater's book in *Review of International Studies*, 25:1 (January 1999) and the review by Nicholas Rengger, *International Affairs*, 74:3 (July 1998). And in a parallel application of Gramsci, Robert Cox, *Approaches to World Order* (Cambridge: Cambridge University Press, 1996).

[5] Ernest Gellner, *Postmodernism, Reason and Religion* (London: Routledge, 1992), p. 90.

Enlightenment can be read as favouring self-determination of states, or, in a scientistic metaphor much beloved of eighteenth thinkers and still with us today, the 'balance of power'. All the forms of political action relevant to domestic *and* international politics can be derived from it: acceptance, reform, revolution. Where the critics see a unity, history has seen a variety.

For this reason alone, we may be suspicious of the critique of the 'Project', itself a hypostatized entity, first cousin of the liberal inquisition. Yet such a critique is very much part of our troubled present, and plays to the very real uncertainties of the post-Cold War epoch. More recently, connections and critiques, drawn from the broader aesthetic and sociological discussion of Enlightenment, have been applied to the international domain.[6] Events of the past few years have, moreover, highlighted the hubris of political commentators and academic analysts alike: a decade after the end of the Cold War, and the proclamation of a new world of peace, democracy and prosperity, the international system finds itself at a point of uncertainty, even crisis. It was said by the Israeli academic and former general Yehoshufat Harkabi that when the Berlin Wall came down this marked the end of two ideologies: in the east, Marxism-Leninism and in the west, political science. The uncertainty of markets, as of security systems, is compounded by an intellectual unease, corrosive both of rational and of democratic endeavour, that pervades the *Zeitgeist*. The fashionable rejection of the 'Enlightenment Project' has, therefore, implications for all areas of human activity, international relations included.

This confusion is evident in the diversity of responses which the events of the late 1980s and 1990s themselves have occasioned.[7] These range from the optimistic, proclaiming a new world order, or an end of history, to analyses in terms of a fragmentation of modern states, a new Middle Ages. Critics on the left emphasise the degree of inequality in the current process of globalization, those on the right the enduring ability of the international system to generate conflict. In several respects these intellectual arguments hark back to those of a century ago. In the 1890s the world lived through the optimism and economic boom of the *belle époque*: a few years later it was plunged into world war, a convulsion from which the further crisis of the twentieth century, World War II and the Cold War, followed. This crisis of the international system was preceded by an unprecedented degree of globalization, in terms of trade, opening of markets, and foreign direct investment. Today that outcome should serve as a warning even if, one may argue, it does not yet set a precedent. Our own *belle époque* has new challenges, not least those of nuclear weapons and environmental catastrophe, but also new forms of knowledge, and political responsibility.

---

[6] For a range of views see *inter alia*, Linklater, *Transformation* and Chris Brown, *International Relations Theory, New Normative Approaches*, ch. 8, 'Critical and Postmodern International Relations Theory' (Hemel Hempstead: Harvester Wheatsheaf, 1992).

[7] There is a wide literature on this issue: see, *inter alia*, Daniel Moynihan, *Pandemonium. Ethnicity in International Politics* (Oxford: Oxford University Press, 1993); Robert Harvey, *The Return of the Strong* (London, 1995); Alain Minc, *Le Nouveau Moyen Age* (Paris: Gallimard, 1993); Dieter Senghaas, *Wohin Driftet die Welt?* (Frankfurt: Suhrkamp, 1994); Mariano Aguirre, *Los Dias del Futuro: La Sociedad Internacional en la Era de la Globalizacion* (Icaria: Barcelona, 1995). I have discussed this further in 'The End of the Cold War and International Relations: Some Analytic and Theoretical Conclusions', in Steve Smith and Ken Booth (eds.), *International Relations Theory Today* (Cambridge: Polity Press, 1995), and in chs. 10 and 11 of *Rethinking International Relations* (London: Macmillan, 1994).

Reassessing the Enlightenment

In any assessment of the Enlightenment, an important distinction, one insufficiently common in contemporary writing on politics, needs to be made here, that of distinguishing the discursive and the real, i.e. not taking the enunciation of ideas—about states, power, nations—as being a history of these phenomena themselves. The history of the past two centuries is *not* primarily the history of ideas, Enlightenment or other, but of socioeconomic and political processes within which ideas played a certain role. It is therefore as empty to ascribe an emancipatory potential to ideas on their own, as it is to ascribe responsibility for the history of the past two hundred years to these ideas: hence the fallacy of the attack on the 'Enlightenment Project' as being responsible for the crimes of two centuries. The idea as such had no impact. Socialism, nationalism, feminism, democracy mean little without the historical and political context in which they emerged. Here, the insight uneasily expressed by IR realism, linking values and morality to power, can be reformulated in a broader sociological context. Enlightenment is, in this sense, what modernity has made of it.

A critical assessment of Enlightenment requires, therefore, not just a discussion of ideas associated with it, but a location of these ideas within a discussion of modernity. That modernity is at once entrapping and emancipatory, the shifting context within which modern politics and international relations have been played out. In what follows, I shall try to relate this to the international, charting the fate of Professor Kant's prognostication. This will involve analysis of the contradictory character of modernity, a critical assessment of the core political value associated with it, liberal democracy, and an engagement with current challenges, theoretical and political. An element of rational, prospective optimism, an Enlightenment reduced in vision but sturdier in resolve, may eventuate.

What such an engagement requires is a linking of the domains conventionally separate: speculative political theory and historical sociology. Put more practically, it means that projects for change and progress need to be linked to the possibilities of society, national and international, as given. Fatalism in the face of the given is as unnecessary as speculation unhinged from practicality and real movement. We need, in Runciman's judicious phrasing most pertinent to IR, to distinguish the 'improbably possible' from the 'probably impossible'.[8] This involves the double assertion—one intellectual, the other sociological: the intellectual revolves around a reassertion, chastened by history and critique alike, of the values associated with the Enlightenment; the sociological involves an assertion that, within the constraints of the contemporary world, and of that modernity which characterizes it, purposive action, linked to agency by individuals, movements and states alike, is possible.

Any one assertion is, on its own insufficient. To claim of modernity on its own a purposive, let alone emancipatory potential, is to fall back into that determinism which has so marred the past two centuries, to deny the possibility *and need* for choice. The series of iconic emancipatory determinisms is familiar and continuing: in times gone by, God, gods, fate; more recently steam, electricity, industrialization, the aeroplane, medicine; today information technology, the global market place. Without an intellectual framework, that delimits analytic and normative options, there can be no adequate response to such determinism. The most important,

---

[8] W. G. Runciman, *The Social Animal* (London: Harper Collins, 1998), p. 189.

repeatedly submerged, response to scientistic determinism is to suppress the human agency which both creates and directs this scientific progress and which can control it.[9] Equally, a focus on values, Enlightenment or other, without regard to the real, social, context of modernity is vacuous. No reader of 'alternative' thinking in the field of IR can fail to note the recurrence of such, in Runciman's terms, 'probably impossible', speculation.

It is in the lack of linkage between these two moments, the philosophical and the real, that lies both the appeal, and weakness, of the critiques to which Enlightenment has been subjected. For conservatives, beginning with de Maistre and Edmund Burke, and continuing through Michael Oakeshott and John Gray, the very appeal to reason does violence to the nature of political life. For troubled or 'agonistic' liberals, with whom contemporary writing is replete, the Enlightenment contains a claim of uniformity and universalism that denies plurality of cultures and normative system. For Marxists, most notably Horkheimer and Adorno, the Enlightenment was in its postulating of a scientific reason, an incipiently totalitarian project.[10] For postmodernists, it represents a claim to a grand narrative, and to a fixity of meaning, that is a product of power and, multiply interpreted, authority.[11]

Each critique converges, even as each claims originality for itself. Each also posits its own alternative, respectively: tradition, pluralism, revolution, anti-foundationalism. Uneasy coconspirators in their positive assertion, these four critiques mask their incompatibility in a shared rejection, linked to the hypo-statization of the 'Enlightenment' itself: hence the pertinence of Habermas' warning, echoed by Gellner, that the apparent advance of postmodernism *beyond* Enlighten-ment all too easily involves support for the irrationalism of the *premodern*—an insight that is sadly evident in the attitudes of many 'critical' political theorists towards religious fundamentalism.

Be it noted, too, that these critiques are hardly novel: they have a history as long as the Enlightenment itself. Perhaps the greatest of many post-1989 conceits is that it is in *this* period alone that the Enlightenment has been questioned. But the crisis of the Enlightenment long predates the end of communism, or the Cold War, or the bacchanalian whirl of postmodernist globalization characteristic of the 1990s. Industrial society in the early nineteenth century, colonial spoliation in the late nineteenth, the collapse of the long peace in 1914, the brutalities of both wars, Auschwitz and Hiroshima—have all been candidates for the end or refutation of the Enlightenment. As Mark Mazower has so brilliantly shown in his history of Europe in the twentieth century, *Dark Continent*, faith in democracy, and in the values of

---

[9] The contemporary variant of this is the obsession with constantly changing IT, as if this acted separately from the plans and profits of monopolistic firms. Objects 'need upgrading', as if this was autonomous of human action and advantage. A similar determinism was evident in the 1970s and 1980s with regard to the nuclear arms race: arguments were made about the need to 'update' and 'modernize' nuclear weapons, as if these had a technological life of their own.

[10] Theodor Adorno and Max Horkheimer, *Dialectic of Enlightenment* (London: Verso, 1979), especially pp. 3–42 'The Concept of Enlightenment'. Habermas, *The Philosophical Discourse of Modernity*, ch. 5, 'The Entwinement of Myth and Enlightenment: Max Horkheimer and Theodor Adorno'.

[11] The classic statement is Jean-Francois Lyotard, *The Postmodern Condition: A Report in Knowledge* (Manchester, Manchester University Press, 1984), where he famously defines postmodern as 'incredulity toward metanarratives'. For one excellent summary see Gregor McLennan, 'The Enlightenment Project Revisited', in *Modernity and Its Futures*, edited by Stuart Hall, David Held and Tony McGrew (Cambridge: Polity in association with the Open University, 1992). For a cogent overview of aesthetic, social and theoretical components see Perry Anderson, *The Origins of Post-Modernity* (London: Verso, 1998).

liberalism and reason, had been virtually extinguished in Europe by the late 1930s.[12] Yet this recognition of repetition is not merely a corrective to antifoundationalist 'presentism', but also suggests a more positive argument: each period of pessimism, and despair, has been overtaken by history, by human agency endeavouring to reconstruct society, and international orders, on rational, Enlightenment, principles. As Walter Benjamin so clearly saw: 'The concept of progress is to be founded in the idea of catastrophe'.[13]

Modernity and its contradictions

As this argument focuses attention on 'modernity' and in particular what is meant by modernity in the opening moments of the twenty-first century, we may begin by addressing the several meanings of this term. A significant part of the intellectual content of modernity derives from the eighteenth century—rationalism, secularism, equality, progress. Here, however, the intellectual contribution of Kant may be linked to that of the two other thinkers who give the term its most comprehensive formulation even as they drew on that Enlightenment heritage, Karl Marx and Max Weber.[14] Both saw modernity as the product not just of intellectual change but of the industrial revolution and the new society, politics, culture it had created. Both asked the question which is central to any social analysis or political programme— within the realities and constraints of this 'modernity' what degree of choice, what kind of freedom, political and otherwise, is possible? Both were concerned to provide analysis of change that was possible. Equally importantly, both Marx and Weber were keen to exclude answers that were, in their view, not possible. As already noted, the twin dangers of any discussion of modernity are fatalism and voluntarism; on the one hand the denial of possibility of any choice or freedom, and on the other the postulation of strategies that are incapable of realization and which may lead to catastrophe.

For Weber, modernity was an 'iron cage', a set of determinations, internal and international, which, above all through bureaucratization, constrained what individuals, or classes, or states could do. This was particularly so in the field of international relations, where military power meant that individual states could do little to alter their positions relative to others. Weber's views on international relations compel study for several reasons. They seek, within a broad understanding of social science, to establish the relations between international relations and other areas of study—the state, culture, economy. In particular, like Marx, Weber regarded the international relations of the nineteenth and twentieth centuries as radically different from those which preceded it. While until recently little acknowledged in realist writings of the UK and US variety, Weber's ideas informed many of the early

---

[12] Mark Mazower, *Dark Continent: Europe's Twentieth Century* (London: Allen Lane, the Penguin Press, 1998), ch. 1, 'The Deserted Temple: Democracy's Rise and Fall'.

[13] Walter Benjamin, *Passages*, vol. 1.

[14] In what follows I draw on Derek Sayer, *Capitalism and Modernity. An Excursus on Marx and Weber* (London: Routledge, 1991) and the debate between Perry Anderson, Marshall Berman and Peter Osborne in *New Left Review*, 144 (March-April 1984) and 192 (March-April 1992). I am especially grateful to Justin Rosenberg for drawing this to my attention and, more generally, for his pioneering work in relating the discussion of modernity to IR.

generation of German-trained realists as well as those of the influential French writer Raymond Aron.

There remain, however, significant problems with his writings, which subsequent history has to some degree brought out—he died in 1920. His belief in nationalism, and in strong, charismatic, leaders was carried to extremes in Nazi Germany: however much he himself can be disassociated from these later developments, the later fate of his theories, like those of Karl Marx, requires reassessment of the theoretical antecedents. Within his theory itself, the very strong argument he makes, on the relation of international conflict to domestic state formation, remains more an assertion than a grounded theory. This problem was to recur when, in the 1970s and 1980s, 'historical sociologists' strongly influenced by Weber were to take further this work on the relation between state formation and international relations. Moreover, while easily recruited by realists in support of their views of international conflict, Weber's stress on the relation of domestic to international politics stands in marked contrast to the attempts by later realists, let alone neorealists, to produce a purely *international* or *systemic* view of relations between states. If Weber remains a classical ancestor of modern international relations, he is one whose very rediscovery by more recent theorists forces us to confront the ambiguities that lie within his theory itself.

Marx, on the other hand, stressed, through his analysis of the development of capitalism, the voluntaristic side of politics and economics. He believed that it was possible for collective human action radically to change history. His conception of modernity rested upon a view of progress within which agency accelerated but could not obviate the transition from one social form to the other, even as this process prepared the basis, at the national and international level, for the supersession of all domination and difference.[15] History must record a contradictory verdict in his case too.

Yet if we can, for present purposes, draw on the two approaches then we can identify the main features of modernity. First, the modern period was a period radically different from the past, a new historical epoch, marked by changes in economics, technology, culture and political life. Secondly, modernity represents a process of change, not only from the old, premodern, to the new, but also within itself: constant change—of technology, values, fashion—is central to modernity. In this sense there is no fixed modernity—no state of economic output, or political institution, or language which, once attained, will be maintained. One of the more curious features of contemporary political life is that of nationalist movements seeking to define a 'true' or 'authentic' identity—as if these could be fixed once and for all in time. Thirdly, modernity is contradictory: for Marx this contradiction was to lead to revolution and a new social order, for Weber it led to enduring and irresolvable conflicts between state and individual, values and reality, sovereignty and peace. Whatever their differences, both accepted that modernity produced conflicts—between classes, nations, other socially constituted groups. Finally, and as part of the novel political and social conditions produced by the arrival of a new era, each stressed the importance of agency within the modern world: for Marx the

[15] I have gone into greater detail on the insights and limits of Marx's view of the international in ch. 6 of *Rethinking International Relations* and in *Revolution and World Politics: The Rise and Fall of the Sixth Great Power* (London: Macmillan, 1999).

agent was class, in particular the working class, for Weber it was the new organised force of industrial society, the bureaucracy.

These four ideas—novelty, change, contradiction, agency—were part of the Enlightenment heritage, and were given impetus by the twin revolutions of the late eighteenth and early nineteenth centuries, the political and the industrial.[16] They were central to the idea of modernity as it then emerged in the middle and late nineteenth century. They thereby contributed to the generally optimistic and forward looking outlook of that epoch. Indeed if there is one thing that, in its different forms, sums up the original view of modernity it is teleology, this belief that history is moving in a discernible direction, towards a goal to which historical dynamic and human agency alike will combine to take us: progress. As has been well argued by Nisbet, progress, a vision of the future, was not so much a distinct idea as a pervasive assumption.[17]

A century of crisis

If we now ask what has happened to this idea of modernity in the ensuing hundred years, where it leaves our discussion for today, we can see how much more complex, how more uncertain, the concept of modernity now is. It is in this practical complexity, one that has evolved over time, not in an abstract and suddenly proclaimed 'anti-foundationalism', that the challenge to Enlightenment lies. Here we can identify some of the ways in which the idea of modernity itself entered into crisis first in the nineteenth century, when modernity transformed Europe and subjugated the rest of the world, and then when it exploded, in war and authoritarian violence, in the twentieth century. For the non-European world the face of the Enlightenment was that of imperial conquest. If the primary failing of modernity was its generation of modern war, its most enduring failing has been the manner in which it has incorporated the non-European world. As recent historical work has so well reasserted, the character of this subjugation was not in spite of, but as a result of, the assumptions of rationalist modernity.[18]

For Europe itself one could say that the twentieth century has been the century of crisis, in marked contrast to the relatively progressive and internationally peaceful nineteenth century. This crisis has indeed come in three phases. First came the buildup to crisis in the explosive contradictions of the *belle époque*, from 1870 onwards, with the rise of industrial imperialism and the militarization of Western society. There then followed what one may term the European civil war of 1914 to 1945, dramatically reflected in two World Wars that engulfed most of the rest of the world, and in the course of which around 80 millions died. This second phase

---

[16] Eric Hobsbawm, *The Age of Revolution 1789–1848* (London: Weidenfeld and Nicolson, 1962).

[17] J. Nisbet, *The Idea of Progress* (New York, 1983).

[18] Mark Cocker, *Rivers of Blood, Rivers of Gold. Europe's Conflict with Tribal Peoples* (London: Jonathan Cape, 1998) links European identity and commercial expansion to the destruction of indigenous peoples; Robin Blackburn, *The Making of New World Slavery* (London: Verso, 1997), in 'Introduction: Slavery and Modernity' (especially p. 4) makes a powerful case for the link between slavery and modernity, showing how, among other things, instrumental rationality, racialized perceptions of identity, market relations and wage labour, consumer society, advertising, even reflexive self-consciousness, all had their origins in the internationalized slave economy.

produced two very different, authoritarian, interpretations of modernity each of which aspired to impose its own version on the world: one was the authoritarian modernity of the right, in Fascism and its various imitators, which lasted from the 1920s in Italy to Portugal in the 1970s. The other was the left authoritarianism of Communism, arising first in Russia in 1917 and then spreading to encompass about a third of the world. This European civil war ended in 1945, with the defeat of the right authoritarian option in most of Europe, but the conflict between liberal capitalist modernity and Communism was to last another four decades. It has only recently ended. No discussion of modernity, the tensions and alternatives within it, can avoid discussion of the Communist movement.

A radical modernity: Communism

It may be too early to provide a confident assessment of what Communism, as a political and economic system, was, but it is a question which must influence any discussion of modernity today. Communism was, in its simplest form, a product of the conflicts generated within and between societies by capitalist transformation of the world. That it was ultimately overwhelmed by other forms of modernity in no way detracts from its own genetic origins in capitalism itself.[19] As a political and ideological project, it was, equally, a version of modernity, a dramatic attempt to mobilize peoples for economic and political development, not only to catch up with the developed capitalist states, but to overtake it: it was, therefore a product of modernity, a radical interpretation of the potential in modernity. It achieved many things, both in developed and in developing countries. One does not see in Havana or Santiago de Cuba the social conditions one sees in Rio de Janeiro. However, Communism was a failure, not only for contingent reasons, but of necessity, because its very programme rested upon a set of illusions, about the inevitability of revolution under advanced capitalism on the one hand, and, on the other, about the possibilities of fundamentally transforming society and human nature. Underlying Communism was a crude scientism, about economic planning, or genetic change, which reflected, in a distorted sense, much of the historical optimism of the nineteenth century.

Communism's achievement, and its relation to modernity, can however also be seen in another respect, namely in the impact it had on its opponents, authoritarian and liberal capitalism. Confronted by a Communist challenge from 1917 onwards, capitalist society was forced to change: it was the Soviet Union which played the major role in defeating Nazi Germany and in so doing brought about the end of authoritarian capitalism; equally the modernization of Western capitalism through the welfare state and the spread of universal suffrage owed much to the fear of Communism's appeal to disenfranchised classes. After World War II Communism continued to make its mark: the abrupt collapse of the western European colonial empires in the 1950s and 1960s was, in part, a result of the challenge that Communism posed to colonialism; the impact of the third world revolutions led by Communism or inspired by it—in China, Vietnam, Cuba, Algeria—provoked major

---

[19] I develop this further in *Revolution and World Politics*.

political conflicts within the developed countries themselves; and the creation of the Common Market owes as much to the perceived need to compete politically and economically with Communism as to anything else. In the Far East, moreover, no account of the rise of the new industrializing capitalist states should omit the central political dynamic, the fear of Communist revolution—be this in South Korea, Taiwan, Hong Kong, Singapore or Thailand. Too much analysis of the success of the Far Eastern economies rests on a purely economic analysis: but we are looking at a phenomenon in the field of political economy, and the 'political' in this case was above all the fear of Communism. The conclusion which this suggests is therefore contradictory and in this sense eminently 'modern': Communism was defeated because it failed to compete adequately with capitalism, yet the very success of capitalism owed much to the Communist challenge. Itself a product of modernity, the greatest, and perhaps most enduring, contribution of Communism to the development of modernity was, consequently, the modernization of capitalism. It defeated authoritarian capitalism before itself succumbing to the liberal variant. In so doing it paved the way for the world of peace and prosperity envisioned today, or so, to some, it appears.

The limits of 'liberal democracy'

We are, therefore, now in a world in which the two authoritarian forms of modernity, fascist or military dictatorship on the right, Communist bureaucratic dictatorship on the left, have been defeated. It is in this context that we now confront the question of what modernity can now mean to us, and what options it provides. Here the focus cannot be only on progress, or regress, in the realm of the international, since the very underpinning of any view of progress at the interstate level presupposes progress at the domestic. The current equation liberal democracy =zone of peace may have much to recommend it: however it can only be sustained with a critical look at the historical, and contemporary, bases of democracy itself. As Kant noted the path to Enlightenment in international relations runs through a reassessment of its domestic, democratic, concomitant. The path to a critical, as distinct from complacent, perspective on modernity similarly entails a questioning, but not rejection, of liberal democratic optimism.

Such an assessment cannot be a simple reassertion of the truths of liberal capitalism, for at least two central reasons. These are the weak links of the liberal optimism of Doyle or Fukuyama. First, there is the need to examine, historically and critically, and within a domestic context, the recipe of liberal capitalism being presented to us today. This can show that, apart from any universal potential or not, this equation of universal suffrage, free market and capitalism is an arbitrary and artificial one; it does not correspond to the history of modernity over the past century and a half. What this examination also reveals is that even within the developed and more established democracies there is no one single model of a 'modern' system. This variety of the modern is evident from an examination of how democracy developed: indeed the question of how we got there is of more than archaeological interest. Such a historicization of democracy is, moreover, linked to its international character. The assumption of most current liberal thinking is that teleological, progressivist, democracy is something that has been growing for many centuries, and has usually come about in a relatively benign and peaceful way. Equally narratives of democratization within countries are usually presented as separate from the broader world-historical context in which they occurred. Yet this world history has to be understood both as competition with other states, and as a product of social changes common to a range of societies that were themselves a product of a shared modernity.[20]

The reality is, of course, that no country in the world was democratic at the beginning of this century, and that some countries have only very recently attained it—if effective universal suffrage is a criterion then neither the United States nor Switzerland were democracies in 1965. France, Belgium, Italy and Japan only became so after the Second World War. This should induce in us a certain degree of historical caution, first about how firmly established systems of democracy really are, and about how easy it may be for other countries, where the objective conditions for democratization do not exist, to establish and maintain such systems. It should, equally, focus attention on the international context for democratization: the growth of democracy was a product of competition between states, of in the first instance war, and of the shared pressures for change common to all industrializing states.

This question of historical evolution applies also to our ideas. Today 'democracy', as summed up in the term 'liberal democracy', is a term that covers at least three groups of phenomena—a range of political conditions, including pluralism, universal suffrage, and elected governments; a set of constitutional guarantees, concerning individual rights, and freedom from censorship, arrest and other forms of arbitrary treatment; and a conception of the economy as a 'free market'. The briefest historical review shows that this, far from being some natural or permanent cluster, is a very recent combination. Athenian democracy excluded 80 per cent of the adult population—including all women and slaves. Nineteenth century liberals had, Mill excepted, great difficulties with universal suffrage, for men, let alone women. The growth of political freedoms, in a country such as Britain, was far ahead of that of political conditions for democracy: plenty of cases of relatively mild dictatorship can be observed today.

As for the 'free' market, many liberals have argued that the state should play an interventionist role in the economy, for reasons of national power or social welfare. The particular contemporary equation summarizing the 'liberal' option—political democracy/political rights/free market—is therefore one possible variant on these themes. Nowhere is this more so than in regard to the role of the state in the economy. In many states that are conventionally seen as partaking of the 'Western' model, the state has played, or now plays, a major role in directing the economy, whether through macroeconomic management and direction, or through welfare programmes, or through appropriation of monies through taxation and state expenditure. Japan is an obvious example of state direction of the economy through forms of planning. Conversely, some of the 'free market' economies of recent years

[20] Year of establishment (first attainment) of democracy: *Argentina; Australia, 1903; *Austria, 1918; Belgium, 1948; *Brazil, 1988; *Canada, 1920; *Chile, 1970; Denmark, 1915; *Finland, 1919; France, 1946; *Germany, 1919; *Italy, 1946; Japan, 1952; Netherlands, 1919, New Zealand, 1907; Norway, 1915; Sweden, 1918; *Switzerland, 1971; UK, 1928(Northern Ireland, 1970); USA, c. 1970.
Note: *Interrupted (except by foreign occupation). *Source:* Goran Therborn, 'The Rule of Capital and the Rise of Democracy', *New Left Review*, 103: May-June 1977, p. 11.

have not been democratic—Chile, Singapore, South Korea. The appearance of democracy—as long-established, national, unitary, teleological—has, therefore, to be replaced by a more fluid and varied picture: recent, international, diverse, constantly changing. This need not challenge the claims of liberal democracy: but it does suggest a far greater degree of contingency, and multiplicity of interpretation, within contemporary political life.

In its assumptions for domestic and international society alike, the liberal capitalist model rested upon a model of modernity that was in the end static: industrialized, increasingly homogeneous, and egalitarian societies would be the norm. But industrialization has given way to deindustrialization and to dramatic falls in the percentage of the population employed in manufacturing: if this posed problems for Marxists, it also yielded an employment and social pattern very different from that earlier envisaged by liberal theories. Equally, the developed countries did not, over the longer run, produce more homogeneous or egalitarian societies: indeed the divisions within them, and most dramatically the social and ethnic divisions within the more developed societies themselves, were to grow wider and more violent. Just as the modernity of the first half of the twentieth century produced Communism and Fascism, so that of the late twentieth century is as much in the gang warfare of Los Angeles as in the tranquillity of Sweden or Austria. Ethnicity too, far from being submerged with modern society, has reasserted itself in many forms, old and new.

The failures of modernity: the international dimension

This brings us to the second broad set of questions about the current model of liberal democracy: its failings at the international level. For if both authoritarian alternatives have been discredited, too much has happened at the international level in the ensuing century to leave this liberal capitalist option unscathed, even assuming we can assume what this model is. In the first place, the optimism of much of nineteenth century thought, including of Auguste Comte, that modernity meant an end to war has proven to be fatally mistaken: the Marxists, and in particular Lenin, were to prove far more correct than mainstream liberal thinkers. The latter believed that industrial society was necessarily peaceful and that only precapitalist societies had an interest in war. On the other hand, the argument about the peaceful character of industrial society implied that this was based on the democratic character of industrial societies: however in 1914, as we have seen, there were virtually no countries in the world which had achieved universal suffrage, and it was to take another half a century for this to be so even in the developed West. Neither of the two maximalist positions on war and modernity were vindicated: instead a contingent relationship emerged, one that may promise a closer association of peace and democracy in the future, but may also presage other, equally modern, phases of war.[21]

---

[21] I have gone into this in greater detail in 'Europe and the International System: War and Peace', in Stephen Chan and Jarrod Wiener (eds.), *Twentieth Century International History* (London: I. B. Tauris, 1999).

If the liberal capitalist model has produced a far more contradictory situation within developed societies, it has, equally, done so on the international scale, as is evident in relations between North and South.[22] One of the assumptions of nineteenth century thinking, including that of Marx, was that the economic model of prosperity would be diffused throughout the world: the whole of Asia would, in Marx's view, duplicate the industrialization of Manchester. Marx was right to recognise the transformative character of capitalism, and to see the potential for industrialization and change in other countries. Yet the pattern of global transformation set in train by modernity has led to greater inequality on a global scale. What we have also seen and continue to see is not such a generalization of wealth, nor a static division into a rich oligarchic North and a poor mass South, but a continuing and growing inequality within the system even as it integrates countries more and more into its productive and commercial systems. Much has been said on this already: suffice it to say here that one and a half centuries of capitalist development have left the world more unevenly developed than ever before and with the concentration of wealth greater than at any previous time. If it is simplistic to argue that capitalism is necessarily incapable of achieving a set of goals— democracy, independence, industrialization, land reform—it is also the case that the majority of capitalist countries have not achieved this, despite many attempts to do so. At the international level, the promise of modernity remains largely that.

New critiques of modernity

These three issues—war, colonial plunder, the widening North-South gap—are what one may term the long-established, or classic, international failures of the liberal democratic variant of modernity. They would, on their own, be enough to raise serious questions about the viability of this model. But the authority of this model has been further undermined over the past few years by other developments, even as the great ideological challenge of the Communist variant of modernity has faded. One, familiar to everyone at the end of the 1990s, is the critique of ecology. Even on the more cautious and moderate evaluations of the ecological crisis challenging humanity, it is evident that the way of life, and the models of development and entitlement, that have dominated our thinking throughout the modern period cannot be sustained. If modernism meant anything it meant a hostility to nature, seen as savage and uncontrolled, even as nature was seen as inexhaustible: we need not surrender to extreme ecological myths, or to ideological variations of how we can reverse modern society, but we have to evolve a new relationship with nature, and a new recognition of the limits to growth and to the environment. We have also to confront, as many ecologists do not confront, the difficulties posed by the

---

[22] According to the UNDP, there has been a striking growth in price and public consumption: six times since 1950, twice since 1975, to a current total of $23,000bn worldwide. In this sense the promise of capitalism, to deliver greater volumes of good and services, has been realised: but 20 per cent of the world's population account for 86 per cent of total expenditure, while the poorest 20 per cent account for 1.3 per cent. Three-fifths of the 4.4bn people in developing countries lack basic sanitation. (*Financial Times*, 10 September 1998).

question of population: it is simple-minded to see this as a problem that can be ignored, or as some imperialist conspiracy.

Secondly, the whole model of society that has underpinned modernity, and indeed the whole of Western thought for the past two thousand years, has come under attack from feminism: second wave feminism revealed, as never before demonstrated, the degree to which the political, economic and social systems, indeed often the very language we use, are based on a sexual hierarchy, from which men benefit. It may be that we are living in a world without revolutionary utopias, but the aim, which is comprehensive but not utopian, of ending this age-long differentiation within our societies is as revolutionary as anything else, and is something that, as much as the ecological critique, challenges our view of modernity. As Juliet Mitchell wrote in her classic article nearly four decades ago, this is the *longest* revolution.[23] Fatuous invocations of a postfeminist world, or relativist denials of gendered oppression, only obscure the necessity for such a transformation.

Finally, we encounter a critique of modernity which, far from seeking to revise or develop it, rejects it, whether in the name of a return to traditional values or in the advance into something called a postmodern world: this critique claims to reject not just the nineteenth century construction of modernity but the Enlightenment intellectual legacy as well. There are certain respects in which this critique of modernity, linked to an assessment of social and intellectual trends at the end of the twentieth century, is valid.[24] First, there is no longer a clear, unitary, model of what constitutes the 'modern'—the goal towards which society, thought, art itself are moving. The sense of historical linearity associated with the nineteenth and twentieth centuries has been eroded—more obviously in the move away from the conventional model of an industrial society. Secondly, the core of this historical optimism, natural science, is more and more contested—from within, by a growing awareness of uncertainty and chance, externally by the erosion of confidence in its ability to resolve physical and social problems. Thirdly, there has been a major shift in the realm of culture—away from a unitary, and homogeneous, modern towards an interest in variety, hybridity, the composite, the playful. This prospective, polyvalent and multicultural redefinition of contemporary culture has been accompanied by a return to concern with tradition, the 'authentic', with heritage. Fourthly, there is a much greater awareness throughout the social sciences of the multiple layers, and sites of power—it is found not just in states and public institutions, but also in families, educational establishments, the media—and of the multiple forms of power, language, symbol, the very denied or repressed being mediations of power as much as money or guns. Finally, in politics as we have seen, the divisions that have defined ideology for the past two centuries have been eroded: the collapse of communism has ended that two centuries of ideological division.

There are, however, substantial difficulties with a postmodernist approach, one that combines a valid identification of shifts in modern society and thought, with exaggerated, and irrational, claims about the nature of the contemporary world. First of all, the postmodernists, for all their talk of a radical break with the politics

---

[23] Juliet Mitchell, 'Women: The Longest Revolution', *New Left Review*, 40: November-December 1960.

[24] There is a large critical literature on postmodernism, most of it blithely ignored by its proponents within the field of IR. I would refer, *inter alia* to Ernest Gellner, *Postmodernism, Reason and Religion* (London: Routledge, 1992), Nicos Mouzelis, 'The Modern and the Postmodern in Social Thought', Department of Sociology, Princeton University, Charles Haar International Sociology Series (Fall 1993), and Peter Dews, *Logics of Disintegration* (London: Verso, 1986).

and epistemology of the Enlightenment, are trapped within modernity: on the one hand, they greatly exaggerate the extent to which the phenomena they draw attention to—change, loss of analytic and ethical certainty—are true of the world as a whole. In this sense postmodernism is yet another conceit of metropolitan intellectuals, as Gellner put it, *Sturm und Drang und Tenure*, IR theory as this season's fashion; on the other hand, the changes they rightly identify as part of the modern world, and particularly changing values and identities, and the importance of language and discourse in constituting social power, are very much features of modernity and have been so for a century or more. In particular, the call for contestation and alterity in the 1990s, associated with much 'critical' theory, is detached from the analysis of modern society: it ignores the history of resistance, nationalist and social, above all Communist, that has marked the twentieth century. In the face of gestural and unanchored critique, the achievements, *and* failings, of such mass contestation merit careful attention. Rather than accepting the overblown claims of postmodernity, the term 'incomplete' or 'second' modernity, associated with Habermas, Ulrich Beck and others, would be more accurate.

The return to traditional or non-Western values is another supposed challenge to modernity. It is perhaps most evident in movements of religious reassertion, as in Iran. Much of this critique of modernity is, in contrast to the ecological and feminist critiques, invalid and confused. One reason is that what appear and present themselves as criticisms of modernity are in fact part of it: while the fundamentalism of Khomeini and other Islamic revolutionaries leads them to deny the modern and call for a return to the seventh century, they are nonetheless part of the modern world in several ways—they operate with the instruments of modern political power, they seek to legitimate themselves through the standard appeals of contemporary mass politics (independence, economic development, popular revolution). Their very conceptual system, for all its archaic appearances, is based on modern, mainly populist, political concepts—revolution, anti-imperialism, defence of human rights, republican government, even 'progress'.

As is already clear from the Iranian case, the Islamic revolutionaries are not very good modernists, and this is why their revolution is already in severe difficulties: yet this is because the criteria by which they have sought to challenge the outside world express, as did those of Communism, a particularly distorted and ultimately doomed set of modern standards. It is also rejected by most modernist young people within Iran. But the reason why the fundamentalist movements have been so successful in mobilizing support, and why they may well come to power in a range of countries, is that while they fail to confront them they claim to address the very real, material and political, problems facing these countries—unemployment, corruption in government, external domination, cultural change. They are part of, not an alternative to, modernity. Their vocabulary and world view is, for all its particularistic appearance, constituted by modernity. If this is nowhere more so than in regard to Islamist movements,[25] a similar argument can be made, however, for other supposedly distinct cultural idioms—be they Confucian, Hindu or whatever.

[25] See on this the work of Aziz al-Azmih, *Islam and Modernities* (London: Verso, 1993); Ervand Abrahamian, *Khomeinism* (London: Tauris, 1993); Sami Zubaida, *Islam, the People, the State* (London: Routledge, 1989). I have gone into similar arguments in *Islam and the Myth of Confrontation* (London: I.B. Tauris, 1996) and *Nation and Religion in the Middle East* (London: Saqi, 1999).

It is in this context that we encounter another case of the dislocation of political theory and social reality in supposed critiques of the Enlightenment Project: for the effort placed by many liberal thinkers on cultural diversity, and hence on the problems of dialogue between them, presupposes a substantive difference that is not necessarily there. The claim to difference reflects not a genuine variety of philosophical outlooks but an instrumental use, a manipulation, of 'difference' by political elites. The much cited contrast of Michael Walzer's between a universal 'thin' and a communitarian or national 'thick' is by the same token deceptive: the particularist 'thick' appropriates much of what is in fact universal—including such values as national self-determination, sovereignty, claims of economic and political injustice—just as every country seeks to define its difference in universal terms—a flag, a capital city, a national airline, a national soccer team and so forth. Every country has its own flag, and gives a national name to its own parliament: but the objects in question are modular, with the same symbolic significance.

The conclusion to this discussion of the antimodern and postmodern challenges to modernity is therefore that, stripped of their exaggeration and demagogy, they reflect issues that are within modernity and are parasitic on its agenda. Different interpretations of such issues of international contention as entitlement to land, or oil revenues, and variant adjudications of the tension between human rights and state sovereignty are *not* a reflection of different cultural values: they reflect different interests, and positions, within a world of shared discourse. The dialogue is *within* not *between*.[26] All regions of the world, developed and developing, participate in the general debate on modernity and on policies, domestic and international, in the contemporary world. One of the many richnesses of modernity is that it both establishes a general, universal and unavoidable, set of questions for every society, but also promotes diversity within regions and countries. It would be just as mistaken to see the problem of modernity as posed in exactly the same way everywhere in the world, or even in one continent, as it would be to deny the common problems, ideological choices and historic contexts, in which each country finds itself.

What this entails is, however, something central to the contemporary discussion of this concept: modernity is not a fatalism, is not a determined set of options. It is rather a context, historical and global, within which a set of options are available, around which states, nations, political parties can develop practical policies and confront their own particular reality. This is true in all three of modernity's constitutive moments—social, theoretical, aesthetic. There is, for example, no one modern language—we have around 10,000 languages in the world. Each is changing, yet each has its contribution. There is no one, single, modern music—again there is diversity, and change, and mutual interaction. Modernity is not a monistic condition, but rather a context for exploring diversity. That possibility, and the diversity it generates, in culture, as in politics, is one part of the legacy of Enlightenment.

---

[26] Exaggeration of this issue is recurrent in contemporary Western political thought. See, for example, John Rawls, 'The Law of Peoples', in Stephen Shute and Susan Hurley (eds.), *On Human Rights* (New York: Basic Books, 1993), and the reply by Jean Elshtain to Andrew Linklater in *Review of International Studies*, 25:1 (January 1999).

The end of the Cold War: agency and progress

It is within this increasingly shared and varied political space, one constituted ideologically and socially by modernity, that human agency has shaped the world over the past two centuries: through movements of nationalism, democratization, revolution, women's emancipation, identity politics on the one hand, and actions of ruling groups, states, and other privileged groups on the other. The battle has been about power and wealth, and has been formulated within, far more than against, the ideas associated with the Enlightenment.

This leads to the question of the contemporary situation, and in particular the international situation after the end of the Cold War. The question that is posed here is how far these major changes have altered our perception of modernity, and indeed the issues that are on the political agenda of countries, developed or developing. My answer, in one phrase, is that the end of cold war has made some changes—above all by removing from the agenda the prospect of a radical, revolutionary, alternative to capitalist modernity. Yet in so doing it has brought us back to the agenda that was central to the discussion of modernity a century or more ago: development, democracy and peace. These are Enlightenment values suffocated by much of modern history, but nonetheless relevant, and practical, in the contemporary situation.

There are many answers possible as to the bearers of agency in the contemporary world: social movements, often overstated by their protagonists, constitute one candidate, as do structural forces, not least markets, with states constituting the longest established option. The discussion of states in IR may be tired or repetitive: it is not avoidable. States remain the focus of political conflict and, under democratic control, the main instruments for human emancipation. Another international focus of any such discussion, combining philosophical aspiration with attention to actually existing mechanisms for emancipation, and with a recognition of a diversity of levels of agency, can be that of the network of institutions, official and nongovernmental, that comprise global governance. In contrast to the ideal of global government, which would propose a single, increasingly centralized, centre of authority, that of governance suggests a set of discrete, overlapping, institutions, which are able, with different competences, to manage the international system. At the core of this system lies, as it has done since 1945, the UN: but even those financial institutions that are formally within the UN system, such as the IMF and the World Bank, act in practice separately from it. The newly created World Trade Organization is not part of the UN system at all, nor are such free-floating but influential bodies as the Bank of International Settlements, or the Group of Seven.

The ideal of global government has, in effect, undergone a triple revision since its initial conception in World War II: first, there is a diffusion of authority, rather than a centralization; secondly, the power of stronger or richer states has become more explicit, be this in the security or the economic spheres; thirdly, the concentration on states alone, characteristic of the UN, has given way to a view of governance, and tentatively of international civil society, in which non-state actors—human rights organizations, multinationals, environmental lobbies, social movements—play a role. The system of global governance that we have today is diverse and constantly changing. Some of it is effective, some is rhetorical, some is outdated. Attempts to reform it, as, for example, over the fiftieth anniversary of the UN, have proven next to impossible. But we cannot dispense with it, or take its setbacks—in the economic and security fields—as reasons for abandoning it.

The system of global governance at the end of the twentieth century rests, as has done any project of human improvement at the international level for the past two centuries, upon four identifiable layers of authority and implementation: states, international institutions comprising states, nongovernmental organizations and, at the core, individual citizens. None can function without the other. To take the second layer first: a great deal of effort has gone in recent years into reorganizing and making more effective the system of international organizations. We can see some successes: the trading bloc of the European Union is a striking international success, whatever may be current doubts about monetary union and persistent mass unemployment; Mercosur and APEC are developing their commercial, if not their political and monetary, integration. The WTO is setting new standards of commercial integration. We have seen, in response to the crises of the late 1990s, an unprecedented degree of coordination between old IGOs, notably the IMF and World Bank, and new bodies, such as the Group of Seven, with regard to global financial management. Contemporary discussion of a new 'financial architecture' reflects a recognition, a result of shifts in thinking by policy-makers and academics alike, of the failure of the neoliberal model.

In two other areas we can see significant change: in the field of international humanitarian law, we see not only an increasingly effective set of international standards, but also institutional development with the setting up of an International Criminal Court; in the field of security in Europe, we have a fine, perhaps over elaborate, example of the superimposition of governance institutions—no less than eight bodies responsible for the security and peace of a Europe, that in the case of some such bodies stretches from Vladivostok to Vancouver. The international effort to protect the peoples of Bosnia and Kosovo in the 1990s—reluctantly embarked on, most imperfectly implemented and maintained—nonetheless marks a practical, and positive, realization of such aspirations. It is ironic that the crowning point of this humanitarian endeavour in 1999 should have been in response to the denial by the Yugoslav state *to its own citizens* of precisely the value which Kant had seen as being the minimum owed to *foreigners*—'Hospitalität'.

All of this is encouraging, up to a point. There are, however, reasons for concern. First, the UN system, of government and governance, has been sorely tested in the post-Cold War world. The major responses to interstate aggression—in Kuwait and Bosnia—have shown the weakened authority of the UN. The Kosovo operation of 1999 had, at best, a tenuous authorization from the Charter and Security Council. It has been the Great Powers, the so-called 'able and willing', who have in the end taken it upon themselves to act, with a loose authorization, perhaps only indulgence, from the UN as a whole. In the absence of a credible UN security role, and of the inability of the Europeans to do anything coherent in the security field, we have fallen back on an improvised recycling of a Cold War institution, NATO, to keep the peace. Secondly, the global governance system has little or nothing to say about what I have identified as the greatest problem of the contemporary world, that of growing inequality. An attempt was made in the 1960s and 1970s to introduce an institutional reform of the world economy, in the New International Economic order: if one looks back at the goals of that campaign—north-south aid, monetary reform, opening of OECD markets to third world exports, investment codes—none has been achieved. It can be argued that another approach, that of neoliberal change and reliance on FDI, has worked: in terms of growth and industrialization, almost inconceivable in the 1970s, this has occurred. But this model is no proof of neoliberalism: first, it was never a free market model, but relied heavily on a form of mercantilism, with heavy state intervention in investment, research and education. It too has its weaknesses: they are ones that are all the greater because of the lack of institutional reform for which the NIEO campaigned.

In a third domain, one also unimagined two decades ago, the achievements of global governance are limited, if not illusory: that of the environment. Global awareness is certainly greater, conferences have been held, NGOs have mobilized. However, to a non-scientist broadly convinced of the seriousness of this issue, the response seems grossly inadequate, too little, too late, too liable to political bargaining. If humanity is indeed destroying the physical and atmospheric environ-ment in which we live, then the irresponsibility, born of indulgent populations in the rich countries, and debilitating interstate competition along the north-south axis, is incalculable. No conferences—Rio, Kyoto, Buenos Aires or anywhere else—are halting the world automobile industry, or the oil producers, or all those five billion or so people who aspire to a life-style of greater energy consumption and waste production. I hope I am wrong: my gut feeling is that we are walking backwards into a catastrophe that no political constituency, and no state, is willing adequately to confront.

This leads to the third and fourth layers of the system of global governance, that of NGOs and that of citizens. NGOs have played, and will play, a central role in global governance, in raising new issues, in pressing governments, relating movements across frontiers. They are not, however, nor can they be, a substitute for states, or international organizations, in the furtherance of these goals. On the one hand, not all non-state actors have as their goals peace, democracy, human rights: some are agents of states, some of business interests, some of irrational and antidemocratic political interests, some are criminals. The second most valuable commodity in the world today, after oil, is narcotics. On the other hand, networks of NGOs, within and between countries, like social movements, will continue to depend not only for their context but for their influence on states. This means a continued attention to the traditional work of politics—parties, elections, governments, law. A global civil society of NGOs may be coming into existence on some issues—the environment, women' rights, development. It is far from harmonious, not always effective, and never independent of the world of states.

At the base of this system of global governance, and here Professor Kant would, I hope, agree with me, is the individual. It is citizens who, among other things, pay the taxes, lobby the governments, enlist in the peace-keeping forces, authorize the major decisions that comprise global governance and world politics generally. There need not be an opposition between a national, polity-based, concept of citizenship and an international one: but there will be choices to be made, between a national and an international interest, and, even more so, there will be competition between the time and effort paid to issues of domestic concern and those of international concern. Here, for all the growth in available information and world-wide communi-cation, we may detect in the 1990s a growing gap, between the focus of citizens on domestic issues and that on international issues. Part of this may be a result of the receding of palpable military threats, of the Cold War. But part is a result of the very character of social change within developed countries, especially as it affects the media: the populations of the US, Britain and other developed countries are less and less educated, concerned, and, I would argue, responsible about international issues. Democratization, and increased emphasis upon the local, the spontaneous, the immediately meaningful, has been accompanied by a narrowing of focus. This is compounded by the grotesque degeneration of television, now the main source of news and political opinion, and of much of the press, as a result of commercialization: the globalization of Murdoch and Berlusconi is antithetical to that of a responsible national and international citizenry.

There is something rotten, and dangerous, in this process, which, in the longer run, will affect not only the functioning of domestic political systems—as exemplified in falling rates of electoral participation—but also of global governance itself. Whether it be in maintaining support for peacekeeping operations, or in sharing sacrifices to reduce world inequality or the environmental threat, the endemic competitiveness of states will be compounded by the ignorance, and self-regarding logic, of national electorates. Here, in inexorable if slow-moving form, the inherent weaknesses of liberal democracy compromise not only the domestic, but the international, realization of an Enlightenment politics.

Conclusion

Where does this leave a prospect of world-wide peace, democracy and prosperity, our modern rendering of the vision of Professor Kant in 1784, fused, in a generic way, with the 'incomplete modernity' of Professor Habermas? A long way off, but not unattainable. As Kant wrote in 'What is Enlightenment?': we do not live in an *enlightened age* but we do live in an *age of enlightenment*.[27] Most of the states in the world today are not liberal democracies of an established kind. There is no reason to presume that those democracies that do exist will necessarily endure for ever: like a building, they require maintenance, renovation, proper use. Developed societies have, however, a model of political organization that can work sufficiently well, and which is compatible with, even conducive to, economic success and sustained growth. The argument is not, therefore, about the desirability of this broad model, but rather about two other things, how to generalize it across the world, to give to all of humanity that which is enjoyed by an elite of states; and, closely related, how to choose from within the range of options that comprise liberal democracy and mixed economies, those policies that are most appropriate for the long-term attainment of the goal. Here the broad agenda of Habermas theory may bear restatement: awareness of macrosocial reality and change, location of the possibilities of social agency, definition in contemporary terms of Enlightenment goals, identification of the continuing tasks of modernity.

A belief in purposive state action, backed by social movements and an informed, participatory citizenry, and, not to be forgotten, by education in all its dimensions, distinguishes Enlightenment from its enemies and defectors, as does the emphasis on

---

[27] *On History*, 'What is Enlightenment?', p. 8.

a continued state role with regard to national and international economic management. Moreover, the concern with equity, between members of one society, and for humanity as a whole, means more today than it ever did, in the face of world inequality and appalling indices of inequality within societies, developed and developing. Finally, as Professor Kant would want to remind us, we may retain—as critics past and present of the Enlightenment do not—a faith in the ability of reason, individually and collectively, to face and influence the challenges facing humanity. Irrationalism is much *à la mode* at the moment, be this in the form of religious fundamentalism, nationalism, neo-Nietzschean pessimism, or postmodernist self-indulgence. The Enlightenment's defenders, who have much to learn from the abuses of reason, have equally a challenge to face in making it applicable, within a democratic form, to the issues of society, domestic and international, today. Whether, how, when, we can move forward to that triumph of reason in perpetual peace, backed by democracy and prosperity, no-one can tell. It is, nonetheless, a fitting focus for political and academic reflection, not least on the cusp of the third millennium.

Marxism after Communism: beyond Realism and Historicism

ANDREW GAMBLE*

Marx always predicted that the development of capitalism as a social system would be punctuated by major crises, which would become progressively deeper and broader until the system itself was swept away. What he could not have foreseen was that the development of Marxism as a theory would also be marked by crises, both of belief and of method, which have periodically threatened its survival. In this respect at least Marxism has achieved a unity of theory and practice. No crisis has been so profound for Marxism, however, as the crisis brought about by the collapse of Communism in Europe after 1989.[1] With the disappearance after seventy years of the Soviet Union, the first workers' state and the first state to proclaim Marxism as its official ideology, Marxism as a critical theory of society suddenly seemed rudderless, no longer relevant to understanding the present or providing a guide as to how society might be changed for the better. Marx at last was to be returned to the nineteenth century where many suspected he had always belonged.

At first sight the collapse of belief among Marxist intellectuals is surprising. After all, Marxism as a distinct theoretical perspective, a particular approach in the social sciences, and an independent critical theory, had long been separate from Marxism-Leninism, the official and ossified state doctrine of the Soviet Union. The various strands of Western Marxism[2] in particular had sought to keep alive Marxism as critical theory, and had frequently turned those weapons of criticism on the Soviet Union itself. 'Neither Washington nor Moscow' was a favourite slogan of the independent Marxist left. Indeed, what defined the so-called New Left which emerged in the wake of the events of 1968, was not just its critique of Western capitalism but its equally strong opposition to Stalinism in Eastern Europe and the former USSR.

But in spite of this attempt to break free from old intellectual shackles, Marxism in general could not entirely escape its association with actually existing socialism and remained deeply marked by the historical accident of being linked in the twentieth century so inextricably with the fortunes of one particular state: the Soviet

---

* I would like to thank Michael Cox, Michael Kenny, and Tony Payne for comments on an earlier draft of this article.

[1] See for example Robin Blackburn, 'Fin-de-siècle Socialism: Socialism after the Crash', *New Left Review*, 185 (1991), pp. 5–67; Robin Blackburn (ed.), *After the Fall* (London: Verso, 1991); G. A. Cohen, 'The Future of a Disillusion', *New Left Review*, 190 (1991), pp. 5–20; Alex Callinicos, *The Revenge of History* (Cambridge: Polity, 1991); Gareth Stedman-Jones, 'Marx after Marxism', *Marxism Today* (February 1990).

[2] One of the most influential characterizations of Western Marxism as a distinctive strand of Marxism is Perry Anderson, *Considerations on Western Marxism* (London: Verso, 1976). For a critical assessment of Anderson's account see Gregory Elliott, *Perry Anderson: The Remorseless Laboratory of History* (Minneapolis: University of Minnesota Press, 1998).

Union. This association was fanned by the opponents of Marxism, who labelled all Marxists (and most social democrats) as Communists and totalitarians, notwithstanding their protestations to the contrary.[3] But the association did have some basis in fact and was reflected most obviously in the ambivalence which the Left continued to display or feel towards the USSR. Even those Marxists most critical of the Soviet Union could not ignore its historical significance and the fact that it appeared to represent some alternative to capitalism, however flawed in its implementation, and a stage of society and history beyond capitalism. Furthermore, in the stand-off between the superpowers after 1945, the very existence of the Soviet Union limited the reach of the United States and created a space for resistance movements and alternative regimes in the Third World. Many Marxists, in fact, supported the USSR not because they admired the Soviet system, but simply because they were opposed to the United States, and because on occasion the USSR did lend support to revolutions, for example in Cuba and Vietnam.[4] Many also gave reluctant support to the USSR because at times it appeared to represent less of a threat to peace than did the United States. During the most intense moments of the Cold War—especially in the early 1980s—many on the Marxist left tended to be less critical of the Soviet Union than the United States for fanning the arms race.

The link which developed after 1917 between Marxism and the interests of a specific nation-state had another major effect: the rise of a rival form of realism in international relations in the shape of official Marxism-Leninism. This offered an account of the international system based upon an instrumentalist account of the relationship between state policy on the one hand and the interests of national capital on the other. The struggle to seize markets, resources, and territory was regarded as the essence of the imperialist era, which Lenin predicted would be the last stage of capitalism. This brand of realism differed from mainstream realist theory in at least three ways: in being more openly materialist, in seeing a close connection between the action of states and their internal character, and offering a broader view of the determinants of state action than just the calculation by elites of their security interests. In the theory of imperialism in particular what states did abroad very clearly reflected the interests of the dominant sections of their national capital and not just something as vague and ill-defined as the national interest. Nonetheless, Marxism-Leninism still viewed the international system in terms of conflict and states, and competing national economies, rather than the global economy or the world system.[5]

It would be wrong therefore to see Soviet Marxism or Marxism-Leninism as having been theoretically opposed to realism. The opposition between it and mainstream realism as it developed in the Cold War era was primarily ideological. The partisans of the two realisms backed different states, but they shared similar assumptions as to how the international system worked, disagreeing only over which

---

[3] A classic example is F.A.Hayek, *The Road to Serfdom* (London: Routledge, 1944)

[4] Michael Cox, 'Rebels Without a Cause', *New Political Economy*, 3:3, (November 1988), pp. 445–460.

[5] The international state system which emerged after 1917 invited the development of realist interpretations. E.H.Carr's attack upon idealism in *The Twenty Years Crisis: An Introduction to the Study of International Relations* (London: Macmillan, 1939) made the case for a realist analysis of international relations and sparked a wide-ranging and still continuing debate. See 'The Eighty Years Crisis 1919–1999', *Review of International Studies*, 24 (1998). In his later history of the Soviet Union Carr went on to provide a systematic defence of the Soviet Union and its policies from a realist perspective.

state played the more progressive historical role. But what made two realisms possible was what made the post-1917 state system different from the state system of the nineteenth century. There was not just a continuation of great power rivalry, but also a contest between universalist ideologies and social systems. This became magnified after 1945 into a struggle between capitalism and Communism, each championed by one of the two superpowers. In this bipolar world the ideological struggle between East and West had a profound impact on domestic politics in all countries, and established a complex network of alliances. Even severe detractors of all great power politics were forced to have an ideological preference for either the United States or the USSR. It was scarcely possible to be even-handed and condemn both equally. And for many, the USSR was not only a key player in the system of states, but the ideological 'other'—one which had a significance and magnetism far beyond its status as another superpower in a two-superpower world.

For this reason the collapse of the USSR had a deep impact not just on the international order but on the ideological arena of world politics as well. Its ignominious implosion appeared to destroy the credentials of the broad Marxist left at a stroke.[6] The triumph of the West and the triumph of capitalism were complete triumphs, and were hailed—and widely recognized—as such. The pulling down of the statues erected to the leaders of Marxism-Leninism was paralleled by the metaphorical pulling down of the theoretical edifices of Marxism in the rest of Europe, as well as the Third World. For radical intellectuals (however distant they might have been from the Soviet Union) the shock was especially great. Politically they may have had little time for the USSR; however, so long as it survived in whatever state of political degeneration, it provided a point of reference for anti-capitalist opposition in the West. Critics did not have to profess loyalty to the Soviet Union; but the fact that it existed allowed them to be critics of their own society— and its disappearance made it far more difficult for them to remain so. How could they when Soviet-style planning had not only failed to deliver the goods but had been openly rejected by the majority of those who had lived under the capitalist alternative for so many years?

In this way the fortunes of the USSR and the fortunes of Marxism became fatally entwined, and this explains why the collapse of the former appeared much more significant than just the collapse of an especially large state. Marxism's critics hailed it as an end of ideology, an end of history. Admittedly, Marxism lived on as the official doctrine of a number of states, Cuba, Vietnam, North Korea and above all China. But in the first three its only purpose seemed to be to justify one party rule, while China, though clinging to centralized party rule, has clearly abandoned the idea of creating an alternative society or economy. Instead from the 1980s it developed a state-led strategy which accepted China's incorporation into global capitalism.[7]

---

[6] Fred Halliday, 'The End of the Cold War and International Relations: Some Analytic and Theoretical Conclusions', in Ken Booth and Steve Smith (eds.), *International Relations Theory Today* (Pennsylvania State University Press, 1995), pp. 38–61.
[7] Manuel Castells, *End of Millennium* (Oxford: Blackwell, 1998), pp. 287–307.

Crawling from the wreckage

What if anything is left from the wreck and does Marxism have any relevance in the new world order which has emerged in the 1990s? One prominent view is that Marxism is now defunct as a political practice and as an ideological doctrine, and that any insights which still inhere in Marxism as a mode of analysis are best dissociated from the Marxist label and incorporated in new forms of social science.[8] Marx might then be used in a manner similar to Hobbes or Machiavelli or Kant, to reinforce an argument, or to offer a particular perspective on the problems of international politics. What would be abandoned would be the pretensions of Marxism to be a self-contained, over-arching theory of the social sciences, an interdisciplinary alternative to mainstream disciplinary approaches, with its own set of concepts, methodology, and special relationship to political practice.

Many defenders of Marxism argue however that the collapse of Communism, far from being a disaster, is in fact a great opportunity to revive the *discourse* of classical Marxism and abandon the *doctrine* of Marxism-Leninism. It liberates Marxism from a false position, tied by association to a state which had long since ceased to have anything to do with Marxism as a critical theory of society, and which represented not a step forward but a step backwards towards a just society. Marxism is therefore set to regain its vitality and its reputation for critical analysis which it enjoyed before the 1917 revolution. No longer linked to the fortunes of any particular state, it can analyse the forces which are shaping the international state system and the global economy in a dispassionate and objective manner, once again understanding the social relations of capitalism as *global* social relations. The analysis does not start from the nation-state; it starts from the global economy. The state is understood once more as one aspect of the social relations which constitute global capitalist society.[9] Marxism has lost its chains, and can speak in its own authentic accents once more to reignite a revolutionary politics.[10]

If Marxism is to have a future, however, it will not be because there is a return to the world before 1914. The global economy is very different today from what it was then, and forms of political struggle and resistance are very different also. When Marxism first emerged it identified the workers' movement as the agent which would overthrow the capitalist system. Marxism at the end of the twentieth century is a theory in search of an agent.[11] It is still capable of providing a searching and often unequalled account of the nature of the global political economy and the structures which shape its development. But as a political practice it is no longer a serious presence and lacks an effective political strategy. Very few parties of any size or significance now call themselves Marxist parties, or adopt a Marxist ideology. The old unity of theory and practice (often precarious in the past) has finally been sundered.

---

[8] This view is very popular among Weberian historical sociologists. See for example John Hobson, *The Wealth of States* (Cambridge: Cambridge University Press, 1997); and 'The Historical Sociology of the State and the State of Historical Sociology in International Relations', *Review of International Political Economy*, 5:2 (1998), pp. 284–320.

[9] Peter Burnham, 'Open Marxism and Vulgar International Political Economy', *Review of International Political Economy*, 1:2 (1994) p. 229.

[10] Hillel Ticktin, 'Where Are We Going Today? The Nature of Contemporary Crisis', *Critique*, 30–31 (1998), pp. 21–48.

[11] Cf. Michael Cox, 'Rebels Without a Cause'.

This may turn out to be an opportunity. The creativity of Marxism has tended to be frozen by realist doctrines such as the theory of imperialism and by instrumentalist accounts of the state, but also by historicist narratives which identified the agent of revolution as the industrial working class, and socialism as the necessary goal of history. To regain its analytical power and its place among other key perspectives with which we try to understand our world, Marxism needs to rediscover what makes it distinctive, its critique of political economy. It does not start from a blank sheet. There is a rich legacy of ideas and approaches within Western Marxism which can be drawn upon. This article will discuss ways in which contemporary Marxist theories, often building on approaches to the international system which developed in the 1970s and 1980s within Western Marxism, are developing new ways of thinking about international politics which transcend the historicist and realist biases of the past.

Transcending historicism

Francis Fukuyama's claim in 1989 (before the opening of the Berlin Wall and the collapse of the Soviet Union) that history had ended was roundly criticized, particularly by postmodernists who saw it as yet another meta-narrative of modernity, but perhaps least by Marxists themselves, who recognised the importance of Fukuyama's question, drawn as it was from Alexandre Kojeve's Marxist interpretation of Hegel.[12] The issue Kojeve and Fukuyama raise is whether the great ideological contests unleashed since the French Revolution over the organization of economic and social life have run their course, with the acknowledgement that the institutions of free market capitalism and liberal democracy are the horizon of modernity.[13] There are no viable alternatives to these forms, no higher stage of human development. Whatever can be achieved in terms of improving the distribution of resources has to be achieved within the limits of these institutions.

These claims strike at the core of Marxism as a political theory of revolution, since the aim of Marx's historical materialism was to demonstrate that there was a stage of human development beyond capitalism which would guarantee the kind of freedoms and opportunities which capitalism had promised but was unable to deliver because of the way it was organized as a class society. Only the abolition of classes and the abolition of the conditions which reproduced class relations in a capitalist society could allow class society with all its inequalities of power and resources to be overcome.

Redressing such social inequalities remains at the core of any Marxist project, but what the debate on the end of history drew attention to was whether Marxists needed to be attached any longer to the particular narrative which for so long had framed its enquiries. This narrative was historicist by adhering to the notion that history had an objective meaning, and was evolving towards an inevitable destination through a series of historical stages. Such historicist guarantees in the past did

---

[12] Perry Anderson, 'The Ends of History' in *A Zone of Engagement* (London: Verso, 1992), pp. 279–376.

[13] Francis Fukuyama, *The End of History and the Last Man* (London: Hamish Hamilton, 1992). The original article was 'The End of History', *The National Interest*, 16 (1989), pp. 3–18.

much to discredit and invalidate Marxist scholarship. The struggle to purge Marxism of this kind of historicism has been a long one; what Fukuyama has succeeded in doing (inadvertently) is reminding his Marxist readers that for Hegel, the meaning of history was revealed only after a particular phase of history is past. Hegel pronounced history dead after the battle of Jena in 1808, because he recognised in the principles of the French Revolution as carried forward by Napoleon's victorious armies the fully developed principles of modernity. What escapes Fukuyama and many of his critics is that the claim that history has ended can only be a judgement on a particular history, and a particular time. At the very moment of the judgement a new process will be under way. What is valid in Fukuyama is his insight that the end of the 1980s was a decisive turning point. A new world was being made, and this involved the supersession of the terms of the ideological battle of the old. What is invalid is his belief that this new world will not develop its own history.

The fall of Communism forced Marxists to acknowledge finally that the confident belief that socialism would involve the replacement of the market by some form of planning, however decentralized or democratically organized, was flawed. This belief was one of the lasting legacies of the 1917 Revolution. Although some Marxists always argued that the Soviet Union was not socialist at all but 'something else', many did believe that it contained certain socialist elements, however distorted and corrupted.[14] Those elements were precisely the elements which prevented it from being a market economy and subject to market disciplines. And for most Marxists (though again not all) socialism was always identified with the existence of a non-market economy—and according to most Marxists this type of economy was either superior in character or in transition to something higher.

In the last ten years, this historicism has almost completely disappeared, and there is now little disposition to think about some stage of human development beyond capitalism guaranteed by the evolution of history. But this does not mean that it is not possible within a Marxist framework to raise questions about what an alternative to capitalism might look like, or what ethical principles may be used to criticise the existing organization of the international order. Two examples of these kinds of writing are the analytical Marxism of John Roemer[15] and the critical theory of Andrew Linklater.[16] Roemer has developed new thinking on the characteristics of a socialist economy. His version of market socialism offers a decentralized model of a socialist economy in which productive assets are publicly owned but in which all economic activity is organized through markets. This is a theoretical exercise, exploring different possibilities in social and economic organization. It starts from the assumption that a political transfer of all assets from private to public hands has occurred. Roemer is not interested in the mechanism by which such a transfer might take place, and those Marxists from the analytical school who have investigated that question have been pessimistic about the political conditions ever

---

[14] Manuel Castells uses the term 'statist' to refer to the Soviet type of economy to distinguish it from capitalist; *End of Millennium* (Oxford: Blackwell, 1998).

[15] John Roemer *A Future for Socialism* (London: Verso, 1994). See also Anderson 'The Ends of History'; Jon Elster & Karl Ove Moene (eds.), *Alternatives to Capitalism* (Cambridge: Cambridge University Press, 1989); See also Christopher Pierson, *Socialism after Communism: The New Market Socialism* (Cambridge: Polity, 1995).

[16] Andrew Linklater, *The Transformation of the Political Community: Ethical Foundations of the Post-Westphalian Era* (Cambridge: Polity, 1998).

arising within democratic political systems which would create electoral majorities for socialism.[17] Nevertheless work on organizational forms which do not prejudge the desirability of different modes of governance has begun to make a significant contribution to the imagining of alternatives to dominant capitalist forms.[18]

Andrew Linklater has developed a very different kind of analysis. He has sought to extend the idea of critical theory developed by the Frankfurt School to issues of international politics.[19] Linklater takes as the most important legacy of Marxism the development of a critical theory which explores the possibility for human emancipation and for creating a universal society, which would include all peoples, which the progress of industrialization has made possible. He argues that it was this insight which gave Marxism its great moral force and which allows the formulation of ethical principles by which existing arrangements in international politics can be judged.[20]

The rejection of historicism by what remains of the Marxist left—and in particular the belief in the historical inevitability of higher stages beyond capitalism—has not of course meant the abandonment of historical materialism. It has rather aided the return to the fundamental contribution made by Marxism to the analysis of social development and to politics. Marxism's great strength, acknowledged by many of its detractors as well as by its advocates, was its incisive analysis of capitalism as an economic and political system, how that system came into existence, the social relations and institutions which defined it, and how these were reproduced and sustained both temporally and spatially.[21] Such a focus is more interested in capitalism as an existing reality rather than socialism as a distant possibility, and therefore more focused on capitalist reproduction rather than capitalist crisis. The adaptability, resilience, flexibility, inventiveness, and dynamism of capitalism as a social and political system take precedence in the analysis over its fragility, vulnerability, sclerosis and imminent demise. The possibility of crisis and the conditions under which it occurs remains a key part of Marxist analysis, but it is no longer considered within the political perspective of immediate political revolution and the transition to socialism, but within the broader context of the conditions of reproduction of capital.[22]

The historicist elements in Marxism previously introduced a strong moralizing tone into the discussion of certain institutional characteristics of capitalism, particularly the market, because this was destined to disappear in the higher stage of socialism. With the discarding of historicism Marxists have been freed to develop a theory of the capitalist economy which no longer demonizes the market, but treats it instead as one tool through which economies are governed. This has opened the way to analyses of the institutional diversity of capitalism, discarding the assumption of an invariant logic of capital, and investigating the contribution which markets make

---

[17] Adam Przeworski, *Capitalism and Social Democracy* (Cambridge: Cambridge University Press, 1985).
[18] Robin Blackburn, 'The New Collectivism: Pension Reform, Grey Capitalism and Complex Socialism', *New Left Review*, 233 (1999), pp. 3–65.
[19] Andrew Linklater, *The Transformation of the Political Community*; and *Beyond Realism and Marxism: Critical Theory and International Relations* (London: Macmillan, 1990).
[20] A forum which critically discusses Linklater's most recent book can be found in *Review of International Studies*, 25:1 (1999).
[21] David Harvey, *The Limits to Capital* (Oxford: Blackwell, 1982).
[22] Robert Brenner, 'The Economics of Global Turbulence' *New Left Review*, 229 (1998), pp. 1–264.

to the reproduction of capital, how markets are embedded in other institutions, how they are constituted and regulated, and how they can be steered.[23]

Transcending realism

One of the distinctive contributions of a Marxist perspective to international politics is its understanding that capitalism from the beginning was global rather than national in its reach. This insight became clouded during the ascendancy of Marxist theories of imperialism, but in the 1970s it was reborn in new theories of how the economic, social and political institutions of capitalism make up a world system[24] or world order.[25] One of the spurs to this has been the development of the discourse around globalization. Marxists can rightly claim that Marx and Engels were among the first nineteenth century theorists who perceived the trends towards globalization not just of economic activity, but of social arrangements, culture and politics. For Marx the creation of the world market was one of the outcomes of capital accumulation. The undermining of existing boundaries of territory and concepts of space was one of the main ways in which new sources of profit were located, and the reproduction of capital assured.[26] Marx's famous passage from the *The Communist Manifesto* is often cited, but it bears repeating, because it encapsulates so well the extraordinary insight which Marx and Engels had into the dynamism of capitalism and its consequences for the political organization of the world economy. Their tone, as many commentators have noted, was more adulatory than critical of the achievements of capitalism:[27]

The bourgeoisie has through its exploitation of the world market given a cosmopolitan character to production and consumption in every country. To the great chagrin of reactionists, it has drawn from under the feet of industry the national ground on which it stood. All old-established national industries have been destroyed or are daily being destroyed. They are dislodged by new industries, whose introduction becomes a life and death question for all civilised nations, by industries that no longer work up indigenous raw material, but raw material drawn from the remotest zones; industries whose products are consumed not only at home but in every quarter of the globe. In place of the old wants, satisfied by the productions of the country, we find new wants, requiring for their satisfaction the products of distant lands and climes. In place of the old local and national seclusion and self-sufficiency, we have intercourse in every direction, universal interdependence of nations. And as in material, so also in intellectual production. The intellectual creations of individual nations become common property . . . The bourgeoisie, by the rapid improvement of all instruments of production, by the immensely facilitated means of communication, draws all, even the most barbarian nations into civilisation. The cheap prices of its commodities are the heavy artillery with which it batters down all Chinese walls . . . It compels all nations, on pain of extinction, to adopt the bourgeois mode of production; it compels them to introduce what

---

[23] Bob Jessop, 'Regulation Theory in Retrospect and Prospect', *Economy and Society*, 19:2 (1990), pp. 153–216; Robert Pollin, 'Financial Structures and Egalitarian Economic Policy', *New Left Review*, 214 (1995), pp. 26–61.
[24] Immanuel Wallerstein, *The Modern World System* (New York: Academic Press, 1974).
[25] Robert Cox, *Production, Power and World Order* (New York: Columbia University Press, 1987).
[26] David Harvey, *The Limits to Capital* (Oxford: Blackwell, 1982) and *The Condition of PostModernity* (Oxford: Blackwell, 1989).
[27] Karl Marx and Friedrich Engels, *The Communist Manifesto* (Harmondsworth: Penguin, 1973), p. 71.

it calls civilisation into their midst, i.e. to become bourgeois themselves. In one word, it creates a world after its own image.

This passage has been rightly cited as one of the first theories of globalization,[28] remarkable for the way in which it draws together economic, political, and cultural aspects of the impact of capital accumulation and understands capitalism as a global system. But for much of the twentieth century the organization of capitalism *as a global economy* has not been central to Marxist analysis. Instead, as argued above, the organization of capitalism as *imperialism*, a more narrow political concept, was emphasized instead.[29] One of the consequences of the collapse of the Soviet Union has been the recognition that the global economy has entered a new phase. For the first time since the early years of the century it can be said to be truly unified, or more accurately as Castells puts it, unified for the first time.[30] In the seventy years after the 1917 Revolution the global economy did not cease to exist, but its organization was marked by the strength of national economies, regional blocs, and in policy terms by protectionism and state regulation. All national economies became relatively closed, particularly in the period up to the 1950s. In the 1960s and particularly after 1971 this structure of the global economy began to break down, and the pressures towards greater openness increased. The discourse of globalization became current, and then dominant in the 1980s. No country or regime appeared able to withstand the pressures for greater openness; the process culminated in the opening of the territories of the former USSR, which followed the previous opening of China (by its Communist Government). The extent of incorporation of many countries continued to vary, but only a very few countries in the global economy, such as Cuba and North Korea, remained significantly closed at the end of the millennium.

In the nineteenth century the growth of the world market went hand in hand with the strengthening of the most powerful capitalist states, and their political and military reach within this world market. While Marxists shared many of the same assumptions as liberal cosmopolitans like Richard Cobden as to the power of global markets to transform the world and undermine nation-states, they were also sceptical about the prospects for a peaceful world of economic interdependence. On the contrary they argued that there was a close connection between economic and political power, and that the state would be used to create favourable conditions for capital accumulation.

The relationship between the global economy and the international state system is a central question in international political economy. Marxists have always argued that there is a close connection between economic and political power although there have been fierce controversies about the degree of autonomy possessed by the state, and whether the state is best understood in terms of the logic of capital or the struggle between classes.[31] But a further controversy which can only perhaps be fully

---

[28] Simon Bromley 'Marxism and Globalization' in Andrew Gamble, David Marsh and Tony Tant (eds.), *Marxism and Social Science* (London: Macmillan, 1999), pp. 280–301.

[29] Tom Kemp, *Theories of Imperialism* (London: Dobson, 1967); Anthony Brewer, *Marxist Theories of Imperialism* (London: Routledge, 1980); Roger Owen and Bob Sutcliffe (eds.), *Studies in the Theory of Imperialism* (London: Longman, 1972).

[30] Manuel Castells *The Rise of the Network Society* (Oxford: Blackwell, 1998), p. 93.

[31] Bob Jessop, *The Capitalist State* (Oxford: Martin Robertson, 1982); *State Theory: Putting Capitalist States in Their Place* (Cambridge: Polity, 1990); Colin Hay, 'Marxism and the State' in Gamble, Marsh and Tant (eds.), *Marxism and Social Science*, pp. 152–74.

appreciated now that Marxism-Leninism and the phase of Marxist realism are over, is whether the focus of the Marxist analysis of capitalism should be the national state and the national economy or the international state and the global economy. Are the social relations of capitalism to be grasped as global or national phenomena?[32] Marx recognised the very strong pressures towards the creation of a unified global economy, and at the same time the fragmentation of political power into a multitude of separate authorities, but left relatively few clues as to how he would have theorized the tension between the two.

Imperialism and war

The tension has been resolved in different ways in Marxist writings. The most influential in the twentieth century was the theory of imperialism, and its variants, which offered a Marxist-realist account of international relations focused on individual capitalist nation-states. Theorists of imperialism argued that the most powerful states used their military and financial capacities to seize as much territory and resources as they could to increase the opportunities for successful accumulation by their own capitalists. The rivalry between the leading capitalist powers was therefore endemic in the system of capital accumulation itself. As the world market was extended and its immense possibilities opened up, the absence of any overarching political authority created fierce competition between states—economic, political, and finally military. The link between capitalism and war became one of the firmest postulates of Marxist analysis, expressed in its classic form in Lenin's immensely influential pamphlet *Imperialism.*[33]

The outbreak of the First World War appeared to vindicate this Marxist analysis, and with the establishment of the Soviet State this became one of its central beliefs and *Imperialism* one of its canonical texts. However there were from the start other ways of analysing the tendencies of the global economy in Marxism, for example those developed by Karl Kautsky, Rudolf Hilferding, or Rosa Luxemburg; these became buried by the rush to canonize Lenin, and the freezing of Marxism-Leninism as a state ideology. The full richness of the Marxist analysis was obscured. Only much later did new theories of the global economy and world order re-emerge.

The thesis of imperialism leading to war had been employed to explain the division of the world into regional blocs in the 1930s and the outbreak of the Second World War, but the theory began to work extremely poorly from the 1950s onwards. The main conflict in the international state system was between the United States and the USSR rather than between the leading capitalist powers (Europe against America) and the great colonial empires were dismantled. The concept of discrete national capitals which underlaid the idea of imperialist powers using economic, political and military means to compete against one another, also began to break down as capital appeared to become more transnational with the emergence of large global companies.

---

[32] Peter Burnham, 'Open Marxism and Vulgar International Political Economy'.
[33] V. I. Lenin, *Imperialism: The Highest Stage of Capitalism* (Moscow, 1917).

The greater openness of the global economy in the 1990s has echoes of the world before 1917, but with some important differences, not least the absence (so far) of the interimperialist rivalry, the aggressive nationalisms and the drift towards war which so marked international politics at the beginning of the century. The economic and organizational structure of capitalism is also quite different; in the course of the twentieth century it has been transformed by the rise of the public limited company, Fordist production methods, the incorporation of science into the production process, and the expanded role of the state in the reproduction of capital.

The more open global economy of the 1990s also contrasts quite markedly with the interwar years, when Marxists predicted that rivalry between the leading imperialist powers would again plunge the world into war. The contemporary (and highly uneven) development of new regionalisms around the three poles of the global economy—Europe, Japan and the United States—has introduced a new tension but hardly matches the regional blocs of the 1930s.[34] The global economy is by no means free of military conflicts which continue to involve several of the leading capitalist states, but there have been no signs of military clashes between these states themselves.

Hegemony

One influential explanation for the lack of conflict in the Cold War era employed the concept of hegemony. The division of the world between the two superpowers helped to suppress the natural conflicts between different capitalist states, and enabled the leading capitalist powers to be successfully united under American leadership to defeat Communism.[35] But some Marxists, like Ernest Mandel, thought that this was an unnatural state of affairs, and predicted that once tension was reduced between the superpowers the old pattern would reassert itself and capitalist states would once again use military power to further the interests of their national capitalists.[36] But although the Cold War has ended and the Soviet Union has been dismantled, there is no sign that the conflicts over trade and investment between the US and Japan, or between the US and the EU, which undoubtedly exist, will be resolved by force.

The concept of hegemony applied to the problems of the more open global economy of the 1970s and 1980s was important in stimulating the development of new approaches which rejected the nation-state as the primary focus, and sought to grasp capitalism once more as a global system of production and exchange.[37] One of

---

[34] Andrew Gamble and Anthony Payne (eds.), *Regionalism and World Order* (London: Macmillan, 1996).

[35] Michael Cox, *US Foreign Policy After the Cold War: Superpower Without A Mission?* (London: RIIA, 1995).

[36] Ernest Mandel, *Europe versus America* (London: Verso, 1968).

[37] Ankie Hoogvelt, *Globalisation and the Post-Colonial World: The New Political Economy of Development* (London: Macmillan, 1997).

the more ambitious attempts to do this was world systems theory.[38] Originating as a critique of modernization theory, it developed a concept of capitalism as a world system in which there was continual conflict between the Centre and the periphery and between the different components of the Centre for control of the periphery. The world system develops through cycles in which at any one time one power may be in a position to unify the centre and exercise hegemony over the whole world system due primarily to its economic dominance, which is closely tied to relative economic performance as measured by trade, productivity, and foreign investment. In world systems theory, the world moves through periods of relative stability and prosperity followed by periods of relative conflict, disorder, and war. The ending of the Cold War on this account does not signal the beginning of a new phase of American hegemony, but a phase in which American power will be increasingly challenged as other states assert themselves.

In world systems theory, capitalism is understood primarily as a system of exchange and circulation, rather than as a system of production. The competition between nation states is conceived still as realists would understand it, but there are many other agents and forces as well which shape the world system. A different approach was developed by Robert Cox. Like world systems theorists, Cox departed considerably from classical Marxism. He treated capitalism as a global system which needed to be understood through specific historical structures (ensembles of ideas, material capabilities and institutions), and at three different levels, (social forces, states and world orders). Cox included nation-states, but widened the analysis to production systems and broader forms of governance, and put special emphasis on the power of ideas. He drew on Gramsci's analysis of national social formations to develop a historical political economy which provided a critical account of how world orders are historically constructed. This approach, as it has been developed by Cox and others, has come to be labelled transnational historical materialism.[39] At its centre is a different concept of hegemony. Cox is more struck by the strength of the forces holding the global order together than in its proclivity to self-destruct, and by the way in which transnational elites seek to win consent for particular visions of the world. He focuses particularly on how hegemony is constructed in a world economy in which political authority is fragmented, paying special attention to how transnational elites are unified through the creation of networks which share ideas, aggregate interests, and facilitate common institutions. These world orders[40] give rise to what the Amsterdam school have called comprehensive concepts of control,[41] such as Keynesianism and neoliberalism, which are then diffused through national

---

[38] Immanuel Wallerstein, *The Modern World System* (New York: Academic Press, 1974); C. Chase-Dunn, (ed.), *Global Formation, Structures of the World Economy* (Oxford: Blackwell, 1989); Immanuel Wallerstein, *The Capitalist World Economy* (Cambridge: Cambridge University Press, 1979).

[39] Andre Drainville, 'International Political Economy in the Age of Open Marxism', *Review of International Political Economy*, 1:1 (1994), pp. 105–132.

[40] Robert Cox, *Production, Power, and World Order* (New York: Columbia University Press, 1987); Stephen Gill, *American Hegemony and the Trilateral Commission* (Cambridge: Cambridge University Press, 1990); 'European Governance and New Constitutionalism: Economic and Monetary Union and Alternatives of Disciplinary Neoliberalism in Europe', *New Political Economy*, 3:1 (1988), pp. 5–26.

[41] Henk Overbeek, *Global Capitalism and National Decline* (London: Unwin Hyman, 1990); Kees van der Pijl, *The Making of an Atlantic Ruling Class* (London: Verso, 1984); Kees van der Pijl, 'Ruling Classes, Hegemony, and the State System: Theoretical and Historical Considerations', *International Journal of Political Economy*, 19:3 (1989), pp. 7–35.

political systems. Monetarism and neoliberalism were not ideas which arose in particular domestic contexts and were then exported. They were fashioned within the transnational networks of the capitalist class and then adopted and adapted within particular countries. Nation states remain important in this world but they are not all-important. There are many other agents, in particular transnational companies and international organizations, the 'organic intellectuals' of the new transnational ruling class. The needs of the transnational business elite for order and predictability leads to the creation of global institutions and the cooption of political groups around the world. One implication of these analyses is that a transnational state is gradually emerging in which key domestic elites have become part of a transnational elite, dedicated to maintaining the institutions of the transnational global economy rather than being concerned with purely domestic interests. The decisive locus of power in such conceptions lies with transnational capital itself; it is its interests and agendas which now drive the global economy and global politics. There are of course many frictions and conflicts, both within states and between them, but these have in general been managed and kept subordinate to the wider aims of ensuring that the global order itself is sustained.

Accumulation and regulation

An important alternative tradition to the emphasis on capitalism as a unified global system have been those traditions in Western Marxism influenced by Gramsci and later Althusser, which have focused on national paths of development, and national social formations, distinguishing between their economic, political, and ideological levels, and analysing the way in which different modes of production are combined. Most influential of these has been the regulation approach.[42] The regulation school developed the concepts of regimes of accumulation and modes of regulation to characterize different national social formations. Regimes of accumulation are interlinked patterns of production and consumption which can be reproduced over a long period; modes of regulation are the rules, norms, conventions, networks, forms of governance, and institutions which organize and sustain regimes of accumulation. With these tools, regulationists have analysed the peculiarities of different national social formations and the types of production system, Fordism and post-Fordism, which characterize them. They show how certain kinds of policies and institutional arrangements protect and insulate societies. In this way the regulation school is part of a broader engagement by Marxists with the historical institutionalists in exploring the specificities of national capitalisms, and whether there are different models of capitalism, which are path dependent and institutionally distinct. The regulation school, although it discusses global trends and global patterns plays down the significance of either accumulation or the market on a world scale, preferring to

---

[42] Bob Jessop, 'Twenty Years of the (Parisian) Regulation Approach: The Paradox of Success and Failure at Home and Abroad', *New Political Economy*, 2:3 (1997), pp. 503–26; Bob Jessop, 'Regulation Theory in Retrospect and Prospect'; Robert Boyer, *The Regulation School* (New York: Columbia University Press, 1990); Michel Aglietta, *A Theory of Capitalist Regulation: the US Experience* (London: Verso, 1979); Alain Lipietz, *Mirages and Miracles* (London: Verso, 1987).

analyse capitalism as a set of interlinked national economies, which are structured through political, legal and cultural relationships.[43]

The reproduction of capital

World systems theory, transnational historical materialism and the regulation approach have been criticised by those Marxists who wish to revive the classical Marxist emphasis on capitalism as a system which is defined by the accumulation and reproduction of capital.[44] These approaches all emphasize the need to understand capital as a social relation—the accumulation of capital means simultaneously the reproduction and extension of the social relationships which constitute capital. These are long-term structures which include the economy, the state, and the household. Theorists such as Ernest Mandel have analysed the long waves of capitalist development, and their punctuation by social, political and economic crises.[45] This Marxist tradition criticises world systems theory for its reliance on a theory of circulation, markets and exchange in its analysis of power in the global system, the Gramscians for the weight they give to ideology and politics, and the regulationists for their emphasis upon national social formations in the reproduction of capital and the imprecision of concepts like Fordism and post-Fordism. Classical Marxism has in its turn been criticized by representatives of these other schools for determinism and reductionism. But it remains a powerful analytical tool for seeking to understand capitalism as a global system of accumulation. A major contribution to this tradition has recently been made by Robert Brenner, seeking to understand the trajectory of capitalist development in recent decades.[46]

Fundamental to any Marxist analysis is its understanding of the economy, how capital is reproduced, how profitability is maintained, and how crises develop. The Marxist insight that the capitalist economy although fragile and unstable is also hugely productive, adaptable and dynamic directs attention to how capitalism reproduces itself. Reproduction of capital has increasingly been conceived in a much broader manner than was once common, in particular through studies of domestic labour and the organization of the household.[47] Classical Marxism continues to emphasize that the driving force of capitalism is the search for profits, to make possible the self-valorization of capital; everything is secondary to this. The driving force is not the creation of a world market; rather the world market is an outcome of the drive for profitability.

---

[43] Michael Kenny, 'Marxism and Regulation Theory', in Gamble, Marsh and Tant (eds.), *Marxism and Social Science*, pp. 35–60.

[44] Peter Burnham, 'Neo-Gramscian Hegemony and the International Order', *Capital and Class*, 45:1 (1991), pp. 73–93; Robert Brenner and Mark Glick, 'The Regulation Approach: Theory and History', *New Left Review*, 188 (1991), pp. 45–99; Robert Brenner, 'The Origins of Capitalist Development: a Critique of neo-Smithian Marxism', *New Left Review*, 104 (1977), pp. 25–93.

[45] Ernest Mandel, *Late Capitalism* (London: New Left Books, 1976); *The Second Slump* (London: New Left Books, 1978).

[46] Robert Brenner, 'The Economics of Global Turbulence'.

[47] Diane Elson, 'The Economic, the Political, and the Domestic: Businesses, States, and Households in the Organization of Production', *New Political Economy*, 3:2 (1988), pp. 189–208; Jean Gardiner, *Gender, Care, and Economics* (London: Macmillan, 1997).

One of the issues raised by the classical Marxist analysis of accumulation is how far this is a process outside politics, essentially ungovernable, a stream which can be dammed and sometimes diverted, but only for a time. Sooner or later the remorseless process of capital accumulation bursts through, subverting all the controls devised to tame it. Historical structures such as welfare states with their employment rights, minimum wages, and social programmes which have been established in so many advanced capitalist countries, although in different forms,[48] may rest on economic foundations which can swiftly be undermined if those who control capital conclude that higher profits are to be made elsewhere. This idea of a race to the bottom, or immiserization as Marx and Engels called it, is regarded by classical Marxists as one of the historical tendencies of the process of capital accumulation, however much it may be delayed or diverted for long periods. Capital always seeks out those circumstances in which costs are reduced to the minimum and profits maximized. The ability of capital to do this depends on a number of factors, including the utilization of new technologies and the speeding up of the pace and intensity of production to increase the exploitation of labour, the transfer of costs to the state (hence to the general taxpayer rather than the individual capitalist), the reorganization of domestic labour, and the discovery of new markets. Under capitalism no pattern remains fixed for ever. Upheaval, crisis, reorganization, innovation are the essence of this most unpredictable mode of production.

The continuing power of classical Marxism to inspire major insights into the shape of international politics can be seen in two major recent works by Manuel Castells and Giovanni Arrighi. Capitalism's dynamism always seems at its greatest in periods of great technological innovation, and the period at the end of the twentieth century with the unfolding of the informational revolution is certainly one of those. At such times all forms of employment can be affected, and huge transfers take place between different sectors of the economy and types of occupation. The consequences are profound for individuals but also for national economies. Castells in the spirit of classical Marxism charts how a fundamental change in the way the mode of capitalism is organized has implications for all aspects of social life— culture, politics, identity, leisure, consumption, technology, work, and households.[49] At the same time for all the dynamism of capital and its ability to subvert all existing patterns of social life, Giovanni Arrighi has also pointed to the persistence of hierarchical patterns and uneven development in the world economy. The rich economies stay rich. In the course of the twentieth century the rank order of the leading capitalist states changed, but not the identity of those states, with one exception—Japan. Otherwise the list is the same in 2000 as it was in 1900.[50] These two works have profound implications for our understanding of international politics and the global system.

---

[48] Gosta Esping Anderson, *The Three Worlds of Welfare Capitalism* (Cambridge: Polity, 1990).

[49] Manuel Castells, *The Information Age: Economy, Society and Culture: vol. I, The Rise of the Network Society; vol, II, The Power of Identity; vol III, End of Millennium* (Oxford: Blackwell, 1996, 1997, 1998).

[50] Giovanni Arrighi, *The Long Twentieth Century: Money, Power, and the Origins of Our Time* (London: Verso, 1994); 'World Income Inequalities and the Future of Socialism', *New Left Review*, 189 (1991), pp. 39–66..

The future of Marxism

Marxism has the resources to detach itself from the ruins of Communism if it moves decisively beyond historicism and realism, building on some of the intellectual traditions of Western Marxism and developing critical theory,[51] but not forgetting its central insight into the nature of society, the social relationships which define the different modes of production which have existed in human history. Many of the other aspects which have defined historical materialism in the past, in particular the historicism which saw capitalism as a stage of development towards socialism and the realism which analysed imperialism in terms of the strategies of national capital and states, have fallen away. But capitalism as a very present reality has not fallen away, and Marxism still offers a crucial set of concepts for understanding it.

What precisely is the nature of this contribution? The microfoundations of Marxism have not worn well, despite the huge investment of time and ingenuity in preserving them. The labour theory of value can be defended as a historical institutionalist account of the social relationships which define capitalism, and in which markets are embedded, but not as a device which allows precise measurement of prices or the modelling of the way in which markets work.[52] Since prices cannot be derived from labour-time values, the microfoundations of Marxism cannot supply a theory of how resources are allocated in markets. But the microfoundations of mainstream economics do not provide an adequate account of the wider institutional context of markets. This is where Marxism can still make a major contribution. It provides an understanding of the nature of power, how it arises and how it is exercised in different modes of production through its analysis of how capital as a set of social relationships is reproduced. Understanding capital as a set of social relationships which are always capable of being contested politically and ideologically, rather than as a quantity of resources which are simply utilised in production, remains its critical insight.

Marxism is still noted for its concern with the dynamics of social systems.[53] More than any other observer in the nineteenth century Marx had an extraordinary grasp of what made capitalism as a mode of production such a subversive and revolutionary force, although even he cannot have imagined what its full effects would be. His intuition that capital would not rest until it had pulled all societies and all sectors into the world market and until it had expelled living labour from the production process altogether by driving towards automation was remarkable when it was written, since capitalism had at that time penetrated a small part of the world, and only in England and a few parts of Europe had industrial capitalism really taken hold.[54] Marx has always been much praised, even by his critics, for the quality of his foresight.[55]

[51] Andrew Linklater, *The Transformation of the Political Community*.
[52] Perry Anderson, *Considerations on Western Marxism* (London: Verso, 1972): Afterword; Ian Steedman, *Marx after Sraffa* (London: NLB, 1977); Ian Steedman *et al.* (eds.), *The Value Controversy* (London: Verso, 1981).
[53] Ankie Hoogvelt, *Globalization and the Post-Colonial World*.
[54] Martin Nicolaus, 'The Unknown Marx', *New Left Review*, 48 (1968), pp. 41–61.
[55] J. A. Schumpeter, *Capitalism, Socialism and Democracy* (London: Allen & Unwin, 1950).

But while Marx was insightful on questions like this he was blind on other questions, particularly nationalism. This may be because Marxism's peculiar strength is derived from its economism. Western Marxists for seventy years have been seeking to deny this and deflect attention away from it. Vulgar forms of economism, in which all politics and all ideology are simply reduced to crude class interest, and the state becomes a puppet in the hands of the ruling class, are uninteresting and have been rightly criticised. But attempts to prove that Marxism contains no economism at all end by throwing away what is still valuable in Marxism—its insistence on the need to understand how modes of production depend upon the continual reproduction of particular social relations which then have particular outcomes in terms of the distribution of power and resources. Marxism in the end has to stand by the claim that the economic power which accrues to the class which controls productive assets is a crucial determinant of the manner in which political, cultural and ideological power are exercised. Many kinds of sophisticated concepts can be deployed to understand the intricacies of the relationship, but in the end if the primacy of the economic is lost, then Marxism loses its distinctiveness and its value in social theory. There are after all many theories of the social which do not privilege the economic, or assume that modern society is to be understood primarily in terms of the way in which the economy is organised. Marxism does make this claim, and although it has often been made rather badly, it is a serious claim, which like Hobbes' claim about sovereignty is a perspective on history and on society which cannot easily be set aside.

Making the most of Marxism as economism does not therefore mean embracing instrumental theories of class, which imply that class itself is the crucial feature of capitalism, and that the people who own property form the ruling class which controls society and politics. What is important about an economistic reading of Marx is the notion of capital as a social relation. It is the reproduction of this social relation, and its invasion into so many spheres of social life and into so many parts of the globe that is one of the most central features of any conception of modernity. The fragmentation of ownership with the rise of the corporate economy and the disappearance of an easily identifiable ruling class is not an objection to Marxism if what is important for Marxist theory is tracing how capital as a social relation is reproduced, imposing the structures within which all agents have to operate, whether in assisting capital or resisting it.

Marxism often lost its way in the past through claiming to be a total science of society, and moreover the only objective and true one. These claims were never credible and have become even less so in a period of questioning of the foundations and truth claims of all theories. Marxism is incapable of explaining all the trends and phenomena of the contemporary world, but it can offer an account of such matters as globalization, inequality, the informational revolution, the changing structure of work, and the changing nature of the state. It also has interesting things to say about the boundaries between the public and the private, and the meaning of non-commodified spheres such as welfare and health—public goods which exist outside the sphere of capital and its operations. But it also provides an understanding as to why any such noncapitalist spheres are never inviolable, and may be subject to political attack and invasion.

A contemporary Marxism needs to direct attention to the potentiality and the limits in the continued spread and development of capitalism as a mode of production. The political interest behind this kind of enquiry has undoubtedly shifted. At one time the perspective was the coming social revolution which would remove the capital relation once and for all. Today's Marxists are more likely to be concerned with how forms of governance at different levels of the international system, global, regional, national, subnational and local, may impose or release constraints on the way in which capitalism operates and is embedded in national and regional societies. This approach would not have been strange to Marx. He recognised the importance of reforms in limiting what capital could do in providing sites of resistance in which other social relations and ideas could flourish. The Factory Acts of the 1840s which set limits on the way in which children and women could be employed in factories were one of the examples on which he commented in *Capital.*[56]

Capitalism as a global system has grown both more interdependent and more fragile. It has generated enormous wealth and enormous knowledge in the last two hundred years which now support a population far in excess of any that has existed in previous human history. At the same time the distribution of the wealth capitalism created has remained highly concentrated and unequal, industrial activities have reached the point where they threaten the life support systems of the planet, and the system of accumulation itself is marked by huge instabilities and imbalances which could still implode in a devastating financial crisis with far-reaching political and economic consequences. Marxist analysis therefore points to the urgent need for new systems of multi-level governance in the global economy to identify, manage and steer these problems. Marxists remain divided in their prognoses. Some are pessimistic and fatalistic about the future of capitalism.[57] It sometimes seems like a giant ship which has slipped its moorings and which drifts on to its destruction because no-one can find a way to steer it or take control. But others are more hopeful.[58] If acts of resistance multiply, new structures and new institutions can be built. It may not be possible to live in the modern world without capitalism, but capitalism need not be a single fate.

---

[56] Karl Marx, *Capital* (Penguin: Harmondsworth, 1976), ch. 10.
[57] Perry Anderson, 'The Ends of History'; Eric Hobsbawm, *Age of Extremes: The Short Twentieth Century* (London: Michael Joseph, 1994).
[58] Pierre Bourdieu, *Acts of Resistance* (London: Verso, 1999); Manuel Castells, *End of Millennium.*

Liberalism since the Cold War:
an enemy to itself?

GEOFFREY HAWTHORN

Many expected that after the Cold War, there would be peace, order, increasing prosperity in expanding markets and the extension and eventual consolidation of civil and political rights. There would be a new world order, and it would in these ways be liberal. In international politics, the United States would be supreme. It would through security treaties command the peace in western Europe and east Asia; through its economic power command it in eastern Europe and Russia; through clients and its own domination command it in the Middle East; through tacit understanding command it in Latin America; and, in so far as any state could, command it in Africa also. It could choose whether to cooperate in the United Nations, and if it did not wish to do so, be confident that it would not be disablingly opposed by illiberal states. In the international markets, it would be able to maintain holdings of its bonds. In the international financial institutions, it would continue to be decisive in the International Monetary Fund and the World Bank; it would be an important influence in the regional development banks; and it would be powerful in what it was to insist in 1994 should be called the World (rather than Multinational) Trade Organisation. Other transactions in the markets, it is true, would be beyond the control of any state. But they would not be likely to conflict with the interests of the United States (and western Europe) in finance, investment and trade, and would discipline other governments. The need to support regimes of 'national security' to curtail the influence of the socialist powers would have gone, and it would be convenient now to encourage liberal democracies and their 'civil societies'. Democracies would be secure allies, and since, it was claimed, regimes of this kind do not go to war with each other, there would be less armed conflict. If a hegemony is 'a fit between a configuration of material', including military, 'power, the prevalent collective image of world order (including certain norms), and a set of institutions which administer the order', there would be a hegemony.[1] The alternatives to liberal capitalism and democracy had been exhausted, war itself perhaps superseded. There was even talk of 'the end of history', and a new long peace.[2] Politically, the world would be a more intelligent place.[3]

Events, of course, continued. Iraq invaded Kuwait. Yugoslavia's republics fought themselves and each other. Wars persisted in Afghanistan, Angola, Uganda and Ethiopia and Eritrea, and started in Congo-Brazzaville, Guinea-Bissau, Lesotho,

---

[1] Robert W. Cox, 'Social Forces, States, and World Orders: Beyond International Relations Theory', in Robert W. Cox and T. J. Sinclair, *Approaches to World Order* (Cambridge: Cambridge University Press, 1996), p. 103.

[2] Francis Fukuyama, *The End of History and the Last Man* (London: Hamish Hamilton, 1992).

[3] James N. Rosenau, *Turbulence in World Politics: A Theory of Change and Continuity* (Princeton, NJ: Princeton University Press, 1990).

Liberia, Rwanda, Sierra Leone, Somalia and Sudan; there were coups elsewhere in Africa; Zaire actually collapsed; and there were uncertainties about the transition in South Africa. There was no firm settlement between Israel and Palestine and at best modest reform in Iran. Vietnam continued to occupy Cambodia, the government in Burma to defy the wishes of its electorate. China pressed its claims in the South China Sea against Brunei, Malaysia, the Philippines and Vietnam. The question of Korea remained unresolved. India and Pakistan were developing their nuclear weapons and demonstrating some ability to deliver them. There were financial difficulties in Russia, continuing recession in Japan, difficulties over China's terms of entry to the WTO, a financial crisis in Mexico and a more severe collapse of confidence in parts of north- and south-east Asia that for a moment was thought to be more widely threatening than any since the 1930s.

Yet by the end of the 1990s, optimists could be confident. Iraq, they could say, had been contained, South Africa had passed more painlessly than many had expected from its illiberal past, Slovenia, Croatia, Macedonia and Bosnia-Herzegovina had been separated and stabilized, and Kosovo, perhaps, would be. Cambodia had been provisionally settled, and if the war in Afghanistan and several of those in Africa had not stopped, these had had no consequence beyond their immediate vicinity. Intermittent threats from North Korea had been offset by greater caution from China, a more conciliatory government in South Korea, and negotiations, however fitful, with the United States. Relations between India and Pakistan had improved and then deteriorated, but the hostility had been largely for domestic display, and there was no open war. Israel and Palestine continued to argue over the implementation of the Oslo accords, but there was less fighting than before. Moderates had strengthened their position in Iran. The Association of South-east Asian Nations brought China into discussions in its Regional Forum and admitted Burma, Laos and Cambodia to its membership. Everyone hoped and many expected that the imbalance in the international economy at the end of the decade, whereby half the annual increase in world demand was being accounted for by private spending in the United States, would be offset by recovery in Japan and western Europe. The economic crisis in Russia persisted, but the IMF was lenient. The crises in north- and south-east Asia had not had the consequences that many feared, either in Asia itself or in the 'emerging markets' beyond; indeed, they produced a will to try to regulate the speculative activities of the hedge funds and the careless interbank lending that prompted them. There was progress in the negotiations on the terms of China's entry to the WTO. Competitive electoral politics appeared to be reasonably secure in most of Europe and Latin America, to have been strengthened in Thailand, and to be establishing themselves in Indonesia. Even those who remained critical of some of the actions of the United States could perhaps have agreed in 1999 that 'with the demise of the Cold War, virtually all the major problems that afflicted Great Power relations over the last half-century have been resolved'.[4]

Liberal theorists of international politics have been accordingly sanguine. Some have argued that the United States' willingness to listen to other liberal states, the 'co-binding' consequences of institutions of international security and economic cooperation, and an increasingly widespread agreement on 'civic values' have

---

[4] John Mueller, and Karl Mueller, 'Sanctions of Mass Destruction', *Foreign Affairs*, 78:3 (1999), p. 43.

together created a 'structural liberalism' that has outlasted the Cold War and been strengthened since.[5] The proliferation of international agents and of the connections between them, some have added, make it appropriate to see power as an expanding resource from which all can benefit rather than as acts in which if there are winners, there have also to be losers.[6] The new liberalism, others have said, makes it possible once again to look forward to a community of states whose members will identify at least as closely with each other's well-being as with their own, to lively civil societies that will act apart from states on an increasingly international stage, and to a 'cosmopolitan', or at least 'cosmopolitical', democracy.[7] Some have even suggested that one could now imagine 'governance without government'.[8]

Liberal philosophers have offered grounds for such hopes. Jürgen Habermas continues to press his belief that individuals can be motivated to abstract themselves from existing political institutions in a 'decentred' public sphere in which they can discover and converge on their true interests in autonomy and agreement.[9] John Rawls, moving from assumptions of self-interest informed by reflection on our moral intuitions from behind a veil of ignorance, through a Kantian ideal of the moral subject to the normative principles of a liberal society, proposes a more pointedly 'political liberalism' in which those who live in the same political society but have different conceptions of the good will agree that they have in the interests of justice 'reasonably' to accept that they cannot seek to convert or otherwise trump each other.[10] Michael Walzer, whose particularist or 'communitarian' starting point is acknowledged in Rawls' decision to start from a liberal society, argues that although 'morality is thick from the beginning, culturally integrated, fully resonant', it does reveal itself 'thinly on specific occasions, when moral language is turned to specific purposes'; and that when excited by the 'vicarious endorsement' of the claims of those beyond one's own community, these can be purposes in common.[11]

[5] David Deudney and G. John Ikenberry, 'The Nature and Sources of International Order', *Review of International Studies*, 25 (1999), pp. 179–96.

[6] Paul Hirst, 'The Eighty Years' Crisis, 1919–1999: Power', in Tim Dunne, Michael Cox and Ken Booth (eds.), *The Eighty Years' Crisis: International Relations 1919–1999* (Cambridge: Cambridge University Press, 1998), pp. 133–48. This is the implication also of Deudney and Ikenberry's argument. 'Realist theories of balance of power, hegemony, sovereignty, and nationalism', they argue, 'fail to capture the core dynamics of the liberal international order'; 'The nature and sources of liberal international order'. p. 195.

[7] For example, Alexander Wendt, 'Collective Identity Formation and the International State', *American Political Science Review*, 88 (1994), pp. 384–96; Commission on Global Governance, *Our Global Neighbourhood* (Oxford: Oxford University Press, 1995); Daniele Archibugi, David Held and Martin Köhler (eds.), *Reimagining Political Community: Studies in Cosmopolitan Democracy* (Cambridge: Polity, 1998). The adjective 'cosmopolitical' is from Carol C. Gould, *Rethinking Democracy: Freedom and Social Cooperation in Politics, Economy and Society* (Cambridge: Cambridge University Press, 1988), pp. 307–28.

[8] James N. Rosenau and Ernst-Otto Czempiel (eds.), *Governance without Government: Order and Change in World Politics* (Cambridge: Cambridge University Press, 1992); Commission on Global Governance, *Our Global Neighbourhood*.

[9] Jürgen Habermas, 'Three Normative Models of Democracy', *Constellations*, 1:1 (1994), pp. 1–10; *Between Facts and Norms: Contributions to a Discourse Theory of Law and Democracy* (Cambridge MA: MIT Press, 1996).

[10] John Rawls, *A Theory of Justice* (Cambridge, MA: Harvard University Press, 1971); John Rawls, *Political Liberalism*, 2nd edn., reprint, 1993 (New York: Columbia University Press, 1996); John Rawls, 'The Idea of Public Reason Revisited', *University of Chicago Law Review*, 64 (1997), pp. 765–807.

[11] Michael Walzer, *Thick and Thin: Moral Argument at Home and Abroad* (London: University of Notre Dame Press, 1994), p. 4.

Onora O'Neill, intent on avoiding the assumptions of a metaphysical or empirically particular kind that are made by Habermas, Rawls and the communitarians, starts from a more abstract, 'non-idealising' and 'banal', conception of agents. Because even the most particular reasons that people have to act, she suggests, presuppose 'a framework of more inclusive and indeterminate principles', because whenever their 'activity assumes a plurality of finite and connected others' they are 'committed to including those others within the scope of their ethical consideration', and because connections in the modern world are as they are, their reasons to act now have a cosmopolitan scope.[12] Not all of these arguments have been intended, like O'Neill's own, to extend to relations across frontiers; but all can be made to do so, and by the new idealists, frequently are. Individuals, the liberals have once again become convinced, are capable of acting rationally in a constructively reciprocal manner, and political frontiers have no moral force.

In the demonstrated commitment of Western states to expanding markets and the extension and eventual consolidation of civil and political rights, the new world is indeed more liberal than the old. But the liberals' own accounts of why this should be have not always exposed the paradox in its having become so. This is especially evident in the politics of 'the new interventionism' and those of the international economy. In the the new interventionism, it is claimed, the tension between order and justice has at last been resolved. In the international economy, the prosperity that ensures them both is secured. The paradox is that these two moves can subvert what they claim to secure.

The new interventionism

The Cold War suspended the argument between those who were committed to a society of sovereign states in which each state defended its government's interests and committed itself only to those rules and institutions of international politics which existed to sustain that sovereignty, and those who aspired to a society in which sovereignty could be superseded in the interests of what had come to be called 'human rights'. The 'rights' were formally acknowledged by most, but their practical extension was a matter for the government of each state alone. The Cold War also restricted the 'self-determination of peoples' to those who happened to find themselves in territories that had been defined as the territories they were by colonial rule. Even where a possible new state, unlike many of the former colonies, might be viable, no further self-determination was considered. Against the insistence of its member states on their sovereignty, there was little effort to meet the United Nations' formal obligation to promote international peace and security, and the attempts that were made were regularly vetoed on its Security Council. A distinction accordingly developed between intervening on humanitarian grounds, which states would not countenance, and intervening to keep a peace; and even intervening to keep a peace was only possible if the states between whom the peace was to be kept

---

[12] Onora O'Neill, *Towards Justice and Virtue: A Constructive Account of Practical Reasoning* (Cambridge: Cambridge University Press, 1996), p. 113, passim. O'Neill is careful to say that this does not presume the justice or virtue of a world state; it is merely 'argument to show that, at least in our world, foreigners count', and why.

were willing. Practical idealism was otherwise restricted to those institutions of the United Nations charged with the welfare of refugees and children and to nongovernmental organisations that were allowed to operate within the bounds of sovereignty and the consent of states. Elsewhere, what had come to be called 'realism' prevailed.[13] Some have suggested that in a different history, the question of when and on what grounds intervention in the internal affairs of a state could be justified might at last have been resolved.[14] There would have been a will to find a balance between the commitment in the United Nations Charter to to international peace and security and the sovereign equality of states, and with the will, a way. The interventions of the 1990s, they argue, failed largely because the Cold War still cast its shadow.

The invasion of Cambodia by Vietnam in 1978 was a move in the Cold War itself. It had been supported by the Soviet Union but opposed by China and the United States as well as by the majority of the members of the United Nations, who regarded it as a simple violation of sovereignty. It was only when the Soviet Union decided to withdraw its support for foreign adventures in the mid 1980s that the violation could be discussed. Vietnam, now weakened, apologised to China for its invasion, and Security Council was able to agree to support a political settlement. Nonetheless, the UN had to acknowledge the existing sovereignties. It was required to manage a transition to elections in 1993 through a Supreme National Council that included both Vietnam's puppet government and the still formally legitimate Khmer Rouge, which Vietnam had usurped (and from which the leader of Vietnam's government in Cambodia, Hun Sen, had himself defected). Since Cambodia had not been put under trusteeship, the United Nations Transitional Authority had merely the responsibility, not the power, to ensure that the contenders kept to the spirit of the agreement. Not given the resources to exercise the responsibility it did have, even though its operation was at the time the most costly of those that had been mounted by the UN, UNTAC had to devolve more than it would have liked to the institutions of the existing government. The outcome of its work in the election in 1993 was to lead to an unsatisfactory coalition between Hun Sen's Cambodian People's Party and the royalists. The deadlock remained unresolved by a subsequent coup by Hun Sen and a second election in 1998.

In Somalia, the end of the Cold War precipitated the dictatorial president into clan enmities that he had himself exacerbated by using both Soviet and American arms to maintain his power. President Bush, having at first resisted American involvement in peace-keeping in the country, changed his mind after his defeat in 1992. The United States was now prepared to act unilaterally, but preferred international support. Support in December 1992 for what became the first humanitarian intervention authorised under Chapter VII of the United Nations charter was unanimous. The intervention, however, was in a state without a state. Inevitably, the

---

[13] There is an excellent summary of this state of affairs in James Mayall, 'Introduction', in James Mayall (ed.), *The New Interventionism, 1991–1994: United Nations Experience in Cambodia, Former Yugoslavia and Somalia* (Cambridge: Cambridge University Press, 1996), pp. 1–24. Mayall follows Bull's distinction between the 'pluralists', upholding the sovereignty of states and international rules and institutions to sustain that sovereignty, and the 'solidarists', aspiring to something more. On the effective statehood of the ex-colonial territories, see Robert H. Jackson, *Quasi-States: Sovereignty, International Relations and the Third World* (Cambridge: Cambridge University Press, 1990).

[14] Mayall, 'Introduction', p. 6, although he is himself sceptical.

forces that were charged with it were drawn into the fights between the clans. They left the country nearly three years later having achieved little beyond the restitution of some devastated agricultural areas.

The Cold War (and Tito's skill) had also suppressed enmities and resentments in the Socialist Federal Republic of Yugoslavia which, it might less persuasively be argued, might otherwise have been resolved. When Slovenia and Croatia declared their independence from the federation in 1991, the international community's long inattention to questions of secession led to a muddle in the course of which, having been faced with unilateral declarations of independence by Slovenia and Croatia, it decided to agree that Yugoslavia had conveniently dissolved itself. (In its acknowledgement of the right of the constituent republics to secede, the constitution of the Federal Republic formally allowed it to do so.) The Serbs then argued that Serbian populations in Croatia and Bosnia-Herzegovina had the right to secede from secession. Having first intervened to keep the peace in fights between the Serb-dominated Yugoslavia, Croatia and the parties in Bosnia-Herzegovina, then on humanitarian grounds, then to prevent further disputes about self-determination, the governments that had become involved in the administration of the collapse of the Federal Republic through the Organisation for Security and Cooperation in Europe, the European Union, and the UN accepted a separate state of Bosnia-Herzegovina and some autonomy within it for the Serbian Republika Srpska.[15]

The interventions in Cambodia, Somalia and the former Yugoslavia in the first half of the 1990s were outcomes of the end of the Cold War, and were guided still by the priorities and conventions that prevailed in that war. So also was Russia's suppression of the attempted secession of Chechnya in 1994. In the intervention later in the decade, however, in the dispute between the Federal Republic of Yugoslavia and the Albanian Kosovans, priorities changed and conventions were broken. Kosovo had a territorial identity and its own structures of government, retained a separate federal status, and was acknowledged in the Federal presidency. In 1989, the government of the Federal Republic suspended its autonomy and made it part of the Serbian republic. Even when Western governments responded in 1997 to the Federal Government's subsequent use of force against the Albanian Kosovars, whose Kosovo Liberation Army had in turn been using force against Serbs in the province, they continued to point to the restrictions in Chapter VII of the United Nations Charter, and refused the Albanian Kosovars' claim to statehood. They demanded the cessation of repression and the withdrawal of Serbian forces. But they also wanted a political settlement that would respect Serbia's territorial unity. To use force themselves, they at first believed, would strengthen Kosovo's claim to independence. When Serbia rejected their demands, and in late 1998 and early 1999 allowed more attacks on Albanian Kosovars, a 'Contact Group' of Western states changed its mind. To their relief and surprise, the Secretary-General of the UN himself told an audience at NATO headquarters in the January that in view of the experience in Bosnia-Herzegovina, the organization should now consider using

---

[15] Mats Berdal and Michael Leifer, 'Cambodia'; Spyros Economides and Paul Taylor, 'Former Yugoslavia'; Ioan Lewis and James Mayall, 'Somalia'; in Mayall, *The New Interventionism*, pp. 25–58, 59–93, 94–124. A full and illuminating account of the events in Yugoslavia in the first half of the 1990s is Susan L. Woodward, *Balkan Tragedy: Chaos and Dissolution after the Cold War* (Washington, DC: Brookings Institution, 1995); I am grateful to Helen Thompson for this reference.

military means to halt internal conflict 'particularly against the wishes of the government of a sovereign state'.[16] This NATO decided to do.

The 'non-negotiable' demands for a new interim settlement at Rambouillet in 1999 included the condition that NATO, supplemented by the OSCE, would oversee its implementation. Force, it was now argued, was justified by the fact that such a settlement was itself necessary to avert a humanitarian catastrophe. The Serbians could not or would not meet the stringent new demands, which in including the provision for an eventual referendum on the province's future, threatened their territorial integrity, and force was deployed against them. The defence that was offered for the demands at Rambouillet, moreover, was new. With the connivance of the Secretary-General of the United Nations, but without seeking the approval of the Security Council, an alliance of liberal powers had taken it upon themselves to enforce the agreement they sought. In June 1999, pressed to do so by the Group of Seven industrial countries and with the agreement eventually of Russia, which secured for the Serbs the removal of any commitment to a referendum in Kosovo, the transfer of authority from NATO to the UN, a refusal to recognise the KLA, and the presence of Russian troops, the Security Council agreed, China abstaining, that Serbia should leave Kosovo to be administered by 'international civil and security presences' under UN authority. The principle of non-interference had been sacrificed to the enforcement of human rights, and an argument had been found to defend the use of arms for humanitarian intervention. Meanwhile, the choice between maintaining the territorial integrity of a sovereign state and allowing the self-determination of part of its population was postponed. Kosovo, still formally part of the Federal Republic of Yugoslavia, was in effect to become a UN protectorate.

These might at first sight seem to be reasons for liberal delight. Even Lee Kuan Yew, always the coolest and often the most intelligent of realists, described the demonstration by NATO in the spring of 1999 that 'no government can act barbarically to its own people' as 'a fundamental advance in international relations'.[17] (Lee forgot that a similar qualification to sovereignty had been allowed for in the Peace of Westphalia.)[18] Yet whatever the arguments for and against the principle of maintaining the territorial integrity of sovereign states, these have not been and cannot be arguments that are consistently applied. In Iraq, it is true, the Western powers have stopped short of allowing the secession of disaffected and persecuted groups in the north and south of the country. With the convenience of NATO airfields in Turkey, whose own 'humanitarian' violations have not been subject to the pressure put on Iraq itself, and the Federal Republic of Yugoslavia, the United States and other Western powers have instead imposed 'no-fly zones' and fierce economic sanctions that can themselves be regarded as a humanitarian abuse.[19] In Yugoslavia, the constitution of the Federal Republic was used as a fig-leaf to allow Croatia, Slovenia and Bosnia-Hertzegovina to secede. But because a larger proportion of Kosovans than Croatians had already expressed their wish to do so, this was not a right granted to Kosovo. Nuclear powers, like China, can be as confident that

---

[16] Marc Weller, 'The Rambouillet Conference on Kosovo', *International Affairs*, 75 (1999), p. 221.
[17] 'Veteran Asian Leader Scorns US policy', *Financial Times*, 19 May 1999.
[18] Leo Gross, 'The Peace of Westphalia, 1648–1948', *American Journal of International Law*, 42:20 (1948), pp. 20–41.
[19] Mueller and Mueller, 'Sanctions of Mass Destruction'.

force will not be used against a country that has 'missiles with nuclear tips' as can those, as in Africa, who know that it will not be used where it cannot prevail.[20]

Inconsistency in a world of variable wills and unequal powers is unsurprising. That the new interventions are self-evidently a function of the power to intervene, however, should give liberals pause. The sacrifice of the principle of non-interference in the affairs of a sovereign state to the principle that human rights should if necessary be enforced against a state that denies them has been defended on principled grounds. In the words of the Secretary-General of NATO, the decision to use arms to force a settlement over Kosovo was 'not about oil, or money, or new trade routes', but 'values'.[21] Carl Schmitt, smarting in Germany in the 1920s under the terms of Versailles and decisions of the League of Nations, had seen the paradox.

When a state fights its political enemy in the name of humanity, it is not a war for the sake of humanity, but a war wherein a particular state seeks to usurp a universal concept against its military opponent. At the expense of its opponent, it tries to identify itself with humanity in the same way as one can misuse justice, peace, progress, and civilisation in order to claim these as one's own and to deny the same to the enemy . . . To confiscate the word humanity, to invoke and monopolise such a term probably has certain incalculable effects, such as denying the enemy the quality of being human and declaring him to be an outlaw of humanity; and a war can thereby be driven to the most extreme inhumanity.[22]

Schmitt was a romantic, and had a detectable nostalgia for a time when enemies were treated with honour. His perception, however, was correct. In Kosovo, NATO worked with the motley KLA, which was itself acting against a sovereign state and except when it suited the 'Contact Group' for it not to do so, against the expressed wishes also of the Western powers.[23] The organization acknowledged that like the Western air forces over Iraq, it was using munitions of depleted uranium whose residue of uranium oxide would have adverse and lasting effects on health.[24] It fought a war to stop ethnic cleansing, and intensified it.[25]

For the application of such means, a new and essentially pacificist vocabulary has been invented. War is condemned but executions, sanctions, punitive expeditions, pacifications, protection of treaties, international police, and measures to assure peace remain. The adversary is thus no longer called an enemy but a disturber of peace and is thereby designated to be an outlaw of humanity.[26]

[20] The phrase is Lee's, 'Veteran Asian Leader Scorns US policy'. Others believe that China fears the precedent set by NATO's intervention in Yugoslavia in 1999, 'Anti-NATO Stance Draws Russia and China Together', *Financial Times*, 10 June 1999.
[21] 'Diplomat at War', *Financial Times*, 15–16 May 1999; 'Blair Doctrine to Tackle Brutal Regimes', *Financial Times*, 23 April 1999.
[22] Carl Schmitt, *The Concept of the Political*, George Schwab (ed., trans.), with a foreword by Tracy B. Strong, reprint, 1932 (Chicago, IL: University of Chicago Press, 1996), p. 54. The limiting case, Schmitt notes, is the war fought to end all wars, which 'degrades the enemy into moral and other categories and is forced to make of him a monster that must not only be defeated but also utterly destroyed. In other words, he is an enemy who no longer must be compelled to retreat into his borders only', p. 36.
[23] Chris Hedges, 'Kosovo's Next Masters?', *Foreign Affairs*, 78:3 (1999), pp. 24–42.
[24] 'Nothing to Worry About, Says NATO', *The Independent*, 15 May 1999.
[25] First estimates are that perhaps 2,000–3,000 people had died in Kosovo before the war began; by its end, perhaps 6,000 Serb soldiers, 2,000 Serb civilians and 100,000 Kosovars might have done so, 'Messy War, Messy Peace', *The Economist*, 12 June 1999, pp. 17–18.
[26] Schmitt, *The Concept of the Political*, p. 79.

This is not to suggest that those against whom NATO's force was deployed over Serbia and Kosovo were themselves innocent of what Schmitt predicted would be described as crimes against humanity. To NATO and many liberals, this was why the interventions were thought to be just. Nor is it to suggest that there was an equivalence of guilt. These are interesting and important issues, and in other contexts crucial. (NATO may however have compromised any subsequent justice in its advance publicity of the evidence against alleged 'war criminals'.) It is simply to say that the conflict between the NATO powers and the Federal Republic of Yugoslavia was political, and that it was political because it was a conflict. The point, as Schmitt put it, is not moral, but existential. There will be many motives for going to war, many reasons given for doing so, and many views on how acceptable these are. (For Schmitt himself, the one acceptable reason was if the enemy threatened 'one's own way of life'.)[27] The fact is that war is the extreme instance of confrontation between friend and enemy, and that it is confrontation, whatever its motive, that is politics. To describe a confrontation of this kind, as those in the alliance have, as principled or 'humanitarian', is merely to describe one or other of the reasons for it. It is not to describe the fact of confrontation itself, which is a fact of power. Against the Federal Republic of Yugoslavia in 1999, the power of NATO was used to enforce a conception of justice (and European interests) against existing international law.[28]

The international economy

Liberals, Schmitt predicted, will avoid talk of power. They will move instead 'between ethics and economics'. 'From this polarity they attempt to annihilate the political as a domain of conquering power and repression ... The state turns into society: on the ethical-intellectual side into an ideological humanitarian conception of humanity, and on the other into an economic-technical system of production and traffic'.[29] He was as correct on the second count as on the first. The advocates of the new international economy have argued that in the aftermath of fixed exchange rates and capital controls, inflation, fiscal laxity, protection and public monopolies are against the interests of all except those who corruptly profit from the 'rents' that such practices allow them to extract. It is simply what John Williamson has called 'common sense' to accept that in a world of deregulated exchange rates and the absence of controls on the movement of capital, financial stabilization and economic liberalization are essential to sustain a sound currency, international banking, a beneficial balance of internal and international trade, and the foreign investment that is essential to growth.[30] This 'Washington consensus', as Williamson called it, has been enforced by the IMF and the World Bank. The two institutions have made it effectively impossible for weaker states to survive unless they observe the

---

[27] Ibid., p. 49.
[28] 'Veteran Asian Leader Scorns US Policy'. Michael J. Glennon, 'The New Interventionism', *Foreign Affairs*, 78:3 (1999), pp. 2–7, is one who accepts that it was proper so to use it.
[29] Schmitt, *The Concept of the Political*, pp. 70, 72.
[30] John Williamson, 'Democracy and the "Washington Consensus"', *World Development*, 21 (1993), pp. 1329–36.

commonsensical conditions that the institutions put upon their lending. More recently, the WTO has made it difficult for states not to lose if they refuse to accept the organization's rules on international trade. The assumption is that the particular constellation of practices that has served the United States so well is a necessary condition of adapting to and succeeding in the new international economy. Countries that are not committed to eliminating subsidies for state-owned enterprises, privatizing what they can, balancing their budgets, lowering their tariffs, regulating their banks and removing restrictions on foreign investment; countries that do not, like the United States itself, provide an educational network that produces large numbers of competent engineers, a financial system that provides venture capital to unproven technologies, generous incentives for managers, and a flexible labour market, will not succeed.

The economic prescriptions are debatable. The east Asian economies, whose growth has (except, so far, in Indonesia) survived the recession into which Japan fell in the early 1990s and the financial crisis that affected several economies in the region later in the decade, have famously done things differently. (The World Bank was in the early 1990s nevertheless reluctant to acknowledge the fact.)[31] So also have several of the more successful economies in Europe, in which in contrast to the United States, the emphasis has been on incremental improvements in the quality of production, strong employers' associations, and different patterns of financing from those in either the United States or east Asia. But not only do the American-directed international institutions insist, in so far as they are able, on the American economic model. They also advocate what they take to be its political corollary, democracy in the American manner. The IMF and the World Bank and most of the regional development banks (with the exception of the European Bank for Reconstruction and Development that was set up to finance post-Communist Europe) have by their charters been prevented from insisting on explicitly political conditions of financial support. As Schmitt would have expected, they express their preferences in legal and administrative terms.[32] But the irresistible implication has been that transparency, accountability, and the establishment and observance of a body of adequate civil law are themselves a function of a democratic politics, and unlikely to be realised under other kinds of regime. It has indeed become conventional in the post-Cold War years to presume that there is what Max Weber would have called an 'elective affinity' between economic liberalization and liberal democracy.

The evidence for the connection is at best ambiguous. Singapore, for example, has an impeccably well-organised, prosperous and resilient economy that in virtue of its size has had no option but to accept the new rules of international finance and trade. Yet the People's Action Party government retains, in its Port Authority, one of the most successful public enterprises in Asia, attempts to restrict the distribution of critical publications, maintains the highest rate of judicial killing in the world, and

---

[31] Robert Wade, 'Japan, the World Bank, and the Art of Paradigm Maintenance: The East Asian Miracle in Political Perspective', *New Left Review*, 217 (1996), pp. 3–36.

[32] World Bank, *Governance and Development* (Washington, DC: World Bank, 1992). In a lecture in Cambridge in 1999, the President of the World Bank took pleasure in his account of how he had managed to persuade his board that corruption was a social rather than political problem, a problem, accordingly, that the Bank could address.

takes effective measures to prevent political opposition.[33] (Singapore casts doubt also, for the moment, on the claim that whatever its political arrangements and cultural dispositions, no society can with closed doors stop what comes in through Windows. It is the first state to make it possible for all its citizens to be on-line, yet attempts to restrict their access. It fears that the Internet will make a transparent, market-based, decentralized and democratic society impossible to resist.)[34] More consequentially, China, for which democracy in anything like the Western manner is still a question, is proceeding with the liberalization of finance, investment and trade.

Liberals might reply that regimes of this kind cannot last. Yet the politics that the liberals favour are themselves unstable. The tacit preference, as the Brazilian Roberto Mangabeira Unger puts it, 'is relative democracy: democracy but not too much'. Too little can concentrate too much power in the state, too much can encourage too much resistance to it. In the one, collusion between finance and business can lead to an unresponsive government. In the other, as in the election of Hugo Chávez to the presidency of Venezuela in December 1998, anger at the inequalities that liberalization brings can revive a taste for popular dictators. Each can undermine the liberal project. The preference is accordingly for constitutional rules and electoral arrangements that keep power in the hands of an internationally controllable and nationally controlling political class, a civil society that presents no threat to that class, 'and media systems that help maintain the people at low levels of political engagement'. Only in a society like Cuba, Unger mischievously but not implausibly observes (or, one might add, like Singapore), in which inequalities have been reduced under a very different kind of political dispensation, might the instability be avoided.[35]

The new international economy, unlike that which existed from the mid 1940s to the early 1970s, is not a politically deliberate creation. It emerged by default. Both directly, however, and by extending the agenda for the Bretton Woods institutions, the United States took advantage of it, and took what control it could. The irony, in the light of the conditions that the IMF and the World Bank imposed on their borrowers, was that Washington proceeded itself to borrow by selling Treasury Bonds to countries in western Europe and east Asia that had no wish to find themselves having to finance the world. John Ruggie has remarked that 'it was the fact of an *American* hegemony that was decisive after World War II, not merely American *hegemony*'.[36] In the absence of any effective competitor, this has been even more true since the 1980s.

---

[33] Christopher Tremewan, *The Political Economy of Social Control in Singapore* (London: Macmillan, 1994); Garry Rodan, 'Elections without representation: the Singapore experience under the PAP', in Robert H. Taylor (ed.), *The Politics of Elections in Southeast Asia* (Cambridge: Woodrow Wilson Center Press and Cambridge University Press, 1996), pp. 61–89.

[34] This is the argument of Thomas L. Friedman, *The Lexus and the Olive Tree* (New York: Farrar, Strauss and Giroux, 1999). The image of closed doors and open windows is Barry Eichengreen's.

[35] Roberto Mangabeira Unger, *Democracy Realised: The Progressive Alternative* (London: Verso, 1998), pp. 68–9, 120. Geoffrey Hawthorn, 'Civil society, development and politics in the South' in Sudipta Kaviraj and Sunil Khilnani (eds.), *Civil Society: History and Possibilities* (Cambridge: Cambridge University Press, forthcoming).

[36] John Ruggie, 'Multilateralism: The Anatomy of an Institution', in John Ruggie (ed.), *Multilateralism Matters: The Theory and Praxis of an Institutional Form* (New York: Columbia University Press, 1993), p. 31.

The persistence of politics

The most optimistic liberals hoped that the post-Cold War world would be one in which a balance between mutually threatening states would be replaced by the pursuit of justice under a single liberal power. War would be superseded by the peaceful establishment of human rights under democratic regimes that would acknowledge the benefits of a liberal international economy. The problems that had afflicted Great Power relations in the previous half-century, not least those that arose in the conflict between order and justice, would have been solved. Now that there were no longer any alternatives to contest, all that remained would be to construct the cosmopolitan democracy that a perpetual peace between consensual republics would allow. In the extravagant imagination of Alexandre Kojève, who began his career as an Hegelian philosopher, ended it as an enthusiastic servant of the embryo of union in western Europe, and inspired Francis Fukuyama, religion would be dead, nature mastered, and the possible contents of life clear for all to see. There would be nothing left to oppose, nothing left to think. Politics would be at an end, and administration would rule.[37]

In almost every respect, these expectations have been mistaken. The military power of the United States is supreme. Its conventional forces are superior to those of any other state, and although others may have nuclear weapons, none has a comparable capacity to deliver them, and none would benefit from doing so against the United States itself. The reach of American conventional forces, however, is not unlimited. It is also far from clear that public opinion in the United States would continue to countenance forays on the ground or even by air into disputes that risk lives and do not affect what is perceived as the security of the United States itself. Both facts were evident in NATO's intervention in Kosovo in 1999. It has accordingly become even more important to the United States that the membership of the organization be enlarged. In this way, other states can be asked to 'share the burden' of military action at the edges of western Europe and beyond that the United States would like to see taken but cannot be sure of being able to commit itself to alone. Meanwhile, NATO's action against Serbia was convenient to those politicians, like the German foreign foreign minister, Joschka Fischer, who see 'the decisive task of our age' in Europe to be that of turning the Union into a state.[38] But the failure of the United States' request that its allies join it in action against Iraq in 1997–98 has shown that the commitment of the existing members of NATO to action outside Europe is unreliable. Despite the initiative of a Partnership for Peace in 1993 and its more recent insistence on enlarging NATO itself, it seems unlikely that the United States will succeed in creating an alliance that is sufficiently wide and reliable to enable it to do what it wants to do. For this reason, and because the United States will want to offend China less than it wants to offend Russia, it also seems unlikely that it will succeed in further strengthening its Mutual Security Treaty with Japan and extending that agreement to other states in east Asia.

---

[37] Alexandre Kojève, *Introduction to the Reading of Hegel* (Ithaca, NY: Cornell University Press, 1980), pp. 159–61; Robert Pippin, 'Being, Time and Politics: The Strauss-Kojève Debate', in *Idealism as Modernism: Hegelian Variations* (Cambridge: Cambridge University Press, 1997), pp. 233–61; Perry Anderson, 'The Ends of History', in *A Zone of Engagement* (London: Verso, 1992), p. 324.

[38] Quoted by Andrew Gimson, 'The Green Man's Burden', *The Spectator*, 19 June 1999, p. 14.

These prospects are unsatisfactory both for those who see the United States as it sees itself, as the guarantor of peace and justice in the post-Cold War world, and for those who are alarmed by this ambition. To the first, it fails to guarantee defence against a conceivably resurgent Russia, an aggressive China, and other dangers that are as yet unseen. To the second, the weakness of such alliances frees the United States to continue to act capriciously in nominally liberal adventures which on their own terms fail and in their consequences, as in Iraq and Kosovo, not only extend suffering rather than contain it but also, in overriding international law, increase the possibility of what an understandably cross Secretary-General of the United Nations described in May 1999 as 'anarchy' in the world.[39] For true liberals, the only solution, towards which there have been no moves in the 1990s, would be for the charter of the United Nations itself to be revised to give a lower priority to the sovereignty of states, for this, if it were to be agreed, would need to be accepted when the occasion arose by the permanent members of the Security Council, for the change to be acknowledged in international law.[40] For others, meanwhile, who fear the absence of an effective balance of power, even the absence of effective power altogether, the best hope is that the present partially unipolar world becomes steadily more multipolar.

This is not to suggest that the least bad future will be to return to the past. During the Cold War, the balance of power in the world was between states with quite different conceptions of economic and political order that directly threatened each other with force. Conceptions of politics and the histories and 'cultures' that might be said to ground these conceptions do continue to be different. That is why Samuel Huntington warned that the post-Cold War world would be one in which a conflict of cultures would replace a conflict of ideologies.[41] But Huntington arguably exaggerated the differences he saw. He also overlooked the contrary effects of the new international economy. Russia is dependent on support from the IMF and in the foreseeable future will continue to be so. China, although naturally exploiting the United States' wish to maintain good relations in order to extract all the concessions it can, is plainly intent on joining the WTO. Even in the larger states in Latin America, Africa and Asia, in Brazil, for instance, or in India, as well as in China, it has been less conceivable in the 1990s than it was in the 1970s that those who believe themselves to be at an irremediable disadvantage in this economy would unite to press for a reform of the international financial institutions in order to protect themselves against the potentially damaging power of the markets in currency, goods and services.

Only a few radical intellectuals, as much at variance with the balance of opinion in the political class in their own countries as with opinion in the North, have even suggested that they should press for such reforms.[42] This is not to say that were reforms to be implemented, the economies of such countries would not benefit,

---

[39] 'Annan Urges Role for UN', *Financial Times*, 20 May 1999.
[40] It is argued that 'sovereignty' is not sensibly seen as an all or nothing affair (Christopher W. Morris, *An Essay on the Modern State* (Cambridge: Cambridge University Press, 1998), pp. 172–227). But whatever the arguments for qualifying it, it allows itself, once these arguments are accepted, to be overridden.
[41] Samuel P. Huntington, *The Clash of Civilizations and the Remaking of World Order* (New York: Simon and Schuster, 1996).
[42] For instance Unger, *Democracy Realized*, pp. 84–6.

though to have the desired effect, the reforms would in turn require changes in the distribution of material advantage within the countries in question that are, in many cases, politically almost equally difficult to imagine. (One should nevertheless note that since the 1980s, the World Bank, appreciating that its original commitment as a bank for 'reconstruction and development' to directly productive investments was increasingly being met by private funds, has for reasons of principle and its own institutional survival concentrated on lending for social amelioration, including the alleviation of poverty.) To suggest that radical reform of the rules of the international economy is now unlikely is rather to say that the short- and medium-term advantages of accepting this economy as it is, together with the power of the United States, the IMF, the WTO, private banks, the markets in currencies, goods and services, and as Friedman and others argue, the new information technology, make it next to impossible to imagine sustained resistance. Only at the margins, in the regulation, for instance, of interbank lending and hedge funds and other sources of potentially destabilizing short-term finance, are South and North likely to agree. Only on this matter, because the South does not want to suffer the effects of forced sudden devaluations, and because the North does not want to have to finance their consequences, is there likely to be some action. In a more multipolar world, however, one might expect that the weaker states would, in negotiations on economic matters, suffer less direct and insistent political interference from the stronger.

In one respect, therefore, Fukuyama was right. In matters of political economy, there are fewer alternatives than there were. Where he and others were mistaken in the euphoria that followed the turn in China after 1976 and the sudden collapse of the Soviet Union and its satellites in 1991 was in supposing that the new international economy would be one in which, within states, there would necessarily be only one kind of politics. A liberal economy does not require a fully liberal democracy, and the liberal democracies that do exist are compromises of a partial, possibly unstable, kind that knowingly stop some way short of affording citizens that 'recognition' which, drawing on Kojève, Fukuyama believed they need and can now receive. But Fukuyama and those who have argued to a similar conclusion have at least seen that politics would continue. The mistake of the more ambitiously cosmopolitan liberals has been to suppose that the new world could be one in which politics would no longer be necessary. Practically, these people's picture appears to be of a gradually extending democracy which would be facilitated by an extension of forums to the world itself, propelled by ever expanding layers of 'civil society'. Theoretically, their picture is guided by the conviction that when freely considered, perhaps in the forums themselves, perhaps in 'civil society', conceptions of the ends of life beyond prosperity converge and eventually coincide. It is a picture of an eventually universal human association whose members come to see that the pursuit of power, even in the pursuit of prosperity, is a thing of the past.[43]

---

[43] There is an excellent account of the senses that have been given to 'civil society' and the incoherent expectations that its advocates have had of it in Lawrence Hamilton, 'Deconstructing "Civil Society": Institutions, Practices, Roles', unpublished Paper (Cambridge, 1999).

The paradox of liberal power

If this is a mistake, which it surely is, the question for a liberal international politics at the end of the century is what kind of mistake it is. The world at the end of the century is one in which nearly three-quarters of states (the most obvious exceptions are Colombia in Latin America and many still in sub-Saharan Africa) retain their domestic authority but in which none is able to achieve what it wants from others by unilateral action; on most matters, even the presently most powerful of all has to seek multilateral support. There are nation-states, in short, and international 'regimes'. Some scholars regard these regimes merely as vehicles in which governments pursue interests that they form elsewhere; some as arenas in which governments seek to derive advantage over others; some as communities in which governments act in concert for reasons that are themselves communal.[44] In part, the arguments are empirical. In NATO's military engagement against the Federal Republic of Yugoslavia in 1999, the United States was arguably acting in the first manner; in the dispute in the WTO in 1999 over Europe's policy on the importation of bananas, it was acting in the second; in responding through the United Nations to Iraq's invasion of Kuwait in 1991, it was acting in the third; in the IMF, it acts in the first two and can convince itself that it is acting also in the third. The arguments, empirical and practical, will continue. In part, however, they are also conceptual. How should one now think of power, and of how is it used?

Realists will accept that the United States must do what, to remain a state in a world of states, any state must do, which is to maintain its power and authority over its own citizens and in so far as it can, over other states also. To do this, it has at least to imagine an opponent, what Schmitt thought of as an 'enemy'. Not to have one, as Schmitt saw, is to cease to be political. And to cease to be political is to cease to act as a state.[45] The difficulty now is that there are few obvious antagonists. The particular difficulty now for the United States (but not for the first time in the twentieth century) is that in the absence of such antagonists, Washington has either to invent them in talk of 'threats to its security' or to insist on its liberal rectitude. Under a weakening liberal president, who like other liberal presidents before him was inexperienced in world affairs, the temptation has proved irresistible. In acting in this way, however, the United States also demonstrates its own weakness, to overcome which it is prompted to act in the same way again, and in so doing, traps itself.

Realists will say that this would be so even if the liberal project were to succeed in the way that the most optimistic cosmopolitans hope. 'Men work nothing well', Machiavelli remarked, 'if not through the necessity' of law and the force of arms;

---

[44] There is a good review of these positions, which the authors describe as liberal, realist and cognitivist, in Andreas Hasenclever, Peter Mayer and Volker Rittberger, *Theories of International Regimes* (Cambridge: Cambridge University Press, 1997). In their case for a new 'structural liberalism' in 'The Nature and Sources of Liberal International Order', Deudney and Ikenberry emphasise the second, adding that the advantages can be absolute as well as relative, and the third.

[45] 'An enemy exists only when, at least potentially, one fighting collectivity of people confronts a similar collectivity. The enemy is solely the public enemy, because everything that has a relationship to such a collectivity of men, particularly to a whole nation, becomes public by virtue of such a relationship', Schmitt, *The Concept of the Political*, p. 28.

'where choice abounds', 'everything fills up with confusion and disorder'.[46] Liberals might reply that were there to be but one law in the world, freely arrived at, and one force to uphold this law, there would be no enemy, and politics in Schmitt's sense would end. The realists will retort that if Machiavelli was right, this would have to be a world in which the need for choice would have disappeared or in which, if it had not, new choices were forbidden. In the meantime, politics continues. The paradox of a liberal hegemony in the post-Cold War world is that it is weak because it cannot convincingly be demonstrated, and in so far as it can be, threatens to undermine the principles on which it is. In the 1920s, Schmitt rightly insisted that the authority of the *Rechtstaat* lies in its opposition to the *Machtstaat*. If a *Rechtstaat* itself becomes a *Machtstaat*, it risks losing that authority. (In the early 1930s, Schmitt himself forgot the point and advocated what he called a 'qualitatively' total state. In his admiration for Hobbes' point of departure, he forgot Hobbes' insistence on the right to defend oneself against the state when it demands one's life).[47] For a world in which liberals dominate, the implication is plain. Nietzsche remarked that if men do not have external enemies, they become enemies to themselves.[48] It is the fate of liberal powers also to become enemies to themselves when they do.

---

[46] Niccolò Machiavelli, Sergio Bertelli (ed.), *Il Principe e Discorsi Sopra la Prima Deca di Tito Livio*, vol. 1 (Milan: Feltrinelli, 1961), p. 136, quoted by Sebastian de Grazia, *Machiavelli in Hell* (Brighton: Harvester Wheatsheaf, 1989), p. 198.

[47] John P. McCormick, *Carl Schmitt's Critique of Liberalism: Against Politics as Technology* (Cambridge: Cambridge University Press, 1997), pp. 249–89. In 1936, Schmitt ended his association with the National Socialist government. By 1944, he appeared to have accepted what in the 1930s he had denied; McCormick, pp. 300–1.

[48] Friedrich Nietzsche, Keith Ansell-Pearson (ed.), Carol Diethe (trans.), *On the Genealogy of Morality*, reprint, 1887 (Cambridge: Cambridge University Press, 1994), pp. 61–2.

Clausewitz rules, OK? The future is the past—with GPS

COLIN GRAY

The confessions of a neoclassical realist

In 1972, Hedley Bull wrote that 'the sources of facile optimism and narrow moralism never dry up, and the lessons of the "realists" have to be learnt afresh by every new generation.'[1] He proceeded to claim, with undue emphasis, that 'in terms of the academic study of international relations, the stream of thinking and writing that began with Niebuhr and Carr has long run its course.' The scholarly problems with classical realist theory are indeed severe.[2] However, it would be a most grievous error to consign such theory to the bin marked 'yesterday's solutions for yesterday's problems.' If the academic study of international relations can find little save period-piece interest in the ideas of the classical realists, that is more a comment upon the competence of scholarship today than upon any change in world conditions.

There is much well worth criticizing in the classically realist theory of international relations and what was once eponymously called statecraft.[3] Any

---

[1] Hedley Bull, 'The Theory of International Politics, 1919–1969,' in Brian Porter (ed.), *The Aberystwyth Papers: International Politics, 1919–1969* (London, 1972), p. 39.

[2] The scholarly literature on 'realism', now generally termed 'classical realism'—with its modern devotees, such as this author, called neoclassical realists—'neorealism,' 'structural realism' (and one day soon, perhaps, neoclassical poststructural realism), is as large as it is largely aridly academic in a pejorative sense. For those inclined to intellectual masochism, I can recommend Kenneth W. Thompson, *Masters of International Thought: Major Twentieth-Century Theorists and the World Crisis* (Baton Rouge, LA, 1980); Robert O. Keohane (ed.), *Neorealism and Its Critics* (New York, 1986); Barry Buzan, Charles Jones, and Richard Little, *The Logic of Anarchy: Neorealism to Structural Realism* (New York, 1993); Benjamin Frankel (ed.), 'Roots of Realism', *Security Studies*, 5, special issue (1995); idem (ed.), 'Realism: Restatements and Renewal', *Security Studies*, 5, special issue (1996); Scott Burchill, 'Realism and Neo-Realism', in Burchill and Andrew Linklater (eds.), *Theories of International Relations* (London, 1996), pp. 67–92; and Stefano Guzzini, *Realism in International Relations and International Political Economy* (London, 1998). These few references are merely the tip of a mighty iceberg of professional activity. For an 'approach' to international relations long condemned by the cognoscenti as simplistic and theoretically severely challenged, 'realism' seems able to attract an endless succession of firing squads. Contemporary theorists of international relations are still looking for that stake to the heart that definitively would dispatch 'realism'.

[3] You know you are in trouble as a scholar when an issue as apparently mundane as the day-by-day working title of your field is widely contested. Each and every title to my field, and subfield, carries some unhelpful baggage. I propose to handle this fact by ignoring it. The text refers to international relations, international politics, international studies, and world politics, without fear, special favour, or subtextual meaning. With respect to my particular corner of the broad field just indicated, I am more particular. Reference in my text to 'strategic' studies, theory, or history, indicates matter connected quite directly to the threat or use of *force*. From time to time, to indicate my liberality of spirit and genuinely holistic perspective upon the subjects that concern me, I refer to 'security' studies. For the record, however, I would like to register a vote for the position that the concept of 'security' studies is unmanageably inclusive. To study 'security' would require the study of everything, a fact which would translate as a thoroughly unfocused study of nothing in particular.

scholar worthy of his or her BISA membership could organize and deliver a sparkling module on the theme of 'Classical Realism: Sins of Omission, Errors of Commission, and Flagrant Ambiguities.'[4] Many of us have bored first-year tutorials with our skilful skewering of balance-of-power theory, the concept of power, and—of course—the national interest. The problem is that with our intellectual rigour all too often we correct the grammar but lose the plot. I will argue that flawed though the principal texts of classical realism may be, when compared with more contemporary would-be master/mistress-works, they have an overriding virtue. To risk the vernacular, they got the big things right enough.

Students reared on the flawed classics written by Thucydides, Sun Tzu, Kautilya, Machiavelli, Clausewitz, Carr, Niebuhr, Morgenthau, Aron, and Kissinger might well be misled on many secondary matters.[5] Authors cannot help but be limited, as well as inspired, by their personal circumstances of time, place, and therefore culture. But, did these paladins of theory capture the core of their subject? Thucydides, for example, tells us in an invented (though probably fairly accurate)[6] discourse that 'fear, honour, and interest' comprise three of the strongest motives for holding on to empire whilst under powerful pressure.[7] It is not at all obvious that eighty years of careful scholarship in the twentieth century, from the immediate aftermath of the First World War to the present day, have produced guidance on the causes of war noticeably superior to that offered by Thucydides. Indeed, recent scholarship by Emanuel Adler in the august pages of the *Review of International Studies* informs us that the key to building the 'conditions of peace' is the construction of security communities.[8] On closer inspection, though, this apparently powerful idea translates rapidly into an unhelpful academic tautology. What Adler has achieved is simply an elegant restatement of the problem. To be told that the conditions for peace can be built via the construction of security communities—because people within such

[4] Such scholars might just notice that some of the more informative critiques of classical realist theory have been written by classical realists themselves. For example, it would be difficult to improve on Ernst Haas, 'The Balance of Power: Prescription, Concept or Propaganda?,' *World Politics*, 5 (1953), pp. 442–77, or Arnold Wolfers, *Discord and Collaboration: Essays on International Politics* (Baltimore, 1962), ch. 10, 'National Security as an Ambiguous Symbol'.

[5] Robert B. Strassler (ed.), *The Landmark Thucydides: A Comprehensive Guide to 'The Peloponnesian War'*, rev. edn. of Richard Crawley (trans.) (New York, 1996); Sun Tzu, *The Art of War*, trans. Ralph D. Sawyer (Boulder, CO, 1994); Kautilya, *The Arthashastra*, trans. L. N. Rangarajan (New Delhi, 1992); Niccolo Machiavelli, *The Art of War*, rev. edn. of Ellis Farneworth (trans.) (Indianapolis, 1965); idem, *Discourses on Livy*, trans. Julia Conaway Bondanella and Peter Bondanella (Oxford, 1997); idem, *The Prince*, trans. Peter Bondanella and Mark Musa (Oxford, 1998); Carl von Clausewitz, *On War*, trans. Michael Howard and Peter Paret (Princeton, NJ, 1976); E. H. Carr, *The Twenty Years' Crisis, 1914–1939* (New York, 1964); idem, *International Relations Between the Two World Wars, 1919–1939* (New York, 1966); Reinhold Niebuhr, *Moral Man and Immoral Society: A Study in Ethics and Politics* (New York, 1932); idem, *The Children of Light and the Children of Darkness: A Vindication of Democracy and a Critique of Its Traditional Defense* (New York, 1944); Hans J. Morgenthau, *In Defense of the National Interest* (New York, 1951); idem, *Politics Among Nations: The Struggle for Power and Peace*, 6th edn. revised by Kenneth W. Thompson (New York, 1985); Raymond Aron, *Peace and War: A Theory of International Relations*, trans. Richard Howard and Annette Baker Fox (Garden City, NY, 1966); Henry Kissinger, *A World Restored: Metternich, Castlereagh and the Problems of Peace, 1818–22* (Boston, 1957); idem, *Diplomacy* (New York, 1994).

[6] See Peter R. Pouncey, *The Necessities of War: A Study of Thucydides' Pessimism* (New York, 1980), ch. 4, and especially Simon Hornblower, *Thucydides* (Baltimore, 1987), ch. 3. Richard Ned Lebow and Barry S. Strauss (eds.), *Hegemonic Rivalry: From Thucydides to the Nuclear Age* (Boulder, CO: 1991), is bold and interesting.

[7] Strassler, *Landmark Thucydides*, p. 43.

[8] Emanuel Adler, 'Condition(s) of Peace,' *Review of International Studies*, 24 (1998), pp. 165–91.

communities do not fight each other (though they might fight people in other such communities!)—is inferior in practical merit to historian Jeremy Black's conclusion that more bellicose societies are more apt to go to war than are less bellicose societies.[9]

It is perhaps a cultural, or psychological, problem for some contemporary scholars that our forebears in theory did such a good job. The problem appears more acute in academic international relations than it does in strategic studies. For example, most modern theorists and practitioners of strategy have little difficulty both in proclaiming the general superiority of Clausewitz over all pretenders to the throne of Top Strategic Thinker and then in taking selectively what they find of most value to them from his often opaque writings.[10] A few contemporary strategic commentators have proclaimed the death of Clausewitz as a theorist with authority relevant for today, but that remains very much a minority position.[11]

The historical focus of this essay is the decade of the 1990s, but lurking not far behind discussion of those years is argument on the essentially contestable question of progress in human affairs. As a neoclassical realist I insist that the game of polities (or security communities) does not change from age to age, let alone from decade to decade. I will stop just short of claiming that the game cannot change, but only by way of a token nod in the direction of never saying never. Paradoxically, perhaps, this stance is not a conservative one. It is alert to the facts of cumulative, sometimes apparently non-linear, change in the character of international relations, including international strategic relations. It denies only the likelihood of change in the nature of those relations. I agree with Ken Booth's helpful light adaptation of the familiar definition of politics by Harold Lasswell: world politics is about '"who gets what, when, [and] how" across the globe'.[12] It was always thus and there is no pressing reason to anticipate a transformation anytime soon.

Agreement with Lasswell-Booth, however, still leaves much terrain for scholarly combat. The formula lends itself to emancipationist, among other, ethically rooted theory, as some scholars endorse and seek to advance particular notions of progress. In addition, though, Lasswell-Booth is compatible with a thoroughly strategic view of history (past, present, and future); that is to say a view that recognizes the importance of the threat and use of force. Such a view, held by this author, agrees with the notably postmodern strategic commentator-theorist, Ralph Peters, when he argues that our humanity is more our problem than our likely salvation. Time and again we humans demonstrate our willingness to do quite literally *anything*. In Peters' words:

---

[9] Jeremy Black, *Why Wars Happen* (London, 1998).

[10] I explain the reasons for the persisting clear superiority of Clausewitz in my *Modern Strategy* (Oxford, 1999), chs. 3–4.

[11] Clausewitz is roughly handled in John Keegan, 'Peace by Other Means?', *Times Literary Supplement*, 11 December 1992, pp. 3–4; idem, *A History of Warfare* (London, 1998); Martin van Creveld, *The Transformation of War* (New York, 1991); idem, 'What is Wrong with Clausewitz?', in Gert de Nooy (ed.), *The Clausewitzian Dictum and the Future of Western Military Strategy* (The Hague, 1997), pp. 7–23. Christopher Bassford has performed nobly as the most recent counsel for the defence. See his articles, 'John Keegan and the Grand Tradition of Trashing Clausewitz: a Polemic,' *War in History*, 1 (1996), pp. 319–36, and 'Landmarks in Defense Literature: "On War", by Carl von Clausewitz', *Defense Analysis*, 12 (1996), pp. 267–71.

[12] Ken Booth, 'Dare not to Know: International Relations Theory versus the Future', in Booth and Steve Smith (eds.), *International Relations Theory Today* (Cambridge, 1995), p. 329.

Technologies come and go, but the primitive endures. The last decade of this millennium has seen genocide, ethnic cleansing, the bloody rending of states, growing religious persecution, the ascendancy of international crime, an unprecedented distribution of weaponry, and the persistence of the warrior—the man of raw and selfish violence—as a human archetype.[13]

Even more chilling than Peters' writings is the conclusion drawn by Joanna Bourke in her recent study of 'face-to-face killing in twentieth-century warfare'. Although Peters argues that 'men like to kill,' he somewhat softens the message by speculating that the 'minority of human beings—mostly male—who enjoy killing ... may be small'.[14] Bourke, however, concludes that 'as this book has attempted to emphasize, warfare was as much about the business of sacrificing others as it was about *being* sacrificed. For many men and women, this is what made it "a lovely war"'.[15]

It is my thesis that in order to understand the 1990s, or the 2090s, study the 1890s, 1790s, and so forth. The future is the past in the ways that matter most. 'Statecraft' and strategy are made of the same ingredients, and work (or fail to work well) for the same reasons, in all periods and among all participants.[16] The most key among the reasons why this should be so is, of course, the common thread of the human factor.

The well of error never runs dry

The industry of academe, indeed the sheer industry of academics, is a potent source of error. Given that the canon (or cannon) lore of international relations already exists in a few 'sacred books,'[17] that careers cannot be advanced simply by intoning that unholy liturgy, and that mere change ever tempts interpretation as transformation, it is not surprising that so much of the new writing in our field is either trivial, or wrong, or both.

Courting the risk, perhaps glorying in the prospect, of being charged for possession of one of Ken Booth's 'nineteenth-century minds at the end of the twentieth-century',[18] I will argue that the idea of realism—in its sensible classical form, not the reductionist nonsense of neorealism[19]—could have equipped scholars to cope well with the 1990s. To read Thucydides, Clausewitz, Aron, and Kissinger, for a terse short-list, allows inoculation by the enduring lore of world politics against misperception of the ephemeral as the lasting.

One function of superior theory is to provide the protection of superior explanatory power against the pretensions and ravages of inferior theory. International

---

[13] Ralph Peters, *Fighting for the Future: Will America Triumph?* (Mechanicsburg, PA: 1999), p. 171.

[14] Ibid., p. 189.

[15] Joanna Bourke, *An Intimate History of Killing: Face-to-Face Killing in Twentieth-Century Warfare* (London, 1999), p. 375. Original emphasis.

[16] An argument that I develop at length and probably in unduly excruciating detail in my *Modern Strategy*, ch. 1.

[17] Booth, 'Dare not to Know,' p. 350.

[18] Ibid., p. 343.

[19] The bible for which view remains, of course, Kenneth N. Waltz, *Theory of International Politics* (Reading, MA: 1979), a book which demonstrates that being elegantly parsimonious in theory building offers insufficient compensation for being wrong.

relations, security studies, and strategic studies, holistically regarded, inherently comprise a practical subject. The test for good theory in this subject could hardly be simpler: does the theory work to offer plausible explanation of, dare one say it, real-world events? Elegance in argument, altitude of moral purpose, weight of quantitative support—are all irrelevant if the ideas at issue are empirically challenged. In the wise words of Charles E. Callwell: 'Theory cannot be accepted as conclusive when practice points the other way.'[20] Faddish concepts have a way of concealing the persistence of old realities, especially when they are perpetrated in new textbooks written by major figures in contemporary academe. For example, the trendy concept of 'global governance' should carry the public warning to students that 'anyone who chooses to take this exciting new concept with more than a grain of salt risks permanent impairment of their understanding of international relations.' In his quaintly titled *Understanding International Relations*, Chris Brown informs his student readers that '[w]e may not have world government, but we do have global governance.'[21] I wonder how much comfort that optimistic claim could provide to Kosovars, Chechens, and Somalis, not to mention Hutus and Tutsis.

The difficulty is that our students are not to know, unless we tell them, that Carr, Morgenthau, and especially Aron, wrote better—yes, better—books than have the theorists of the 1990s. The texts of classical realism offer superior explanatory reach and grasp, because they are better grounded empirically. Similarly those students are not to know that (classical and neoclassical) realism is not simply one among a potentially infinite number of 'approaches' to international relations. It may be academically sound and ecumenical for teachers to treat all theories as if they were created equal, with each capable of delivering salvation. The fact is, however, that for a practical subject like international relations, poor—which is to say impractical—theories are at best an irrelevance, and at worst can help get people killed.

There is a voluntarism in recent writing about international relations that is as attractive as it is perilous. To quote Brown again, he advises that 'we need to pay serious attention to the implications of the view that knowledge is constructed, not found, that it rests on social foundations and not upon some bedrock of certainty.'[22] At one level, such advice is a sound invitation to exercise healthy scepticism.[23] At another level, though, Brown opens the floodgates to fallacy and mythmaking. There is an obvious and rather trivial sense in which knowledge has to be socially constructed. Knowledge is what we decide it is. However, unless one totally debases the meaning of 'knowledge,' it is not useful to propagate the silly idea that we can 'construct' knowledge at will. There is knowledge as 'truth', in the sense of valid most-case generalizations, which the practitioners of international relations ignore at their, and our, peril. For example, Clausewitz advises that in war political goals can only be achieved if they are effected instrumentally by the securing of suitably

---

[20] Charles E. Callwell, *Small Wars: A Tactical Textbook for Imperial Soldiers* (London, 1990), p. 270.
[21] Chris Brown, *Understanding International Relations* (London, 1997), p. 121.
[22] Ibid., p. 119.
[23] Bruce G. Blair offers a persuasive reason why such scepticism is desirable. Writing about my field of strategic analysis, Blair argues plausibly that '[a]s in any field that straddles science, policy, and politics, the temptation to overreach is unusually strong. High demand for unwaffled answers creates a market for study products that package immature theories as final, easily digestible truth'. *The Logic of Accidental Nuclear War* (Washington, DC: 1993), p. 288.

matching military objectives.[24] When policymakers elect to disdain that nugget of strategic 'knowledge' about means and ends, as did NATO for ten weeks from March to June in 1999, policy will not succeed and people will suffer gratuitously as a consequence.

Understanding of the nature of world politics and strategy is not, in a meaningful sense, socially constructed knowledge. That nature is what it is, and it is what it has been for millennia. Bold theorists, brave optimists, moral crusaders, as well as simply the simple, which is to say the ignorant, may find my claim quite shocking: theoretically primitive, morally irresponsible, and blind to the evidence of benign change, and so on and so forth. To be more specific, I believe that much of the misunderstanding of the meaning of the course of recent history and much of the faulty prediction stems from the popularity among scholars of some powerful myths and probable myths. A less polite way of making this point would be to claim that those scholars do not understand their subject as well as they should—certainly as well as they would had they read and inwardly digested Aron's *Peace and War* at an impressionable age.

For the same class of reason why today no murderous sociopath will sign-up for the label 'terrorist', so no scholar will choose to recognize himself or herself as a propagator of myths. Some reader resistance to what follows is therefore likely.

Old fallacies rarely die: myths, probable myths, and half-truths

This discussion explores and explains many of the errors and much of the imprudence in current scholarship on international relations with reference to popular myths, or probable myths, and half-truths. These fallacies cluster around the subject of whether history is essentially cyclical or is more arrow-like; around the reasons why the human condition might be improving; and around beliefs about military power.

The megamyth of benign historical transformation

It might be more accurate to refine this claim to apply to the megamyth of benign and irreversible historical transformation. Many scholars of international relations, in some cases probably subconsciously, underwrite the myth of inevitable and, taking a medium to long view (i.e. temporary setbacks are recognized), inexorable improvement in the human security condition. Truly this is the master myth that opens the door to a host of lesser myths which, in succession with fashion or ephemeral evidence, appear to support it.

It is as commonplace to mistake the plain evidence of change for progress in some normative sense, as it is to flatter oneself that history actually has turned at a 'turning point' in one's own lifetime. In 1994 I delivered an inaugural lecture which downplayed the significance of the very recent conclusion of the Cold War and

---

[24] Clausewitz, *On War*, pp. 81, 605–10.

advanced the unremarkable principle that bad times always return in world politics.[25] In point of fact, my lecture was grossly and unduly NATO-centric, because
very bad times indeed occurred in the 1990s for many peoples in the Balkans, the
former USSR, and Africa.

The core of this megamyth is the appealing notion that we can improve our
collective and individual security condition on a global basis.[26] This belief is fed by
what amounts to a disdain for historical experience, our understanding of which is
not all socially constructed at will (e.g., Nazi Germany did lose the Second World
War and the USSR did collapse). The problem is one of time-frame and, of course,
particular individual and societal circumstance. For many of us today, the future
looks even brighter and more prosperous than is our distinctly tolerable present.
However, we neoclassical realists contest neither the fact of good times for some, nor
of good times rolling for quite a while. The argument, rather, is that 'bad times
return'. The point has been made with exemplary clarity in a recent essay by Donald
Kagan.

If one lived, say, in 450 or even in 440 BC, one might very well have made what would have
been an intelligent prediction: that democracy was the road of the future. Then the Athenians
lost the Peloponnesian War, and democracy stopped. That was the end of democracy until
the American Revolution. It is worthwhile remembering, therefore, that *great historical
reversals can happen.*[27]

Not all scholars recognize that to observe the present is not necessarily to observe
the future. The future is made from the past, that is to say our present, but it is
unlikely to comprise simply 'today, only more so'. Such a view is what my late
colleague Herman Kahn used to deride as a 'surprise-free projection'. To explain,
the 1930s in Germany were, of course, 'made' in the 1920s, which in turn were
'made' by The Great War. With the benefits of hindsight-foresight we see the origins
of Nazi Germany in the (German) myth of an undefeated army in 1918 and in the
Weimar Republic, just as we see the several holocausts of 1945 rooted in the new
Germany of the 1930s. At the time, indeed at all times, however, the future that will
be made creatively from the ever-moving present is not quite so clear. Eliot A.
Cohen has a plausible grip on the matter when he argues that '[t]here is simply much
more contingency in international politics than we are willing to admit.'[28] Even if in
principle the future is predictable at some level of specificity useful for policy detail
today, we lack the tools—if you like, we lack the social science—to do the job.
Moreover, even if there is a futurologist of genius among BISA members, we have
no way of knowing who he or she may be. Also, one should not forget a caveat
about self-negating prophecies. 'Futures' that are widely and authoritatively
endorsed as probable, are massively at risk to negation by purposefully spoiling
action.

Although we neoclassical realists are apt to endorse Edward Gibbon's opinion
that 'history . . . is indeed little more than the register of the crimes, follies, and

---

[25] Colin S. Gray, *Villains, Victims and Sheriffs: Strategic Studies and Security for an Inter-War Period*
(Hull, 1996), esp. pp. 16–17.
[26] For example, see Andrew Butfoy, *Common Security and Strategic Reform: A Critical Analysis*
(London, 1997). This book is as well intentioned, as appealing, and as moderate and reasonable, as it
is hopelessly 'off piste' for the rougher realities of strategic history.
[27] Donald Kagan, 'History is Full of Surprises', *Survival*, 41 (1999), p. 142. Emphasis added.
[28] Eliot A. Cohen, 'The "Major" Consequences of War', *Survival*, 41 (1999), p. 145.

misfortunes of mankind,'[29] typically we are not pessimists, at least we are not near-term pessimists. Realists do not believe that Humankind in History is embarked on some grand voyage towards an ideal future condition of peace and harmony. We believe that the twentieth century demonstrates, yet again, the truth—yes, the truth, not socially constructed 'knowledge'—in our reading of the security story of past, present, and future. Indeed, we witnessed actual—*not socially constructed*—holocaust/ genocide; and as late as the 1980s we might have witnessed actual holocaust on a truly global scale. The danger of nuclear war was real, if incalculable. Following the demise of the evil, but happily sickly, empire of the Soviets, a necessarily temporary geopolitical condition of quasi-US hegemony has allowed the peril of global nuclear holocaust a rest (not definitive retirement—a topic to which this essay will return).[30] The holocausts of the 1990s have been less global and explosive than was the possible one which dominated our concerns in the 1980s, but they have been actual, rather than virtual. Also, the beastliness of this decade emphatically has been in-the-face personally primitive and postmodern. Chechnya, Bosnia, Rwanda, and Somalia comprised a ghastly combination of Homer and Tom Clancy.[31]

Our security story is not all grim, however. The twentieth century has been appalling, with crimes against humanity committed, book-end like, by the British Empire in Southern Africa and by Serbia in Kosovo, with much worse way-stations in between. Nonetheless, the strategic and general security history of this century might well have recorded events so unhappy that the actual history would appear benign. Specifically, whether or not it was a happily and repeatedly deeply contingent accident, it was a thrice-fold fact that the right side won each of the three great wars of the century. I claim that the human security condition was much improved, albeit only for a while—which is all that can be achieved—by the repeated defeat of Germany, and then by the defeat of the Soviet Union (for defeat it was). Realists aspire neither to improve humankind, nor to establish *for all time* a peace with security based upon the essentially contestable concept of justice. Realists know that a secure peace can only be established and maintained for now, and that despite our best educated, and certainly 'prudent' endeavours, still historical contingency is likely to ambush us in the future.[32] Such generic pessimism is fully consistent with optimism over our ability, as prudent players, to survive history's accidents well enough. If we could see off Imperial and Nazi Germany, and then the abominable heirs of Lenin—in the last case without need for (nuclear) combat—then there have to be grounds for hope. That hope, however, cannot extend to irreversible establishment of a world free from fear. Wars to end wars are a nonsense. If scholars of international relations do not know this, then they are overdue for attendance at an academic 'boot camp' with the classics of realism.

The megamyth of the transformation of world politics has some obvious religious affiliations and overtones. Another way of expressing this myth is as an 'endist' vision. For various reasons and in various respects, so we are invited to believe, the

---

[29] Edward Gibbon, *The History of the Decline and Fall of the Roman Empire*, ed. J. B. Bury (London, 1909), I, p. 84.

[30] On the past and future of nuclear history, see Colin S. Gray, *The Second Nuclear Age* (Boulder, CO: 1999).

[31] Robert D. Kaplan, 'The Coming Anarchy,' *Atlantic Monthly*, February 1994, pp. 44–76, and Peters, *Fighting for the Future*.

[32] Aron advises that 'prudence is the statesman's supreme virtue.' *Peace and War*, p. 585. This is not to suggest that the content of prudent behaviour is self-evident.

old order passeth away (has passed/is passing/will pass/will probably pass—one needs to watch the declension carefully). 'Endist' visions on sale in the 1990s have included

- An end of *History* as we know it, as great ideological struggles are overtaken by the definitive triumph of liberal democracy fuelled by capitalism.[33]
- An end of *major war*—usually defined as great wars between states—because the costs are too high, the prospective gains are too low, and states are of sharply diminishing relevance to international security affairs.[34]
- An end to *the utility of the use of force* in international relations, if not in all human relations, because of sundry taboos, the maturing of the legal and moral 'war convention,' and the strengthening of popular controls over public policy.[35]

These *fin de siècle* visions proclaiming the death of bad old habits can be interpreted to amount, synergistically, to the claim that the long and bloody reign of *strategic history* at last has ended/is ending/is probably ending. Readers of an 'endist' persuasion are advised that the institution of war is a chameleon—to borrow from Clausewitz[36]—able to adapt with apparently effortless ease to altered circumstances. War's nature as organized violence for 'political' (or what corresponds to what we understand by political today) goals survives untouched by radical shifts in political forms, motives for conflict, or technology.[37] Recognizable 'war' predated, and will postdate, the modern states' system. Readers are warned that if they are seeking an 'endist' transformational theory capable of slaying strategic history—the history that is influenced by the threat or use of force—they will need a very grand and inclusive theory indeed.

Hamburger heaven: countries with 'MacDonald's' do not fight each other

Reductionist syllogisms easily can exceed a culminating point in sensible judgment. For example, consider the elegant formula which holds that (1) capitalism fuels democracy, (2) democracies do not fight each other, therefore (3) capitalism is a vital condition for peace. In a world both rational and reasonable this syllogism would have much to recommend it, notwithstanding its vulnerability to neo-Marxist assault.

The theory of the 'democratic peace' has much in common with its close relatives in theories of capitalism sponsoring democracy, and of maritime polities or trading

---

[33] Francis Fukuyama, *The End of History and the Last Man* (New York, 1993).

[34] John Mueller, *Retreat from Doomsday: The Obsolescence of Major War* (New York, 1989); Michael Mandelbaum, 'Is Major War Obsolete?,' *Survival*, 40 (1998–99), pp. 20–38.

[35] 'I propose to call the set of articulated norms, customs, professional codes, legal precepts, religious and philosophical principles, and reciprocal arrangements that shape our judgments of military conduct, *the war convention*.' Michael Walzer, *Just and Unjust Wars: A Moral Argument with Historical Illustrations* (New York, 1977), p. 44. Original emphasis.

[36] Clausewitz, *On War*, p. 89.

[37] I prefer to thicken Hedley Bull's workmanlike definition of war as 'organised violence carried on by political units against each other' with the addition of 'for political motives'. *The Anarchical Society: A Study of Order in World Politics* (New York, 1977), p. 184. For a very different, culturalist, view of war, see Keegan, *History of Warfare*.

states being especially likely to find democracy both practical and practicable.[38] What the 'democratic peace' most has in common with those cognate theories, alas, is a hefty measure of irrelevance. Democracy worthy of the name is not about to conquer the globe, any more than capitalism worthy of the name can command compliant political change, or countries can choose a maritime orientation. I exaggerate, but not by much. Popular democracy as practiced, albeit imperfectly, in North America and by the members of the European Union, unfortunately is not a vision that can be caught by many greedy, or liberty-loving, others. So, even if the proposition is true that democracies do not fight each other, world politics is not in the process of thoroughgoing capture by the ideology of democracy. It is not surprising that democratic institutions are absent, say, from China, and a sham or bad joke in Russia. What is surprising is that so many Western scholars and business people should have expected otherwise.

I am not advancing an absolutist argument. Of course, political culture and its institutional expression can change over time; they can even change, fairly reliably, abruptly on command (witness the course of modern Germany and Japan). In the truly long term, or as a result of catastrophic events, anything is possible.[39] But a transformational theory of world politics keyed to an early universal triumph of popular democracy, has to be an awfully bad bet. An advancing tide of success for democracy that leaves even a very few islands of recalcitrant authoritarian polities behind it, would be about as useful for peace with security as a deterrent effect that worked well nineteen times out of twenty. A good, even excellent, record would not be good enough. Just one old fashioned 'greater power' that was a non-democracy could spoil a decade or longer, much as just one failure of deterrence might promote a substantial blemish on a whole century or more.

The problems with the theory of the 'democratic peace' are all too familiar. First, as suggested above, there is the structural and cultural difficulty that not all polities are plausibly susceptible to capture by democratic ideas and practice—and a most-cases success rate would mean failure. Second, democracy is not an either-or political condition. There is no magical metric, no alchemical algorithm, that can tell scholars when a polity has breasted the tape to be counted as a democracy. In point of fact, every polity in the world would score somewhat differently on a democracy rating, were we even able to agree on how polities would be graded. The

---

[38] A recent variant on this intriguing theme is presented in Peter Padfield, *Maritime Supremacy and the Opening of the Western Mind: Naval Campaigns that Shaped the Modern World, 1588–1782* (London, 1999). If Padfield overreaches on the evidence available concerning possible links between liberal values at home and maritime success, so does Spencer R. Weart in his study, *Never at War: Why Democracies Will Not Fight One Another* (New Haven, CT: 1998). Especially useful on the theory of the democratic peace are Peter T. Manicas, *War and Democracy* (Oxford, 1989); Michael Brown, Sean M. Lynn-Jones, and Steve E. Miller (eds.), *Debating the Democratic Peace: An 'International Security' Reader* (Cambridge, MA: 1996); and Michael W. Doyle, *Ways of War and Peace: Realism, Liberalism, and Socialism* (New York, 1997). This important debate cries out for empirical assistance. The literature on the causes of war probably would be improved if it contained fewer entries by philosophers of international relations (e.g., Doyle, just cited, or Hidemi Suganami, *On the Causes of War* [Oxford, 1996]), who tend to add elegantly to opacity, and more by first-rate historians (e.g., John Brewer, *The Sinews of Power: War, Money and the English State, 1688–1783* [New York, 1989], and Charles E. Esdaile, *The Wars of Napoleon* [London, 1995]).

[39] Scholars differ on the feasibility of swift radical change in political (or strategic) culture, in part because they differ on what they mean by culture. My current view may be found in my article, 'Strategic Culture as Context: The First Generation of Theory Strikes Back,' *Review of International Studies*, 25:1 (1999), pp. 49–69.

third region of difficulty, perhaps grounds for scepticism, is the non-trivial matter of plausibility in theory. Specifically, what is the mechanism of cause and effect that is supposed to generate the democratic peace? At this juncture, empirical concerns raise their embarrassing heads. Empirically it may appear to be true that democracies (hopefully, defined carefully!) do not wage war on other democracies. But, why should that be so?

If scholars could produce a 'cast of thousands' by way of well-attested case studies to 'test' the 'democratic peace,' though admittedly it is extraordinarily difficult to explain a negative (why did war *not* occur?), that would be one thing. As things stand, however, the case-study evidence is historically wafer-thin. Given that accessible history is most barely populated with polities that might even qualify as candidates for a list of democracies, it is not surprising that the potential, let alone the actual, database for this theory is embarrassingly sparse. It is precisely because the plausible historical database is so thin, that the quality of theory, the plausibility of its explanatory reach and grasp, is so important. Rephrased, the fewer the likely looking facts, the better sounding the explanation needs to be.

If we know anything for certain it is that decisions for war never rest upon perceptions of the democracy rating of the candidate enemy. The ideology, or political culture, of the enemy often is important, but most typically as a conditioner of behaviour or, more often, as an *ex post facto* rationale for belligerency. For example, both the Second World War and the Cold War had a large and richly veined moral dimension. Neither conflict, however, was waged by any polity for moral reasons. Nazism may have been at stake from 1939 to 1945, but none of Germany's foes who had a choice in the matter chose to fight in order to eradicate the Nazi ideology.[40]

While there may be some limited merit in the theory of the democratic peace, on balance it warrants labelling as a probable myth. There is no evidence to suggest either that democracies do not fight other democracies because they are democracies, or that democracies fight non-democracies because they are not democratic. More troubling still for the theorist is the weight of evidence which casts doubt on the proposition that bellicosity correlates with authoritarian forms of government.[41]

The theory of the democratic peace does not withstand close scrutiny when viewed from any angle. In fact the theory reminds this author of the old saying, 'Indians go in single file, the one I saw did.' Aside from the almost cheap shot to the effect that the evidential base for the theory is meagre and eminently contestable, one needs to worry at the core question of how does the theory attempt to explain the democratic 'causes' of peace. Two leading answers are prominent, albeit of an 'it

---

[40] Richard Overy has attempted a brave, and unusual, treatment of the moral dimension of the Second World War, as ch. 9 in his *Why the Allies Won* (London, 1995). He argues that '[w]hatever the rights and wrongs of the Allied cause, the belief that they fought on the side of righteousness equipped them with powerful moral argument (p. 312)'. In conclusion, Overy asks rhetorically, '[b]ut can there be any doubt that populations will fight with less effect in the service of an evil cause? (p. 313).' Overy is surely right to flag the importance of the connection between the will to fight and a confidence that justice is on our side. The problem is that in practice belief in the justness of one's cause has proven to be entirely unrelated to the character of that cause.

[41] Edward N. Luttwak is probably right with his characteristically robust claims that '[t]here is simply no connection between the form of domestic politics and the propensity to wage war by choice. As the historical record shows, dictatorships can be impeccably peaceful and democracies can be fiercely aggressive.' *Strategy: The Logic of War and Peace* (Cambridge, MA: 1987), p. 188.

stands to reason' kind. Democracies might be expected to be peace loving, because when 'the people' who must bear the costs of war are able to shape, even control, high policy, they can be trusted to demonstrate and vote for the blessings of the prosperity and personal safety associated with peace. In addition, so some will argue, government truly answerable to properly empowered and duly emancipated common folk, should be governments swayed by the humane human values that lurk within most of us. In other words, democracies make policy with an eye on cost-effectiveness and humane values' audits largely absent from the domestic processes of authoritarian polities.

The problem with the twin focused argument just outlined is that it is not true, at least it is not plausibly true enough. Authoritarian polities are not indifferent to the costs of war or the prudent assessment of the national interest, far from it. For example, Adolf Hitler was as obsessed with public opinion, and as worried about the consequences of public disapproval, as is Bill Clinton.[42] The strange idea that dictators can ignore domestic constituencies needs to be quashed once and for ever. Also, the idea that human beings are 'good,' but only governments are 'bad,' requires prompt burial. The Wars of Yugoslavian Succession in the 1990s may have been masterminded by evil (but popular) dictatorial leaders, but generally they were conducted ferociously on all sides by 'ordinary' Serbs, Croats, Bosnian Muslims, and Albanian Kosovars. I shall return to this theme.

Globalization: truth with two faces

Globalization is not a myth. However, it is a truth, at least a half-truth, that bears a message more of menace than of hope. When promoted by enthusiasts, Anthony Giddens, for example, in his vapid and undisciplined 1999 BBC Reith Lectures, the concept of globalization lends itself too easily to summary dismissal as a faddish and trivializing celebration of the obvious. Fashionable sociologists like Giddens, as well as some contemporary theorists of international relations, may flatter themselves with the conceit that they have discovered this rather amorphous bunch of processes that can be retailed to the credulous as globalization.[43] Long before these theorists 'discovered' globalization, British and French statesmen actually practiced it strategically in an episode known to us as The Seven Years' War (1756–63). Whether information travels electronically around the globe in nanoseconds, or is

---

[42] See Ian Kershaw, *The Hitler Myth: Image and Reality in the Third Reich* (Oxford, 1987), and John Lukacs, *The Hitler of History* (New York, 1998), ch. 7.

[43] The best, and most even-handed, terse review of the relevant theories known to this author is provided by the editors in John Baylis and Steve Smith (eds.), *The Globalization of World Politics: An Introduction to International Relations* (Oxford, 1997), pp. 1–11 (ch. 1 by Jan Aart Scholte also is useful). 'Globalization,' meaning many things to many people, has been a buzz-word of the 1990s. Nearly every contemporary textbook on international relations makes extensive use of the word, generally reverentially. Readers interested in illustration of my point could do worse than refer to Janne E. Nolan (ed.), *Global Engagement: Cooperation and Security in the 21st Century* (Washington, DC: 1994), for a glimpse at the sources of what has passed for a vision of foreign policy in the Clinton years; James H. Mittelman (ed.), *Globalization: Critical Reflections* (Boulder, CO: 1996); Brown, *Understanding International Relations*; and Lynn H. Miller, *Global Order*, 4th edn. (Boulder, CO: 1998).

carried by frigate in weeks or even months, would not seem to affect the quality of 'globality'; if I dare a neologism. Anglo-French unpleasantness in the 1750s and the 1760s was expressed, by central design, literally on a global playing field.

If The Seven Years' War fails to impress, try the history of geopolitical theory. Speaking at the Royal Geographical Society on 25 January 1904, Sir Halford Mackinder expounded the first of his three variants of truly global geostrategic theory.[44] To consider ideas and action in parallel, today's gurus of globalization might recall that in 1943 Mackinder wrote a prescient article in *Foreign Affairs* on 'The Round World and the Winning of the Peace', in which he postulated a geostrategic standoff between an Atlantic world and much of a Eurasia dominated by the USSR.[45] The 'globality' of it all was underlined in June 1944 when, only nine days apart, the United States led the two greatest amphibious operations in history at locations half a world apart (D-Day on 6 June, and the invasion of Saipan in the Marianas on 15 June). None of this is intended to belittle or discredit contemporary ideas on globalization. But it is to say that strategic thinkers and doers long have 'been there/done that'.

Genuinely global thought and action is not exactly an innovation of the 1990s. The issue, of course, is not globalization itself, but rather its meaning and implications. Many of the factual claims advanced by globalization theory can be admitted readily enough. There is no doubt that economic autarky is less feasible for more states than was the case in the past. Similarly, it cannot be doubted that modern information technologies (IT) have rendered states more porous than in days of yore. There are senses in which states are less sovereign than much of international law assumes them to be, and that societies and individuals almost everywhere—unless they are seriously IT-challenged—are accessible to information, ideas and hence potential influence from geographically distinct places. In the view of some people, a global politics, economics, and perhaps even culture, is emerging which transcends the traditional constraints of time and place—which is, in practical effect, placeless, beyond geography.[46]

Provided the brush-strokes are kept broad and fast moving, characterizations such as that just offered are fairly plausible. But, even if the vision is plausible, we have to ask the classic strategist's question, 'so what?'. With respect to cultural and hence political identity, what is the evidence for the death of nation-state loyalties? The 1990s provided ample evidence of the decline in authority of loyalty to, even just bare tolerance of, multinational and sometimes federal polities. But the beneficiary of transferred loyalties does not appear to be a 'global village' polity. An increasing political clout for more local loyalties is a trend not much improved in its implications for a benign 'globality', when set in the context of a more organized regionalism. For all the rhetoric and scholarly speculation about globalization, the contemporary reality is an unattractive mixture of classic Balkanization—not excluding the less-than-United Kingdom—and a drift towards regional superstates.

---

[44] Halford J. Mackinder, *Democratic Ideals and Reality* (New York, 1962). See also Geoffrey Sloan, 'Sir Halford Mackinder: The Heartland Theory Then and Now', in Colin S. Gray and Sloan (eds.), *Geopolitics, Geography and Strategy* (London, 1999), and Geoffrey Parker, *Geopolitics: Past, Present and Future* (London, 1998).

[45] Reprinted in Mackinder, *Democratic Ideals and Reality*, pp. 265–78.

[46] Martin Libicki, 'The Emerging Primacy of Information', *Orbis*, 40 (1996), pp. 261–74.

A regionalization of world politics, if that is what is underway, is a step more plausibly down the road to *1984* than it is to the global village as a true global security community.

Some of the current rather breathless literature on globalization reveals a classic misunderstanding of the inherently Janus-like quality of technological innovation. The railways and the electric telegraph shrank brute geography in the nineteenth century. By 1914 they had bound Eurasia from Lisbon to Vladivostok, and indeed much of the world was 'on line' via underseas cables. Sad to relate, however, those wonders of nineteenth-century science and technology also enabled mass armies to be transported, fed and kept in ammunition, and operationally commanded over great distances.[47] The same kind of point applies to wireless, to aircraft, and now to the computer.

The IT story that lies at the heart of most current globalization theory happens to refer to the same technologies that are triggering the latest Revolution in Military Affairs (RMA).[48] IT can, in one sense, transcend the erstwhile geographical discipline of distance and therefore time, but fundamentally it is a blank page, an empty bottle in which to place messages of our all too human choice. The computer, indeed the Internet and general exploitation of the electromagnetic spectrum, will not miraculously rescue the human race from a *strategic* history that, on the evidence, is endemic to the human condition. The globalization facilitated by modern science and electronic engineering can no more lead to a technologically mandated peace than could the invention of the wheel, the railway, the telegraph, or any other class of machine. The only scenario for a (rapid) process of globalization that would create a global security community, is some variant of the story line in the 1996 movie, *Independence Day*. In the event of an absolutely unmistakable threat from outer space, then, but only then, would our humanity unite us politically rather than divide us.

---

[47] Edwin A. Pratt, *The Rise of Rail-Power in War and Conquest, 1833–1914* (London, 1916); Paul M. Kennedy, 'Imperial Cable Communications and Strategy, 1870–1914', in Kennedy (ed.), *The War Plans of the Great Powers, 1880–1914* (London, 1979), pp. 75–98; and Martin van Creveld, *Command in War* (Cambridge, MA: 1985), ch. 4. Writing in 1905, a Lt. General on Germany's Great General Staff explained what the electric telegraph meant for operational command. 'The former and actually existing danger of failure in the preconcerted action of widely separated portions of the Army is now almost completely removed by the electric telegraph. However much the enemy may have succeeded in placing himself between our Armies, or portions of our Armies, in such a manner that no troops can get from one to the other, we can still amply communicate with each other on an arc of a hundred or two hundred or four hundred miles. The field telegraph can be laid as rapidly as the troops are marching and headquarters will hear every evening how matters stand with the various Armies, and issue its orders to them accordingly.' Rudolf von Caemmerer, *The Development of Strategical Science during the 19th Century*, trans. Karl von Donat (London, 1905), pp. 171–2. The events of the first week of September 1914 were to demonstrate the vanity in this confident expectation that modern technology would eliminate much of the friction that impedes efficient communication in time of war.

[48] On the thesis of an information-led RMA, see Stuart E. Johnson and Martin C. Libicki (eds.), *Dominant Battlespace Knowledge* (Washington, DC: 1996), and John Arquilla and David Ronfeldt (eds.), *In Athena's Camp: Preparing for Conflict in the Information Age* (Santa Monica, CA: 1997). Williamson Murray, 'Thinking About Revolutions in Military Affairs,' *Joint Force Quarterly*, 16 (1997), pp. 69–76, and Colin S. Gray, 'RMAs and the Dimensions of Strategy', *Joint Force Quarterly*, 17 (1997–98), pp. 50–54, are much more sceptical.

I fight, therefore I am human

It should be as obvious to everyone today as it was to neoclassical realists in the early 1990s, that the departure of the deeply unlovely USSR has had as great a significance for global power relations, as it has had no implications whatsoever for the nature of those changed relations. The 1990s were yet another of modern history's shake-down cruise periods following a protracted passage of arms— thankfully, only a *virtual* passage in this latest case, though the arms were real enough. If one was to attempt to rate modern postwar 'ordering' endeavours on an ascending scale of merit from 1 to 5, it would be plausible to allow Vienna and Paris 1814–15 an all but perfect 5, Versailles 1919 warrants a clearly failing grade of 1 (or 2 at the most), Yalta and Potsdam 1945 rates a 4, while 1989–91, a reordering period bereft of a formal settlement, probably deserves a grade of 3. The leading difficulty in 'marking' the statecraft of the early 1990s is that really it is too soon to tell. President George Bush, the largely accidental beneficiary of the prudent grand strategy pursued during his years of impotence as Vice President, and earlier, was not much attracted to 'this vision thing.' No vision, or statecraft, *à la* Bush, is, of course, preferable to poor vision. Still, The New World Order to which Bush spoke very briefly *en passant*, was strictly notional. There were senior officials in the Bush Administration who had a clear vision of a lasting American hegemony comprising the desirable meaning, architecture, and implications of a New World Order. Such a robust vision, however, at least as explicit inspiration for US policy, was judged too embarassingly hubristic for contemporary sensibilities abroad as well as too expensive.[49]

History repeats itself in that great conflicts come and go, and they are succeeded, or concluded, by more or less grand 'ordering' designs that cope more or less well with the would-be disruptive traffic of their period. It is a vital matter, as Brian Bond argues in his study, *The Pursuit of Victory*, that statesmen—if I may be forgiven the twin sins of eponymity and sexism—should understand how to win the peace as well as win the war.[50] Nothing lasts for ever, especially in the architecture of relations of power that principally organize world politics, but some postwar 'orders' endure much longer than do others. The most important principle (with *caveat*) for peacemaking is to try to ensure either that every essential polity/interest-player is tolerably satisfied with the political settlement, or that polity/interest-players who are certain to find the settlement intolerable will be unable to make significant mischief on any time-scale of relevance. For example, a 'Carthaginian Peace' can do the job

---

[49] The Bush Administration was much embarassed by the revelation in Patrick E. Tyler, 'US Strategy Plan Calls for Insuring No Rivals Develop', *New York Times*, 8 March 1992, pp. A1, 14. The authority of the Pentagon's hegemony plan was denied promptly. See Patrick E. Tyler, 'Senior US Officials Assail Lone-Superpower Policy', *New York Times*, 11 March 1992, p. A6. This was a truly brief bid for glory! Words, of course, are one thing, the reality of American hegemony is something else.

[50] Brian Bond, *The Pursuit of Victory: From Napoleon to Saddam Hussein* (Oxford, 1996).

admirably, provided it truly is 'Carthaginian'.[51] If you know that you are not of Roman quality, it is unwise to attempt to impose a 'Carthaginian Peace'.

Sad to say, a proclivity to combat helps define the human condition. The 1990s were just another post-war decade and—if we are prudent and fortunate—the twenty-first century will be just another 100-year period. To repeat the primary refrain of this essay, a benign transformation in the human security condition is not about to happen. No matter what your transformational agency-of-choice happens to be, on the evidence available you are wrong. Humans will not learn the ways of peace, following the simplistic proposition that peace is a matter of education, even of education by doing;[52] peace will not be enforced by awesome technologies; and peace will not be ours by default because wars happily and conveniently proceed through obsolescence to become terminally obsolete. War and strategy are eternal, albeit eternally changing as they adapt to new circumstances.[53]

To believe that war, understood broadly,[54] largely is yesterday's problem and yesterday's solution,[55] is not unlike believing in all but eternal life guaranteed strictly by non-divine skills. Both are possible, but they are so improbable as to merit no weight in our planning. It can be difficult to advance neoclassical realist nostrums without appearing cynical, patronizing, or both. However, we realists would wish special note to be taken of the fact that in the twentieth century the 'civilized countries' proceeded from a Great War to end wars;[56] into a second Great War twenty years later which included an effort at genocide worthy of the title; and then into a virtual, or Cold, War which, had it turned hot, through a 'nuclear winter' effect might have ended life on planet Earth.[57] We humans have demonstrated that we are capable of committing, and are contingently willing to commit, any and every abomination. Furthermore, we have demonstrated this fact recently. The neoclassical realist, at least this neoclassical realist, admits that in the long term anything is possible. But for the next several decades it would be prudent to invest in

[51] The problem with the Versailles 'order' of 1919 was that in deadly fashion it combined the elements of humiliation of the vanquished—who were not convinced that they had been properly vanquished—with an unrealistic requirement for protractedly robust postwar 'ordering' on the part of the victors. It might be said that there was nothing much wrong with Versailles; the difficulty lay not with the treaty, but rather with the lack of will for enforcement by the international community. This excuse, though strictly true, is not persuasive. Prudent peacemakers do not design a post-war 'order' that leaves most political parties among the vanquished committed to its overthrow. Such an absence of political stake in the new order all but guarantees that 'bad times' will return sooner rather than later. James S. Corum, *The Roots of Blitzkrieg: Hans von Seeckt and German Military Reform* (Lawrence, KS: 1992), is instructive. Scholars of international relations have devoted too much attention to the causes of war, a subject that does not lend itself to useful assault, and far too little to the making of more lasting periods of (postwar) 'order'. The latter is a vital topic on which a great deal of useful work could be done. For a praiseworthy venture into the realm of 'orders', see Torbjorn L. Knutsen, *The Rise and Fall of World Orders* (Manchester, 1999).

[52] Adler believes that learning is key to the arrival of peace. '[L]ike all practices it [peace] can be arrived at through *learning* … In other words, peace is socially constructed.' 'Condition(s) of Peace,' p. 168. Original emphasis. Would that Adler were correct.

[53] This is the central theme in Gray, *Modern Strategy*.

[54] War is a legal, certainly a customary concept. *Warfare* might be the better term.

[55] It may no longer be fashionable to say this, but in the words of B. H. Liddell Hart, '[t]he function of war is to settle disputes'. *The Revolution in Warfare* (London, 1946), p. 42.

[56] G. W. Gong, *The Standard of 'Civilization' in International Society* (Oxford, 1984).

[57] US Congress, House of Representatives, Committee on Science and Technology, Subcommittee on Natural Resources, Agricultural Research and Environment, and Committee on Interior and Insular Affairs, Subcommittee on Energy and the Environment, *Nuclear Winter*, *Joint Hearing*, 99th Cong., 1st session (Washington, DC: 14 March 1985).

residual military force for 'order', all the while one hopes for changes in human hearts and culture.

The 'death of strategy,' which is to say the demise of the political demand for strategy, has been anticipated from the mid-nineteenth century until today. In the aftermath of great conflicts, many among the best and the brightest in the scribbling class discern no obvious need for rude soldiery, or strategic reasoning, in a world that appears to present no strategic problems. Daniel Johnson offers an explicit statement of this recurring fallacy when he identifies false alternatives thus:

The Cold War was fought by warriors who never went to war. Intellectuals, that is, who are faced with an uncomfortable choice: obsolescence in a world which values their ideological polemics and treatises on strategy as little as the campaign medals of the retired officer; or a new career, perhaps as historiographers or critics of the martial arts they once practised.[58]

Or, perhaps we would prefer just to cultivate our gardens. There may be much to recommend a new career, but the reason advanced by Johnson does not figure in such an inclination. Strategic thinkers and doers alas are not obsolescent. They were missing from the action in the Balkans in the Spring of 1999, but that is another matter entirely.

In its strategic dimension the megamyth of transformation appears in several variants.

First, the past decade has witnessed yet another burst of speculation by scholars concerning the health of the social institution frequently called 'major war'. As Eliot Cohen and others have noticed, point scoring in this particular debate is extraordinarily sensitive to language.[59] As so often is the case, the scholars who can win the definitional combat are likely to win the debate. If, by 'major war', one means what the first half of the twentieth century intended by 'total war'—*grande guerre* for existence among the greater powers—then, yes, the nuclear discovery certainly rendered 'major war' obsolescent, at least. Of course, obsolescent, or even obsolete, does not mean impossible. Several defence communities expended huge effort over forty years of Cold War preparing as rationally—though arguably not reasonably— as they could to conduct just such a war as competently as they might prove able. Arguably, a tolerably good job was done by all. Nuclear-age defence preparation proved compatible with a protracted condition of non-(hot) war. Quite possibly, the peace was kept during the Cold War despite the extant strategic theories, plans, and capabilities. I am not claiming that deterrence 'worked'. We do not and really cannot know.[60]

If one sidelines fine points of definition and adopts the position that major war can refer not only to great, possibly protracted, and bloody conflicts, but also to brief passages of arms that have major consequences, then its demise appears distinctly improbable. Furthermore, one needs to venture into the mire of postmodernity and abandon a fixation upon regular state-to-state conflict, focusing instead on the (somewhat) organized violence for political motives that defines

---

[58] Daniel Johnson, 'Liberalism's Tragic Lack', *Times Literary Supplement*, 9 April 1999, p. 30.

[59] Cohen, '"Major" Consequences of War'.

[60] In which respect see Fred Charles Iklé, 'The Second Coming of the Nuclear Age,' *Foreign Affairs*, 75 (1996), pp. 119–28, and Keith B. Payne, *Deterrence in the Second Nuclear Age* (Lexington, KY: 1997).

warfare.[61] Such a commonsense expansion of theoretical domain exposes the prospective longevity of our all too human will to fight—at least for major stakes— if only irregularly and therefore typically in tactically small-scale engagements.

Journalists who feed on exciting copy and whose grasp of international politics frequently appears to have been shaped strictly by the most recent of events, may be excused believing that the world ever can be remade anew. But scholars should know better. It is true that interstate wars are rare occurrences in the current era. However, it would only take one or two such rare events to spoil a decade, or even a century. Major war, employing every class of weapon in the arsenal, remains possible in a world where states remain the final arbiters of their own security. The reason why the United Nations could be allowed to assume such apparent significance at the close of NATOs air campaign against Serbia in 1999, was precisely because the issues at stake for the leading members of the Alliance were less than truly serious. Serious matters of national security are not submitted for assay, let alone action, if they might be impacted by an unfriendly veto. Overall, the current burst of *Moralpolitik* as favoured by baby-boomer leaders in the United States and Britain, means nothing in particular for the future of world politics (or even of 'global governance'). Moral imperialism, provided it is cheap, can be indulged in a period that is permissive of such frivolity. We neoclassical realists are not at all opposed to doing good. Rather are we opposed to doing good if the price is high and there are more pressing purposes of security requiring military attention.

Again on the principle of never saying never, let us not bury totally the possibility that major war is obsolescent/obsolete *and therefore very unlikely to be employed as an instrument of policy*. The consequentialist qualification is vital. Many an obsolescent, even obsolete, social institution limps on with varying degrees of grace. Consider the British monarchy. Given the appalling human record in the twentieth century, and given the absence of powerful theory explaining why the future must, or even is likely, to be notably different, we realists will keep the jury out on the trial of 'major war' for at least a couple of centuries to come.

Second, and as a somewhat inchoate variant of the argument above, it may just be a *déformation professionelle*, but repeatedly over the past century and a half scholars and other pundits have declared a declining utility to the threat and use of force.

This uneasy compound of fact, value, and prediction can take the form of generalizations about new security agendas and how the traditional military dimension of security has lost (or is losing) pride of place as principal concern to political, economic, cultural, environmental or some other dimensions.[62] Leaders of

---

[61] Hedley Bull advises that '[v]iolence is not war unless it is carried out in the name of a political unit. Also, he insists that 'violence carried out in the name of a political unit is not war unless it is directed against another political unit.' *Anarchical Society*, p. 184. Although such juridical concerns can have great practical significance for the applicability of the limitations in the 'war convention,' they can impair achievement of a more relevant understanding of warfare. Although he overreaches in his argument, Peters does provide a useful wake-up call to Western scholars in his *Fighting for the Future*.

[62] For example, see Barry Buzan, *People, States and Fear: An Agenda for International Security Studies in the Post-Cold War Era*, 2nd edn. (Boulder, CO: 1991); Ole Weaver, Barry Buzan, Morten Kelstrup, and Pierre Lemaitre, *Identity, Migration and the New Security Agenda in Europe* (London, 1993); Barry Buzan, Ole Weaver, and Jaap de Wilde, *Security: A New Framework for Analysis* (Boulder, CO: 1998); David A. Baldwin, 'Security Studies and the End of the Cold War', *World Politics*, 48 (1995), pp. 117–41; and idem, 'The Concept of Security', *Review of International Studies*, 23 (1997), pp. 5–26.

all political parties in the United States and Britain in the 1990s celebrated the end of the Cold War by proclaiming the arrival of political peace, promptly seizing a large peace dividend, and demonstrating no real interest in defence policy. Such belated recognition of the utility of force as there has been pertains to the official rediscovery that even moral crusaders need sharp swords. Because moral force alone fails the strategy test (i.e., it does not work), evil dictators need to be bludgeoned by heavy ordnance. If humanitarian intervention for the forcible doing of good becomes all the rage—which it will not, because it is far to costly in relation to its dubious effectiveness—then military security would recover some lost ground in legitimacy, albeit for an unsound reason.

The case of humanitarian intervention shares with all military subjects sub-servience to the eternal lore of strategy. Recall Theobald von Bethmann Hollweg's infamous apologia of 4 August 1914 when he told the Reichstag that 'necessity knows no law'.[63] With profit for understanding world politics one could rewrite the German Chancellor's honest, if impolitic dictum, to read, 'necessity knows only the lore of strategic effectiveness'. Whether or not an exercise in attempted coercion enjoys the blessing of the UN Security Council, strategy, or one might usefully say 'Clausewitz, rules'! Readers of this essay who are not strategic theorists or defence analysts may have noticed that the Great Man came under renewed assault in the 1990s.[64] Yet again, agents of the transformational myth have been working overtime. If war, organized violence, or the threat or use of force for 'political' purposes—select your favoured language—has been/is being shown the door by the vigorous working of sundry antistrategic factors, then it should follow that war's greatest theorist must be yesterday's man.

The urgency of public demand for military security can vary on the scale from apparently zero to immediate and overriding of most other considerations. The scholars who periodically discover accurately enough that military security appears not to matter very much today, are akin to people who decide that because the weather now is fine the days of bad weather obviously have passed. Competent strategic analysts, who I am tempted to assert have to be neoclassical realists, can fall into the trap of responding to scepticism expressed by agents of any of the many variants of the transformational myth by overpressing the evidence extant on future threats. Let us be clear: competent neoclassical realists today do not emphasize the need for military security because they *know* that 'China is coming,' or 'Russia is coming back', as the leading challenge to US global hegemony and the international order supported by that hegemony. What competent neoclassical realists truly *know* is that just as all political vacuums eventually are filled,[65] so every hegemonic international order eventually decays and is challenged. There is scope for argument on the timing and political identity of the challenge, but not as to its eventual appearance.

Although active and intensive demand for military security is irregular, even rare, for most societies, for some it always reappears. Happy accidents of geopolitical location certainly allow some relatively quiet neighbourhoods, but for the globe as a whole bad times invariably return. To help guide superior performance for those

---

[63] Quoted in Walzer, *Just and Unjust Wars*, p. 240.
[64] Bassford, 'Landmarks in Defense Literature', is an outstanding defence.
[65] Kissinger, *Diplomacy*, p. 548.

'bad times', when the threat or actual use of force is a dominant concern, the writings of a Prussian Major General, first published 167 years ago, provide the outstanding source of inspiration. In *On War*, Clausewitz was right enough on the essentials of his subject. Indeed, he was so right that he has no plausible competitors among strategic theorists.[66] The analogy between Clausewitz for strategic studies and Aron and Morgenthau for international relations is no less valid for being hugely unattractive to many scholars today. In the same way that Clausewitz explains strategy and war for all times, so Aron and Morgenthau tell their readers most, possibly all, that they really need to know. Before the firing squad draws its ammunition, I must add the explanatory point that of course Clausewitz's *On War* has its limitations, as do Aron's *Peace and War* and Morgenthau's *Peace Among Nations*. However, we do not seek perfection, rather do we seek good enough explanations of human misbehaviour in the realm of world politics.

The third spoke in the wheel of military oriented mythology is the persisting idea that particular weapons are unusable. This variant of the megamyth of transformation appears frequently in the guise of the belief that there is a taboo prohibiting, certainly inhibiting, the threat or use of weapons of mass destruction (WMD). Most of the pertinent literature addresses alleged taboos against chemical and nuclear arms.[67] The peril in this myth lies in the implications of its very plausibility. There is a taboo that has emerged since the 1960s that stigmatizes nuclear weapons, while a taboo against chemical arms is nearly half a century older. Unfortunately, these taboos do not extend into the domain where we need it most, which is to say into a commanding role over the hearts, minds, and policies of those desperate for a general respect or a specific protection against the well armed world of G-8 countries. A taboo, or taboos, proscribing WMD most probably is extant among all those who are not motivated to break it. Readers may notice that this is broadly the most serious of difficulties with the approach to the control of arms that we know as (negotiated) 'arms control'. Most people, including most political leaders, are horrified at the prospect of the threat, let alone the use, of any kind of WMD. But, most people, including most political leaders, favoured peace over war in the late 1930s. Under the press of perceived necessity, be it idiosyncratically personal to a leader, or genuinely of wider moment, no taboo is worth the ink expanded in its praise by scholars.

The danger in tabooist reasoning among Western academics is that they risk convincing themselves of that which is not true. We are encouraged to repose confidence in a rather fuzzy culturalist belief that, for example, nuclear weapons have not been, and cannot be, used because of the operation of a nuclear taboo.[68] A plausible consequence of such a position is blindness to the attractions of WMD to

---

[66] 'One Clausewitz is still worth a busload of most other theorists'. Richard K. Betts, 'Should Strategic Studies Survive?', *World Politics*, 50 (1997), p. 29.

[67] T. V. Paul, 'Nuclear Taboo and War Initiation in Regional Conflicts', *Journal of Conflict Resolution*, 39 (1965), pp. 696–717; Richard Price and Nina Tannenwald, 'Norms and Deterrence: The Nuclear and Chemical Weapons Taboos', in Peter J. Katzenstein (ed.), *The Culture of National Security: Norms and Identity in World Politics* (New York, 1996), pp. 114–52; and Richard M. Price, *The Chemical Weapons Taboo* (Ithaca, NY: 1997).

[68] In 'Norms and Deterrence,' p. 140, Price and Tannenwald assert confidently that '[t]the strength of the nuclear taboo and the odium attached to nuclear weapons as weapons of mass destruction render unusable all nuclear weapons …' Certainty, probability, and value, are thus confused.

those for whom necessity knows no taboo.[69] Speculation that the marvels of military effectiveness allowed by information-led armed forces translate as a strategic obsolescence for WMD are exactly wrong[70]—except, that is, for us information-rich G-8 folk, who are decreasingly interested in employing WMD.

It is all too human to organize to fight and even to enjoy combat (especially vicariously). Alas, the belligerent quality to humanity includes a rare, but genuine, willingness to wage major war, including major war with WMD. There is no point in shouting that 'war does not pay'. For most people, most of the time, such a claim is a self-evident truth. The trouble is that we humans are so gripped by some of the less attractive features of our nature as to be obliged to function according to a notion of prudence that has to include a willingness to fight.

On the lethality of optimism

From different angles this essay has assaulted the multifaceted myth of the possibility, probability, let alone actuality, of benign transformation in human security affairs. This megamyth has spawned interconnected undercooked theories of, for example, complex interdependence, globalization, emancipation, and the rest, all of which tend to share the features of innate attractiveness, some existential merit, but overarching signal error on the essentials. The evidence for synergistic trends suggesting a peaceable future were quite strong on the eve of the Wars of the French Revolution and Empire, the First World War, and in the 1920s and 1930s.

If scholars of international relations wish to conjure up fantasies of security futures radically different from past experience, such is their privilege. However, as professional students of their subject they should be held to account when they confuse fact and value, and they should know better than to risk misinforming students with airy visions of non-existent alternatives. History is a realm of contingency that lends itself to intriguing counterfactual theorizing. For example, had Britain's RAF not resisted successfully the pressures in the 1920's against maintaining service independence, its Army-oriented counterfactual alternative might well have been fatally overcommitted to the protection of the BEF in 1940.[71] The consequences truly might have warranted description as awesomely awful. This military operational and strategic example of counterfactual speculation offers the prospects of an alternative course of events, but not of an alternative nature to the course of events. Too much of the contemporary scholarship in our field betrays either indifference to, or even rank ignorance of, the way that world politics and strategic history 'works'. Four points summarize my argument.

First, although change in international politics—in the distribution of power, in the political culture of key polities, in the technological and economic contexts, and so forth—matters, it does not matter to the degree that it can transform the nature

---

[69] Tabooist argument is taken to task in Gray, *Second Nuclear Age*, ch. 4.

[70] I tackle this issue directly in my 'Nuclear Weapons and the Revolution in Military Affairs', in T. V. Paul, Richard J. Harknett, and James J. Wirtz (eds.), *The Absolute Weapon Revisited: Nuclear Arms and the Emerging International Order* (Ann Arbor, MI, 1998), pp. 99–134.

[71] I thank Richard P. Hallion for this example. See his 'Air Power Past, Present, and Future,' in Hallion (ed.), *Air Power Confronts an Unstable World* (London, 1997), p. 7.

of final cost than other economies with either easy access to excellent roads or to the world's oceans.

A large number of Soviet industries were also located in the more peripheral and distant parts of the former USSR, and had been placed there for reasons which had little to do with economic rationality and everything with national security or the need to exploit a crucial raw material. This raised the obvious question—what would happen to these and the people employed in them, if, and when, they were exposed to the forces of supply and demand? Take the industries and the three million people living north of the Arctic circle. There is no way that a market economy could sustain either. The military facilities there would have to be closed and the mining towns reduced in size. But how would the surplus citizens be moved south? And who then would employ them? Furthermore, what was one supposed to do with the several cities and their populations (again usually a long way away from the centre) whose only purpose had been to produce a single item, such as tanks, nuclear missiles, and the like that were no longer needed in a new international system where cooperation rather than hostility was becoming the norm and where Russia simply could not afford to maintain a huge defence budget? There was no easy answer to this, or, as we shall see, to a number of other problems facing Russia after 1991.

The IMF takes the lead

Late 1991 therefore found the Soviet Union disintegrating and its economic system in chaos. Into this environment stepped the International Monetary Fund and sundry advisors with the 'Cure', one which had been implemented elsewhere in Central Europe (notably Poland) without killing the patient. So why, it was reasoned, should the same medicine not be equally effective in reviving Russia? But why did the West decide to use the IMF, rather than any other body, to be its point man? There were at least three important reasons.

One, clearly, was to justify the Fund's existence.[23] Set up in the immediate post-war period to manage the fixed exchange rate regime of the post-war economic order, by the 1970s and the abandonment of that regime in favour of floating rates, the IMF appeared to have lost its raison d'etre. It had become, in effect, an organization without a clear mission.[24] The collapse of communism in Eastern Europe in 1989, followed two years later by the implosion of the USSR, at last seemed to provide it with one. Moreover, the Fund had already gained valuable experience in the 1980s putting together structural adjustment packages for the heavily-indebted economies of Latin American and Poland, and it was felt that it would be able to do the same again for the Russian economy.[25]

---

[23] In Nigel Gould-Davies and Ngaire Woods, 'Russia and the IMF', *International Affairs*, pp. 1–2.

[24] Harold James, *International Monetary Co-operation Since Bretton Woods* (Oxford: Oxford University Press, 1996).

[25] On Poland, see Jeffrey Sachs, *Poland's Jump to the Market Economy* (Cambridge, MA: MIT Press, 1993).

The IMF's willingness to shoulder the burden of the Russian transformation was also opportune from the point of view of US policymakers. President Bush, recall, had put all his eggs in the now-shattered Gorbachev basket; caught off-guard by the abrupt turn of events, the US administration swam with the tide and backed Yeltsin's bold reform efforts. However, by the time Clinton took office in January 1993, he had neither the inclination, nor the authority, to craft a brand new approach to the Russian economic transition.[26] Hence, shifting the responsibility to the IMF made perfect political sense, especially for an administration more concerned to focus on domestic issues rather than foreign ones. Furthermore, even though the US had enormous influence in the institution (and could thus determine IMF policy towards Russia) it was unwilling to lend large amounts to support Russian reform. Working through the IMF, therefore, permitted the US to push Russia in a direction it hoped it would go, but without having to fork out huge sums of money itself. Indeed, far from being particularly generous, the Americans overall tended to leave the generosity to their various allies—especially Germany; not because Germany was richer, but because Germany had to reward Russia for not standing in the way of unification between 1989 and 1990.[27]

It was also believed, finally, that if the US could work through a body like the Fund this might reduce popular Russian opposition to economic reform. The political logic here was quite straightforward. If America was seen to be imposing painful reform upon its vanquished foe, then there was every chance this would be used by Russian communists and nationalists alike to attack the reform programme—using anti-Americanism as the obvious vehicle for doing so. If however the IMF was seen to be in the vanguard of change, this might lessen the political reaction to reform from within Russia itself. Whether this was a reasonable calculation or not was not at all clear. However, the assumption was that if change was seen to be coming from an ostensibly independent, multilateral institution and not the US, this would make the reforms more palatable.[28]

How well-suited the IMF actually was to carry out the job it had been allotted is, of course, a moot point. The organization after all 'had no more experience than any other institution in supporting the transition from communism to capitalism'.[29] The Fund was also an economic instrument at heart. Hence, it was not equipped or required to think about the political implications of its decisions. Nor was it asked to reflect about the larger strategic questions and the West's more general interests in making Russia a stable partner in the international system. It had one brief and one brief alone: to sit down with the authorities in Russia and provide them with irresistible arguments (under pressure) as to why they should abandon the economic habits of a lifetime and go for the market.[30]

---

[26] For a more sympathetic account of Clinton's policy towards post-communist Russia, see Michael Cox, ' The necessary partnership? The Clinton presidency and post-Soviet Russia', *International Affairs*, 70:4 (1994), pp. 635–58.

[27] Of the $150bn that Russia owed the West in 1999, 40 per cent was held in Germany.

[28] How successful this was is examined by Peter Reddaway in 'Visit to a Maelstrom', *The New York Times*, 10 January 1994.

[29] See Nigel Gould-Davies and Ngaire Woods, 'Russia and the IMF', *International Affairs*, p. 2.

[30] See Michael Camdessus, 'Russia's Transformation Efforts at a Turning Point', *IMF Press Release*, 29 March 1995.

The Cure

The Cure—known by its critics as 'shock therapy'—consisted of a Holy Trinity of policies: monetary stabilization; liberalization; and privatization. Most of these policies, generically known as the Washington consensus, had already proved their effectiveness in a wide variety of other circumstances.[31] And the hope obviously was that they would be equally effective under conditions in Russia. Let us deal with each in turn.

Monetary stabilization was seen as the most pressing of the policy troika. Money after all is the essence of capitalism, and without stable money the price system cannot work and investment cannot take place. One thing that the state can and must do is introduce a stable currency; in particular it must prevent hyperinflation. Given the problems with measuring price levels and money supply, an easy way to check whether a country is succeeding in price stabilization is to make the currency convertible and use the exchange rate as the nominal anchor of your stabilization programme. This has the virtue of simplicity—everyone from the Wall Street banker to the street-corner babushka knows what is the rouble/dollar exchange rate on any particular day. Certainly, given the resource constraints under which even the IMF must operate, using the stability of the exchange rate as a signal for how reform is doing in Russia was attractively simple.

The second supporting leg of the tripod was liberalization, and involved lifting restrictions on business activity, domestic and international. Price controls would thus be removed and subsidies ended. Restrictions on new business formation would also be scrapped, and private businesses given free access to foreign trade. Quotas and duties on exports would in turn be eliminated and import tariffs lowered. Liberalization of foreign trade was important because import competition would force the monopoly suppliers inherited from the Soviet economy to become competitive or go out of business. Free trade would reveal Russia's comparative economic advantage and would draw resources into the sectors with growth potential. Trade liberalization was also a prerequisite for the influx of foreign investment and technology that Russia urgently needed.[32]

Finally, privatization meant the transfer of economic assets into private ownership in order to unleash entrepreneurship and to create competitive markets.[33] Inspired in large part by what had been happening in other parts of the world throughout the 'deregulating' 1980s, privatization aimed to sell off State enterprises to whomever was willing to buy them, while those enterprises which stayed in state hands would be weaned off subsidies and given hard budget constraints. At the same time, bankruptcy legislation would be introduced and enforced to ensure the closure of loss-making firms and the redistribution of their resources (machinery, premises and labour) to more efficient producers. Though this formula may have

---

[31] See *World Bank Development Report: From Plan to Market* (Washington, DC: World Bank, 1996).

[32] Non-Communist Russia's exports however continued to be very 'Soviet' in nature: about 45 per cent in any one year being in oil and gas and 15 per cent in metals. Moreover, the revenues earned privately from the sale of these commodities were not reinvested back into their respective industries. For a critique see Yurii Yeremenko, ''Bessmyslennost' eksporta dlya Rossii' {Exports are senseless for Russia], *Ekonomichekaya Gazeta*, no. 33, 1996, pp. 2–3.

[33] See Roman Frydman and Andrzej Rapanczynski, et al., *The Privatization Process in Russia, Ukraine and the Baltic States* (Budapest, Central European University Press, 1993).

worked elsewhere, in Russia it faced a serious problem: there were no private agents with the capital necessary to purchase enterprises. This meant that state-owned firms had to be either sold to foreigners—a politically difficult path to follow—or given away to domestic buyers at below market value. This is precisely what happened with the result that the privatization process essentially became a vehicle for the legitimization of the seizure of state assets by the more energetic members of the old communist-industrialist nomenklatura.

Overall, then, the IMF approach focused primarily on macroeconomic policies. Questions of market regulation and institution-building were to be postponed to a later date. It was argued that premature moves to increase state control—before liberalization was completed—would merely provide a cover for communist reactionaries to reimpose a state-controlled economy. It was assumed that the institutional infrastructure (laws, regulatory agencies, etc.) was either in place already, or could be built quickly—either imported or driven by the enlightened self-interest of the new elites.[34] The underlying assumption was that getting the incentives right would lead to the emergence of economic agents who would have a vested interest in creating institutions to protect their long-term property rights. Thus in a neat display of recursive logic, the provision of a rule of law was treated as endogenous to the transition model. The demand for secure contracts would create the supply of institutions to provide them.

Democracy from above or Yeltsin rules—OK?

One of the real and many paradoxes of the West's approach to economic reform in Russia was that while it made great play of the need for more economic choice, it put an enormous amount of pressure on Russian decision-makers to go down one particular path. Equally, while Western policymakers talked easily about the need for democracy and greater political freedom in Russia, the form of democracy they promoted was especially elitist in nature.[35] This had a particular impact both upon the way the reforms were introduced and perceived within Russia itself. Indeed, whereas in East-Central Europe, shock therapy was introduced by governments that came out of parliaments elected in post-1989 free elections, in Russia the reform programme was mostly implemented by presidential *ukaz*, by a man who until the age of 59 had been a leading functionary of the Communist Party. The Russian legislature was treated not as source of legislation and a vehicle for democratization, but as an annoyance that was to be avoided at all costs. There were no fresh elections to president or congress after the collapse of the Soviet Union. The first new elections came in December 1993—two years after the launch of shock therapy; two months after the previous parliament had been dispersed by force; and under a constitution hand-crafted to maximize President Yeltsin's powers. Russian voters expressed their discontent by electing a legislature dominated by communists and

---

[34] For an uncritical but revealing examination of this self-serving notion see Maxim Boycko, Andrei Shleifer and Robert Vishny, *Privatizing Russia* (Cambridge, MA: MIT Press, 1996).
[35] I have explored this issue in more detail in my 'Russia's Flawed Democracy', *Current History,* October 1998.

nationalists, with Vladimir Zhirinovsky as the leading vote-getter. Knowing that the parliament would have little influence over the composition of the government, voters had little incentive to behave responsibly.

While some reform programmes in Russia were introduced by means of laws passed by the legislature (most notably the 1992 voucher privatization programme), most were introduced by presidential decree (most notoriously, the second-wave of privatization by means of shares-for-loans auctions in 1995). Bureaucratic institutions charged with implementing the reforms such as the Central Bank or the State Privatization Committee were not directly accountable to the parliament, or to anybody in particular.

Significantly, however, these characteristics of the new Russian political system were not seen as problems but instead regarded as virtues by Russia's Western advisors. In fact, in their eyes, it was absolutely vital to by-pass all potential opposition to economic reforms coming (as they feared) from conservative groups with a vested interest in the pre-1991 *status quo*—that is communist bureaucrats and workers in subsidized industries (such as military plants). And such impediments, it was believed, could only be overcome with speed, international leverage and by a highly presidentialist system which vested great powers in the man at the top—in this case Yeltsin. This model of vested interests blocking reform certainly looked plausible. It also looked familiar. That was the pattern of social interests that had undermined Gorbachev's reform efforts in the 1980s. It was also typical of the political economy of protectionist coalitions in Latin America—entrenched elites and periodically-mobilized urban masses.

As it turned out, these fears proved groundless. To all intents and purposes, the old Soviet military industrial complex was politically disembowelled by the rapid collapse of communist institutions and proved totally unable to defend their interests in the transition economy. As for the masses, they proved politically inert despite (or perhaps because of) shattering social changes, a massive fall in living standards, and tremendous uncertainty about their future well-being.[36] Indeed, some radical critics of shock therapy have argued that this is precisely what the reforms were intended to do; to literally bludgeon any potential social opposition into submission. After all, people who are worried about keeping their job, or feeding their family, are less likely to resort to political violence. Whatever the truth, the workers did not rise up.[37] Nor did anybody else. The serious opposition, in the end, did not come from communist reactionaries or proletarian discontent, but from some of the very elites who led the original charge towards the market economy. Using the privatization programme to secure their control of industrial and financial assets, this group with close ties to Yeltsin proved extremely resistant to genuine market reforms—largely because genuine reform would have challenged their new-found monopoly position. However, before examining the consequences of their actions, let us first examine the reforms in practice.[38]

---

[36] Sarah Ashwin, *Russian Workers: The Anatomy of Patience* (Manchester: Manchester University Press, 1999).

[37] See Simon Clarke, *New Forms of Employment and Household Survival Strategies in Russia* (Coventry: Centre for Comparative Labour Studies, 1999).

[38] See also Anders Aslund (ed.), *The post-Soviet Economy: Soviet and Western Perspectives* (London: Pinter, 1992).

Capitalism in command?

How, then, did the Russian reformers do when it came to implementing shock therapy? Better than one would have expected, but worse than one would have liked, and not well enough to save Russia from financial collapse in 1998.[39]

Liberalization had the most dramatic initial effect. Most price controls were lifted on 2 January 1992, and the rudiments of a market economy quickly surfaced. Not all prices were freed up however: energy prices for example were fixed for several years, while housing and utilities remained price-controlled. Measures to liberalize foreign trade were also undertaken. This led to a flood of imports—including food—and soon accounted for about half of all consumer spending. After a year's hiatus there was also an export boom, as producers switched their sales of oil, gas, metals, and chemicals from the CIS to hard-currency markets. There were however a number of obvious flaws in the programme of liberalization. For one thing, small businesses did not flourish, unlike in Poland where they became a vital engine of growth. Organized crime and bureaucratic regulation also did much to undermine Russian entrepreneurship. And while some effort was made to encourage foreign investment, the barriers—from political obstruction to the lack of legal protection—always remained high. Consequently, there was no great rush by Western firms to invest in Russia and by 1998 Russia had cumulative foreign investment of some $6 billion—less than Hungary, a country one tenth its size.

Stabilization took longer than liberalization to accomplish. The rouble was quickly made convertible into dollars, but inflation clocked 1,600 per cent in 1992, wiping out people's hard-earned savings. It was not until 1995 that the money supply and budget deficit were reined in, and inflation (monthly, not annual) came down to single digits. This stabilization was a house built on sand, however, since the tightening monetary policy was accompanied by the dollarization and demonetization of much of the economy. Many people kept their savings in dollars and many businesses conducted their transactions in dollars. Barter also spread apace, and by 1997 accounted for 50 per cent of all transactions in some industrial sectors (especially energy). Arrears also became a money-substitute: arrears to suppliers, to tax authorities, and in paying wages to one's workers.

In 1995, on the advice of the IMF, it was decided to finance the budget deficit in a non-inflationary way—by issuing treasury bonds (GKOs) rather than by printing money. On the surface, everything looked fine. From 1995 the rouble held its value against the dollar within the corridor announced by the Central Bank; it even appreciated in real terms. But this had its downside and very soon two parallel economies began to emerge: one monetized, taxed, and recorded for the international community; and the other hidden from view, demonetized, and at best paying taxes in kind, in goods and services, at local level. Gaddy and Ickes have referred to this barter system as a 'virtual economy' since it was based on subsidized, value-destroying enterprises. But one could equally argue that the financial sector was almost 'virtual' as well, particularly in light of the collapse of the banking system in August 1998.[40]

[39] For a more positive assessment see Anders Aslund, *Russia's Economic Transformation in the 1990s* (London: Pinter, 1997).

[40] Clifford Gaddy and Barry Ickes, 'Beyond the Bailout: Time to face Reality', *Foreign Affairs*, 77 (1998), pp. 53–67.

Even more worrying was the fall in industrial production. GDP plunged alarmingly in 1992, with a cumulative loss in economic output of between 40 and 50 per cent. Recovery only began in 1997, and then with an anaemic GDP growth of 0.8 per cent. Federal tax revenues also plummeted from 25–30 per cent of GDP in 1989 to 10–12 per cent by 1997, even though spending was still running at 15–18 per cent. These problems however tended to be explained away by the reformists. Thus the slump, they argued, was merely a product of changes in statistical reporting: formerly managers overreported output for the planners, now they under-reported output for the tax man; and to the extent that the output fall was real, it reflected an end to the production of non-goods like nuclear submarines and busts of Lenin. Likewise, the fall in government revenue was nothing to be too concerned about either. The Russian state's share in GDP was too large anyway for an economy at its level of development, or so it was argued. The government, moreover, had to learn that it must get out of the business of subsidizing farms or paying the utility costs of residents in economically non-viable parts of the old communist economy.

This brings us to the issue of privatization. Hailed as a major victory for the reformers, within the space of a few years up to 70 per cent of productive assets had been transferred out of state ownership into private hands. The privatization took place in three phases.

First, there was the conversion of state firms into private corporations at the stroke of a pen. The shares of these firms were held by federal and regional governments, or given to other firms (suppliers and customers). Gazprom, Russia's largest company, was privatized in this manner already in 1990, with the incumbent directors acting as trustees for the federal government's 40 per cent stake in the firm. Most of Russia' commercial banks were also created in this way, and they grew fat through currency speculation, handling government accounts, and trading in treasury bills.

Second, there was the voucher privatization programme of 1992. Citizens were given vouchers which they could use to bid for shares in former state enterprises, now registered as private corporations. Unlike the Czech scheme, however, workers and managers could opt to acquire a majority of the shares in their own firm, using a combination of vouchers and ploughed back profits. Seventy per cent of firms chose the worker-manager buyout. However, in most of them control over the shares was quickly concentrated in the hands of a small group of managers.

Third, there was privatization through cash sales, beginning in 1994. As we have already noted, the government was reluctant to sell to foreign investors while Russian buyers lacked the necessary capital. Thus in 1995 the privatization 'tsar', Anatolii Chubais, decided to go with the idea of swapping packets of shares in some leading oil and metals companies in return for loans from Russian banks. The transactions reeked of corruption: the prices were low relative to the firms' quoted earnings, and most of the auctions were by an affiliate of the bank organizing the bidding. Furthermore, much of the money that the banks were lending to the government came from state coffers. The loans-for-shares scheme enabled the Moscow-based banks to move into the industrial sector and try their hand at wealth creation. After the hiatus of the 1996 presidential election campaign, during which the oligarchs circled the wagons to ensure Yeltsin's re-election, privatization sales resumed.[41]

---

[41] For a critical examination of the consequences of privatization see Joseph R. Blasi, Maya Kroumova and Douglas Kruse, *Kremlin Capitalism: The Privatization of the Russian Economy* (ILR Press, Cornell University Press, 1996).

The 1998 August crisis

In spite of this very patchy record, Western advisors were brimming with optimism five to six years after the collapse of the USSR. One noted Western economist close to Yeltsin wrote effusively in 1995 about how Russia had become a market economy.[42] A year later two other apostles of neoliberalism predicted a new Russia boom.[43] Even in 1997, the IMF seemed to be brimming with good cheer.[44] True the reforms had been uneven in their consequences, but that, according to the optimists, was only to be expected. After all, one could not hope to make a fine market omelette without cracking a few eggs along the way. The political situation was also far from hopeless. Hence, while the Russian Communist Party remained strong, it did not pose a serious threat to the reforms or to Yeltsin who was re-elected to the presidency in 1996. In spring 1997 moreover a new reformist government led by First Deputy Prime Minister's Anatolii Chubais and Boris Nemtsov launched a second liberal revolution designed to tackle the yawning state budget deficit, boosting tax collection while cutting subsidies to energy users. In the same year, the Russian stock exchange surged by a full 85 per cent. And a year later, in March 1998, Yeltsin replaced premier Chernomyrdin, the grandfather of Gazprom, with Sergei Kirienko, a move which provided the opportunity for a renewed surge of Western optimism that another political barrier to the reform programme had been removed.

Yet all was not well, as even the youthful Kirienko was to admit on taking office. Russian reformers might have scored a few victories, he accepted: nonetheless many of those who had been the beneficiary of change—the new oligarchs—were now standing in the way of further radical surgery. They were not even paying their taxes, while most of the money they were making was flooding out of Russia into Western bank accounts. Nor, he argued, could serious people turn a blind eye to the fact that Russia was living on the 'never, never' with a foreign debt now standing at well over $140 bn and rising. Workers were also not being paid, and while a few at the top were getting fabulously wealthy, living standards for the overwhelming majority of Russians were continuing to decline. The outlook he concluded was by no means rosy. Others agreed. *The Economist* was one, and in the summer of 1998 published a particularly alarming report about the state of Russia. Its conclusions were bleak, alarmist even. Russia, it opined, stood on the edge of an economic precipice, with the rouble about to collapse, foreign investors beginning to panic and 'intelligent Muscovites' talking seriously (and for the first time in five years) about a financial and political crisis that could only be settled by force of arms. What it called a 'nightmare scenario' faced Russia and the only way of avoiding it was by taking even more thoroughgoing measures.[45]

For once the experts (unfortunately) managed to get Russia right, and within a month of *The Economist* hitting the news-stands in July, Russia was facing a

---

[42] Anders Aslund, *How Russia Became a Market Economy* (Washington, DC: Brookings Institution, 1995).

[43] Richard Layard and John Parker, *The Coming Russian Boom* (New York: The Free Press, 1996).

[44] So optimistic were the reformers that in September 1997 it was predicted that fairly soon Russia would need no further IMF funds. See Yeltsin's statement in *RFE/RL Newsline*, 18 September 1997.

[45] 'Russia's Crisis: Could it Lead to Fascism?', *The Economist*, 11 July 1998.

meltdown of epic proportions.[46] The immediate cause of the August crisis was the chronic fiscal deficit, in turn the product of an essentially unreformed economy in deep recession that produced little wealth, and a government unable to tax those profits that were being made. Experts are still divided over whether the August crisis was inevitable given Russia's deep structural flaws, or if it was just bad luck, the product of unfavourable international circumstances and some poor policy responses. Arguably the leading two policy errors, made back in 1995 and sustained to the bitter end, were fixing the rouble exchange rate at too high a level, and the decision to finance the yawning government deficit through international borrowing. Vladimir Popov has shown that the ratio of the rouble exchange rate to purchasing power parity (PPP) rose from around 50 per cent (the level of most East European currencies) to 70 per cent between 1995 and 1997.[47] This priced Russian manufactures out of export markets and exposed them to fierce import competition. Inevitably this led to a massive trade deficit (by mid-1998 Russia was running a $5.8 bn deficit). To add to its woes, Asian stock markets started to fold in October 1997, causing a Gadarene flight from emerging markets by international investors. Then, to make matters worse, Russia was hit badly by the ongoing fall in the price of oil from an average of $18 a barrel to a mere $11 by the end of 1998. This not only weakened Russia's trading position, but sent out a signal that it might not be able to underwrite its spiralling international debts.

In light of these trends, there were increasing calls for a devaluation of the rouble—from maverick economist Andrei Illarionov to financier Boris Berezovsky. Outside observers, however, discounted these concerns, operating on the assumption that Russia was too big to fail. They believed that the international financial institutions would always rally to shore up the reform efforts of the Yeltsin administration, and the rouble exchange rate was taken as the chief indicator of those efforts. A devaluation would cause panic in international markets, and would produce precisely the crisis it was supposed to avoid. Indeed, the IMF came through with a $22.6 bn aid package (approved by the IMF board on 20 July), including $4.8 bn in ready cash, which it was confident would protect the rouble against speculative attack.

Concerns over the rouble's stability were also reflected in the market for treasury bills (GKOs). GKO nominal rates averaged 63 per cent in 1996, fell to a low of 26 per cent in 1997 (when inflation was 11 per cent), but started to rise again in 1998. The rate hit 130 per cent by June, by which time the total stock of GKOs was about $40 bn, of which about half were held by foreigners or by Russian banks who had borrowed from foreigners to buy the bonds. The GKO pyramid was by then a full-blown Ponzi scheme, with new bonds being used to pay the interest on old bonds. By June the government was finding it hard to find buyers for GKOs even at rates in excess of 100 per cent. This left interest payments accounting for some 30 per cent of federal spending. In July 1998 to reduce the exposure to a possible rouble devaluation they managed to convert $6.4 bn of GKOs into Eurobonds at 15 per cent interest, denominated in dollars. That still left $11 bn of GKOs falling due by the end of September.

---

[46] See for example Marcus Warren, 'Russians Sleepwalking into Crisis', *The Daily Telegraph* (London) 18 August, 1987.
[47] Vladimir Popov, 'Will Russia achieve fast economic growth?', *Communist Economies and Economic Transformation*, 19:4, 1998, pp. 421–49.

In return for its bailout, the IMF insisted on an emergency package of spending cuts and tax increases to bring the fiscal deficit below three per cent of GDP. Meeting on 15 July, the State Duma accepted 12 of the government's proposed bills and rejected only two. Yeltsin anyway announced his intention to enforce by decree the tax increases which the Duma had rejected.

In the second week of August, as Russian government officials dispersed for their vacations in exotic corners of Europe, George Soros dropped a bombshell with his 13 August letter to the *Financial Times* predicting that Russia would have to devalue the rouble. On 17 August the Russian government announced a 90 day moratorium on foreign debt payments, a suspension of GKO payments, and allowed the rouble to devalue from $6 to $9. The financial system froze up, prices shot up, and by 9 September the rouble had fallen from $6 to $21.

After the crisis, or what went wrong?

The August crisis dealt a deadly blow to economic reform. Two seasoned analysts summed up the situation with devastating accuracy. The collapse of the currency, they noted, had finally put paid to the 'the big capitalist lie' that the market had succeeded in transforming Russia. The dream was over.[48] Few seemed to disagree. Some feared—and talked openly about—a return to Stalinism,[49] while others speculated about the more likely rehabilitation of a middle Gorbachevian way between communism and capitalism.[50] The collapse in Russia was also interpreted by many as serving notice on the much larger neoliberal economic project directed and overseen by the IMF. Certainly, coming when it did, in the midst of the Asian crisis, the implosion in Russia was regarded as having a significance that far outweighed its more immediate impact on the Russian economy. As *The Wall Street Journal* noted at the time, although the Russian economy was relatively minute in global terms—accounting for less than 2 per cent of world output in 1998—the impact of the situation there was bound to be great. Indeed, the paper very much feared that the events of August might easily set off a chain reaction that could end in a worldwide recession, if nothing was done to prevent it.[51]

While the August crisis shattered the Russian banking system, disrupted Russia's trade with its neighbours and pushed many firms into bankruptcy, dire predictions of hyperinflation, starvation, and economic turmoil did not materialize. A major crisis should have major consequences. After all, the dictionary definition of a crisis is that it is the critical stage in a disease after which the organism either recovers or dies. In this sense, the August crisis was most peculiar. The Russian economy did not recover, of course. On the other hand, it did not die. Even so, there was little to celebrate. Living standards remained low, and continued to fall. Investment slumped.

---

[48] Mark Franchetti and Peter Millar in *The Sunday Times* (London), 30 August 1998.
[49] George Friedman, 'Russian Economic Failure Invites a New Stalinism', *International Herald Tribune*, 11 September 1998.
[50] Adrian Karatnycky, 'The Rise of Russia's Third Force—Gorbachevism', *International Herald Tribune*, 15 September 1998.
[51] 'How Russia's Market Set Off a Global Chain Reaction', *The Wall Street Journal Europe*, 22 September 1998.

The middle class that had been created after 1992 was virtually wiped out. And what had once been the world's second-largest economy was now reduced to the level of a Brazil or Mexico. Meanwhile, the majority of the population slipped into survival mode.

The IMF, naturally enough, insists it did nothing wrong. The problem, it argues, was never its advice but rather the failure of the Russian government to follow its advice.[52] Moreover, in its view, there was really no alternative to what it originally advocated. But this is plainly absurd. On the one hand, this assumes there was no other middle way between neoliberalism and central planning; on the other, it ignores the simple fact that its own remedies—whether they were applied in Russia or not—have always tended to lead to indebtedness, inequality and impoverishment.[53] Thus even if its medicine had been swallowed completely (and much of it was) it would still have had pretty appalling consequences.

In Russia there were of course very specific problems and here it might be useful to distinguish between two phases in the so-called transition. In phase one—primarily 1992—Russian government policy was really quite simple: to stabilize the situation as quickly as possible. By 1995 the contours of the post-Soviet political regime had been established. It was only in this second phase, especially after April 1995, that IMF money started to flow into Russia in large quantities. By then, unfortunately, most of the damage had already been done. Yeltsin had become 'our man in the Kremlin'. The West had imposed its own particular brand of elitist democracy. And the oligarchs had taken over. At this point, the IMF now began to lend more and more money to the Russian government, just to keep it afloat. Thus between 1993 and 1994, it lent $3 bn in the form of a Systematic Transformation Facility. This was followed by a $6.5 bn stand-by loan in 1995, and an Extended Fund Facility commencing in 1996 which was to dispense $18.5 bn over three years. IMF approval was also taken as a green light for other sovereign and commercial lenders to continue to do business with Russia and to lend the Russian government even more money. Inevitably, the debt grew and by spring 1999 Russia owed $15 bn in Eurobonds, $11 bn in Finance Ministry bonds, $38 bn to the London Club and $26 bn to the Paris Club.[54] Nor did this include Western bank purchases of domestic GKOs, which together with all other loans amounted to something close to $150 bn.

In effect, the international community bailed out the sinking ship of state and helped keep Boris Yeltsin in office between 1992 and 1996, a period in which some fortunes were made but which saw little lasting progress towards real structural reform. Certainly, the IMF were aware that the Russian government was failing to meet all the conditions attached to its loans; nonetheless, money continued to be released at quarterly intervals, although some tranches were delayed for a few months. Loan agreements with foreign governments are confidential documents, and it will be up to future scholars to reconstruct the precise record. However, it seems *prima facie* that the IMF fell into the trap of moral hazard. Once the Russian government realized that it could fudge compliance with loan conditions, it made it that much harder to try to make the conditions stick the next time round. The loans,

---

[52] See my 'IMF Meeting Weighs Results of Past Seven Years', *Jamestown Foundation Monitor*, 1 December 1998.

[53] See Charlotte Denny, 'Mountains of Debts', *The Guardian* (London), 6 August 1999.

[54] *Reuters*, 2 June 1999.

most likely, will never be recovered. There is also a very real danger that Russian politicians will seek to blame those who advanced the loans for their own economic mismanagement. According to a Public Opinion Foundation poll, when Russians were asked in 1998 whether the IMF had brought benefit or harm to Russia, 17 per cent said benefit, 19 per cent harm, and 46 per cent didn't know. By March 1999 however opinion had shifted: 14 per cent now said benefit, 43 per cent harm, and 28 per cent had no opinion.[55]

We thus seem to have the worst of all possible worlds: on the one side stands Russia, trapped by a huge overhang of debt that can only retard its recovery; on the other is the West, locked into an embrace from which it cannot escape, with a recalcitrant debtor that shows no signs of mending its ways. Ordinary Russians also feel cheated. They have been forced to give up what they once had—limited though that undoubtedly was—but have gained very little in return. The only people it seems who have no regrets are those Western advisors who helped get Russia into the mess it is now in. But perhaps even they should be regarded less as monsters and more as victims of their own false consciousness, and of a particular economic ideology that brooked no dissent. Certainly, in the climate of the early 1990s, there was no way that the US in particular was going to contemplate any other option for Russia than the one that was ultimately pursued. The central thrust of policy was the promotion of global trade liberalization—the creation of NAFTA, the conversion of GATT into the World Trade Organization and the opening up of the rest of the world to American products and ideas. Even if anyone had understood the possibility of another model for Russia, it would have created conceptual, not to mention political, dissonance to have voiced an alternative given the prevailing economic orthodoxy of the time.

Conclusion

According to some commentators, the failure of market reform in Russia can only lead to increased tension between an increasingly resentful Russia and the West, especially if the current impasse increases the political influence of the Russian Communist Party and its nationalist allies. This indeed would seem to be the view of the US itself, whose original support for economic reform was based not just on material considerations or the belief that capitalism is a good thing, but an assumption that a reforming Russia would be a friendly and cooperative Russia. Thus it follows, that if Russia is not reforming, it is bound to be, or at least more likely to become, hostile.

This argument is not without some basis in fact, and one can point to Russia's opposition to NATO expansion, its awkward behaviour in the Balkans, and its sale of arms to regimes hostile to the West, as proof that an unreformed Russia is likely to be an unfriendly Russia. But this would be a one-sided conclusion. Russia might not be as compliant as many in the West would hope. On the other hand, it has not turned out to be much of a problem either. And for a good realist reason: it is simply not in its interest to be a problem. At least two factors need to be mentioned

---

[55] *The Washington Post*, 4 April 1999.

here. The first is Russia's debt to the West. Dependent and indebted states have few choices and even fewer options, and as long as Russia needs regular injections of Western money to sustain it, it is unlikely to bite the hand that feeds it. There is also the question of the new class ruling Russia. While the oligarchs might have been a critical factor undermining serious reform, this does not mean they want a fight with the capitalist world. Let's not forget, they have to put their money somewhere, and as long as the opportunities remain better outside Russia than in it, Russian foreign policy is likely to be guided by pragmatists with a stake in Western stability rather than nationalists hostile to the Western project. Finally, there is the even more basic problem of capabilities. In the end, the Soviet Union lost the Cold War because capitalism proved to be more productive than Soviet-style socialism. Economics is also likely to play an equally important role in shaping Russia's post-Cold War relations with the West: and as long as post-Soviet Russia continues to decline economically while the West continues to prosper, it simply won't have the capacity to upset the *status quo*. As Vaclav Havel has pointed out, a weak and demoralized Russia is less likely to be a problem for the rest of the world than a strong Russia. 'Better an ill Russia than a healthy Soviet Union' he once noted. Whether the Soviet Union was ever really healthy is a matter of conjecture. What is not in doubt is the seriousness of Russia's illness and thus its continued inability to play a serious role in world affairs.

Europe after the Cold War: interstate order or post-sovereign regional system?

WILLIAM WALLACE

The changing structure of European order poses, for any student of international relations, some fundamental questions about the evolution of world politics.[1] Concepts of European order and of the European state system are, after all, central to accepted ideas of international relations. Out of the series of conflicts and negotiations—religious wars, coalitions to resist first the Hapsburg and then the Bourbon attempt at European hegemony—developed ideas and practices which still structure the contemporary global state system: the equality of states; international law as regulating relations among sovereign and equal states; domestic sovereignty as exclusive, without external oversight of the rules of domestic order. The 'modern' state system, modern scholars now agree, did not spring fully-clothed from the Treaty of Westphalia at the close of the Thirty Years' War; it evolved through a succession of treaties and conferences, from 1555 to 1714. It remains acceptable, nevertheless, to describe the European state order as built around the Westphalian system.[2]

In the twentieth century, these rules have been modified but not replaced. The European state system—which was the international state system until almost a hundred years ago—has expanded into a global state system. The UN and other global institutions are based upon recognizably similar assumptions to those which governed the eighteenth- and nineteenth-century European orders, modified at the margins to limit the exclusive nature of domestic sovereignty and to give some large states more say in some institutions.

As this European system has extended across the globe, however, the now-regional European order has mutated. Divided into spheres of influence between two hegemonic powers after 1945, its Western states—under a benevolent American hegemony—accepted shared institutions, and limits on their sovereignty, which have crept gradually closer to the central issues of national sovereignty as their economies have integrated and their societies become more interdependent. The significance of this development for our understanding of international relations as a whole has to some extent been limited by the reluctance of most international relations scholars

---

[1] Earlier drafts of this article were presented as a 125th anniversary public lecture at the University of Wales, Aberystwyth, and as a paper for the third Pan-European International Relations Conference in Vienna in September 1998. I am grateful to Helen Wallace and Franziska Hagedorn for additional comments.

[2] There is a substantial recent literature reassessing the development of the Westphalian system. See, for example, Stephen D. Krasner, 'Westphalia and All That', ch. 9 in Judith Goldstein and Robert O Keohane (eds.), *Ideas and Foreign Policy* (Ithaca, NY. Cornell University Press, 1993); Alexander Murphy, 'The Sovereign State as Political-territorial Ideal: Historical and Contemporary Considerations', ch. 3 in Thomas J. Biersteker and Cynthia Weber (eds.), *State Sovereignty as Social Construct* (Cambridge: Cambridge University Press, 1996).

to examine the regional international relations of Europe in much detail, and the predisposition of most students of European integration to start from Brussels and work outwards, rather than start from the changing European context and work in.

The technological and economic changes which constitute the phenomenon of globalization have had a particularly intense impact on the European region, for evident reasons. Core Western Europe—the Rhine valley and delta, reaching across the Western Alps into northern Italy and the Mediterranean coastline from Barcelona to Genoa, and across the Channel into southern England (the economic geographers' 'European banana')—is one of the world's most densely-populated regions, as well as one of the world's most prosperous regions. The population of the EU-15 is, at 371 million, 40 per cent higher than that of the United States, living within a territory 35 per cent the size.[3] The market and border regimes developed within Western Europe over the past fifty years are peculiarly favourable to the development of cross-border links. The 'light touch' border controls between the United Kingdom and its European partners are matched in their relaxed character outside Europe only on the US-Canada border. Between France and Germany, the Netherlands and Belgium, border controls have long since ceased to operate.

For students of globalization, therefore, the European region represents either a model which other regions are likely to follow, or an exception which demonstrates the importance of regulatory and border regimes, and of institutions and rules, in governing global development. The current expansion of this framework of regional institutions, regulations and regimes across the former socialist states of eastern Europe, as well as its extra-territorial extension across Europe's dependent periphery to the east and south, offers a further case-study from which international relations scholars may wish to draw broader conclusions.

Though the European region has now become an intensely institutionalized order, the EU is not unchallengeably the defining European institution. Ten years after the Cold War ended, European political and security issues are managed as much through NATO as through the EU. The focus in this article is on the challenges to national governments and international institutions which the European region now presents, to which the EU and its member governments have to respond: the con-tinuing transformation of (West) Europe through economic and social integration and technological change; the transformation of central and eastern Europe since 1989, as they have reoriented their political systems, economies and societies towards the West; and the efforts which Western institutions—most importantly NATO and the EU—have made since then to accommodate the drive by post-socialist regimes to 'rejoin the West'. It then outlines some alternative scenarios for the future development of European order, relating them to competing theoretical assumptions about the dynamics of politics and international relations.[4]

---

[3] This includes the almost-uninhabited Arctic regions of Sweden and Finland; the EU-12, before the 1995 enlargement, had 350 million people living in an area 25 per cent the size of that occupied by 263m Americans. Population density in the Netherlands and North Rhine-Westphalia is close to that of Singapore.

[4] For evidence on the transformation of Western Europe, I have drawn extensively on chapters contributed to William Wallace (ed.), *The Dynamics of European Integration* (London: RIIA/Pinter, 1990), and on chapters contributed to Helen Wallace and William Wallace (eds.), *Policy-making in the European Union* (4th edn: Oxford University Press, forthcoming 2000). Other sources I have found particularly useful include Ole Tunander and others, *Geopolitics in Post-Wall Europe: Security, Territory and Identity* (London: Sage for PRIO, 1997), and the earlier studies by Hugh Miall, *Shaping the New Europe* (London: RIIA/Pinter 1993) and Christoph Bertram, *Europe in the Balance*

Rethinking Europe

Ten years after the end of the Cold War, the European region is moving towards a new pattern of international relations. Western Europe's established system of highly-institutionalized multilateral politics is being gradually expanded, to incorporate or associate the former socialist states to its east and south-east. But its structure, boundaries, and component units remain unclear. It is arguable that the region within which the modern state system emerged is now moving towards a post-modern and post-sovereign political system, in which authority will be shared among different levels of government—and in which the Westphalian concept of sovereignty will have disappeared, with a more diverse and open international civil society emerging in its place, with multiple levels of authority and governance. If the European region is now moving away from such operating assumptions in a radical way, then we have evidence for a revolutionary transformation of the established state system, which might in time extend to other regions.[5]

Realists reply, however, that the apparent emergence of a benign and civilian European international society, institutionalized through the EU, depends upon the continuation of American political and security leadership, institutionalized through NATO.[6] The relationship between the EU and NATO is one of the least well-defined aspects of contemporary European international politics: rarely discussed within governments, let alone between the two international institutions. That is partly because any clarification of the institutional relationship would redefine the political relationship between the US and the major European governments (by which I mean Germany, France and Britain, and in the second rank Spain, Italy and the Netherlands); which all of these governments, for different reasons, were reluctant until very recently to address.[7]

Realists also reply that the political authority of national governments, as representatives of states, remain only marginally impaired by the development of economic and social interdependence; and that major governments still define and control the European international agenda. They see the compromises which emerged out of the Treaty of Amsterdam, and even more the political manoeuvring over appointments to the European Central Bank, as evidence that a new interstate order is emerging, based upon intensive multilateral bargaining among representatives of states—very different in style from the eighteenth and nineteenth century

---

(Washington: Carnegie Endowment, 1995). See also the interesting group of essays on *New European Orders, 1919 and 1991*, edited by Samuel F. Wells and Paula Bailey Smith (Washington: Woodrow Wilson Center/Johns Hopkins, 1996).

[5] Robert Cooper, *The Post-modern State and the World Order* (London: Demos,1996), lays particular stress on the transformation of security relations in the European region as providing evidence of an emerging post-sovereign order. This paper was originally written as a planning paper within the British Foreign and Commonwealth Office.

[6] Josef Joffe, 'Europe's American pacifier', *Foreign Policy*, Spring 1984, pp. 64–82.

[7] On the centrality of the American security guarantee to West European integration, see Alfred Grosser, *The Western Alliance: European-American relations since 1945* (London: Macmillan, 1980); Anton de Porte, *Europe Between the Superpowers: The Enduring Balance* (New Haven, CT: Yale University Press, 1986); Geir Lundestad, *Empire by Invitation: The United States and European Integration, 1945–1997* (Oxford: Oxford University Press, 1998).

European state systems, but not different in principle.[8] The transformation of Europe, for them, consists in the partial disengagement of the United States since the end of the Cold War, in the gradual emergence of Poland as a major player alongside the major West European governments, and in the changing positions of Russia, Turkey and now-independent Ukraine on the periphery of the regional system.

Perhaps the most remarkable aspect of developments within the European regional system in the late 1990s is the speed of change, without shared concepts of where changes may lead to or what eventual shape of society or order should be pursued. The retirement of Helmut Kohl has removed from European politics the last protagonist for a federal political union in Europe, born of the bitter historical experience of the Second World War. Yet paradoxically West European states appear to be moving further away from the old intergovernmental model as their political leaders become more hesitant about where they may be moving to. A single currency has been introduced within the West European EU, without agreement on the political or economic implications of its introduction. Cooperation among police, intelligence agencies, customs and border/immigration agencies is growing rapidly, without any consensus about the implications for concepts of citizenship or democratic accountability. Economic and social transborder interactions continue to rise, while democratic politics remains stubbornly territorial; transnational elites coexist with surges of national populism. Even defence integration, since the Franco-British St. Malo declaration of December 1998, is at last coming onto the West European agenda.

Both the EU and NATO are committed in principle to radical enlargement to incorporate the former socialist states of central and eastern Europe, but without accepting that enlargement will necessarily transform the character of both institutions. The nation state remains the only accepted basis for legitimate representation in such institutions; but across Europe 'suppressed' nations are challenging the established structure of recognized nation-states. Within Western Europe several states are becoming looser entities, while in Eastern Europe weak states continue to emerge from national aspirations and discontents. The break-up of Yugoslavia may not yet have ended; the status of Kosovo and Montenegro hovers between autonomous region and independent state. Malta is now reviving its application to join the EU, alongside Cyprus, Slovenia, Estonia, Lithuania and Latvia; four of these are also pressing to join NATO. Accession to European institutions of a succession of states with populations and GNPs much smaller than those of sub-state entities within other member states—Catalonia, Lombardy, Flanders, Scotland, Bavaria—may strain the principle of sovereign equality, and the privileged position of states within the European system, to breaking point.

A number of underlying contradictions within the established West European multilateral (and multilevel) order should be noted:

---

[8] This is the underlying argument of Andrew Moravcsik, *The Choice for Europe: Social Purpose and State Power from Messina to Maastricht* (Ithaca, NY: Cornell University Press, 1998). See also Andrew Moravcsik and Kalypso Nicolaidis, 'Explaining the Treaty of Amsterdam: Interest, Influence, Institutions', *Journal of Common Market Studies*, 37:1 (1999), pp. 59–86.

- States have ceased to act as gatekeepers between domestic and international politics in intra-European relations; but the dominant framework for political debate and political recruitment nevertheless remains the state.
- Substantial areas of previously national decision-making and regulation have been transferred into multilateral bargaining within international institutions; but mechanisms of political accountability have been left behind within nation-state structures.
- Transnational elites have flourished within this open West European space; transgovernmental coalitions have become a normal aspect of multilateral politics. Cross-border personal ties and communications hold European politics and economics together to a far greater degree than in the eighteenth and nineteenth century European systems. Yet for the mass of Europe's population identity, loyalty and culture remain firmly anchored in national symbols and institutions.
- Integration of policy areas formerly considered intrinsic aspects of domestic politics into multilateral European institutions has moved a long way over the past 15 years, affecting law and order, border controls, and currency. But the core issues of 'high politics'—foreign policy and defence—have so far remained clearly under state control, 50 years after the West European Union was founded, 30 years after European political cooperation began.

There is evidence here to support either a modified Realist approach or a trans-formationalist Idealist approach to an understanding of European international politics. Students of West European integration have long grappled with the problem of interpreting patterns of shared policymaking which from one perspective look functional and transnational, but from another perspective intergovernmental. Any attempt to describe and define the emerging character of this wider post-Cold War Europe is faced with a similar dilemma.

The transformation of Western Europe

Cold war rhetoric, before 1989, spoke conventionally of the 'two halves of Europe'. The reality exposed by the political and economic collapse of socialist regimes was that the countries to the west of the Iron Curtain represented the core of Europe—economically, politically, socially and culturally—as they had done for 1,000 years before 1945.[9] The institutions which had 'integrated' eastern Europe, CMEA and the Warsaw Pact, rapidly collapsed; successor regimes clamoured to be allowed to join Western institutions, from the Council of Europe to the key institutions of NATO and the EU. The first postsocialist governments had very little idea of the implications of joining such institutions, let alone the constraints on their newly-regained sovereignty which they would impose. It is thus the West European system which is now in the process of expansion eastwards to form the basis of the post-Cold War regional order. The evolution of the West European system, both before and since

---

[9] The argument here is set out more fully in ch. 2 of William Wallace, *The Transformation of Western Europe*, London: RIIA/Pinter 1990.

1989, provides one of the most important indicators of the likely shape of this wider emerging order.

The most distinctive governmental characteristic of this regional system is its intensive multilateralism. Geographical concentration and excellent transport links make it easy for national elites, from heads of government down, to interact in person, by phone or by video link, as regularly as they need. In 1998 prime ministers met together six times in the European Council, each time for the better part of two days: conference diplomacy of an intensity unimaginable a century ago.[10] It has been a commonplace for 15 years that foreign ministers meet each other more often than they meet their colleagues within their own national Cabinets: in the General Affairs Council of the EU (which meets between 15 and 20 times a year), in informal meetings of EU foreign ministers, alongside their prime ministers in European Councils, in WEU ministerial meetings—and for those from larger states also in G8, in contact groups such as that which has handled the Bosnian conflict. Finance ministers have come to interact more intensively as the EU has moved towards a single currency; central bankers have become a collective body. Even interior ministers by the late 1990s were meeting as a group every two to three months, attending each other's seminars and conferences, on first name terms with each other.

If interaction were only among ministers, then it might still be possible for government to play two-level games, addressing different messages to separate domestic and foreign audiences. But the two audiences overlap, swap information, form transgovernmental coalitions, respond to transnational lobbies. European governance is above all governance by committee: through multilateral negotiation, mutual accommodation, intensive and extensive consultations and exchanges of information. Senior civil servants in all important national ministries in all West European states travel incessantly, up to two to three days per working week. Their diaries are shaped by the round of regular multilateral meetings, and the bilateral consultations which supplement them. Mutual interpenetration of governments and state administrations has extended further into joint training schemes, exchanges of personnel among national ministries, secondment from national administrations to the Brussels institutions of officials who later return to senior positions in national capitals. Alongside these, and out of these, have grown transgovernmental elite networks; centred around shared expertise, shared party groups, or shared administrative needs or client interests.[11] No other international region, no group of established states, has experienced this phenomenon of political and administrative interaction.

---

[10] At the time of writing five European Councils were calendared in 1999, including a special European Council entirely devoted to judicial cooperation, measures against cross-border crime, and asylum and immigration policy, in Tampere, Finland in October. Most European heads of government also meet at the semi-annual NATO summits; those of the larger states meet with the US President and others in G8. Bilateral meetings build personal links, and coalitions, in between multilateral conferences.

[11] Fiona Hayes-Renshaw and Helen Wallace, *The Council of Ministers* (London: Macmillan, 1997); M. P. C. M. van Schendelen (ed.), *EC Committees as influential policy-makers* (Aldershot: Ashgate, 1998); Wolfgang Wessels, 'An Ever Closer Fusion? A Dynamic Macropolitical View on Integration Processes', *Journal of Common Market Studies*, 35:2 (1997), pp. 267–99; Simon Hix and Christopher Lord, *Political Parties in the European Union* (London: Macmillan, 1997).

As the massive literature on West European integration has demonstrated, Western Europe as an international system has been undergoing an autonomous transformation over the past half-century, well underway before the geopolitical transformation of 1989–91. This process of transformation, both of the formal conduct of relations among states and of informal transborder interactions, surged further forward in the 1980s, and has continued through the 1990s. Western Europe has now moved far away from the nineteenth century state-to-state model. Some scholars, it is true, draw comparisons between the integrated economy and transnational elite of pre-1914 Europe and the circumstances of Europe today.[12] But economic barriers between European states were high in the years before 1914, border posts well defended.

The international community of contemporary Western Europe displays a number of distinctive features. Levels of transborder economic interaction are qualitatively higher than within any other international region.[13] The expansion of regional trade in the 1960s, as tariff barriers were removed, has been reinforced by the development of integrated production across the region, with self-consciously 'European' companies producing finished articles from components procured from across the region, to sell across the region. The 'common market' achieved by 1970 has been succeeded by the 'single market' achieved by 1992, built through the harmonization and mutual recognition of previously-national regulations, food and safety standards, testing and inspection procedures. This European process has been paralleled by 'global' negotiations within GATT/WTO and OECD; which have in practice more closely resembled bilateral US-European negotiations, through which the US Administration has attempted to reconcile European regulations with American interests.

Measured by the standards of interstate relations rather than by those of an established federation, levels of transborder social interaction across Western Europe are also extraordinarily high. In nineteenth century Europe aristocrats and plutocrats moved across the continent, with the socially-excluded—Jews, urban unemployed—struggling across frontiers or leaving for the New World as migrants and refugees. The great mass of the population within European states however lived, worked and died entirely within their state boundaries, unless they were conscripted into military service abroad or—as after the First World War—the boundaries of their state changed around them.

We now have strong evidence of shifting concepts of social space within Western Europe. Tourism has moved decisively from a national to a European frame; sport (and sports stars and supporters) now operates as much on the European level as the national. Cross-border work patterns have developed, both for professional elites and for manual jobs like building workers and truck drivers. Some millions of well-to-do Europeans now own second homes outside their 'home' state; hundreds of

---

[12] See, for example, chapter 2 of Paul Hirst and Grahame Thompson, *Globalization in Question* (Cambridge, UK: Polity, 1996).

[13] Integration of the Canadian and Mexican economies with that of the United States is in some ways comparable, institutionalized within the North American Free Trade Area (NAFTA). But the overwhelming size of the American economy within NAFTA limits the extent of mutual economic integration. The relative autonomy of the European single market within the world economy—the ratio of external trade to GDP—is comparable to that of the American economy. The EU is not however the world's largest integrated market, as Brussels officials like to claim; India and China, though less prosperous, represent larger internal markets in population terms.

thousands of northern Europeans have settled in retirement around the northern shore of the Mediterranean, echoing the larger numbers from the northern US who have retired to Florida.[14] Rising levels of intermarriage have pushed West European governments into complex negotiations on common rules for the division of property and the custody of children on divorce. Cross-border shopping has mushroomed, exploiting differential tax rates. Student exchange continues to rise.[15]

Transborder communications have been transformed both by technological advance and through deliberate policy. 'Trans-European Networks' (TENs) is the title of an EU programme and budget line, as well as a description of the removal of the bottlenecks left around national borders by the strategic transport planning of nineteenth century states. The European traveller may now cruise along the motorways which cross Western Europe's historic battlegrounds: from Paris past the Somme to Waterloo and Brussels, from Kaiserslautern to the supermarket in Metz or Verdun. Trans-Europe Expresses (TEEs) take civil servants and businessmen, tourists and students, from Amsterdam to Basle, Milan to Munich; the opening of the Channel Tunnel has made it quicker to travel from London to Brussels and Paris than to Edinburgh or Plymouth.

The loosening of border controls foreseen in the Treaty of Rome has led gradually on to their further weakening, under the pressure of people and traffic crossing them, and from there to their effective disappearance, indeed deliberate abolition: not only among states with particular historical and geographical links (Benelux, the UK–Ireland and Nordic Travel Areas) but more widely through the 1985 Schengen Agreement and the 1997 Amsterdam Treaty. This loss of *national* control over the movement of citizens and aliens has been balanced by the growth of transnational cooperation among state law-enforcement agencies: police, customs, immigration, intelligence services, judicial administrations, interior ministries—the guarantors of domestic order, learning to work together now that domestic order can only be guaranteed through extensive international cooperation.[16]

One should however recognize that national differences remain important, national (and linguistic) boundaries still easily observable in patterns of exchange. Transborder labour mobility is 'sticky', in terms of the expectations of labour market economists, with levels of movement far lower than within North America in spite of the much smaller physical distances involved. Comparison of Western Europe's degree of economic and social integration with that of the United States puts into perspective how far away it remains from the United States of Europe which American and European enthusiasts in the late 1940s wanted to create.

The limits of political community are also evident in the weakness of European-level media, with the consequent absence of a shared public debate across this half-established West European space. Language barriers, cultural reference points, still sharply differentiate the reception and interpretation of news. The number of

---

[14] See for example Keith Hoggart and Henry Buller, 'Retired British Home Owners in Rural France', *Ageing and Society*, 15 (1995), pp. 325–53. France, the largest state by physical area within the EU, is host to the largest number of expatriate second homes; followed by Italy, Spain and Greece.

[15] *Student mobility in the European Community*, 27th Report of the Select Committee on the European Communities, House of Lords, 1997–98 (London: HMSO, HL-116 1997–8).

[16] Monica den Boer and William Wallace, 'Justice and Home Affairs', ch. 18 in Wallace and Wallace, *Policy-making in the European Union* (4th edition: Oxford University Press, forthcoming 2000); *Dealing with the Third Pillar: the Government's perspective*, 15th Report from Select Committee on the European Communities, House of Lords, 1997–8 (London: HMSO, HL-73 1997–8).

Europeans who watch television from outside their home country remains minute; the *Financial Times*, the nearest Western Europe has to an international newspaper, prints in several countries but sells less than 100,000 copies in Europe outside Britain. National media, from newspapers to TV, respond to and reinforce national images and assumptions, interpreting the same event in different ways to different audiences.

Can one discern, as optimists for European integration would hope, the growth of a Europe-wide civil society? Here again the evidence is ambivalent. The integration of European elites—intellectual, economic, even political/administrative—has already been noted. Some European social movements have become more than loose coalitions, most of all in the environmental field; the ability of Greenpeace to mobilize protests across several West European states against BP on the Brent Spar issue was as impressive as it was mistaken. Some of the many European lobby groups which cluster around Brussels have come to form effective transnational networks; the European Round Table, for example, operates for its self-consciously European companies from one capital to another.[17] But a strong national 'stickiness' is evident here, too. Cultural and political values differ widely from one national/state community to another. Animal welfare issues move British citizens to demonstrate, but not French; the international development movement in northern (and Protestant) Europe is not only more active, but focuses on different issues than its counterparts in the south. Different diasporas—Turks in Germany, Algerians in France, South Asians and Cypriots in Britain—orient domestic politics in different directions.

Some institutions which might in principle be thought natural motors for integration—banks, universities—are so strongly rooted in national institutions and national traditions as to prove deeply resistant to international integration. Cross-border bank mergers in Europe have proved far more difficult than mergers among companies. University collaboration and exchanges have struggled to overcome different assumptions about teaching, funding, academic hierarchy, and relationship to the state; there remain, for example, scarcely any professors from other European states in French and German universities, while British lecturers are challenging Italian treatment of non-Italian academic staff before the European Court of Justice.

The European Union is pursuing the idea of building 'European citizenship', espoused by the EC 20 years ago. European passports have been harmonized, and Europe's citizens now file through its external borders in lines differentiated from those from third countries. The Maastricht Treaty gave EU citizens resident in other member states the right to vote in local and European elections, while officials from justice and interior ministries have negotiated common rules on divorce and child custody to cope with rising intermarriage. But many obstacles remain before one can talk dispassionately of a single European space for citizens. Distinctive national tax regimes complicate cross-border employment; registration requirements in several member states complicate the establishment of residence and the ownership of property. Ethnic minorities are subject to different treatment in different states, and

---

[17] Sonia Mazey and Jeremy Richardson, 'The Logic of Organization: Interest Groups', ch. 11 in Richardson (ed.), *European Union: Power and Policy-making* (London: Routledge, 1996); Mazey and Richardson (eds.), *Lobbying in the European Community* (Oxford: Oxford University Press, 1993).

have different degrees of entitlement to legal protection and to the acquisition of citizenship.

Western Europe can be said to represent a post-sovereign state order, rooted in the emergence of a loose regional sense of political community, a highly-integrated regional economy and intense mutual interaction among different levels of national, subnational and European-level governance. But it has not yet displaced the state as a dominant point of reference, in political or social life. The major step forward taken in 1999 to a single currency for most EU member states, managed by a European Central Bank, may take it further away from the Westphalian model, bringing fiscal policy, larger elements of taxation, and economic management as such, much more directly onto the European level. But the representatives of national governments are likely to remain for some time the major players in this complex game of multilateral multilevel politics that characterizes the transformed political system of Western Europe.[18]

The transformation of central and eastern Europe

The collapse of central European regimes in 1989–90 witnessed a brief flowering of social movements and popular demonstrations, often led by dissidents who had established contacts with sympathizers in Western Europe in the difficult conditions of the 'second Cold War' of ten years before. This wonderful surge of social movements however subsided as enthusiasm gave way to the hard choices of political and economic transition, presented by inexperienced politicians to unprepared electorates. Most dissidents failed to adapt to the compromises and the grind of day-to-day politics. They thus gave way to more conventional politicians, who knew how to organize national politics and rebuild state structures, and to play the tunes of national reassertion while negotiating the terms of association with Western institutions.

One paradox evident in central and eastern Europe after 1989 has been the reassertion of national sovereignty and independence within a political and economic framework which depended on access to sovereignty-constraining Western institutions. A linked paradox is that the achievement of full sovereignty for ex-socialist states—particularly for states emerging out of former federations, such as Estonia, Slovenia, Macedonia—has depended on their acceptance by Western institutions as appropriate associates, even as potential candidates for future membership. Another has been the perceived importance of state- and nation-building in the process of transition, within a context in which state institutions had been partly discredited by socialism, and national unity was hard to rebuild among those who had survived 50 years of socialist domination through different compromises with the regime.

Commitments to Western integration were made well before the implications of integration for national autonomy were understood. In the first flush of post-socialist optimism, central European governments seem to have hoped that the West

---

[18] I have developed this argument at greater length in 'The Sharing of Sovereignty: The European Paradox', *Political Studies*, 47, special issue on sovereignty, pp. 503–521, 1999.

would welcome them with few conditions and with open arms. The negotiations on Trade and Cooperation Agreements between the EU and the Polish, Czech and Hungarian Governments, during the course of 1990–91, were thus a painful and disillusioning experience. Willingness on the part of post-socialist governments to adopt Western models, in part or in full, as the processes of legal and administrative transition rebuilt structures of domestic sovereignty and redefined the boundaries between state and civil society, was met by the imposition of detailed conditions by the EU, by NATO, by the EBRD and other Western bodies.[19]

The process of transition in the countries between Germany and Russia has therefore become one in which the targets set have been imposed from the outside, from the dominant West, supported by externally-provided advisers and training programmes. Brief initiatives for cooperation within the region—the Italian-initiated 'Pentagonale', the Visegrad group—have given way to competition, to gain preferred access to Western markets and institutions, and preferred status and attention in the major West European capitals. Once the first flush of euphoria had evaporated, in 1990–91, most governments of 'the lands in between' concluded that dependence on the West was a strongly preferred alternative to dependence on the East—on Russia. Memories of the uncertain interwar years, when overlapping claims to unite national groups with ambitiously-drawn state boundaries entrenched regional insecurity, reinforced this emerging consensus that security, and prosperity, were to be found through formal integration with their Western neighbours, accepting the conditions and limitations on sovereignty which they imposed.[20] Transition, in effect, has become a process which ends in incorporation—of the weak states of central and eastern Europe into the structures established to manage Western Europe.[21]

Over the nine years since Poland first moved to a non-socialist government, patterns of informal integration have already done much to reorient the geographically closer and more economically-advanced states within the region into West Europe's economic and social space. Seventy per cent of Poland's trade in 1997 was with the West; Czech and Hungarian trade was even more strongly Western-oriented. Western investment had flowed most strongly into these three countries but also into Slovenia, Croatia and the Baltic states, and more hesitantly into the Balkans. Polish factories which had formed part of the Warsaw Pact's military-industrial complex are now making sub-assemblies for Western aircraft firms; Skoda, transferred to German ownership, is becoming one of the most successful units within Volkswagen. Western tourists in large numbers have learned to enjoy the scenery (and the lower prices) of Prague, Budapest and Warsaw, or of skiing in the Tatras and the Carpathians. Smaller numbers from the region have moved across the West: students on scholarships, migrants working legally or 'on the black', families

---

[19] Ulrich Sedelmeier and Helen Wallace, 'Policies towards Central and Eastern Europe', ch. 14 in Wallace and Wallace, *Policy-making in the European Union*, 3rd edn. 1996; Jan Zielonka, 'Policies without strategy: the EU's record in eastern Europe', ch. 9 in Jan Zielonka (ed.), *Paradoxes of European Foreign Policy* (the Hague: Kluwer, 1998). See also Stuart Croft and others, *The Enlargement of Europe* (Manchester: Manchester University Press, 1999).

[20] The government of Slovakia until after the 1998 elections provided one exception to this development, seeking accession but rejecting the political conditions attached. The government of Croatia maintained a similar position into 1999. Serbian Yugoslavia has of course provided a far sharper exception, resisting all Western conditions and pressures, and making no effort to seek access to Western institutions.

[21] Karen Henderson (ed.), *Back to Europe: Central and Eastern Europe and the European Union* (London: UCL Press, 1999).

visiting those who fled or were displaced during and after the Second World War and who have now established themselves in the comfortable West to which their relations aspire.

On almost all measures this is, in the late 1990s, a relationship of highly asymmetrical interdependence: of Eastern dependence on the West, without significant Western dependence on the East. Poland accounts for 1 per cent of German external trade, for less than 1 per cent of EU external trade as a whole. The entire ex-socialist region, from Frankfurt an der Oder to Vladivostock, accounts for some 10 per cent of the EU's trade—with a classic asymmetrical trading pattern, oil and gas, other raw materials and semimanufactures flowing west, machinery and finished products flowing east. Central European economies have opened to Western investment, accepting that prized local companies become part of Western multinationals—even substantial parts of the Czech brewing industry—without gaining substantial stakes in Western economies in return. Experts travel east to advise, train and teach; would-be experts travel west to learn.

But where does Europe end?

Western Europe—or, the West, since for security issues through NATO the US is a central player in the reshaping of Europe—has responded to this opening up of the regions to the east with deep ambivalence. In the autumn of 1989, when the prospect presented itself of four central European states (these were then the German Democratic Republic, Poland, Hungary and Czechoslovakia) detaching themselves from the 'Eastern bloc' and attaching themselves to the West, enlargement of Western institutions through the reincorporation of historic central Europe appeared welcome and manageable. As other states further east and south-east followed, Western ambivalence grew. The Baltic states, with sponsors in the Nordic countries, historic ties with Germany and exile groups in Britain and North America, present a special case: small enough to incorporate without excessive cost, self-evidently in need of Western security provision. Slovenia, relatively prosperous, small, Catholic, closely linked to Austria, Italy and Germany, has also succeeded in presenting itself as returning to the West—in spite of an awkward dispute with the Berlusconi government in Italy over the restitution of Italian property from before the frontiers were redrawn half a century ago. Croatia, similarly Catholic, with a substantial diaspora in southern Germany and a long-established position as a holiday destination for West European tourists, has so far failed to establish a similar position: held back by its direct involvement in the conflicts of ex-Yugoslavia, by the authoritarian tendencies of its government, and by its treatment of its Serbian minority.

Those countries without direct frontiers with ex-Cold War Western Europe, geographically more distant, with less easily-exploitable cultural or human ties, have found it harder to gain or to hold the attention of Western institutions and governments. South-eastern Europe has presented a particular anomaly. It was economic crisis and political weakness in Greece and Turkey which led to the Marshall Plan of 1947; the geopolitics of Cold War Europe which crystallized in the years which followed attached Greece and Turkey to 'the West', as members of NATO and the

Council of Europe and as the first associates of the infant EEC. Post-Colonels' Greece succeeded, through skilful political advocacy, in overcoming the negative *Opinion* of the EC Commission and gaining full EC membership in 1981. Post-Generals' Turkey was less skilful, with a far weaker case: economically more backward, politically even less stable, with fewer emotional chords to strike with West European elites about claimed contributions to European history and civilization. Greece thus became a full member of both major Western institutions eight years before the opening up of socialist Europe began; while a discontented Turkey remained as a key Western ally, the home country for over two million of the EC's population, its application for EC membership resubmitted in 1987 and blocked not only by the Commission's negative assessment but also by determined Greek obstruction.

Geopoliticians need not be too concerned with defining exact boundaries within an international system marked by spheres of influence, heartlands and border regions. Institutionalization however requires hard decisions. States must either be accepted into full membership of regional institutions, or excluded, unless a mutually-acceptable form of association can be found. The electorates of Switzerland and Norway, secure in their prosperity and national identity, have chosen association with the EU rather than full membership.[22] The Swiss, and Irish, Swedes, Finns and Austrians, have similarly chosen to remain outside NATO. Turkish political leaders on the other hand perceive their state as excluded from the EU, and bitterly resent the inferior status of association which is offered. Russian and Ukrainian leaders as fiercely resent the opening of NATO membership to Poland but not to them, and challenge the implicit assumption that the economic and political privileges of EU membership will extend across the lands between Germany and Ukraine but be denied to those beyond.

Enlargement raises difficult questions of institutional capacities as well as of regional international relations. Concerns that enlargement would undermine the decision-making capabilities of the European Community, as well as destroying its delicate internal balance, have preoccupied existing members and Brussels officials since enlargement began. Five years' experience of Greek intransigence, reinforced by Spanish and Portuguese accession, persuaded Margaret Thatcher and other heads of government to accept further moves away from unanimity to qualified majority voting in the 1986 Single European Act. Jacques Delors as President of the Commission sought in 1988–9 to define a form of closer association for the member states of the European Free Trade Area which would provide them with a satisfactory alternative to seeking full membership; but even before these negotiations were completed the Austrian government had decided that full membership was the only satisfactory outcome, with the Finnish, Swedish, Norwegian and Swiss governments also reconsidering their position.[23] Further enlargement, incorporating another 10–15 states into an institutional framework designed for six close neigh-

---

[22] In both cases against the preferences of their governmental and economic elites, which sought the influence which follows from a seat at the table in multilateral policymaking, and feared the long-term political and economic costs of accepting the extra-territorial jurisdiction implied by association.

[23] Helen Wallace (ed.), *The Wider Western Europe: Reshaping the EC-EFTA Relationship* (London: Pinter, 1991); Anna Michalski and Helen Wallace, *The European Community: The Challenge of Enlargement* (London: Royal Institute of International Affairs, 1992).

bours, threatens—so some within the original members have argued—fatally to weaken the capabilities of the institution they clamour to join.

The narrower scope of NATO makes eastern enlargement in some ways less traumatic. Association, through Partnership for Peace, was offered not only to Russia and Ukraine but also to the trans-Caucasus and Central Asian successor states to the Soviet Union. But pressures from Poland, in particular, and from supporting lobbies within the US, pushed the Atlantic Alliance to move towards full enlargement: initially only to three states, but with others in south-eastern Europe and the Baltic pressing for similar access to NATO's consultative mechanisms and integrated military structures, and for similar security guarantees. NATO, like the EU, is thus now faced with the dilemma that half-promises of future membership raise expectations that will eventually have to be satisfied, while denial that membership may even be a long-term prospect is seen as discrimination, even exclusion.

Abolition of internal frontier controls within Western Europe further complicates the question of Europe's outer border. The principle on which the Schengen Agreement was based was that the lifting of internal controls would be accompanied by 'compensatory measures' at the common external frontier: raising, for critics of the evolution of European immigration and asylum policy, the prospect of a 'Fortress Europe' from which outsiders would be more and more rigorously excluded.[24] Pre-accession negotiations between the EU and east European applicant states have paid particular attention to border controls; the German government has made it a condition for the relaxation of controls on the Polish-German border that the Poles should tighten controls on their border with Ukraine. A sharp line is therefore being drawn between insiders and outsiders, between the privileged who may move around Europe's internal space and the unprivileged, queueing for visas and for entry, outside. The question of where 'Europe' stops is thus difficult to evade, or to answer in terms of peripheral regions and associated territories. Institutional membership or exclusion, freedom of movement or denial of entry, will clearly mark the outer boundaries of the emerging European order.

During the Cold War the question of Europe's extent and boundaries was easily resolved. The 'iron curtain' represented 'Europe's' effective eastern frontier; the nations and states behind it were remembered as 'captive', but accepted as excluded for the foreseeable long-term future. Article 237 of the Treaty of Rome (repeating the language of Article 98 of the 1951 Treaty of Paris) clearly stated that 'Any European State may apply to become a member of the Community'; but none of the drafters envisaged that the European Community might expand beyond the then-20 or so members of the Council of Europe.[25]

In the post-1945 period the concepts of 'Europe' and of 'the West' had been elided; the European intellectual diaspora which settled in the United States in the 1930s and 1940s wrote and taught on 'Western civilization' and 'the Atlantic

---

[24] Malcolm Anderson, et al., *Policing the European Union* (Oxford: Clarendon Press 1995); *Visas and Control of External Borders of the Member States*, 14th Report of the House of Lords Select Committee on the European Communities, 1993–4 (London: HMSO, HL-78 1993–4).

[25] Jean Monnet's *Memoirs* (London: Cape, 1978) are unclear on how wide a Community he was prepared to envisage. François Duchene, in *Jean Monnet: the First Statesman of Interdependence* (New York: Norton, 1994), ch. 5, suggests that he did not care greatly about the number of smaller countries incorporated, provided that it was built around France and Germany and expanded to include Britain.

Community'. In the 1980s dissident intellectuals successfully reinvented the concept of 'Central Europe', cleverly defined as 'that region geographically in the centre of the Europe, which belongs spiritually to the West, which is under the political domination of the East'.[26] Gorbachev and the reforming Russians around him were meanwhile talking about 'our common European home', a region which for them should include Russia but might well in the long-term exclude North America. The continuing framework of the Conference for Security and Cooperation in Europe, which had grown out of the Helsinki Conference of 1972–4, defined its wider 'Europe' as from Vancouver to Vladivostock.

This mental reconstruction of Europe, of competing claims to geographical inclusion, cultural and historical affinity, to be credited in economic access and aid and in security provision, remains an area of continuing contention and confusion. One West European reaction to the lengthening queue of applicants to Western institutions was to float the competing concept of 'core Europe': the rich and densely-populated states around the Rhine valley and delta, the Rhone, the routes across the Alps and the north-western Mediterranean around which European prosperity, high culture and high politics has revolved since the establishment of Charlemagne's Western empire. Its French and German proponents pictured a multi-tier structure for this wider Europe, a western core with an eastern periphery extending outwards through second-tier membership of Western institutions to external associates. Western policymakers have been preoccupied with consolidating their own achievement of regional integration, potentially threatened by enlargement to incorporate a succession of smaller, politically and economically weaker states.

The re-emergence of central and eastern Europe, rolling east and south-east into Asia, have forced Western policymakers to rethink their mental maps, to return to the old question of 'Where does Europe end?', most of all to the dilemmas posed by the semi-European states of Russia and Turkey. Russia is too important to exclude, too large to include; neither NATO nor the EU, neither the US nor Germany, have yet defined a coherent strategy in the face of incoherent Russian political and economic circumstances. Responses to all South-Eastern European states have been coloured by the breakdown of Yugoslavia; 'the Balkans' provide a familiar image from European history of murderous conflicts and chronic instability. Greece's position as a full member of Western institutions, its frontiers touching Bulgaria, Albania, and former-Yugoslav Macedonia, as well as Turkey, has made Western responses more difficult. It rules out any attempt to draw the boundaries of institutionalized Europe along the old fault line between Western and Eastern Christendom, as many (in Germany particularly) would have preferred.

One of the strongest indicators of the incoherence of Western responses to the reshaping of Europe was the acceptance by the EU of Cyprus and Malta as priority candidates for accession, at the Corfu European Council in 1994: a late-night decision, pressed on tired foreign ministers by the Greek Presidency and accepted by Heads of Government into the Council Communiqué. The Cyprus dispute has become a central issue in Greek–Turkish relations, with Turkish troops and Turkish

---

[26] The successful efforts of these dissident intellectuals to influence opinion in Western Europe is described in Tim Garton Ash, *The Uses of Adversity* (Cambridge: Granta, 1989). For an early Western attempt to reopen this geopolitical question, see Hugh Seton-Watson, 'What is Europe, where is Europe?' *Encounter*, (July–August 1985), pp. 9–17.

subsidies supporting the otherwise-unrecognized 'Turkish Republic of Northern Cyprus'. Cyprus itself is further south than Tunis, further east than Moldova and Belarus, its east coast 200 km from Lebanon, its prosperity as a financial centre intimately entwined with Russia and the Middle East. Cypriot entry to the EU will not prove possible without a resolution of its divided status, without also a resolution of the question of Turkey's future association or membership with the EU. American perceptions of Turkey as a key ally, and of the EU as a subordinate part of the US-led Western community, have led to repeated support from Administration officials for its EU application, thus exposing divisions between these two Western institutions. The parallel priority accorded to mini-state Malta also raises the uncomfortable prospect of granting a seat at the Council table to a second Luxembourg, a small state with domestic politics much more idiosyncratic than those of Luxembourg, its 371,000 population equivalent to that of a small Italian or German city.

Then there is Europe's near South, across the Mediterranean, historically more often a highway linking its littoral states than a border between Europe and non-Europe. Ninth century Moors extended their reach northwards across Spain into France, as well as into Sicily; nineteenth century France, Spain and Italy extended their reach southwards across North Africa. Present-day Algeria, as part of France, was formally included within the EEC when the Treaty of Rome was signed; though the French Government failed to persuade its American ally that the war of independence then underway came within the framework of the Atlantic Treaty. Population explosions, social and economic disruption across North Africa have brought several million Moroccans, Algerians, Tunisians, Mauritanians within the boundaries of the EU; thousands of others struggle each month to follow them, across the narrow straits of Gibraltar and Sicily. All of the states around the southern Mediterranean depend economically on the EU, as asymmetrically as the EU's eastern neighbours; but none are ever likely to be accepted as candidates for membership.[27]

One of the responses of the EU's southern members to the reorientation of their northern partners eastwards was to launch new initiatives for Mediterranean partnership. The Euro-Mediterranean Conference in Barcelona in November 1995, an initiative of the Spanish EU Presidency, brought the 15 EU members together with 12 'Mediterranean partners' (including Jordan, the Palestinian Authority and Israel, but not Libya) to agree on a 'comprehensive Euro-Mediterranean Partnership . . . through strengthened political dialogue on a regular basis, the development of economic and financial cooperation and greater emphasis on the social, cultural and human dimension.'[28] Substantial financial transfers from EU funds were promised, estimated at two-thirds of those committed to central and eastern Europe; though

---

[27] The Moroccan government addressed a letter of enquiry about future membership to the EC Commission in 1987, which referred to the contribution which Morocco had made to European civilization—treating contemporary Morocco as the successor state to the Moorish kingdom of Spain. So far as I am aware, it did not receive a formal answer. On Morocco's application, see George Joffe (ed.), *Morocco and Europe*, Centre for Near and Middle East Studies, SOAS, London, 1989; and A. Bahaijoub, 'Morocco's Argument to join the EC', in George Joffe (ed.), *North Africa: Nation, State and Region* (London: Routledge, 1993), pp. 235–46.

[28] Final Declaration, Euro-Mediterranean Conference, Barcelona, 29/11/1995. See also Ricardo Gomez, 'The EU's Mediterranean Policy: Common Foreign Policy by the Back Door?', ch. 8 in John Peterson and Helene Sjursen (eds.), *A Common Foreign Policy for Europe?* (London: Routledge, 1998).

political difficulties, problems of absorption by weak state administrations, have limited distribution since then. American determination to retain control over Israeli-Palestinian negotiations, while depending on the EU and its member states to provide the greater part of international assistance to the Palestinian Authority, has blighted the proposed political dialogue; intractable internal conflict within Algeria has blocked it further. But this intense dependent relationship remains, exerting a counterpull to eastern enlargement and a constant reminder that Europe's southern border is as difficult to define as its eastern.[29]

One of the central ambiguities within the Atlantic alliance, now as in the 1950s, is the extent of its shared responsibilities in the Mediterranean. American deployment of troops to Europe, for logical operational reasons, has shifted since 1989 from the central front to the south; the Sixth Fleet more than any other military force assures the security of the Mediterranean, and projects American power across the Middle East. Loose and overlapping concepts like 'Eurasia', 'Euro-Mediterranean', 'the eastern Mediterranean', 'the Near East' and 'the Greater Middle East' encapsulate loose thinking over shared responsibilities and policy preferences. The southern borders of Europe, the southern extension of its developing institutions and their dependent associates, are likely to be as troublesome a source of confusion and disagreement among Western governments as the eastern.

What structures for European order are now emerging?

It is at least clear that the politics and structure of post-Cold War politics within the European region will not, as John Mearsheimer predicted, resemble those of pre-1939 Europe.[30] There are of course some evident similarities. Poland is again emerging as an important—and difficult –state: the key player among the accepted EU applicants, with 40 million of the 100 million population of all 11 central and east European associates, with by far the largest agricultural sector, with a political class less willing to swallow all the conditions the EU wishes to set than its counterparts in the Czech Republic and Hungary.[31] Russia and Turkey again present problems at the periphery; South-Eastern Europe (the Balkans) has returned as a preoccupation. But the balance of power is not returning as the guiding principle of this new European order—unless pursued subtly through the multiple negotiations and coalitions of institutionalized European policymaking. German political leaders have been careful to place their approach to their eastern neighbours within this established multilateral framework. Hungarian political leaders have worked to prevent ethnic disputes overflowing into interstate conflict—successfully in relations with Romania, less successfully in relations with Slovakia and Yugoslavia/Serbia. Only in the former Yugoslavia have old patterns of pre-1945 conflicts re-emerged. The greatest failure of both NATO and the EU in managing the transition from

---

[29] Esther Barbé, 'Balancing Europe's Eastern and Southern Dimensions', ch. 8 in Zielonka (ed.), *Paradoxes of European Foreign Policy*.

[30] John J. Mearsheimer, 'Back to the Future: Instability in Europe after the Cold War', *International Security*, Summer 1990, 5–56.

[31] Clare McManus, 'Poland and the Europe Agreements: the EU as a Regional Actor', ch. 7 in Peterson and Sjursen, *A Common Foreign Policy for Europe?*

Cold War order to post-Cold War order has been their uncertain approach to the successive conflicts in eastern Croatia, Bosnia and Kosovo.

To some extent what we are witnessing within the European region—or at least within Western Europe—resembles the 'new medieval' model of a European society set out by Hedley Bull, in which authority, loyalty and identity are diffused away from the monolithic structure of the sovereign state to supra- and sub-state entities, within a shared framework of values and rules.[32] It is clear that this emerging European order will be 'institution-rich', interacting through political rather than military conflict, through diffuse political differences rather than direct interstate rivalries. Cross-border interaction between nongovernmental organizations, politicians, journalists, officials and ministers has substantially eroded the classical distinction between the domestic and the international. Regional European politics is characterized by intense transgovernmental transactions, in which substate entities as well as national administrations play an active part.[33]

It is also clear that within this emerging order states will continue to play an important, though not exclusive, role. State administrations will manage the complex mechanisms of multilateral negotiation and multi-level governance; state institutions will continue to provide the framework for political recruitment, political debate, representation and accountability. Even for Europe's largest states, however, sovereignty in the full nineteenth century sense has long since disappeared. Community law runs throughout the EU, implemented as fully as federal law within the United States and extended extraterritorially across the EU's associates.[34] Governments take collective decisions, often by unanimity but increasingly often by qualified majority vote; the link between governmental responsibility for foreign policy and accountability to national parliaments for those decisions has thus been broken, as ministers explain to parliaments that they have done their best to represent national interests but have been outvoted. The Brussels institutions—the European Commission, the EU Council Secretariat, the NATO and WEU Secretariats, the European Parliament—have limited autonomous influence and an ambivalent image, but nevertheless play a significant part in this new level of politics and policymaking. The commitment in the 1997 Treaty of Amsterdam to upgrade the post of EU Council Secretary-general to include the function of a 'High Representative for the common foreign and security policy', and the appointment to that post in 1999 of Javier Solana (former Spanish foreign minister, and Secretary-general of NATO) mark a further step in the transfer of influence from separate national capitals to shared institutions.[35]

The proliferation of small and weak states across central and eastern Europe represents one of the most intractable problems in expanding Western institutional

---

[32] Hedley Bull, *The Anarchical Society: A Study of Order in World Politics* (London: Macmillan, 1977), pp. 254–5. Fred Halliday, in *Rethinking International Relations* (London: Macmillan, 1994), ch. 5, traces this interpretation of European international society back to Edmund Burke.

[33] Helen Wallace, 'The Pattern of Policy', ch. 1 in Wallace and Wallace, *Policymaking in the European Union*, 4th edn.

[34] This is not to imply that it is implemented without question in every member state; but US federal law is not implemented unquestionably throughout every state within the USA. It is only 40 years since the National Guard had to be mobilized in southern states to enforce the supremacy of federal law over state legislation. What is most remarkable is that Community law is so widely accepted by national courts and administrations, without any comparable sanctions.

[35] Article 26, Treaty of European Union, as revised in the Treaty of Amsterdam 1997.

structures east and south-east, and in maintaining a balance between sovereign equality and effective multilateral policymaking. European institutions face the challenge of a widening imbalance between strong and weak states, between large and small, prosperous and poor: of state-units claiming sovereignty, and representation in regional institutions on that basis, without resources in terms of population, economic development, military forces, even administrative capabilities, to support that claim.[36] The combined population of eleven of the twelve states whose applications the EU is currently considering (leaving aside Poland) is smaller than that of Germany; their combined GDPs are smaller than that of the Netherlands. The prospect of an enlargement process which could take NATO and EU membership to more than 30 member states, the majority of which are poorer and less populated than North-Rhine/Westphalia, strains the distinction between sovereign and non-sovereign entities to the limit. Hence the rumbling discussion within the EU over changing voting weights and representation between large and small members; though this has not yet surfaced within the 'consensual', effectively American-led, NATO.[37]

How far is it likely that European institutions themselves will become the dominant level of governance, rather than the vehicles through which national actors, representing diffuse but still recognizable state interests, pursue advantage? That, I suggest, depends above all on the future relationship between NATO and the EU: on whether issues of force, power, violence, remain predominantly matters dealt with through a hegemonic American power, or whether civilian European institutions are forced to develop capabilities for hard security and power projection. Political transactions *within* Europe have developed the quality we now observe because politico-military relations between Western Europe and other states— Russia, the Middle East—have been handled primarily by the United States, and because relations between West European governments and the United States have themselves been managed within a framework of multilateral institutions and shared values. Civilian-power Europe has been able to develop its semi-sovereign, semi-medieval patterns of intense transgovernmental politics because questions of force and of external threats have been left to the Atlantic alliance, countered predominantly by American power and American defence expenditure.

The relationship between NATO and the EU, between the United States and its European allies, remains one of the least well-explored questions about Europe in the 21st century, in spite of a wealth of academic and policy studies. Europe without the United States is more likely to move towards a more explicit federation, necessarily with a larger common budget and a stronger federal policymaking structure. Europe with the United States will be able to avoid grappling with these hard choices, managing intensive regional governance through further development

---

[36] This is not entirely a new phenomenon. Franz Lehar's opera, The Merry Widow, was after all a skit on the pretensions of Montenegro to independent statehood; the plot revolves around a leading bankers' widow being left a large proportion of the state's domestic capital.

[37] This threatened to be a major issue in the 1996–7 EU Intergovernmental Conference (IGC), with the German and French governments expressing concern that with the current weighting of votes favouring smaller countries it would be possible after further enlargement for a qualified majority of votes to carry a decision against states representing the majority of EU citizens. The confused endgame negotiations at Amsterdam, in June 1997, however agreed to postpone this issue until a further IGC. Brendan Smith, *Politics and Policymaking at the 1996–7 European Union Intergovernmental Conference* (London: LSE Ph.D thesis, 1999), ch. 5.

of the multilateral institutions it has already established.[38] So long as the United States continues to relieve European governments and institutions—through its leadership of NATO, and the maintenance of NATO as itself a European institution—of the necessity of confronting the hard questions of high politics and military power, of maintaining regional order and preparing to meet external threats, then the EU itself can remain a civilian power, a focus for intergovernmental bargaining and a vehicle through which national governments concert their policies. If US and West European interests were however explicitly to diverge, if the mood of American politics were to shift towards political and military withdrawal or to posing demands for burden-sharing and subordination to American global leadership which European political leaders found too oppressive, then the institutional structure of post-Cold War Europe will have to be built upon a much firmer, single-centred foundation.

The complexity of the choices involved, the unwillingness either of American or of West European policymakers to confront them, explains the deliberate indirection with which the wider European order has so far been negotiated. Disjointed incrementalism is the policy style of practical men, who recognize that the great questions of politics are often best avoided for as long as possible. Neither the EU nor the Atlantic alliance have adopted a strategic view of enlargement. The EU has shuffled from European Council to European Council, spelling out a 'Pre-accession Strategy' in 1994 to prepare the applicant states for future membership while postponing negotiation on how the EU itself might adjust to enlargement, and saying nothing about a timescale for entry. After the Amsterdam Treaty had been agreed the Commission in July 1997 published, in successive volumes of its *Agenda 2000* report, its proposals on the necessary adaptation of the existing EU to enlargement and its opinions on each applicant state's readiness for membership. Negotiations on entry for the first six candidates got under way in early 1998, with a minimum timetable for completion, ratification and entry estimated at 2003–2005, and divergent views on how rapidly others might follow on behind.[39] The EU has thus approached the incorporation of eastern Europe reluctantly and indirectly, so far avoiding the question of where it may draw the definitive border in 10–20 years' time.

Two reformulations of NATO's 'strategic concept', in 1991 and 1999, and a NATO 'Study on Enlargement' in 1995 have left the alliance still confused about how many further members it should accept, unhealthily dependent on shifting moods within the US Administration and Congress. The 1995 NATO 'Study of Enlargement' set out the prospect of a European institutional order built around the twin pillars of NATO and EU, concluding that 'ideally, in the long run, the memberships of NATO and the EU should coincide.'[40] In the process of transformation and enlargement, however, NATO and the EU have diverged. The conditions attached to

[38] For contrasting views on the post-Cold War development of transatlantic relations, see Christopher Coker, *The Twilight of the West* (Boulder, CO: Westview, 1998), and John Peterson, *Europe and America: The Prospects for Partnership* (London: Routledge, 2nd edn 1996); or *The Future of Transatlantic Relations*, Task Force report (New York: Council on Foreign Relations, 1998), and William Wallace and Jan Zielonka, 'Misunderstanding Europe', *Foreign Affairs*, 77:6 (1998), pp. 65–79.

[39] This process is detailed in Alan Mayhew, *Recreating Europe: the EU's Policy towards Central and Eastern Europe* (Cambridge: Cambridge University Press, 1998).

[40] 'Study on NATO Enlargment', *NATO Secretariat,* Brussels, September 1995.

NATO accession were progressively reduced, the cost estimates sharply lowered; allowing the three candidates accepted in the first round to enter on a timetable which fitted the desire of NATO's leading member to celebrate appropriately the 50th anniversary of the signing of the Atlantic Treaty, in April 1999.

NATO is thus enlarging much more rapidly than the EU, but with a much less clear sense of what the implications of enlargement may be for the alliance. The assumption remains, at least in public, that NATO will remain essentially unchanged by enlargement; though change is evidently underway, most visibly in the crowd of 'Partners' who assemble on the edges of NATO meetings and in the formal meetings of the NATO-Russia and NATO-Ukraine Joint Councils. Disjointed incrementalism is the preferred approach; NATO has, its defenders claim, adapted successfully to changes in its strategic tasks and environment since 1989, maintaining alliance solidarity during the ex-Yugoslav conflict and learning from the complex requirements of that conflict. Further incremental adjustment may continue to serve its purposes sufficiently well. Academic analysts may argue that the European-American relationship needs to be reshaped and strengthened into an Atlantic Union, lest it drift into disgruntled confrontation.[41] Policymakers are content that it has so far adjusted to a reduction of American forces in Europe to a third of their strength in 1989, and has managed disagreements over policy towards the Middle East, Turkey and Central Asia without public confrontation.

The unanswered questions of European foreign policy thus interrelate. The United States is a key player in European relations with its defining semi-European neighbours—Turkey, Ukraine, Russia—and in relations with its Arab and Muslim Mediterranean neighbours. The management of enlargement of both the EU and NATO, the evolution of mutually satisfactory associations with those on the European periphery which do not come in, depend upon the maintenance of an active, mutually confident relationship between European governments and Washington. Perceptions from Washington, of Turkey as a strategic ally in the 'Greater Middle East' which should be rewarded with early membership of the EU (as US officials have repeatedly declared), of Russia as a Pacific as well as a European power, of politics in the Middle East, differ significantly from perceptions in the major European capitals. But provided that European political leaders can continue successfully to avoid confrontation with Washington, and can rehearse the rhetoric of transatlantic solidarity even while practising the pursuit of European interests, then hard choices about European defence and foreign policy may not be necessary.[42]

In the absence of an overall strategy, the experiences of Bosnia and Kosovo have done much to shape government assumptions, at least in the short-term. The impact of Kosovo in 1998–9 may prove significant in pushing reluctant governments forward; unless second thoughts and domestic distractions lead governments to drift away from the commitments they made in the heat of the conflict. The British and French governments, shaken by the weakness of European military capabilities in an emergency, and by American unilateralism in negotiations with President Milosevic

---

[41] Charles Kupchan, 'From European Union to Atlantic Union', ch. 10 in Zielonka (ed.), *Paradoxes of European Foreign Policy*.

[42] Jan Zielonka, *Explaining Euro-paralysis: Why Europe is Unable to Act in International Politics* (London: Macmillan, 1998).

as the crisis developed, launched at St. Malo in December 1998 a defence initiative intended to merge WEU into the EU, to raise through closer integration and specialization European defence capabilities, and so to contribute to greater European autonomy within the Atlantic alliance. Leading Western governments held out half-promises to the states of south-eastern Europe—including Albania and Macedonia—of eventual membership both of the EU and of NATO, as well as of a generous programme of economic assistance for post-conflict reconstruction in the region. That in turn should give greater urgency to completion of the first round of EU enlargement, placing the negotiations within a strategic framework which EU member governments had until then preferred to ignore.

Tracing the direction in which West European governments and the US are drifting, it is possible to discern the outlines of a future European regional order. Without fully appreciating the implications of commitments half-made, West European governments have now pledged themselves to extend the reach of European institutions across all the states between Germany and Ukraine, and between Austria and Greece. Merger of WEU and EU in the proposed Intergovernmental Conference of 2000 would create a framework for extending security across that region in parallel; leaving for transatlantic negotiation the question of whether NATO should expand to include these new EU entrants, or should halt enlargement in order not to bring the boundaries of the Western alliance to the borders of Russia, or alternatively should aim to expand beyond to bring both Ukraine and Russia within a military framework with which both are now formally associated.

Many within the West European governments would be happy to move towards a regional order within which both Russia and Turkey were full members of the security framework, but neither full members of its politico-economic framework. The importance of Turkey and Russia to European stability, the overlap of Russian and Turkish minorities into institutionalized Europe, leave the question of how to accommodate these two states as in many ways the most difficult issue to face in constructing a stable post-Cold War European order. Governments will therefore attempt to postpone hard decisions, hoping that crises—over Russian minorities in Baltic states, over Cypriot entry into the EU—will not force them to choose one option or the other. The idea that institutionalized Europe's hard outer border should be drawn across Cyprus, or that the border between Estonia and Russia (or between eastern Poland and western Ukraine) should mark the dividing line between the rich West and the excluded east is not one that Western ministers want to accept, even though these are the borders towards which current policy is drifting.

The integration of Europe has been managed by elites, with mass publics enjoying the benefits that integration brings without always supporting the challenges to national identity which they also pose. Shared values, geographical propinquity, and increases in cross-border movement, have provided sufficient sense of political community to support the gradual emergence of a new level of government, managed multilaterally by representatives of national governments alongside supranational institutions. The extension of integrated institutions and patterns of multilateral policymaking across a further 100 million people in another dozen states will stretch this sense of shared community—the necessary foundation for a post-sovereign regional system—to the limit. Larger financial transfers from west to east, shifts in industrial production, will provide ample opportunity for populist politicians in the west to protest against the conspiracy of elites which manages the consociational politics of institutionalized Europe.[43] Yet the passage of time, and the provision of growing prosperity, have carried western Europe's reluctant voters much further than they expected or wished over the past forty years; barring economic depression or external military crisis, it may well be that they will continue to follow reluctantly the path quietly set by their leaders.

What is emerging, therefore, is a post-sovereign regional system. But it is one which depends crucially on the provision of security from the outside, on being able to focus on striking internal bargains without confronting external demands. It remains to be seen whether the United States will be willing to continue to provide external security far into the twenty-first century, or whether European governments will be content to accept its provision on American terms. To this extent the Realists are right: politico-military questions are ultimately controlling. What West European governments and societies have demonstrated is that once the problem of mutual insecurity is resolved, it is possible to move away from state-to-state international politics through the development of multilateral institutions and the dismantling of frontier controls. The hardest test for supporters of civilian power, multilevel governance, and international civil society will not be whether Western Europe can succeed in extending its established patterns of interaction across the east European applicants—though that is hard enough. It will be whether this emerging post-sovereign Europe can extend stability, prosperity and mutual trust further, across its dependent periphery, with or without the cooperation of the United States.

---

[43] Paul Taylor, *The European Union in the 1990s* (Oxford: Oxford University Press, 1996), ch. 2.

Where is the Third World now?

CAROLINE THOMAS[1]

As we enter the new millennium, the Third World, far from disappearing, is becoming global. The dynamic of economic driven globalization is resulting in the global reproduction of Third World problems. Growing inequality, risk and vulnerability characterize not simply the state system, but an emerging global social order. This is part of an historical process underway for five centuries: the expansion of capitalism across the globe. Technological developments speed up the process. The demise of the communist bloc and the associated rejection of 'real existing socialism' as a mode of economic organization have provided a specific additional fillip to the reconfiguration of the 'Third World'. The 1980s, and more particularly the 1990s, have witnessed the mainstreaming of liberal economic ideology via the Washington consensus.[2] This approach to development has been legitimated in several global conferences such as United Nations Conference on Environment and Development (UNCED) and the Copenhagen Social Summit. It has been applied practically through institutions such as the International Monetary Fund (IMF), the World Bank and World Trade Organization (WTO). In its wake we have seen a deepening of existing inequalities between and within states, with a resulting tension—contradiction even—between the development targets agreed by the United Nations (UN), and the policies pursued by international organizations and govern- ments to facilitate such results.

The article is divided into three parts. The first part identifies where the Third World is now, arguing that it is in fact being globalized. The second part examines the global architecture which defines the dynamics of this process. Part three examines contending ideas about how the crisis of globalization of the Third World might be addressed. A comparison of solutions defined broadly as reformist and transformist highlights the political framing of the problem and solutions.

---

[1] I am grateful for the comments of an anonymous *RIS* reviewer, to the editors of the Journal and friends and colleagues who commented on various drafts, especially M. Mohamed Salih, Steve Morris, Nana Poku, Jeremy Smallwood, Steve Thomas, Heloise Weber, and Peter Wilkin.

[2] The term 'Washington consensus' was coined by John Williamson, of the Institute for International Economics. It refers to a particular recipe for development growing in popularity in the 1980s and especially in vogue in the 1990s. It has been explained and summarized succinctly by Paul Krugman in 'Dutch Tulips and Emerging Markets' *Foreign Affairs*, 74 (1995), pp. 28–9: 'By "Washington" Williamson meant not only the US government, but all those institutions and networks of opinion leaders centered in the world's *de facto* capital—the International Monetary Fund, World Bank, think tanks, politically sophisticated investment bankers, and worldly finance ministers, all those who meet each other in Washington and collectively define the conventional wisdom of the moment . . . One may . . . roughly summarize this consensus . . . as . . . the belief that Victorian virtue in economic policy—free markets and sound money—is the key to economic development. Liberalize trade, privatize state enterprises, balance the budget, peg the exchange rate . . .'.

Third World: what, where, whom?

The term 'Third World' was used in 1952 by Alfred Sauvy to refer to the third estate or common people before the French revolution. The term embraced notions of political powerlessness, economic poverty and social marginalization. In the early post-colonial period, the term was adopted to refer to a self-defining group of mostly post-colonial states, united psychologically in common opposition to colonialism and imperialism. Within the context of the ideologically bifurcated world of the Cold War, this group necessarily occupied a political space between the First World capitalist states and Second World socialist states. Through non-alignment it attempted to maintain a distance and independence between the two superpower blocs, and where possible to benefit from this bifurcation.

Two key characteristics distinguished these Third World states. Firstly, on account of their position in the world economy they perceived themselves as vulnerable to external factors beyond their control, and to decisions and policies—primarily economic—which they did not own. These external factors included the great powers, the IMF, the world market, foreign multinationals and banking institutions. Secondly, these states were the home to the majority of the world's poor who endured every day survival risks associated with grave social problems. These two shared characteristics prompted interrelated and shared concerns: the desire to exercise greater control over national economies, and to accelerate national development via policies such as the consolidation of a large state sector and import substitution. A key part of the strategy to address these concerns was the call in 1974 for a New International Economic Order (NIEO). This was swiftly followed by the Charter of Economic Rights and Duties of States (CERDS), designed to empower economically weak states by reducing risk and vulnerability and by asserting national economic sovereignty.[3]

Interstate polarization

Notwithstanding the demise of the bipolar Cold War context, the collapse of the Second (communist) World, and the abandonment of a Third World development strategy based on the state sector, the term 'Third World' still has meaning today.[4] The goals sought through the NIEO and CERDS remain elusive. Characteristics which distinguished Third World states a quarter-century ago now apply to a wider group of states than ever before. At a broad level, and despite marked heterogeneity, the current Third World grouping now embraces many states from the former

---

[3] See Yearbook of the UN, 1974 (New York: UN Information Office); Caroline Thomas, *New States, Sovereignty and Intervention* (London: Gower, 1985) p. 122.

[4] See any edition of the monthly publication Third World Resurgence (Penang, Malaysia: Third World Network); Eric Toussaint, *Your Money or Your Life: The Tyranny of Global Finance* (London: Pluto, 1999); Julian Saurin, 'Globalization, Poverty and the Promise of Modernity', *Millenium*, 25: 3 (1996); Ankie Hoogevelt, Globalization and the Post-colonial World (Basingstoke: Macmillan, 1997); Caroline Thomas and Peter Wilkin (eds.), *Globalization and the South* (Basingstoke: Macmillan, 1998).

Second World.[5] The general pace of globalization in the 1980s and 1990s, and the particular trajectory of capitalist expansion, have in addition increased risks for a broader group of countries, and for a wider band of humanity. Interstate and intrastate inequality have deepened. These Third World states house eighty five per cent of the global population, including the overwhelming majority of the world's poor, and produce only 20 per cent of world GDP. They lack general progress in national development. Three billion people in these countries lack basic sanitation; one and a half billion lack clean water; a billion or more are without adequate food, housing, healthcare; and twenty per cent of children do not learn to read and write.[6] While acknowledging differentiation within this inclusive Third World grouping, in broad terms these states remain economically weak, politically powerless and socially marginalized.

These states also continue to share the experience of vulnerability to external factors, especially the risks associated with functioning in the global market. They do not exert meaningful influence in global governance institutions. Third World states do not enjoy a significant voice in the IMF, World Bank or WTO. Consequently they do not author decisions which affect them in the most profound ways. The G7 drives the global economic policy agenda, even though 'The G7 countries, plus the rest of the European Union, represent a mere 14 per cent of the world's population. Yet these countries have 56 per cent of the votes in the IMF Executive Board . . . The rest of the world is called upon to support G7 declarations, not to meet for joint problem-solving'.[7] The US is still the only state which can exert unilateral veto power at the IMF.

The sense of risk and vulnerability experienced by Third Word states, both in relation to the IMF and to private bank and non-bank lenders, has been magnified by the recent financial crises in East Asia, Russia and Brazil. Yet there has been no commensurate feeling of opportunity. The legitimacy of the IMF, routinely in question, has been further eroded on account of the perceived lack of distance between IMF and US policy agendas on the one hand, and the needs of Third World states on the other. In the case of South Korea, for example, some have seen IMF actions as 'an abuse of power to force Korea at a time of weakness to accept trade and investment policies it had previously rejected'.[8] IMF restructuring of East Asian economies has enabled First World companies to take advantage of bargain-basement priced East Asian companies. In 1998, US and European companies mounted over $30 billion in take-overs of Asian companies—a fourfold increase on 1997.[9] This has been described by one commentator as 'the greatest global asset swindle of all time'.[10] The Asian crises have also heightened awareness of the ability of a handful of relatively new private financial actors such as hedge funds to exert such leverage that they can force currency devaluations at a breathtaking pace, undermine national economic policy and erode national development.

[5] See Christopher Clapham, 'Degrees of Statehood' *Review of International Studies*, 24 (1998), pp. 143–57; and Laszlo Andor and Martin Summers, *Market Failure: Eastern Europe's Economic Miracle* (London: Pluto, 1998).
[6] UNDP, Human Development Report, 1998 (Oxford: University Press, 1998) p. 2.
[7] Jeffrey Sachs, 'Stop Preaching', *The Financial Times*, London edition 1, 5 November 1998, p. 22.
[8] See Martin Feldstein, 'Refocusing the IMF', *Foreign Affairs*, March/April 1998, p. 32.
[9] Walden Bello, 'The TNC World Order: Will it Also Unravel?' prepared for the Democracy, Market Economy and Development Conference, Soeul, Korea, 26–27 February 1999.
[10] Robin Hahnel, 'The Great Global Asset Swindle', *ZNet Commentary*, 23 March 1999.

It is sobering to reflect that no former Second or Third World country has joined the ranks of the First World countries in a solid sense. While a handful have increased their economic power, this has not been matched by influence in key global governance institutions. Global success in massively increasing consumption is not being reflected in access of the majority of states to the benefits of this growth. The explosive widening of the gap between rich and poor states (and between rich and poor people) evident over the last fifty years has been exacerbated in the 1990s. Deepening interstate inequality both reflects and reinforces the systemic con-figuration of risk and opportunity. The UNDP reports that 'No fewer than 100 countries—all developing or in transition—have experienced serious economic decline over the past three decades. As a result *per capita* income in these 100 countries is lower than it was 10, 20, even 30 years ago'.[11] There was a moment when the achievement of East Asian states suggested that the economic gap between First and Third World states could be closed, but recent crises have shattered that hope. GDP growth in East Asia as a whole fell from 4.3 per cent to −6.2 per cent in the short period 1997–8.[12] The ESCAP 1999 regional survey shows that over the same period, the percentage of population in poverty has risen dramatically, as labour market displacement has been massive. For example in Indonesia the percentage in poverty has risen from 11 per cent to over 40 per cent, and unemployment from 4.7 per cent to 21 per cent. This is particularly tragic given the unique gains that had previously been made in the region to promote growth with equity and lift millions of people out of poverty.

The attempted integration of the 'transition' economies of Central and Eastern Europe and the Commonwealth of Independent States into the emerging global economy has so far relegated these states to the ranks of Third World rather than First. These states have acquired the characteristics of extreme vulnerability to the workings of the global market, and deepening poverty and inequality. Output in most of them remains below pre-transition levels, and unemployment is very high and rising.The painful process of transition has been undertaken without the cushion of public provision previously in place, and in the case of Russia with the disadvantage of highly corrupt government officials committed to the capital flight of public funds for private enrichment. The number of people in poverty in Russia has increased from 2 million to well over 60 million over the 1990s.[13] By 2000, it is expected to reach 20 per cent of the population.

No First World country has joined the ranks of the Third World. Yet even for First World states, the risks accompanying globalization[14] have been brought into sharp relief—witness the contagion effect in financial crises, the collapse of the US hedge fund Long Term Capital Management in September 1998, and job losses due to mergers, efficiency gains and even the withdrawal of Asian investments. Importantly, however, First World states enjoy a voice in global governance.

---

[11] UNDP, 1998, p. 37.
[12] United Nations Information Services, 8 April 1999.
[13] James Wolfensohn, World Bank President, described this increase as 'enormous'. See press conference at the beginning of the spring summit of the IMF and the World Bank, 22 April 1999.
[14] For a very interesting discussion of how in this era of advanced modernity, when genuine material needs can be satisfied, risks are being produced in society to an extent previously unknown, see Ulrich Beck, Risk Society (London: Sage, 1992).

Hence, in the post-Cold War context, Third World states, far from disappearing, have increased numerically and in terms of geographic spread. Third World status has effectively been globalized. The picture is highly differentiated, but central characteristics of vulnerability to the workings of the global market, and lack of meaningful influence in global governance institutions, are shared by a growing group of states. Yet an exclusive focus on interstate polarization hides the increasingly global social configuration of inequality, risk and opportunity. Globalization of the Third World can be seen in the life experience of people, as well as in the experience and condition of states. There is a First World within Third World states, and increasingly there is a Third World within First World states. In identifying where the Third World is now, we must be mindful of this intrastate polarization.

Intrastate polarization

Over the last fifty years, and more particularly over the last decade, differentiation/stratification has increased at the intrastate as well as interstate level. This is as true for the First as for the Third World countries. The dynamic of economic driven globalization has led to a global reproduction of Third World social problems, while at the same time aggravating socioeconomic divisions within weak states. Concentration of wealth, and social exclusion, seem to be part of a single global process. With the exception of a few East Asian tigers, the success of states, whether of First or Third World, measured in terms of GDP *per capita*, has not been reflected in their societies at large. This intrastate differentiation increasingly reflects the degree of integration of various social classes and geopolitical regions within the emerging global economy. Thus for each human being, their respective position in the global economy has an enormous impact on their perception and their experience of risk and opportunity.

In defining the Third World from the human aspect, our concern is with those human beings for whom poverty is the norm, for whom vulnerability and risk are defining features of their daily existence, wherever they are located territorially. Their search for security has both qualitative and quantitative aspects. At one level it is about the fulfilment of basic material needs; at another, the achievement of human dignity, which includes personal autonomy, control over one's life, and unhindered participation in the life of the community. Human security is pursued as part of a collective, most commonly the household, sometimes the village or the community defined by criteria such as caste or religion. At the global level the state is the community which is given legitimacy to represent the interests of human beings and further their search for security. Such human security is indivisible—it cannot be pursued by or for one group at the expense of another.[15]

Global economic integration is directly impacting on human security. Patterns of systemic inclusion and exclusion of people can be mapped with reference to the means of economic sustenance. Robert Cox provides a useful categorization of the

---

[15] For more on this see Caroline Thomas and Peter Wilkin (eds.), *Globalization, Human Security and the African Experience* (Boulder, CO: Lynne Reinner Press, 1999); and Caroline Thomas, *Human Security in a Global Economy* (London: Pluto, forthcoming 2000).

world's producers in a global economy[16]: there is firstly a core workforce of highly skilled people integrated into the management process; a second level of precarious workers located where business is offered the greatest incentives in terms of lowest labour costs or environmental controls; and the rest, the expanding pool of people in the First and Third World states who are excluded from international production (the thirty seven million unemployed plus the low skilled in the rich countries; and the billion under- or unemployed, the marginalized in the poor countries).[17]

The core refers to those people who are able to take advantage of the opportunities which global economic integration presents. James Gustave Speth of the UNDP has written that 'An emerging global elite, mostly urban based and interconnected in a variety of ways, is amassing great wealth and power, while over half of humanity is left out'.[18] Within this group also sit the super-rich. The world's richest two hundred and twenty five people have a combined wealth equal to the annual income of 47 per cent of the world's people.[19] Eighty three of these ultra-rich people, i.e. over a third, are non-OECD citizens. Forty three are in Asia, 22 in Latin America and the Caribbean, 11 in the Arab states, four in Eastern Europe and the CIS, and two in sub-Saharan Africa.[20]

The core of people who are already reaping the benefits of the globalization process will be able to advantage themselves further by their ability to exploit lifelong learning opportunities, and to tap into ongoing technological advance and the related communications revolution. Thus uneven access to technological advance intensifies disparities between states, and also between different groups of people within states. The ESCAP Survey 1999 identifies the future as internet commerce. Yet out of the world's 5.9 billion population, there are only 50 million internet users, and over 90 per cent of internet hosts are in North America and Western Europe. Eighty per cent of people worldwide still do not have access to a telephone.[21]

Cox's second category, precarious workers, comprises those people who may gain temporarily from the globalization process by job creation, but who remain very vulnerable due to the pace of change in the demand for skills, and labour market conditions. Their numbers are as disappointing as is their insecurity of employment. Transnational corporations directly employ only 3 per cent of the global labour force.[22] Export processing zones provide opportunities, but the conditions of employment are poor. Moreover these zones act as a magnet for migration, and this can create social problems when the expected opportunities do not materialize. For example, in China, deepening differentiation between the export-oriented coastal region of the east and the rest of the country is stark, and there is a growing problem of urban unemployment. Mergers and acquisitions consume an increasing proportion of Foreign Direct Investment (85 per cent of the global total in 1997, and 67 per cent of the total going to the Third World countries), and unlike greenfield investment often result in job losses rather than job creation. The push to

---

[16] Robert Cox, 'Civil Society at the turn of the millennium: prospects for an alternative world order', *Review of International Studies*, 25: 1 (1999) p. 9.

[17] ILO, World Employment Record 1998–99 (Geneva: ILO, 1998) p. 1.

[18] B. Crossette, 'UN survey finds world rich–poor gap widening', *New York Times*, 15 July 1996, p. 55.

[19] UNDP, *Human Development Report*, 1998, p. 30.

[20] UNDP, 1998, p. 30.

[21] *African Development Bank Report*, 1998, p. 172.

[22] Panos Institute, *Globalization and Employment*, Briefing no. 33 (London: Panos Institute, May 1999), p. 6.

liberalize trade results in capital seeking out the location where it can reap the best advantage. This pits country against country, and even divides individual states— and therefore citizens—within a federal structure. An example of the latter is Brazil. When the new Governor of Rio Grande Do Sul decided to try to renegotiate contracts with Ford, other states within Brazil were quick to compete for the investment by offering more attractive loans and infrastructure to the company.

The outlook for Cox's third category, the expanding pool of people marginalized by the process of global economic integration, is bleak. For them, risk and vulnerability are increasing, and there do not appear to be opportunities. In the words of ILO Director General Michel Hansenne, 'The global employment situation is grim, and getting grimmer'.[23]

Social exclusion of the most vulnerable is intensifying: the old, the young, the disabled, ethnic minority groups, the less skilled, and across all these groups there is a bias against women.[24]

Education and training can create opportunities to overcome labour market exclusion. The OECD classifies 25–40 per cent of its adults as 'functionally illiterate', that is without the necessary skills to function in the modern work environment, and thus excluded from the advantages globalization offers.[25] If this is the situation in countries where virtually all children have the opportunity to go to primary and secondary school, the scenario for the rest of the world is very frightening indeed. One hundred and twenty five million primary school age children worldwide never attend school. Another 150 million drop out before they can read or write.[26] Globally, this is over a quarter of the world's children. Yet there is marked differentiation across region, country and districts, and along other fault lines such as gender. In sub-Saharan African states, fifty per cent of school age children are not enrolled in schools. The average man in Africa has less than three years schooling, the average woman less than a year. Given that the greatest population growth takes place amongst the poor who have least access to education, then without immediate remedial action we can expect differentiation to become more entrenched and to cascade into future generations.

This differentiation will also cascade into the future due to the pernicious influence of malnutrition, recently called a 'silent emergency' by UNICEF.[27] Malnutrition is affecting the development potential of the globe, as it impacts on learning ability. China alone has more malnourished people than all of sub-Sahara Africa put together. Recent crises are further eroding significant gains against malnutrition in East Asia, Russia and the US. The 1990s have seen a growth in the number of children affected world-wide. Malnutrition is a routine consequence of the day to day ordering of access to resources; there is nothing unusual or exceptional about it, except in specific situations such as war. But none of this is inevitable. The South Indian state of Kerala provides a shining example of what can be achieved in terms of human development even in a low *per capita* situation. (What the Kerala example also reveals is how such local policies can be influential in

---

[23] Ibid, p. 5.
[24] ILO, *World Employment Report*, 1998–99 (Geneva: ILO, 1999), p. 9.
[25] Panos Institute, *Globalization and Employment*, p. 5.
[26] Oxfam International, *Education Now, Break the Cycle of Poverty* (Oxford: Oxfam, 1999).
[27] UNICEF, *The State of the World's Children 1998* (New York: Oxford University Press, 1998), p. 17.

enabling some states within a federal system to take advantage of opportunities offered by globalization).

But risks endured by marginalized people, particularly in Third World states, result not only through exclusion from the economic globalization process, but also by the way in which that process directly undermines their ability to be self-sufficient. An example is the privatization of the commons.[28] A notorious recent example is the redrafting of the Mexican constitution in the context of liberal restructuring in the run up to the North Amerian Free Trade Association (NAFTA). This was done to stop government redistribution of land to the landless, and to facilitate privatization of previously communal land. While the resulting Chiapas uprising[29] hit the global headlines, other examples can be cited from all over the world illustrating the violation of the rights of indigenous communities, landless peasants, fishing communities, in order to further the interests of the holders of capital.

Thus what we have seen is the expansion of the number and geographical domain of states characterized by vulnerability to external factors beyond their control and to policies which they do not own. We have also witnessed intrastate differentiation within First and Third World states between people who are able to take advantage of the opportunities offered by global economic integration, and those who are marginalized by the process. The dynamics of this differentiation process are defined by a global architecture. It is to that architecture that we now turn.

Global architecture

The UN has set a target of a 50 per cent reduction in the number of people in absolute poverty by 2015. It is questionable whether the model of development pursued in the 1980s and 1990s, that is export-led growth based on free capital mobility, can deliver this outcome. The model requires high and sustained growth to achieve this level of poverty reduction. African economies, for example, would need to grow at an estimated seven per cent a year on average to reach the UN target by 2015.[30]

Yet given the trends outlined in the previous section, can we be confident that even if such growth were achieved and sustained, that it would translate into a 50 per cent reduction in poverty? The historical evidence suggests not. This raises a legitimate concern as to whether the mechanisms in place to tackle poverty and promote development are adequate to the task. The scope, depth and speed of the changes that have been, and continue to be, introduced in development policy are breathtaking; their legitimacy is open to question,[31] and the future of billions depends on them.

---

[28] See Michael Goldman (ed.), *Privatizing Nature* (London: Pluto, 1998).

[29] On the Chiapas uprising, see Lynn Stephens, 'Between NAFTA and Zapata: Responses to Restructuring the Commons in Chiapas and Oaxaca, Mexico', in M. Goldman, ibid, pp. 76–101.

[30] African Development Bank Report, 1998; and Economic Commission for Africa (ECA) Executive Secretary K. Y. Amoako, press conference, 6 May 1999, Addis Ababa, at UN ECA conference.

[31] See several contributions on transparency and accountability of the IMF, World Bank and WTO in John Cavanagh, Daphne Wysham and Marcos Arruda (eds.), *Beyond Bretton Woods* (London: Pluto, 1994).

Throughout the 1980s and 1990s key First World states and the international institutions which they dominate have presented global economic integration as the best, the most natural and the universal path towards growth and therefore development for all humanity. This is to be promoted through liberalization of trade, production and finance. The blueprint has been marketed with the powerful language of 'There Is No Alternative', or TINA, and to a large extent it has been accepted by Third World governments desperate for external finance. Voices of opposition have been neutralized, often by the incorporation of the language of opposition into the mainstream presentation. For example, those concerned about the environmental or social sustainability of growth find their objections neutralized by the presentation of the problem as the solution.

An increasingly conscious coordination of policies is evident in the work of the IMF, the World Bank, other regional multilateral development banks, the WTO and a growing number of other arms of the UN system, most recently the UNDP and UNCTAD. These institutions are operationalizing the new approach to development. To different degrees and in different ways, key international institutions have been changing their general orientation, their institutional structures and their policies to facilitate movement towards a world in which for finance, if not for people, national economic sovereignty is an anachronism.[32]

The integration process which they advocate has been underpinned philosophically by the so-called Washington consensus (see note 2), a particular brand of liberalism which privileges freedom defined in terms of private power and the individual, and which attacks the public realm and associated ideas of collectivity and society. Within this vision, inequality in itself is not a problem, and may even be desirable as it will unleash entrepreneurial abilities which will contribute to maximizing global wealth creation. Ultimately everyone will benefit.

Structural and institutional reform of national economies

The IMF is the lynchpin in the implementation of the new vision. Going beyond its original mandate to provide short term balance of payments support, it has co-ordinated with the World Bank in the 1980s and 1990s to promote fundamental structural and institutional reforms of national economies world-wide to better reflect the dominant vision of market-led rather than state-led development. These changes redraw the social as well as the economic map, profoundly altering the relationship between state, market and citizen. Beginning with Latin America and Africa in the 1980s in the context of the debt crisis, the IMF and the World Bank turned their attention to the economies in transition post 1989, and more recently to East Asia.

Conditioned structural adjustment loans[33] have enabled these institutions to advance the role of the market, and redesign the role of the state to support the

---

[32] For a critical assessment of the changing focus of the IMF, see Feldstein, pp. 20–33; also Devesh Kapur, 'The IMF: A Cure or a Curse?', *Foreign Policy*, 77: 2 (1998), pp. 114–29.

[33] The literature on structural adjustment is extensive, and the arguments will not be rehearsed here for lack of space. See the two volumes of theory and case studies, Paul Mosley, Jane Harrigan and John Toye (eds.), *World Bank and Policy-Based Lending* (London: Routledge, 1991).

creation of an enabling environment for the private sector.[34] Key components of IMF and World Bank packages include privatization of public services and public assets, liberalization of trade, finance and production, deregulation of labour and environmental laws, and the destruction of state activism generally in the public realm. The export-led growth expected from these changes would generate the foreign exchange income necessary to keep up debt repayments. Essentially these institutions have been applying a blueprint, a standard remedy for problems which may in fact be different depending on the specific country. This blueprint, very clear in the IMF's handling of the East Asian crisis, is based on the incomparable experience of Latin America over a decade earlier.[35]

Trade liberalization

IMF/World Bank structural adjustment policies are in tune with their vision of the emerging world trade system based on free trade. James Wolfensohn has remarked that 'together, we (the IMF and the World Bank) must work with and support the work of the World Trade Organisation which is so critical to the trading arrangements and future of our client countries'.[36] The global push for trade liberalization is reinforced and supported by the movement towards increased regional liberalization, for example NAFTA. From 1948 to 1997, 76 free trade agreements were created or modified, and more than half of these came into being after 1990.[37] The momentum is increasing.

In the 1980s the central role of trade was evident in the liberalizing trend of the Uruguay Round, and more recently in the World Trade Organisation. The Uruguay Round brought down barriers to agricultural trade, instituted trade-related investment measures (TRIMs) and trade-related intellectual property rights (TRIPs). A new round of trade talks is being sought under the WTO by the First World states, keen to bring even more new areas into the agreement. The EU Commission is pushing for a new 'Millennium Round' of comprehensive trade negotiations. Topics under suggestion include investment and competition policy and government procurement. It is interesting to note that the First World states, having failed to get an agreement on investment at the OECD,[38] have identified the WTO as the appropriate locus for this issue. In discussions in the WTO working group on investment, First World states have pushed for new rules to make it mandatory for all WTO countries to give foreign investors the right to enter and establish themselves with 100 per cent ownership, for foreigners and foreign firms to be treated at least as well as locals, and for prohibitions on restriction of the free flow of capital.

---

[34] The Corner House, *The Myth of the Minimalist State* (Dorset, UK: Corner House, 1998), Briefing no. 5.

[35] For more on this see Kevin Watkins, *Economic Growth with Equity: Lessons from East Asia* (Oxford: Oxfam, 1998).

[36] James Wolfensohn, 'A Proposal for a Comprehensive Development Framework: Discussion Draft', (Washington, DC: World Bank, 21 January, 1999).

[37] ECLAC/CDCC/UNIC, 1997, p. 6.

[38] For a critique of the Multilateral Agreement on Investment proposed by the OECD, see Caroline LeQuesne, *Reforming World Trade: The Social and Environmental Priorities* (Oxford: Oxfam, 1996), p. 21.

Finance

Public overseas development assistance is at its lowest level in fifty years, and falling sharply: in 1998, the figure stood at $33 billion, 40 per cent down on 1990, and equivalent to 0.25 per cent of the GDP of First World countries.[39] Most Third World countries find it exceedingly difficult to raise money. But as public finance has been dwindling, private flows have soared, with private lenders and investors taking advantage of opportunities created by the financial deregulation pursued by Third World governments in response to the policy prescriptions coming from the IMF and G7. Financial deregulation has prompted mergers and acquisitions. These have contributed to the growing concentration of wealth in the 1990s.

In assessing these private flows, several key points have been identified by Anderson, Barry and Honey.[40] Firstly, the volume of private flows, plus their proportion of overall flows, has surged. Private flows grew from US $44bn in 1990, to $256bn in 1997. By 1996 they accounted for over 85 per cent of resource flows, dwarfing public flows. Second, short-term portfolio flows have been the fastest growing, surging from 3.2bn to 45.7bn. These short-term flows are speculative rather than long term and productive, and as such have been concentrated in 12 countries—the 'emerging markets', the preferred terminology of the World Bank's International Finance Corporation. The rest of the Third World countries have been unable to attract private foreign investment. Thirdly, there has been a huge proliferation of new financial instruments and institutions in the 1980s and 1990s. The leverage they can exert is significant, with the potential to pose a challenge not only to individual countries, but to the stability of the entire global financial system.

Some international supervision of private finance has developed, but this has not kept pace with financial deregulation. Efforts are underway to build on the Basle Capital Accord of 1988 which provided a minimum standard for bank health,[41] but as yet these have not resulted in concrete developments due to disagreement about how to measure risk.[42] Supervision of non-bank private finance is meagre, existing mainly within the national domain. The January 1999 Basle Committee for Banking Supervision Report on Highly Leveraged Institutions, commissioned by the central bankers of the industrialized countries following the LTCM collapse, advised sounder risk management practices by banks and other lenders to highly leveraged institutions. It did not recommend regulation of the hedge funds themselves.[43] When LTCM collapsed in September 1998, the US Federal Reserve Bank hosted a meeting of the creditors. While it has denied funding a rescue package, its role is very sensitive and unclear.

[39] James Wolfensohn, Press Conference, World Bank, Washington DC, 22 April 1999.
[40] Sarah Anderson, Tom Barry and Martha Honey, 'International Financial Flows', *Foreign Policy in Focus*, 3, 41, (December 1998). The figures in this paragraph are taken from Anderson *et al.*
[41] See Bill McDonough, Chair, Federal Reserve Bank of New York and Chair, Basle Accord, 'Issues for the Basle Accord', Federal Reserve Bank of New York, 1998 Annual Report, pp. 3–12; and *The Economist*, 'Capital ideas: What's Cooking in Basle', 17 April 1999, p. 12.
[42] The Economist, 'Basle Brush: Banking Regulation', *The Economist,* 1 May 1999, p. 115.
[43] See *The Economist*, 'Capital Ideas: What's Cooking in Basle', 17 April 1999, p. 12.

Solutions

Given increasing inter- and intrastate economic polarization, many wonder in whose interests the current global economic architecture is working. Civil society groups have been calling for the reform of global governance institutions and their policies for two decades. What is new now is that debate is also taking place amongst concerned champions of existing strategies. Particularly in the wake of recent financial crises, critical questions have been raised about at the speed and appropriateness of global economic integration. The rewards have been enjoyed by a few, the gains have been made at the expense of stability, and the overall quality of life.[44]

A critical assessment of the Washington consensus was offered in January 1998 by Joseph Stiglitz, Senior Vice President and Chief Economist at the World Bank. In a public lecture entitled 'More Instruments and Broader Goals: Moving Toward the Post-Washington Consensus', Stiglitz argued that:

We seek increases in living standards—including improved health and education—not just increases in measured GDP. We seek sustainable development, which includes preserving natural resources and maintaining a healthy environment. We seek equitable development, which ensures that all groups in society, not just those at the top, enjoy the fruits of development. And we seek democratic development, in which citizens participate in a variety of ways in making the decisions that affect their lives.[45]

This position was reiterated a year later in a discussion document put out by James Wolfensohn.[46] Using the analogy of a balance sheet, Wolfensohn suggested that the left-hand side presents the language of finance ministers, that is macroeconomic data such as National Income Accounts, Balance of Payments and Trade Statistics, while the right hand side presents social, structural and human aspects. The emphasis in the 1980s and 1990s has been on the left hand side; as we enter the next millennium, he believes we must now consider both sides together. In other words, growth is necessary but not sufficient. This is evident in the World Bank proposal for a Comprehensive Development Framework the better to balance the macroeconomic and human aspects of development, and to increase ownership by broad-based consultation with stakeholders.

Broadly speaking, we can identify reformist and transformist positions on what might be done to address the problem of globalization of the Third World, though neither group is monolithic. The former, emanating from the G7, the World Bank and the IMF, is more limited in scope and nature, focusing mostly on technical modifications to existing policies and general risk management The latter, emanating from civil society groups in First and Third World states, tend to be more imaginative, far-reaching and directed at changing structures. At base, the reformist approach is informed by 'the fundamental belief that a market-based system provides the best prospect for creating jobs, spurring economic activity, and raising

---

[44] David Korten, When Multinationals Rule the World (London: Earthscan, 1995); also, see an interesting collection of views on the differential benefits of trade liberalization in Annie Taylor and Caroline Thomas (eds.) *Global Trade and Global Social Issues* (Routledge: London, 1999)

[45] Joseph Stiglitz, More Instruments and Broader Goals: Moving Toward the Post-Washington Consensus, WIDER Annual Lectures, 2, p. 31 (Helsinki: United Nations University 1998).

[46] Wolfensohn, A Proposal, 1999.

living standards in the US and around the world'.[47] Transformists do not share the fundamental belief in the market system. For them, 'The global financial crisis presents an opportunity to rethink and reshape the rules of the international economy so that they benefit people and the environment'.[48] What is at stake is the relationship between market, state and society. Transformists support the agenda articulated 24 years ago by Third World states in the CERDs, but they go further: they want national and local authorship and ownership of, and control over, development policies.

In order to compare and contrast the ideas of both groups, it would be useful to consider their respective views on some key issues of mutual concern: debt, finance, trade and investment. This comparison highlights the political framing of the problem of, and solution to, the globalization of the Third World.

Debt

Reformist and transformist positions on the debt burden of the poorest countries are quite different, reflecting very different views on how best to promote development.[49] Reformists continue to advocate the macroeconomic reform strategies designed by the IMF and World Bank. They are committed to the basic framework of the IMF/World Bank Heavily Indebted Poor Country initiative (HIPC). This initiative, launched in 1996, was designed to bring debt down to sustainable levels, as a reward for successful implementation of macroeconomic reform over a six year period. Reformists are committed to the creation of an investment climate attractive to the private sector, particularly foreign investors, and to this end they advocate the tying of debt relief to successful adherence to IMF Enhanced Structural Adjustment Facility (ESAF) programmes. They are opposed to blanket debt relief or debt cancellation. Transformists on the other hand, see the macroeconomic reform strategy as fundamentally flawed, because it ignores human development impacts. They reject the link between IMF ESAFs and debt relief, seeing these as inherently contradictory. For them, Fund/Bank adjustment programmes are part of the problem, and cannot be part of the solution. They support blanket debt relief and/or cancellation. The transformist position has been gaining ground recently as the Jubilee 2000 NGO campaign impacts on public opinion in G7 countries. The campaign has been joined by several powerful voices from international and national politics, such as the Pope, Jesse Jackson and Desmond Tutu, as well as celebrities such as Mohammed Ali and U2.

The IMF and the World Bank, mindful of growing public concern in G7 countries over debt, and of the disappointing results of HIPC initiative, have launched a review of the HIPC. They have asked governments and NGOs for written input to the review process, seeking responses from interested parties to a

---

[47] US Treasury Secretary Rubin, 'Remarks on the Reform of the International Financial architecture to the School of Advanced International Studies', Princeton University, 21 April 1999.

[48] 'A Citizens' Agenda for Reform of the Global Economic System', sometimes referred to as the Declaration on the New Global Financial Architecture, December 1998; Friends of the Earth (US), Third World Network, Institute for Policy Studies, USA.

[49] Merrill Goozner, 'Poorest Nations Mired in Big Debt', *The Chicago Tribune*, 19 March 1999.

series of specific questions. Similarly, G7 governments, aware of the growing public support for the Jubilee 2000 campaign, have put forward multiple suggestions for modification of the HIPC. The UK government, for example, supports the continued link with successful adherence to an ESAF programme, but advocates a reduction in the timescale before a state can receive relief from six to three years. Benefit should also be conditional on a government which is seeking relief signing a Social Code of Conduct to ensure that money released from debt servicing is spent on education and health. G7 countries generally support the idea of selling IMF gold to finance modifications to the HIPC, but disagree over how much should be sold.

Transformists see the HIPC and the modifications under suggestion as 'providing far too little far too late'.[50] Kevin Watkins of Oxfam points out that after three years of operation, only three countries have benefited from the HIPC, and of them, one, Uganda, now finds itself back in an unsustainable debt position. Transformists argue that real solutions to the debt problem must involve deeper debt reduction, and the delinking of debt relief from IMF-ESAF programmes.

Transformists also advocate a move away from consideration of debt-to-export ratios when calculating the debt distress of a country, and its replacement by a focus on the budgetary burden of debt.

When Mozambique qualifies for debt reduction (in 1999) it will save only $11m on a total debt service bill of more than $108m. In a country where one in five children die before the age of five, and where half the primary school age children are out of school, debt will continue to absorb more budget resources than health and primary education combined. Defining such a state of affairs as 'debt sustainability', as the framework does, is as absurd in economic terms as it is unacceptable in moral terms.[51]

Oxfam has suggested a 10 per cent cap of the share of government revenue devoted to debt servicing.

With respect to the debt reduction IMF-ESAF link, transfomists argue that the link should be abolished since the IMF 'has consistently prioritized monetary targets over human development goals'.[52] They argue that ESAF programmes intensify the poverty of certain groups. User fees in health and education reinforce stratification and marginalization. Moreover, by the IMF's own assessment, over the period of operation of these programmes from 1981–95, the debt burden of the poorest states in sub-Saharan Africa almost doubled as a share of GNP.[53] Not only do they impact negatively on human welfare, but they fail to deliver debt reduction. In place of the ESAF link, transformists suggest earlier and deeper debt reduction for countries willing to transfer savings from debt relief to education, health and water. In other words, there should be an explicit pro-poor incentive. This would benefit not only those people directly involved, but ultimately the global development effort. Currently, sub-Saharan Africa spends four times as much on debt repayment as it would cost to provide universal primary education. 'Using debt relief to finance education would provide real opportunities for the 40 million African children

[50] Kevin Watkins, 'Riderless horses and a third world handicap', *The Observer*, UK, Sunday 18 April 1999.
[51] Ibid.
[52] Ibid.
[53] Jubilee 2000 Coalition Afrika Campaign, 'Letter to members of the United States Congress', 11 March 1999.

denied an opportunity to go to primary school, helping create a platform for social and economic recovery'.[54] Transformists support independent scrutiny of government expenditure on health and education.

Trade

The reformist position is that trade liberalization is necessary for maximising global growth and therefore global welfare, and thus the momentum for liberalization must be maintained. The pattern of distribution of the global gain is not of central importance. Trade must be free, and the liberalization agenda must be pushed forward to cover new areas. This will be facilitated by expanding ownership of the agenda by development of a broader consensus. Most G7 governments, the WTO and the EU have undertaken consultations or discussions with civil society groups (mostly from the G7 countries) active in the trade debate. Former Director General Ruggiero of the WTO has initiated outreach activities by the organization. In March 1999, the WTO held two high level symposia with civil society groups: one on trade and the environment, the other on trade and development. Ruggiero has also initiated talks with Third World civil society groups. The US Trade Representative Barshevsky has also met with civil society groups on substantive issues relating to WTO ministerial conferences. The European Commission has in turn initiated active consultation with civil society representatives. All these exchanges are designed to increase support for further trade liberalization (and in the case of the US, to promote support for fast-track negotiating authority).

The transformist position is that growth is not the exclusive goal; that trade must be fair—not free; that governments must be free to choose not to trade and to pursue self-sufficiency if they have a mandate from citizens to take that path; that governments following trade liberalization must decide the appropriate pace; and that a redistributive mechanism should be put in place to compensate those states which lose out under the pursuit of global advantage.[55]

Transformists insist as well that the global trade regime does not embrace all members in an equitable fashion. The consensus decision-making at the WTO is understood as the 'consensus of the Quad', that is the US, Japan, EU and Canada, and this results in mistrust and lack of confidence. Transformists want development to be put at the centre of the trade liberalization agenda. Ruggiero, meeting with NGOs from LDCs on 1 February 1999, said that inclusion of development concerns in the WTO system is necessary to bring a human face to the process of globalization, and conceded the need for more civil society involvement given that trade rules are increasingly affecting day to day lives.

Transformists are waiting to see if these words get translated into action at the WTO. Unpleasant wranglings over the choice of Director-General Ruggiero's successor have raised concerns over lack of transparency and democracy in the

[54] Watkins, *Riderless horses*, 1999.
[55] See for example, Herman Daly, 'Globalization versus Internationalization: Some Implications', November 1998, available direct from School of Public Affairs, University of Maryland, College Park, MD 20742-1821, USA.

decision-making machinery of the organisation.[56] There is also the fear that the First World states are driving the WTO agenda at a speed and in a direction which pays insufficient attention to the interests of many members, and that the marginalization of development concerns will continue.[57]

Finance

For reformists, liberalization of finance remains the central goal, but it is acknowledged that some technical efforts or new tools or facilities might be appropriate to diminish the occurrence of destabilizing disruptions, contagious crises and general financial risk. Suggestions for reform however are hardly radical. In the view of Hans Tietmeyer, President of the Bundesbank, 'sweeping institutional changes are not needed to realise these improvements'.[58] US Treasury Secretary Rubin suggests that 'reform is not going to involve a single dramatic announcement but a collection of actions over time. Some of these have already been taken or are in process of happening. Others will take shape going forward'.[59] The sort of thing Rubin had in mind were the IMF's new Supplemental Reserve facility, and the Contingent Credit Line. The emphasis is on preventing crises before they arise by the adoption and maintenance of sound macroeconomic policies, sound debt management practices, sustainable exchange rate regimes and the development of supervisory regimes. Reformists not surprisingly oppose the reintroduction of national capital controls which they believe detract from the long-term goal of strengthening the global financial system via further liberalization. Moreover, they regard such controls as damaging to a country's capacity to attract foreign investment.

Hans Tietmeyer has put forward the idea of a financial stability forum to strengthen surveillance, coordination and supervision of the international financial system. This would contribute to reduction in systemic risk and to crisis prevention. Attendance would initially be limited to G7 countries, plus regulatory bodies, but eventually other national authorities, probably the emerging market economies, would be invited to join the process.[60] This forum has a feature common to global governance institutions: so many countries and so many of the world's people would not be represented there in a meaningful way. As such, it is severely limited in what it can deliver. Jeffrey Sachs has remarked that what is needed is 'a dialogue of the rich and poor together, not just a communion of the rich pretending to speak for the world'.[61]

The transformists' ideas about finance are more far-reaching. Their starting point is that the needs of individual states as determined by national governments must be given priority over the needs of capital. International capital must be firmly

---

[56] For a detailed report of the process of selecting the new director-general of the WTO, and an
      examination of the surrounding controversy, see Chakravarthi.Raghavan, 'Trade: From Rule-based to
      Rule-less System?', *South-North Development Monitor*, 4, 6, 7, and 10 May 1999.
[57] WTO, 'Seattle Preparations Enter New Phase' *WTO Focus*, 37 (January-February 1999) pp. 2–3.
[58] Robert Chote, 'Forum to help prevent Crises Agreed', *Financial Times*, London, 22 February 1999.
[59] US Treasury Secretary Rubin, 'Remarks', 21 April, 1999.
[60] Robert Chote, 'Forum', *Financial Times*, London, 22 February 1999.
[61] Jeffrey Sachs, 'Stop Preaching' p. 22.

regulated, they believe, and financial liberalization must take place only at the pace appropriate to the local conditions. Capital in the end must work for the majority of people; thus it must be predominantly productive rather than speculative, and long-term rather than short-term in nature. A clear exposition of these ideas appears in 'A Citizens' Agenda for Reform of the Global Economic System'. This calls for action at the national, regional and international levels 'to regulate international capital in order to reorient finance from speculation to long-term investment, reduce instability and volatility, enhance local and national political space, keep private losses private'.[62]

At the national level, governments—according to the transformists—should be allowed and encouraged to pursue regulations and measures that restrict short-term capital mobility. The examples offered in the Agenda include implementation of taxes, establishing capital controls and setting exchange rate regimes. At the regional level, the Agenda recommended the establishment of regional crisis funds. At the international level, the Agenda called for the establishment of an international bankruptcy mechanism, the provision of debt reduction delinked from IMF/WB conditions, the reform of the IMF, and the establishment of a speculation tax.

Some national measures have already been implemented by a few governments in the Third World. The reinstitution of capital controls has been attempted in an effort to decrease national vulnerability to some major problems resulting from liberalization. This goes against conventional economic theory and the wishes of the IMF and World Bank, and sometimes occurs after heated domestic disagreement about the best way forward. The government of Chile for example, put capital controls in place and believes these probably helped the country ride out the Mexican crisis more effectively.[63]

The Malaysian government in September 1998 also introduced a set of measures based on the system existing in China.[64] The Central Bank of Malaysia pegged the Malaysian ringgit at 3.80 to the US $; overseas dealing in the ringgit was prohibited; Malaysian residents were restricted in the amounts of money they could take out of the country (and also in the purposes for which it could be taken out); and the capital and profits of foreign investors were deliberately locked into the Malaysian market for a year. These controls were eased at the beginning of February 1999 with a graduated levy, or exit tax, on foreign investments in Malaysian stock.[65] The Malaysian government claims that these measures contributed to an increase in reserves, an improved current account balance and a balance of trade surplus. Indeed, in its view, these were the 'only reasonable option for Malaysia, or any small country who finds its currency under attack'.[66]

At an international level, there is a campaign underway for a speculation tax on the world's major currencies to discourage short-term capital movements. The idea of a tax on international currency transactions was proposed in the late 1970s by Professor James Tobin of Yale University.[67] The Tobin tax, as it has come to be

[62] A Citizens' Agenda for Reform of the Global Economic System, 1998.
[63] Anderson *et al.*, *International Financial Flows*.
[64] Martin Khor, 'Within the Third World, Malaysia's Case Could Help Ailing Brazil', *Third World Network Features*, 10 March 1999.
[65] For details see Ian Stewart, 'Malaysia Loosens Capital Controls', *The Australian News*, 5 February 1999.
[66] Malaysian Government, 'The Tiger Fights Back', *Financial Times*, London, 28 March 1999, p. xiv.
[67] Anderson *et al.*, *International Financial Flows*.

known, would place a small tax on all foreign exchange transactions, and would have the effect of reducing short term movements of money. With over a trillion dollars a day being exchanged in international currency deals, this tax would be lucrative. The money yielded from it could potentially be used in civil sectors such as health and education.[68]

Foreign direct investment and corporate accountability

Reformists identify foreign direct investment by transnational corporations as a central part of the strategy to promote global economic integration, foster growth and create employment opportunities. Such corporations, they argue, create wealth and goods for the global good, and as far as possible an environment should be created for their successful operation. This of necessity must entail removing restraints on their activities and allowing them to be self-regulating global actors seeking out global advantage in a borderless world. By way of contrast, trans-formists define the role of foreign investment as helping the community in which it takes place by contributing to locally and nationally determined sustainable develop-ment strategies. Corporate decisions impact directly on the social, cultural, environ-mental and economic conditions of much of humanity, and as such they must show sensitivity to broader goals than profit. Governments must have the right to regulate investment, establish measures to redirect and improve the quality of FDI flows, review and renegotiate international institutions and agreements concerning invest-ments, participate in the establishment of core standards of behaviour for TNCs and their effective monitoring and enforcement, and re-examine corporate structure and activities.[69]

The case for the modification of corporate practice to take account of values and goals other than profit has gained strength over the last decade with the explosion of knowledge about corporate operations and perceived corporate complicity in the oppressive policies of many Third World regimes. Ken Sara Wiwa's struggle and death on behalf of the Ogoni people in Nigeria highlighted possible connections between extraction of raw materials by transnational corporations, physical repression by security forces, environmental degradation and general human rights violations. The activities of BP in Colombia have also come under the spotlight. Other examples have been the subject of campaigns by non-governmental groups: for example, the use of child or prison labour for production of goods for export to the markets of the First World states. In response to this, reformists have argued for the private regulation of corporations. At the World Economic Summit, Davos, Switzerland, January/February 1999, Kofi Annan called on corporations to abide by core values—human rights, environment and labour standards.[70] Annan, like other

[68] See http:/www.cyberus.ca/choose.sustain/Tobin.html#697731.
[69] A Citizens' Agenda for Reform of the Global Economic System, 1998.
[70] Kofi Annan, 'The Secretary-General's Address to the World Economic Forum', UN press release, 31 January 1999.

reformists, sees private regulation as serving businesses, employees and society as a whole.

A patchwork quilt of private codes is slowly evolving. These embrace codes established by individual companies such as Levi Strauss,[71] to others developed for certain industries such as the chemical industry or toy manufacture.[72] Others are more inclusive private international standards (ISOs). The ISO standards are interesting because, while private in origin, they accrue a degree of public legitimacy even though they lack any requirement for public or independent scrutiny. Examples are the ISO 14000 Series which provides standards for environmental management, and the SA8000, the Social Accountability standard on workers rights.[73]

Transformists argue that public corporate accountability is imperative if corporate practice is to take account of values other than private profit. They regard self-regulation of corporations via voluntary codes as wholly inadequate and open to abuse, not only within the Third World but also within the First. Hence transformists advocate a global code of conduct or global guidelines similar to those suggested by the now defunct UN Centre on Transnational Corporations prior to the UNCED. This recalls moves in the UN in the 1970s by Third World states to establish a Code of Conduct for transnational corporations.

Conclusion

We have a problem. As we enter the next millennium, we are witnessing a reconfiguration of the Third World in the context of an emerging global economy. Defined in terms of states, the Third World has expanded to embrace the former centrally planned economies of the Second World; defined from the human aspect, it now includes growing numbers of marginalized people in First as well as Third World states. The intensification of economic polarization between and within states is a key feature of the contemporary global social landscape. The UN target for halving the number in absolute poverty by 2015 will not be met. In an increasingly coordinated fashion, key global governance institutions, and the interests they represent, are overseeing a process of increased economic, political and social stratification. They are complicit in this outcome.

---

[71] Craig Forcese, Commerce with Conscience (Ottawa: ICHRDD, 1997); Andrew Ross (ed.) *No Sweat* (London: Verso, 1997).
[72] Panos Institute, *Globalisation and Employment*, p. 18.
[73] Ibid., p. 18.

Table 1: *The world's priorities? (annual expenditure, $US bn)*

Basic education for all	6[a]
Cosmetics in the USA	8
Water and sanitation for all	9[a]
Ice cream in Europe	11
Reproductive health for all women	12[a]
Perfumes in Europe and the USA	12
Basic health and nutrition	13[a]
Pet foods in Europe and USA	17
Business entertainment in Japan	35
Cigarettes in Europe	50
Alcoholic drinks in Europe	105
Narcotic drugs in the world	400
Military spending in the World	780

Note: [a]Estimated additional annual cost to achieve universal access to basic social services in all developing countries.
Source: UNDP, 1998, p. 37.

Reformists accept that life is unfair, but transformists argue that it doesn't have to be. The importance of history is clear, but current choices are also very significant. These choices are being made by global governance institutions, by a handful of states, by powerful corporate actors and by the 20 per cent of the world's population who exercise consumer choice in the global market place. While acknowledging the global reproduction of Third World problems, we must not forget that the overwhelming majority of poor people live in the Third World states. They did yesterday, they do today, and in the absence of remedial action, they will tomorrow.

Whatever happened to the Pacific Century?

ROSEMARY FOOT AND ANDREW WALTER*

Typical of the opposing trends that have been a part of the decade 1989 to 1999, many of the states in the Asia-Pacific in these ten years have shifted from 'miracle' status to crisis. From being the political and economic model for other countries in both the developing and the developed world, they now signal how best to avoid the less savoury pitfalls of rapid development. The miracle status, deriving from two decades or more of impressive growth rates on the basis of a presumed distinctive politico-economic model, was supposed to herald a Pacific Century. The key characteristics of this new era were a newfound regional coherence and a related transfer of economic and above all political power from the Atlantic community towards Asia-Pacific. The crisis, in turn, is seen as marking the end of that shift in the economic and political centres of gravity.

Despite the starkness of these contrasts, we argue that the idea of the Pacific Century was always overstated in economic, but especially in political terms. Two particular currents of thought in international relations contributed to this overstatement: developments in international political economy encouraged the presumption of a close correspondence between economic and political change, and the resurgence of interest in culture led to a search for the distinctively Asian values that were perceived to be at the root of that economic success. This tendency to overstatement has also shaped reactions to the economic crisis that is seen as beginning in 1997. In fact, many of the underlying weaknesses in certain of the East Asian political-economic models were present well before the events of 1997. In what follows, we subject the concept of the Pacific Century, which reached its zenith in the late 1980s, to renewed scrutiny. We argue that the interlinkages among the economic, political and security dimensions are more complex than the unidirectional claims at the base of this concept have tended to suggest.

The Pacific Century idea

Would one have expected in the 1950s that our focus on the American century would have given way, some three decades later, to an absorption with the Asia-Pacific? Many saw this as heralding the Pacific Century, a century that not only would pose a challenge to the dominant explanation about the path to growth, but also that would

* The authors would like to thank Jonathan Aronson, Stephan Haggard, Stuart Harris, Michael Leifer, and Robert Wade, together with the editors of this Special Issue, for valuable comments on an earlier draft.

mark a major shift in structural power—that is, in the norms and rules of behaviour that would characterize international society.[1] The locus of world power was perceived to be shifting towards Asia, away from the Atlantic and particularly the United States. These perceptions were especially startling because Japan's comprehensive defeat in the Second World War, years of civil war, foreign intervention and ultimately Communist victory in China, and the Korean and Indochina conflicts, all suggested rather that Asia would be condemned to persistent instability and impoverishment. US political and economic linkages across the Atlantic were of much greater importance than those across the Pacific. European integration and the Atlantic alliance held out the prospect of a continued deepening of the Atlantic 'community' and its entrenchment as the dominant locus of global political and economic activity.

Even by the late 1960s, this picture remained largely true. Despite Japan's rapid economic recovery, this was generally put down to the inevitable catch-up of a comparatively backward economy, and its manufactured goods still had a reputation for poor quality. Dominant images of Asia reflected those contained in Gunnar Myrdal's three volume study, *The Asian Drama*,[2] published in 1968, with its focus on Asia's overwhelming, impoverished population, and low technological base. Although in retrospect we can point to the beginnings of export-led growth in the early 1960s in some East Asian developing countries, Myrdal's conclusions were widely shared at the time.

It was the dramatic reversal of the outlook for Asia's material prospects that was essential to the emergence of the Pacific Century concept. During the 1970s, it was becoming increasingly apparent that the pessimistic image of Asia seriously underestimated Japan, leading to the publication of such pathbreaking studies as *Japan as Number One*.[3] During the golden age of the postwar boom, 1950–73, Japan's real GDP grew at 9.3 per cent per annum, compared with 3.6 per cent for the US and 4.9 per cent for the OECD average. Over the same period, Japan's volume of exports grew 15.4 per cent per annum, compared with 6.3 per cent for the US and 8.6 per cent for the OECD average. Japan had far outpaced Britain and France in terms of economic size: in the 1970s, Japan became the world's number three exporter (behind West Germany and the US) and the number two in terms of both manufacturing and total output. The apparent Japanese economic challenge to the US itself provided the subject of many studies, feeding American self-perceptions of relative decline and giving a powerful boost to studies concerned with the institutional and normative consequences of a US inability to sustain a hegemonic role. Measured at current exchange rates, Japanese *per capita* income appeared to be soaring past that of the US (see Figure 1).[4]

The emergence of Japan as an 'economic superpower', as Henry Kissinger termed it in 1973, was the essential prerequisite for the emergence of the concept of the Pacific Century. During the 1970s, this interest in Japanese advancement spread to

[1] For reasons that will become apparent, our focus will primarily be on Asia-Pacific rather than the Pacific rim, except where attention to Latin America is pertinent to our argument.

[2] Myrdal, *The Asian Drama: An Inquiry into the Poverty of Nations* (New York: Twentieth Century Fund, 1968).

[3] Ezra F. Vogel, *Japan as Number One: Lessons for America* (Cambridge, MA: Harvard University Press, 1979).

[4] 'PPP' comparisons, which take into account national prices, suggest Japanese real income still remains below that of the US.

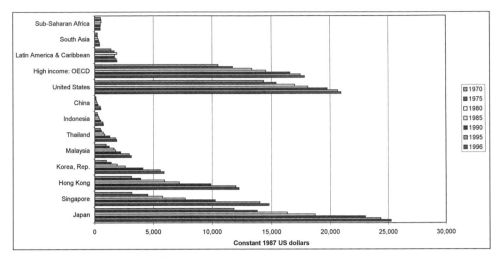

Source: World Bank data, 1998.

Figure 1. *Real GNP per capita growth, 1970–96 (constant 1987 US dollars).*

the smaller developing countries and economic territories of East Asia. The 'four tigers' of Hong Kong, Singapore, South Korea, and Taiwan were also experiencing rapid rates of growth and apparently rapid economic convergence with the West. Attention focused in the 1980s on the other ASEAN countries and China, where growth rates were also taking off (see Figure 1 and Table 1). During the 'lost decade' of growth in Latin America and the bulk of the developing world in the debt-ridden 1980s, developing East Asia continued to grow at rates comparable to Japan after 1950 (7.7 per cent 1980–90 and 10.2 per cent 1990–96). The success of the tiger economies in manufactured exports, combined with Japan's earlier successes in penetrating Western markets in such key industries as steel, automobiles and electronics, underpinned growing US and European concern about a loss of competitiveness in these industries. A literature emerged which explained this East Asian success story in terms of a broad competitive advantage in manufacturing.[5]

With the striking success of Thailand, Malaysia and Indonesia, soon followed by China, it was evident that a broader regional pattern of rapid growth was emerging. As the World Bank noted in 1993, 'if growth were randomly distributed, there is roughly one chance in ten thousand that success would have been so regionally concentrated.'[6] Although various explanations for this pattern were to emerge, the notion of an East Asia led by a dynamic Japanese economy in a 'flying geese' pattern dominated popular images and academic literature.

One prevalent view was that Japan had discovered a superior and neomercantilist model of economic development, a model successfully copied by its neighbours, in

[5] For example see Roy Hofheinz and Kent E. Calder, *The East Asia Edge* (New York: Basic Books, 1982).
[6] World Bank, *The East Asian Miracle: Economic Growth and Public Policy* (Washington DC: World Bank, 1993), p. 2.

Table 1. *Trends in long-term economic development, selected Asia-Pacific Countries, 1965–96.*

	GNP		Value added			Private con- sumption	Gross domestic fixed invest- ment	Exports of goods and services
	Average annual % growth		*Average annual % growth*			*Average annual % growth*		
	Total 1965– 96	Per capita 1965– 96	Agri- culture 1965– 96	Indus- try 1965– 96	Services 1965– 96	1965– 96	1965– 96	1965– 96
China	8.5	6.7	4.3	11.0	11.1	7.6	10.5	11.1
Hong Kong, China	7.5	5.6	..	..	..	7.6	8.2	11.3
Indonesia	6.7	4.6	3.9	9.1	7.5	7.1	8.9	5.6
Japan	4.5	3.6	−0.1	4.6	4.8	4.2	4.7	7.7
Korea, Rep.	8.9	7.3	2.0	13.8	9.0	7.5	12.1	16.1
Malaysia	6.8	4.1	3.7	8.5	7.0	6.1	9.9	9.5
Philippines	3.5	0.9	2.4	3.6	3.9	3.7	4.5	6.3
Singapore	8.3	6.3	−1.4	8.6	8.3	6.6	9.6	12.2
Thailand	7.3	5.0	4.1	9.7	7.4	6.3	9.1	11.2
Argentina	1.2	−0.3	1.3	1.0	2.4	..	..	4.8
Brazil	4.6	2.4	3.5	4.6	5.4	4.6	1.7	8.6
Chile	3.3	1.6	3.7	2.9	4.3	2.8	3.8	8.0
Mexico	4.1	1.5	2.3	4.6	4.2	3.7	3.8	7.9
Developing Countries:								
East Asia & Pacific	7.4	5.5	4.1	9.7	8.3	6.7	9.4	8.8
Latin America & Carib.	3.3	1.1	2.7	3.3	4.0	4.0	2.0	5.2
Middle East & N. Africa	1.1	−1.8	4.4	0.0	2.0	..	..	..
South Asia	4.6	2.2	2.8	5.5	5.6	4.1	5.3	6.2
Sub-Saharan Africa	2.7	−0.2	1.7	2.6	3.3	2.9	−1.1	2.1

Source: World Bank, World Development Indicators, 1998, CD-Rom.

part (particularly in the ASEAN countries) through the transfer of Japanese capital and technology.[7] In his influential *MITI and the Japanese Miracle* (1982), Chalmers Johnson identified successful Japanese industrial policy as the key. Although later books placed more emphasis upon Japanese private sector innovation and manage-

---

[7] Chalmers Johnson, *MITI and the Japanese Miracle* (Stanford, CA: Stanford University Press, 1982); Robert Wade, *Governing the Market* (Princeton, NJ: Princeton University Press, 1990); Alice Amsden, *Asia's Next Giant: South Korea and Late Industrialization* (New York: Oxford University Press, 1989); E. Vogel, *The Four Little Dragons: The Spread of Industrialization in East Asia* (Cambridge MA: Harvard University Press, 1991).

ment techniques,[8] this literature entrenched the idea that Japan had discovered a superior way of making things and of organizing the relationship between state and market. Robert Wade's *Governing the Market* (1990) argued that the rest of East Asia had successfully copied important aspects of efficient state interventionism from Japan, helping to explain their success in manufacturing. Much of the literature argued that the provision of 'patient capital' to strategic industries via a state-managed banking system, involving some 'financial repression', was part of the explanation. Others, such as Ronald Dore, pointed to the cultural foundations of the Japanese model.[9]

The political aspects of the model were emphasized in the idea of the 'strong state', comparatively autonomous of domestic interest group pressures (unlike the US and most of the developing world), providing the basis for this efficient interventionism.[10] Others emphasized a causal link between the economic miracle and the prevalence of authoritarian political regimes in the region. 'Asian values', which prioritized growth above political freedom, also produced 'growth with equity', particularly compared with the Latin American countries on the other side of the Pacific. In 1990, China, Indonesia, and South Korea each had Gini indices of about 34, much lower than the 50s typical of highly unequal Latin American countries like Brazil, and comparable to OECD countries.[11] For many commentators, it was increasingly unclear how the West could presume to claim any moral superiority for its liberal model when the results it produced were economically and perhaps socially inferior. The 'soft authoritarian' implications appealed to many Asian governments, even to some in Japan, and of course China. Government officials in Singapore and Malaysia took up the argument with enormous verve, comparing and exaggerating the differences between industrious, chaste, family-centred Asians and lazy, high spending, low investing, violent, self-centred and welfare-dependent Westerners.[12] Once seen as the cause of economic stagnation, Confucianism had become a key explanation for the Miracle.[13] For different reasons, Western conservatives, postmodernists, and communitarians had some sympathy with such arguments. The American journalist Robert Elegant urged Westerners to:

take a profound lesson from the patient perseverance that is central to the Asian ethos: the tenacious accretion of power and virtue that lies beneath the dazzling surface of present day Asians . . . Asian societies do change, sometimes dramatically. But they change only after attaining an almost mystical consensus regarding their new course—and the old values

[8] Notably James P. Womack, et al., *The Machine That Changed the World* (New York: Rawson Associates, 1990).

[9] Ronald Dore, *Taking Japan Seriously: A Confucian Perspective on Leading Economic Issues* (London: Athlone, 1987).

[10] See Stephan Haggard, *Pathways from the Periphery* (Ithaca, NY: Cornell University Press, 1990); Peter Evans, *Embedded Autonomy* (Princeton, NJ: Princeton University Press, 1995).

[11] World Bank, *World Development Indicators 1998* (Washington DC: World Bank, 1998; CD-Rom). The Gini index measures the extent to which the distribution of income (or, in some cases, consumption expenditures) among individuals or households within an economy deviates from a perfectly equal distribution. An index of zero represents perfect equality and an index of 100 implies perfect inequality.

[12] Two similar versions of this argument are Kishore Mahbubani, 'The Dangers of Decadence: What the Rest Can Teach the West', *Foreign Affairs*, 72:4 (1993) and Bilahari Kausikan, 'Asia's Different Standard', *Foreign Policy*, 92 (Fall 1993).

[13] P. L. Berger and H.-H. Hsiao, *In Search of an East Asian Development Model* (New Brunswick: Transaction Books, 1987).

endure. Individualistic Westerners living in laissez-faire societies are unaccustomed to arriving at fundamental decisions by such patient and profound processes.[14]

This economic, cultural and political challenge would, some claimed, have dramatic consequences for international relations. The breakdown of the Bretton Woods system, the oil price hikes of 1973 and 1979, together with Washington's inability to prevail in Vietnam, to halt the decline in its nuclear superiority, or to sustain political coalitions of support in such bodies as the United Nations, appeared to highlight the challenge from Asia. More specifically, Asian trade practices, and particularly Japan's, were seen as highly resistant to external pressure for change.[15] America's major allies in Western Europe seemed similarly troubled, their introspection compounded by slow growth and rising unemployment. Robert Gilpin argued that the challenge was at the global level and, if history was any guide, would likely result in an extension of the economic competition to the military realm.[16] Others such as Richard Rosecrance suggested that countries like Japan embodied a new type of postrealist, 'trading state' model, a threat of a different kind to the US.[17] The success of China's economic reform programme provided a further, and possibly even more worrying, long-term attack on American influence in the region and globally. America's destiny, therefore, was as a significantly diminished giant: militarily constrained by the 'Vietnam syndrome' and strategic multipolarity, able to sell only agricultural products, software and services to Asian consumers on the basis of a continually depreciating dollar, and increasingly dependent upon Asian savings to fund its trade and fiscal deficits.

By the late 1980s, then, the American Century was apparently giving way to a Pacific Century. It is important to note that East Asia's eclipse of Latin America as the major developing region in the world economy was a key aspect of this. Not only was the US being economically eclipsed; the Western hemisphere as a whole appeared to be in long term decline, and 'the Pacific' was now seen in distinctly Asian terms. By 1994, the APEC region accounted for 38 per cent of world population, 56 per cent of world GDP, 46 per cent of world trade, and 65 per cent of world FDI inflows. East Asia was perceived as the dynamic core of this new Pacific economy, with Latin America marginalized and the US economy and institutions seen as degenerate. Put at its most graphic, we were witnessing the torch of leadership being passed from the Atlantic to the Pacific countries, particularly to those on its western rim.

This perception was given a further boost by the end of the Cold War in three related ways. First, it increased the focus on regions generally as the removal of strategic bipolarity more fully exposed the regional patterns that had lain dormant or unnoticed underneath.[18] New regional institutions such as APEC emerged, but

---

[14] Elegant's *Pacific Destiny* (1990) quoted in Alexander Woodside, 'The Asia-Pacific Idea as a Mobilization Myth' in Arif Dirlik (ed.) *What is in a Rim? Critical Perspectives on the Pacific Region Idea* (Lanham, MD: Rowman and Littlefield, 1998), p. 38.

[15] For a discussion, see C. Fred Bergsten and Marcus Noland, *Reconcilable Differences? United States-Japan Economic Conflict* (Washington DC: Institute for International Economics, 1993).

[16] Robert Gilpin, 'International Politics in the Pacific Rim Era', in *Annals of the American Academy of Political and Social Science*, 505 (September 1989), p. 67.

[17] Richard N. Rosecrance, *The Rise of the Trading State* (New York: Basic Books, 1985).

[18] See Louise Fawcett and Andrew Hurrell (eds.), *Regionalism in World Politics* (Oxford: Oxford University Press, 1995).

there was also clear evidence of a desire to promote narrower East Asian institutions explicitly aimed at excluding Western, and particularly the US presence. This was related to the growing influence of Japanese trade, aid and investment linkages with its region, and the likelihood of an emerging 'Yen bloc', with its implied challenge to dollar hegemony.[19] Second, the end of the Cold War clarified the political and cultural challenge from Asia, and called into question the Western and especially the US government's assumption that the end of the Cold War would represent another 'end of ideology', when claims about the universality of values and the existence of an international community could be made real. Finally, it reinforced the presumption of an increased importance for geoeconomics compared with geopolitics, which emphasized the salience of the Asian challenge. At the first APEC summit in Seattle in 1993, President Clinton spoke of East Asian states as dynamos rather than the vulnerable dominoes they once were.[20] Some international political economy literature emphasized the negative economic legacy of the Cold War for the US: government spending and an industrial base heavily skewed towards the defence sector and dual-use technologies, reducing the competitiveness of American industry in the new civilian markets and technologies in which East Asia excelled.[21] Even the Soviets saw the writing on the wall. Gorbachev's speech in Vladivostok in summer 1986, a time when it was already plain to the new Soviet leadership that the label superpower hardly deserved to be attached to it, somewhat plaintively reminded his audience that the USSR was also a Pacific power occupying one quarter of the Asian landmass.

To summarize, the concept of the Pacific Century was generally underpinned by the following propositions. First, the spreading economic miracle from Japan to the developing countries of East Asia implied a successful formula of economic development different to that promulgated by the West. A combination of successful learning from the Japanese experience and unique 'Asian values' were seen as behind this success and led to far greater attention to the 'Asian values' debate than would otherwise have been the case. Second, the rapidity of economic growth in Asia-Pacific, and particularly the emerging economic pre-eminence of Japan, would enable this group of countries not only to resist Western influence, but to exercise itself growing influence over international institutions and outcomes. Material (economic) power would enable Asia-Pacific to challenge the key norms and institutions of postwar international order, hitherto Western-dominated. Third, the emerging economic and political coherence of Asia-Pacific as a region would facilitate both Japanese political influence within and beyond the region, and the ability of the region as a whole to mount such a challenge.

---

[19] See Rudiger Dornbusch, 'The Dollar in the 1990s: Competitiveness and the Challenges of New Economic Blocs', in *Monetary Policy Issues in the 1990s* (Kansas City, MO: Federal Reserve Bank of Kansas City, 1989).

[20] Quoted in Mark T. Berger and Douglas A. Borer (eds.), *The Rise of East Asia: Critical Visions of the Pacific Century* (London: Routledge, 1997), p. 1.

[21] Michael Borrus and John Zysman, 'Industrial competitiveness and American national security', in Wayne Sandholtz *et al.*, *The Highest Stakes* (New York: Oxford University Press, 1992).

The East Asian challenge in retrospect

Although there is a significant portion of truth in this early 1990s picture, some of the analysis was controversial and at times superficial. Moreover, this exaggeration of the degree of change associated with the idea of a Pacific Century may have contributed to the onset of the economic crisis in the late 1990s. It certainly contributed to the failure to see it coming. We deal below with the various claims concerning the East Asian challenge, before turning to consider the implications of Asia-Pacific regionalism.

Japan and Asia-Pacific as challenger

The economic success of Japan and many of the developing countries in the region was indisputable, but its broader implications were less clear than much of the political economy literature suggested. Underlying the notion of Japan as an 'economic superpower' lay certain conceptions of the relationship between economic and political power in the international system. In the 1970s, academics followed practitioners like Kissinger in asserting the diminishing importance of military power and traditional security factors in international politics, compared with economic issues and power. Keohane and Nye argued this was true under conditions of 'complex interdependence', and claimed it was difficult for military superpowers such as the US to gain leverage over economic issues through 'linkage' with security issues.[22] To the extent that power was increasingly issue-specific, Japan and an integrated Europe could be seen as 'civilian superpowers', fostering multipolarity in economic issues. At the same time, strategic bipolarity had led to military stalemate. Others were less sceptical than Keohane and Nye about the possibilities for issue-linkage. Gilpin, for example, argued that, in the longer term, American dependence upon Japanese finance would:

further weaken American power and strengthen the Japanese...Whatever decisions the Japanese make regarding the use of their growing financial power will have profound significance for the future of the international economic and political system.[23]

There are a number of problems with such analyses. First, even putting aside the recent renaissance of the US economy, much of the commentary of the 1970s and 1980s significantly exaggerated the extent of US (and European) relative decline. Much of the declinist literature took the aberrant situation of 1945 as the base point of comparison, but the US weight in the world economy showed relatively little change if 1930 or 1960 were used instead. Second, too much was read into phenomena such as the overtaking of Atlantic by Pacific trade flows, which received great emphasis in the debate. This overlooks that the US and Europe are more integrated via foreign direct investment (FDI) than trade, although the reverse is true for the

[22] Robert O. Keohane and Joseph S. Nye, *Power and Interdependence: World Politics in Transition* (Boston, MA: Little, Brown, 1977).
[23] Robert Gilpin, *The Political Economy of International Relations* (Princeton, NJ: Princeton University Press, 1987), pp. 337, 338.

Table 2. *US majority-owned nonbank affiliate local sales of goods and services vs. US exports, by destination in 1994.*

Destination	Local affiliate sales ($m)	US exports of goods and services ($m)	Ratio of local sales to exports
Europe	516,754	123,479	4.18
Germany	113,179	19,229	5.89
UK	147,599	26,900	5.49
East Asia	204,301	156,610	1.30
Japan	88,280	53,488	1.65
Korea, Taiwan, Singapore, Hong Kong	50,161	59,595	0.84
China	2,520	9,282	0.27
Latin America	91,832	92,555	0.99
Argentina	10,086	4,462	2.26
Brazil	29,238	8,102	3.61
Mexico	27,022	50,844	0.53
Canada	134,197	114,439	1.17

Note: In these US Commerce Department definitions, 'Europe' includes the EU plus other western, central and eastern European countries. 'East Asia' includes the East Asian Pacific Rim, including ASEAN countries, Oceania, and the Indian sub-continent. 'Latin America' includes other Western hemisphere, except Canada.
Source: US Department of Commerce, Bureau of Economic Analysis, *US Direct Investment Abroad, 1994 Benchmark Survey, Final Results* (Washington DC, May 1998), table III.F2; US Department of Commerce, International Trade Administration, website tables, 1999.

US and East Asia. As Table 2 shows, although US exports to Asia-Pacific now greatly exceed those to Europe, a much greater proportion of sales by US-owned firms to 'European' customers occurs through the channel of FDI rather than cross-border exports. American multinational corporation (MNC) affiliates based in the UK alone sold almost as much to UK-based customers in 1994 as the total amount of US exports to East Asia as a whole. This asymmetry has contributed significantly to American frustration with Asian trade practices.[24]

Third, the literature tended to focus on the Japanese and Asian challenge in a few high-profile sectors in Western trade politics. This may have reflected more the ability of sectors like automobiles, steel and electronics to exercise voice and organize protectionist responses than a sober assessment of the seriousness of the 'threat'. Clearly, many Western economic sectors were comparatively unchallenged, including most services and many high technology industries, although the long run difficulties of the US semiconductor sector (and even automobiles) were exaggerated.[25] In addition to all this, the Asian crisis has revealed serious weaknesses in the previously vaunted Asian model, explored further below. In fact, Japanese

---

[24] On this question, see Dennis J. Encarnation, *Rivals Beyond Trade: America versus Japan in Global Competition* (Ithaca, NY: Cornell University Press, 1992).
[25] With the obvious qualification that the revival of important parts of manufacturing industry in the US may be due in part to the seriousness of the challenge and the adoption of Japanese manufacturing techniques.

economic stagnation since the beginning of the 1990s pointed towards such weaknesses well before the crisis hit in 1997.

Economic, political and security linkages

Even if we can all agree that the US declined relative to its overwhelming position at the end of World War II, this needed to be distinguished from US power over outcomes in world politics. No torches of leadership had really been passed at the time that the Pacific Century was being proclaimed. The US remained and still remains the principal guarantor of regional security and economic growth in Asia-Pacific, and the leading shaper of the global system. Washington plays a dominant or at least a major role in all of the security questions that affect the Asia-Pacific region, including the problems associated with China-Taiwan reunification and the Korean peninsular, and the dispute over the ownership of islands in the South China Sea. The ASEAN Regional Forum (ARF), significant as the first major multilateral security forum for the region and in undertaking an important role in confidence building, nevertheless has found it impossible to make itself relevant to the resolution of the North Korean crisis, or to the Taiwan question because of China's objection, and has played only a superficial role in the South China Sea dispute. Dominant aspects of the Cold War security framework for the region, such as the US-Japan, and US-South Korean security alliances, remain in place and seem unlikely soon to be removed despite the transformation in US-Soviet relations after the Cold War.

It is important to recognize that the US often found itself unable to use this dominance in the security realm to achieve economic and other policy changes on the part of its allies. However, while East Asia could often resist external pressure for change, these US allies have proved remarkably unwilling to challenge Washington in many issue areas. Explicit linkage by the US has often proved unnecessary, since its allies feel sufficiently dependent upon American military power to refrain from disrupting relations in areas such as trade or finance. For example, predictions that Japan/East Asia would wield financial power to demand changes in US policy never materialized, even at the height of the US's 'twin deficits' and of allied dissatisfaction with various US policies in the later 1980s. Japan's financial 'power' proved a chimera: the Louvre accord and its aftermath demonstrated rather the determination of the Japanese authorities to intervene to support the dollar when private Japanese capital flows faltered, without any substantive American *quid pro quo*.

The economic rise of East Asia tended to reinforce rather than displace the Cold War era substructure of economic, political and military linkages with the US. Most states in the region remain highly dependent upon the continued openness of US markets, as well as the US security umbrella. China's rise has increased the importance of the latter for many states in the region, including Japan. The dependent relationship with the US has conditioned many of Japan's aid decisions, which tend to be either supportive of, or at least do not cut across, US security interests in the region. Any Japanese attempt to use its aid flows to enhance potentially distinctive political interests in developing East Asia is further constrained by the legacy of

Japanese imperialism. Finally, in domestic political terms, Japan's party system, the constitutional constraints on the use of force and emphasis on economic rather than military means as a way of achieving national objectives all weaken its ability to assume a larger security or political role, either globally or regionally.

Strong states and Asian values

There are also significant problems with claims about Asian values, not least because of the numerous points of conflict of an ethnic, religious, linguistic or political kind in the Asia-Pacific together with the long debate that has taken place in the West on the relationship between rights and duties, individualism and social order. The Asian values argument soon revealed itself to be dominated by governing elites and was strongly countered by domestic opposition forces, many of whom saw it simply as a means of justifying authoritarian political systems. One such opposition politician, Kim Dae Jung, now President of South Korea, argued strongly against the need for authoritarianism on cultural grounds, pointing to Asia's 'rich heritage of democracy-oriented philosophies and traditions'.[26] The Nobel Peace Laureate and leader of Burma's National League for Democracy Party, Aung San Suu Kyi, stated that 'when democracy and human rights are said to run counter to non-Western culture, such culture is usually defined narrowly and presented as monolithic'.[27] Even those that had taken note of these authoritarian arrangements in the successful Asian economies qualified the implied causal relationship.[28] Indeed, a general worldwide trend towards democratization in the immediate post-Cold War period also embraced South Korea, Taiwan and Thailand—a further potential source of division within the region, as some states seek to embrace this path and others try to eschew it.

Domestically, the 'strong state' argument also overlooked key sources of weakness and vulnerability. Some analysts' work cast doubt upon the view of the comparative omnipotence of Japan's MITI in guiding the market, such as Daniel Okimoto's *Between MITI and the Market*.[29] While falling into the same trap of over-generalization as the Asian values argument, Paul Krugman's widely read *Foreign Affairs* article of 1994 also suggested that the 'miracle' was mainly due to the mobilization of labour and capital inputs into production by a 'Soviet'-style state. This version of the strong state argument rendered it less attractive and also raised questions about the Asian unlocking of the secret of rapid productivity growth.[30] At

---

26 Kim Dae Jung, 'A Response to Lee Kuan Yew—Is Culture Destiny? The Myth of Asia's Anti-Democratic Values', *Foreign Affairs*, 73, Nov./Dec. 1994. For a similar point, see Amartya Sen, 'Our culture, their culture', *New Republic*, 1 April 1996, pp. 27–34.

27 Aung San Suu Kyi, 'Freedom, Development and Human Worth', *Journal of Democracy*, 6:2 (1995), p. 15.

28 Stephan Haggard, *Pathways from the Periphery* (Ithaca, NY: Cornell University Press, 1990), ch. 10. See also Svante Ersson and Jan-Erik Lane, 'Democracy and Development: A Statistical Exploration' in Adrian Leftwich (ed.) *Democracy and Development* (Cambridge: Polity Press, 1996).

29 Daniel Okimoto, *Between MITI and the Market* (Stanford, CA: Stanford University Press, 1989).

30 Paul Krugman, 'The Myth of Asia's Miracle', *Foreign Affairs*, 73 (1994), pp. 62–78. This article publicized work by Young and others (see A. Young, 'The Tyranny of Numbers: Confronting the Statistical Realities of the East Asian Growth Experience', *Quarterly Journal of Economics*, 110:3 (1995), pp. 641–80.

Japanese prompting, the World Bank undertook a major study in 1991, published as *The East Asia Miracle* report (1993), which also took a critical view. The report interpreted East Asian success as a challenge to Bank orthodoxy, and acknowledged a significant role for the state. However, it also placed emphasis on the market-consistency of the successful aspects of East Asian industrial policy interventionism, and noted some of the conspicuous failures of such intervention throughout the region, particularly in the ASEAN countries. Most important, the report maintained, was the promotion by East Asian governments of export-orientation. Latin America's recent embrace of export orientation, often interpreted as learning from East Asia, was much closer to this aspect of the report than any other; indeed, state interventionism in Latin America was widely interpreted as a failure.

The report did not satisfy fully either those who felt East Asian growth demonstrated the superiority of the market, or those who claimed it underrated the guiding role of the state. In retrospect, however, and particularly in the wake of the recent crisis, the *Miracle* report was more balanced about some aspects than originally thought. It rightly pointed out the difficulty of demonstrating hard counterfactuals that would favour the industrial policy interpretation, though as noted above, it accepted that some intervention had accelerated development. It rejected the notion of a single East Asian model, noting the great diversity of policy practice throughout the region. Its main mistakes were elsewhere. Although it pointed to the dangers of governments providing implicit or explicit guarantees against economic failure to private sector investments and even implied criticism of the strong state and soft authoritarianism arguments, the overall tone of the report cast a positive gloss on these characteristics.[31] Its gravest misunderstanding, as we explain later, was to claim that there was 'strong prudential regulation and supervision' in the financial sectors of most Asian countries.[32]

Literature that emphasized the domestic political and cultural foundations of growth also sometimes undervalued the international environmental factors that favoured development in East Asia compared with other parts of the developing world. The severe external (for Korea, Singapore, Thailand, and Taiwan) or internal (for Malaysia and Indonesia) security concerns which many countries in the region faced during the Cold War and beyond provided a powerful incentive for hard work, high savings and national reconstruction. The bilateral security relationships with the US at the same time eventually helped to stabilize the region, and also led the US to provide positive incentives for outward-orientation on the part of East Asian allies, most notably via substantial aid and relatively open markets for Asian exports. In addition to the international political context of East Asian development, the low resource endowment of Japan and the NICs created a heavy dependence upon raw materials imports from abroad (and in turn, US security), and a need to export manufactured goods.

International institutional outcomes

Nor did East Asian economic success and resources translate into significant

---

[31] World Bank, *The East Asia Miracle*, ch. 1.
[32] Ibid., p. 16.

influence on international regimes and institutions. Japan in particular was asymmetrically integrated into the world economy, with key manufacturing sectors dependent upon continued access to US and European markets, although Japanese manufactured imports from other OECD countries were comparatively low. This meant that Japan (and arguably most of East Asia in general) was much more dependent upon the GATT trade regime than were the US and Europe. Much US and European 'new protectionism' and unilateral market-opening demands were focused on East Asia from the early 1980s, some of which were successful in gaining Asian concessions. The very success of East Asian exports increased their dependence upon the GATT, though decreasing the willingness of the other major actors, particularly the US, to abide by GATT rules and spirit.

Similar points can be made about the role of East Asia in the Bretton Woods institutions. The situation here is possibly even more anomalous than in the GATT/WTO regime. Japan became the second most important member of the IMF as measured by IMF quotas and voting rights as late as 1992, and in the late 1980s became the world's largest aid donor in dollar terms, including through the World Bank. Japan has been much less attached to Fund and Bank policy conditionality than it has to GATT rules, as reflected in its desire to fund the *Miracle* report. Although Japan hoped this report would demonstrate the potentially positive role of the state in economic development, as noted above, it did little to dislodge the neoliberal 'Washington consensus' in the Bank and IMF. Again, Japan's financial preeminence in a major multilateral institution did not translate into substantial political influence.[33]

This Japanese weakness left developing East Asian countries vulnerable to the shift of the Bretton Woods institutions towards the promotion of good governance, transparency and accountability in the early 1990s. Indeed, this concern, linked with 'new world order' emphases on human rights and democracy, explains much of the resort to the 'Asian values' argument and illustrates that side of it which was borne out of insecurity rather than strength. Although on the eve of the Asian crisis, most were less dependent than other parts of the developing world upon multilateral finance, they still perceived a threat to the Asian model and to Asian political systems.

It could be argued that Japan's growing dominance of bilateral aid and private capital flows to the region has enabled it to protect its nearest developing neighbours from the strictures of Washington-based policy conditionality (see Table 3). Importantly, Japan became China's largest bilateral aid donor from the early 1980s. Its 1992 ODA Charter stressed the need to promote democracy, human rights, and the free market, though in practice it much prefers 'quiet diplomacy'. Furthermore, in the Asian financial crisis of 1997–8, Japan was conspicuously unable to protect East Asian developing countries from IMF conditionality, and from US pressure for political change. Although it floated the idea of an Asian Fund in 1997 to provide much-needed liquidity to the Asian developing countries, it was vigorously opposed by the US, which interpreted it as a threat to the IMF's and its own ability to influence policies in the indebted Asian countries. In the face of this opposition, also

[33] See Robert Wade, 'Japan, the World Bank, and the Art of Paradigm Maintenance: The East Asian Miracle in Political Perspective', *New Left Review*, 217 (May-June 1996), pp. 3–36.

Table 3. *Distribution of net bilateral non-military aid to Asia by four major members, $bn, 1996.*

Recipient	Total OECD flows	US	Japan	France	Germany
		Four major donors:			
Cambodia	252.6	28.0	71.3	52.1	14.2
China	1,671.1	0.0	861.7	97.2	461.1
India	1,025.1	6.0	579.3	14.8	51.2
Indonesia	1,062.6	−57.0	965.5	28.4	−106.0
Korea, Dem. Rep.	9.1	0.0	0.0	0.0	0.9
Korea, Rep.	−149.2	−54.0	−127.9	10.1	16.0
Lao PDR	147.5	3.0	57.4	16.4	22.9
Malaysia	−453.1	0.0	−482.5	3.5	7.5
Myanmar	45.3	0.0	35.2	2.1	1.5
Nepal	236.3	15.0	88.8	2.0	25.7
Pakistan	338.6	−101.0	282.2	5.4	15.8
Philippines	748.3	46.0	414.5	27.4	106.6
Singapore	11.9	0.0	8.5	0.0	2.5
Sri Lanka	279.3	4.0	173.9	−1.6	15.8
Thailand	803.1	3.0	664.0	10.4	23.2
Vietnam	469.7	0.0	120.9	67.3	52.8

Note: Net flows of resources are defined as gross disbursements of grants and loans minus repayments on earlier loans, which explains the negative signs for some cells.
Source: World Bank, World Development Indicators, 1998, CD-Rom.

forthcoming from Europe, Japan withdrew the proposal, only to reintroduce it with a value of $30 bn at the end of 1998 when IMF programmes and their associated conditions were already in place (with the exception of Malaysia).

One could ask further whether a Japan-led fund with no policy conditions attached (as the initial proposal appeared to suggest) was in any case in Japan's interest. The wartime legacies that constrain Japan's relations with its developing neighbours might lead one to expect that Japan would be quietly insistent upon multilateral institutions as the vehicle for recycling capital and providing policy conditionality, to introduce a political buffer between itself and its poorer neighbours. But requiring few conditions for borrowing from the Suharto government of Indonesia looked more like the Asian periphery being able to dictate the terms of Japan's regional role than of any real ability of Japan to exercise influence. It also reflected a desire to bail out heavily overlent Japanese banks: by mid-June 1997, total outstanding Japanese bank loans to Asian developing countries were $271 bn, representing 110 per cent of total Japanese bank capital. By comparison with Japanese and European banks, US banks were not exposed.[34] Overall, Japan's problematic involvement in its region constrains its ability to exercise power.

---

[34] OECD, *Economic Outlook, June 1998* (Paris: OECD, 1998).

Table 4. *Regional trade blocs, intra-bloc exports ($m and percentages)*.

Region	1970	% of total	1980	% of total	1985	% of total	1990	% of total	1996	% of total
APEC	56,020	56.9	353,778	57.6	491,623	67.7	897,427	68.5	1,706,692	73.1
EU	76,451	59.5	459,469	61.0	421,641	59.3	985,128	66.0	1,275,696	61.5
NAFTA	22,078	36.0	102,218	33.6	143,191	43.9	226,273	41.4	436,805	47.5
MERCOSUR	451	9.4	3,424	11.6	1,953	5.5	4,127	8.9	17,151	22.8
ASEAN	1,201	19.7	12,016	16.9	13,130	18.4	26,367	18.7	77,221	23.2

Source: World Bank, World Development Indicators, 1998 CD-Rom.

Regionalism in Asia-Pacific

Perhaps the greatest effect of the perceived and partly real shift in the balance of economic power towards East Asia was not on multilateral institutions, where Asian influence is weak, but in regional institutional developments since the late 1980s. The burgeoning literature on regionalism in the 1990s often pointed out that Asia-Pacific increasingly dominated world trade and foreign investment flows, and that the regional orientation of these flows was increasing. Suddenly, matrices of world trade flows by regional bloc began to appear, which suggested that intra-regional trade flows in the APEC region had now overtaken those within the EU (see Table 4). Almost as soon as it was born, APEC had become the world's most important economic region, and one apparently more self-contained than the European Union.[35]

Japan led the way in developing an intra-regional network of trade and investment. After 1985, the high Yen and perceptions of growing protectionism in the West pushed Japanese companies to search for lower cost production locations in the region. Investment to NE and SE Asia increased six-fold between 1985 and 1989; by 1990 Japan had a dominant presence in Indonesia, Malaysia and Thailand.[36] As noted above, these private capital flows were complemented by official Japanese aid flows, and Japan gradually began to displace the US as the major market for regional manufacturing exports. A surge of FDI flows from the four tigers to the ASEAN countries and China in the 1990s confirmed this emerging regional network of trade and investment.

Regional institutional development

Regional institutional developments followed this pattern of regional market integration: unofficial organizations such as PAFTAD, PBEC, and PECC made up

[35] See R. Garnaut and Peter Drysdale (eds.), *Asia-Pacific Regionalism* (Pymble: Harper Educational, 1994).
[36] Mark Borthwick, *Pacific Century: The Emergence of Modern Pacific Asia* (Boulder, CO: Westview Press, 1992) p. 513.

of business people, academics and officials operating in private capacities, pushed forward the concept of an official forum.[37] This resulted in APEC, established in 1989, stemming from a joint Japanese-Australian proposal to create a regional institutional response to the perceived weakness of the GATT and to regional developments elsewhere in Europe and North America. Although APEC was envisaged as involving very limited formal institutionalization, it was nevertheless interpreted as the first step towards a governance structure for managing this increased regional economic interdependence. Almost immediately, some voices in the region, most notably Malaysia's Prime Minister Mahathir, proposed a more narrow 'East Asian Economic Caucus' (EAEC) that would exclude the Caucasians (the US, Australia, Canada and New Zealand). East Asia seemed poised to develop its own distinct voice in global economic affairs, as a counterweight to the long-standing dominance of the US and Europe on such questions.

This activity in the economic field was swiftly matched by actions on the security front. In 1992, the idea of establishing a multilateral security structure in the Asia-Pacific was first mooted to manage this transition to the post Cold War era, a possible reduction in the US presence, and the rise of Japan and China.[38] In 1994 the ASEAN Regional Forum (ARF) held its first gathering, seen as a major achievement because it was the first, inclusive, multilateral security institution in the region. Moreover, it was established in the teeth of opposition not only from the United States, which wanted to retain a security order based on its bilateral alliances, but also from a China suspicious of multilateralism in most issue areas, and particularly in the security field.

These regional institutional developments were indeed remarkable, especially given their virtual absence during the Cold War period (with the exception of ASEAN); but the implications were often exaggerated. First, on the security side, although the ARF has the important objective of building trust among its member states at a time of strategic change, it relies on a formal commitment that the ARF will only move forward its agenda of developing confidence-building measures and engaging in preventive diplomacy at a pace that is 'comfortable' to all participants, and on the basis of non-binding voluntary agreement. Its normative commitment to the protection of participants' sovereignty and non-interference in internal affairs similarly contributes to the glacial pace at which the organization advances its aims. A prime objective for Japan and a number of the other East Asian states at the outset was to keep the US involved in regional security; the ARF's incrementalism if anything enhanced this need. Its name also reflected the dominant organizational role of the ASEAN 'middle powers', and the absence of any region-wide agreement that the major states of the region were acceptable as alternatives.

On the economic side, the Malaysian proposal for an EAEC was also opposed by the United States. But more importantly, it was also opposed, albeit usually more diplomatically, by most of Malaysia's East Asian neighbours. The dependence of

---

[37] Full versions of the following acronyms are: PAFTAD: Pacific Trade and Development Conference; PBEC: Pacific Basin Economic Council; PECC: Pacific Economic Cooperation Conference; APEC: Asia Pacific Economic Cooperation.

[38] See Michael Leifer, *The ASEAN Regional Forum: Extending ASEAN's Model of Regional Security*, Adelphi Paper no. 302, (London: IISS, 1996); Rosemary Foot, 'China in the ASEAN Regional Forum: Organizational Processes and Domestic Modes of Thought', *Asian Survey*, 38:5 (May 1998), pp. 425–40.

Japan, Singapore and Korea upon US markets and security meant that any regional economic forum should include the US, to ensure its continued presence in East Asian affairs. The export dependence of most East Asian countries, as noted earlier, also heightened these countries' dependence upon GATT/WTO multilateralism. Although both the EAEC and APEC stemmed from the widespread fear that the contemporary impasse over agricultural and other trade issues in the Uruguay Round of the GATT might threaten the very existence of this regime, the EAEC proposal threatened to make this even more likely. Discriminatory regionalism of the European and North American kind was rejected in favour of a form of 'open regionalism', in which any regional liberalization agreements would be passed on automatically to all GATT members. In this way, open regionalism within APEC could complement without detracting from GATT/WTO multilateralism. The Eminent Persons Group of APEC, in which economists were strongly represented, proselytized the benefits of open regionalism as compared with the discriminatory regionalism practiced by North America and Europe. Less mentioned, however, was that the open regionalism model made a virtue of political weakness, and how it considerably diminished the Asian character of regionalism in the Pacific.

Also exaggerated was the degree of regional economic integration already achieved. Statistically it was true that APEC's 'intra-trade' ratio exceeded that of the EU, but like was not being compared with like. As more and more countries are added to APEC, including countries as large as the US, Japan and China, it is hardly surprising that APEC's share of world trade and investment flows is very large, and that its intraregional trade ratio is high. The *reductio ad absurdum* of this line of argument is that the intratrade ratio of the whole world is 100 per cent. The real question is whether a particular regional entity makes a substantial difference both to intraregional and extraregional relationships, as the deeper form of institutionalized regionalism of the EU clearly does. Including FDI stocks and financial flows would suggest that the Atlantic region remains much more highly integrated than the Pacific. Certainly intraregional trade and investment within Asia-Pacific grew very rapidly from the early 1980s, but these were largely driven by more rapid growth in East Asia compared with the rest of the world, rather than any large increase in their 'regional bias'.[39] Regionalization driven by rapid growth alone may be a fair weather phenomenon, vulnerable to periods of slower growth and economic crisis.

Finally, aggregate figures purporting to show high levels of integration in Asia-Pacific can obscure large inequalities of income, wealth and opportunity between and within countries. In thinking about who was a part of the Pacific century, some ethnic minorities and women were often not touched by it or touched by it in a way that further impoverished their existence. Some countries or geographical areas— such as North Korea, Burma, the interior of China, deliberately or not, remained outside of it. Indeed, the 1990s saw a considerable increase in the inequality of income distribution in many Asian economies, blurring any sharp distinction with Latin America. Such inequalities also make regional political and economic cooperation more difficult.

---

[39] For more detail, see Andrew Walter, 'Regionalism, Globalization, and World Economic Order', in L. Fawcett and A. Hurrell (eds.), *Regionalism in World Politics* (Oxford: Oxford University Press, 1995), pp. 74–121.

All of the above imply continuing severe constraints on the possibilities for deeper integration in Asia-Pacific, and particularly on the possibilities for political leadership within East Asia. In comparison with Germany, Japan is less well integrated into international society, and its relations with its neighbours remain much more complicated today by the legacy of the Pacific War than are Germany's in Europe. Even the 'flying geese' image has negative connotations for countries like Korea and China, since it implied a pattern led and controlled by Japanese financial power, multinational firms, and technology. In this sense, Japan's complicated relationship with its neighbours is more comparable to the US relationship with Latin America than with Germany's relations with its EU partners. If, on the other hand, China were to press further its role as regional hegemon, the willing regional acceptance of this dominance would be severely conditioned by fears of its demographic weight, the large numbers of territorial disputes it has with its neighbours, its strategic nuclear capacity, and the numerical superiority of its armed forces. China's use of force against neighbouring states on a number of occasions since 1949 and its past adherence to an interventionist political ideology create further suspicions. This combination of economic and political/security factors promotes the desire to keep the US engaged in the region, through multilateral institutions, and bilaterally.

Asian drama revisited?

Today, as the meaning and consequences of the Asian financial crisis are still working themselves out, the Asian model and Asian values are being seriously questioned, both from within many countries of the region and from without. It would be far too strong to suggest we have come full-circle back to the pessimistic predictions of Myrdal's *Asian Drama*. Yet it is not an exaggeration to say that many of the proclaimed strengths of the Asian model only a few years ago have become perceived as serious weaknesses that need to be addressed before rapid growth can be resumed. As for Japan, any return to growth levels approaching those of the US and even Europe within the next few years would be seen as a minor miracle.

The Asian model as liability?

The Asian crisis has revealed what area specialists had long known. These were not all strong states in a real sense, many of their decisions were not taken for reasons of public interest, but often for private, political or personal gain, and the 'miracle' was grounded in specific historical circumstances. Those who argue that corruption, cronyism, protectionism, and authoritarianism cannot explain the regional crisis since they existed before it must be right at one level. Yet the crisis also leads us to question previous theories that characterized these or similar variables more positively, or at least saw them as relatively unproblematic. It may simply be that the costs of inefficient interventionism and of weak political systems could be borne during the high growth period.

Just as there was no single Asian model, nor is any single explanation of the crisis equally convincing for all countries. There were common negative shocks to the region from 1996, which produced a rapid slowdown in export growth for most of developing Asia, particularly Thailand. The unravelling of the Japanese miracle from the late 1980s, with the bursting of the Japanese property and stock market bubble, was one source of this. Japanese productivity growth had fallen dramatically in the 1970s and again in the 1980s, although substantial weaknesses in the Japanese economy—especially in banking and real estate—were masked by the success of key manufacturing sectors. The Asian developing countries had mostly weathered previous developing country crises quite well, but the sheer size of Japan's economy compared with the rest of East Asia, and the growing dominance of Japanese FDI flows and bank lending in regional capital flows, made it unlikely they could escape the consequences of an endemic crisis in Japan. Others point to the rise of Chinese export competition, often said to have caused further adjustment difficulties for its developing country neighbours. However, it is likely that declining Japanese growth, rising inflation, and the appreciation of the US dollar were more important in eroding competitiveness.

Unfortunately, financial market actors often did lump countries in the same basket. Contagion spread from Thailand to other countries as investors perceived new weaknesses in previously unaffected countries, including Russia, Brazil and Argentina, and Korea in Asia. As is now well-documented, the main form of capital withdrawal was international bank lending, particularly in the interbank market.[40] It is untrue that international banks made no distinctions at all, as Singapore, the Philippines and Taiwan were less affected by the general contagion. However, it is arguable that the financial market actors were particularly susceptible to the amateur political economy and sociology associated with the hubris of the 'miracle' years; it should not be surprising that they were equally susceptible to pessimism and panic as the conventional wisdom was reversed.[41] In this sense, one consequence of the hubris associated with the Asian model and the Pacific Century in the 1980s was that it made a bubble and its subsequent bursting more likely.

The 'Washington consensus' view, most clearly associated with Alan Greenspan at the US Federal Reserve, key officials at the US Treasury, and the IMF, and not without an element of Schadenfreude, is that the Achilles heel of the Asian model was excessive government interventionism. In this respect it is not dissimilar to their earlier characterization of import-substitution models in Latin America in the 1980s. Excessive state-driven or sanctified investment, related and risky short-term international borrowing, high levels of corruption and 'crony capitalism', protected domestic markets (especially financial sectors), and inappropriate maintenance of pegged exchange rates, all figure prominently in such analyses. In Asia, such arguments are widely seen as driven by US sectoral interests which perceive an opportunity to open East Asian markets to foreign investment, and which thereby threaten to unravel what was, undeniably, a large number of developing success stories. Not lost on Asians either is the convenient implication of the Washington consensus that Western bank lending and regulation is not at fault.

[40] IMF, *International Capital Markets* (Washington, DC: IMF, 1998), ch. 2.
[41] Charles Kindleberger, *Manias, Panics, and Crashes: A History of Financial Crises* (London: Macmillan, 1990), provides an historical overview of the susceptibility of financial markets to such conventional wisdoms.

Whatever the merits of the argument, there seems little doubt that the crisis has further entrenched this Washington consensus, despite the fact that various Western critics have sought to defend the Asian model against the Washington and Wall Street wreckers. Robert Wade, for example, argues the crisis is largely the result of financial liberalization inappropriately encouraged by the US and IMF, liberalization that has proven incompatible with the 'high debt' East Asian model. Others have sought to argue that the crisis was caused by reckless Western bank lending and inadequate supervision.[42] While many can agree with Wade's latter point, there were also powerful domestic forces pushing in the same direction in a number of countries. After all, it was domestic banks in Asia that intermediated most of the international capital flows during the boom years from 1991–96, providing large profits in this sector and fuelling the rapid growth that regional political leaders desired. By the end of 1996, net outstanding international bank credits to banks in Hong Kong, Singapore, Thailand, Korea and Indonesia amounted to $219 bn, $116 bn, $78 bn, $59 bn and $12 bn respectively. For Thailand, 76 per cent of this debt was acquired over 1994–96 alone.[43] The *Miracle* report of 1993, though it noted the dangers of providing explicit and implicit guarantees to debt-financed investments, was representative of the pre-crisis literature in praising the 'strong prudential regulation and supervision' typical in the region.[44] Today's official conventional wisdom is described by the IMF:

The problems facing Asia's distressed banking systems are the legacy of years of bad lending practices and inadequate supervision that led to high lending growth and risk taking.[45]

The critics are correct that the IMF has had its own agenda to push, and that Western and Japanese bank regulation were inadequate. However, poor Asian financial regulation also played a role in the crisis. Combined in some cases with pegged exchange rate policies and assumed government guarantees of various kinds, a dangerously rapid buildup of unhedged external debt developed. Over 1994–96, the growing Asian reliance upon potentially volatile international bank lending to sustain the domestic boom created a vulnerability to combined currency and debt crisis that proved disastrous (see Figure 2). Although IMF policy mistakes deepened the crisis, the initial buildup of leverage occurred as a result of the Asian boom and the perception on the part of lenders and borrowers alike that the rapid accumulation of debt was relatively riskless.[46] In retrospect, therefore, the institutions of the Asian developmental states proved unable to manage the consequences of large debt capital inflows, reflecting an inability to 'govern the market' in this important area.

This conclusion holds whether one believes the buildup of indebtedness was primarily due to crony capitalism and implicit guarantees on the one hand, or

---

[42] Robert Wade and Frank Veneroso (1998), 'The Asian Crisis: The High Debt Model Versus the Wall Street-Treasury-IMF Complex' *New Left Review*, 288 (March/April 1998), pp. 3–23; Ha-Joon Chang, 'The Hazard of Moral Hazard', *Financial Times*, 7 October 1998.

[43] IMF, *International Capital Markets*, 1998, p. 31.

[44] World Bank, *The East Asia Miracle*, p. 16.

[45] IMF, *International Capital Markets*, 1998, p. 34.

[46] See Jenny Corbett and David Vines, 'The Asian Crisis: Lessons from the Collapse of Financial Systems, Exchange Rates, and Macroeconomic Policy', forthcoming in Richard Agenor, Marcus Miller, David Vines and Axel Weber (eds.), *The Asian Financial Crisis* (Cambridge, UK: Cambridge University Press, 1999). As Figure 2 shows, portfolio flows have also proved highly volatile, but as with FDI, they do not raise the same threat of default as does international bank lending in hard currencies.

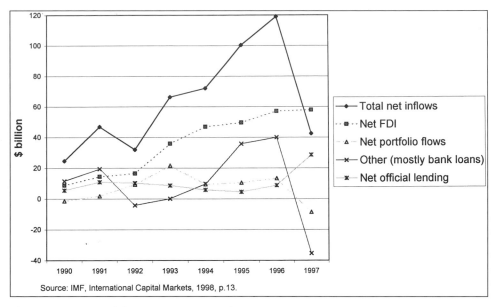

Figure 2. *Net capital flows to emerging market Asia.*

Western bank recklessness on the other. As is now well known, financial and political mismanagement has been particularly evident in Japan for almost a decade. An excessive dispersion of political power and ineffective management in both the public and private sectors has been endemic, including in Japan's most venerated key ministries. Capital account liberalization was, in Thailand's case, due to the desire to promote Bangkok as a regional financial centre, notably through the Bangkok International Banking Facility from 1993. In Thailand and Korea, credit growth in under-regulated non-bank financial intermediaries was a particular problem (and this was not an area where foreigners were pushing for liberalization). Capital account liberalization also places a premium upon central bank credibility, but in the foreign exchange crises of 1997, Asian central banks proved insufficiently autonomous of political interests. In contrast, the financial sectors of some Latin American countries, with a much stronger foreign bank presence, considerably improved supervisory regimes, and a lesser dependence upon international bank lending, proved much less vulnerable to debt crisis.

Although the crisis casts more doubt upon the virtues of short term capital mobility than upon trade and FDI liberalization, it is unlikely that many countries will go down the Malaysian and Chinese paths of stricter capital controls once the crisis abates. Brazil has so far resisted any such return to the old ways, despite the depth of the crisis there. The four NICs have little interest in a policy that would set back their entry into the ranks of developed countries, and their financial and service sectors. Even the developing countries will find it difficult to separate trade from capital account liberalization (China has suffered from continuing and substantial illegal capital flight, for example), not to mention the various opportunities for corruption and rent-seeking that capital controls provide. In addition, the perceived need to take more active steps to promote foreign investment in the crisis-hit countries makes it difficult to maintain strict capital controls. Finally, pressure to liberalize the capital account from the IMF and US is likely to remain considerable, since they reject the argument that capital flows *per se* are to blame. If so, the high-debt model may have to adjust, and steps will be taken in the direction of greater foreign presence in domestic financial sectors, and tightened monitoring of foreign borrowing. Korea and Thailand are moving rapidly down this path, and at present are recovering more quickly than Malaysia or Indonesia.

Political repercussions

This sapping of confidence and weaknesses in economic policy and institutions has powerful political repercussions. The boom itself gave increasing voice to domestic opposition groups within a number of East Asian countries, who as we noted above, were acutely aware of the way in which the Asian values argument was being used to bolster the political *status quo*. Indigenous challenges mounted by nongovernmental groupings of various kinds quickly exposed both the instrumental nature of the claims, the diversity of views in the region, and range of experience. As Amartya Sen has written, 'there are no quintessential values that apply to this immensely large and heterogeneous population, which separate them as a group from the rest of the world'.[47] These intellectual challenges, and not just the economic crisis, have undermined the ability of leaders to promote their particular interpretations of Asian values, contributing to the passing of this debate almost as quickly as it arrived.

However, the crisis has generalized this dissatisfaction. As Paul Krugman has noted, it is easy to look competent during booms, and there is little doubt that rapid growth helped to draw attention away from the failures of state intervention and the costs of corruption and of political authoritarianism. The argument that strong states caused rapid growth was always problematic; however, the collapse of growth now threatens to weaken already fragile polities. Having hitched their political legitimacy to their claimed ability to produce rapid growth with equity, governments of the region became vulnerable to any serious downturn, or indeed to any significant diminution of the equity aspect. The boom produced greater inequalities of income and wealth in recent years, reducing an important domestic aspect of legitimacy. The increasingly conspicuous wealth and corruption at the top provided a focal point for this dissatisfaction, particularly once growth collapsed, as the removal of President Suharto in Indonesia has strongly borne out. Even Singapore's Lee Kuan-Yew recently noted 'certain weaknesses in Confucianism...when you use public resources through your official position to do your duty to your family and be loyal to your friends.'[48] All success stories may carry the seeds of their own unravelling; resisting generalized corruption in government may be easier for authoritarian political leaders than resisting the demands of their adult children.

Of course, the vulnerabilities of the political systems in East Asia to delegitimation vary enormously. The exposure of the Suharto family's cynical manipulation of the Asian model for its own enrichment in its later years rendered it

---

[47] Sen, 'Our Culture, Their Culture', p. 32.
[48] Lee in *Time Magazine* 16 March 1998, and quoted in François Godemont, *The Downsizing of Asia* (London: Routledge, 1999) p. 107.

highly vulnerable to internal revolution as millions were returned to poverty on the back of the crisis. The obliteration of the distinction that used to be made between Indonesian technocratic management under Suharto and the plundering of the Philippines by the Marcos family may well be unfair to the former, but hard distinctions between the success stories and the failures in the region (and outside it) now seem less convincing.[49] Whatever happens in Indonesia will be enormously consequential for the region, and for organizations such as ASEAN. For individuals too, the economic shocks of 1997–99 have been defining moments for many of Asia's middle classes, encouraging a rethinking of the basis of the East Asian miracle and the wisdom of allowing political leaders relatively free rein in the absence of strong legal regulation. Evidence that there was considerable unrecorded indigenous capital flight from 1996, (particularly from Korea and Malaysia) also casts doubt upon simplistic assertions about Asian solidarity and upon conspiracy theories regarding the attack on Asia by 'international' investors.[50]

As Minxin Pei has pointed out, political change following from crisis has been the norm rather than the exception in postwar East Asia.[51] Those states best placed to respond to this crisis with its widespread social consequences will be those that base their legitimacy on more than high economic growth and that can rely on consensual and not repressive means of building support for the hard policy decisions that have to be made. Not ignoring the vastly different ethnic and cultural makeup of Korea compared with Indonesia, there is a significant political difference between South Korea's ability to implement reforms without widespread political and social upheaval, and Indonesia's struggle with both the economic crisis and the need to legitimate a new political order. As Chinese leaders confront the toughest aspect of their reform agenda—dealing with the inefficient state-owned enterprises—at a time of regional economic uncertainty, it will be a hugely difficult task to defuse the grievances of the newly-unemployed in the absence of institutional mechanisms for channelling such complaints. High levels of corruption—a major source of the demonstrations in 1989—have already undermined the political legitimacy of the Party. China's rapid buildup of debt and high levels of nonperforming loans make it vulnerable not only to financial distress but also to further political disorder should growth slow significantly.[52]

The end of the Cold War, as noted above, eroded the willingness of the US to turn a blind eye to the negative aspects of authoritarian government in Asia. Gone is the convenient distinction in US foreign policy between communist totalitarianism and pro-Western authoritarianism. Pressure for change has come bilaterally, and through international institutions with extended normative ambitions in the area of democratic enlargement, good governance and transparency, enhanced environmental and human rights protections and the like. These issues served to identify a number of East Asian states as targets to powerful external and increasingly influential internal critics: one consequence of dynamic growth for example had

---

[49] This point is made by Stephan Haggard, 'Business, politics and policy in East and Southeast Asia', in Rowen, *Behind East Asian Growth*.

[50] IMF, *International Capital Markets*, 1998, p. 17.

[51] Minxin Pei, 'Constructing the political foundations of an economic miracle', in Rowen, *Behind East Asian Growth*, pp. 45–6.

[52] See Nicholas Lardy, *China's Unfinished Economic Revolution* (Washington DC: Brookings, 1998), pp. 193–203.

been land degradation, urban air pollution, forest depletions, pesticide con-
tamination, and declining ground water levels.[53]

At the same time as the propensity for Western interventionism has increased, the
weakness of regional institutions in Asia-Pacific further limits the capacity of East
Asian countries to resist. APEC and ASEAN have been left looking like fair-weather
forums. We should not exaggerate this weakness, since just as it is easy to look
competent in good times, most look incompetent in bad times. However, lack of
leadership in the region increased the ability of the US to dictate the terms of rescue
packages. The exposure of Asian corruption and inefficiencies further undermined
Japan's ability and willingness to push a different view to the Washington consensus
regionally, and in international institutions. At home, the anaemic Japanese
economy sapped Japanese self-confidence at the same time as America's—at least in
the economic realm—soared, and has further eroded Japan's ability to protect (if it
should wish to try) East Asian interventionism from US pressure for liberalization.

Pacific Century: myth or reality?

Just as the virtues of an elusive East Asian model were exaggerated in the past, there
is a considerable danger today of going too far in the other direction. There is little
doubt that some circles in the US and Europe have felt considerable relief over
Asia's recent difficulties. An important element of reality was captured by the
miracle story: rapid postwar growth in Japan and later in other East Asian
developing countries is undeniable, as is their attention to the development of
human capital and high savings rates. Furthermore, in comparison with the Cold
War period, important regional institutional developments occurred in the 1980s
and 1990s which in the security field could eventually contribute to greater
transparency and the development of shared understandings.

Key aspects of the Pacific Century idea came from outside the region, and we
have argued that dominant currents in Western social science thought contributed to
its propagation and reception. Perceptions outpaced reality, and gave the misleading
impression that what economists persist in calling the 'stylized facts' of a synthetic
Asian model could persist. Politicians both in Asia itself and in the West had a
vested interest in various aspects of this distorted picture, and the dramatic shift in
the balance of power in the global political economy and in international regimes
that it appeared to entail. We have argued that, although the economic achievements
of East Asia must be acknowledged, this failed to translate into substantive political
power, in large part because of the particular constraints upon Japan. This weakness
and vulnerability helps explain the first steps towards regionalism in East Asia at the
end of the 1980s, when the international political and strategic environment was
changing rapidly. Yet it is not as simple as this: regionalism was also a product of
perceived Asian strength as well as vulnerability. Indeed, without this strange
combination of strength, vulnerability, hubris and misperception that reigned in
Asia-Pacific in the last decade, it is unlikely that the necessary regional political
coalitions could have been formed across such diverse societies.

---

[53] Gareth Porter, 'The Environmental Hazards of Asia Pacific Development: The Southeast Asian
Rainforests', in *Current History*, 422 (December 1994), pp. 430–4.

Where the Pacific Century idea has proven most misleading is in the implication of a Pacific community, which has proven difficult to establish, especially among states divided by more features than those which bring them together. The economic determinism behind the Pacific Century concept represented wishful thinking in this respect. Indeed, the economic crisis has put even those reasonably successful subregional mechanisms for building community, such as ASEAN, under strain as governments concentrate on their own individual solutions to the dilemmas they face.

Thus, the Pacific Century has not arrived and is not likely any time soon. East Asia has not been eclipsed and will no doubt rebound. Furthermore, there is little doubt that its economic strength enabled it to resist US and general Western pressure for liberalization to a much greater extent than Latin America, and this will most likely continue once growth returns. But the last few years have shown that rapid growth does not solve all problems and creates many new ones. In particular, although economic strength enabled East Asia to resist American pressure for change in economic policy, it did not enable East Asia to exercise broader influence in international affairs. It is in this sense that economic materialist conceptions of power have proven especially misleading, and it underlines the distinction between relational and structural power in international relations.[54] This helps to explain the paradox of East Asia's perceived challenge to the West: on the one hand, its ability to resist demands for change at home, but on the other its inability to articulate alternative international norms and to establish institutions consistent with 'Asian interests', whatever these might be. It is in this sense, above all, that the American century that Henry Luce first pointed to in 1941 has not yet run its course.[55]

---

[54] Susan Strange, *States and Markets* (London: Pinter, 1998), pp. 24–9.
[55] A recent series of articles assessing the American century is contained in *Diplomatic History* 23:2 and 3 (Spring/Summer 1999).

Still the American Century

BRUCE CUMINGS

At the inception of the twenty-first century—not to mention the next millennium—books on 'the American Century' proliferate monthly, if not daily.[1] We now have *The American Century Dictionary*, *The American Century Thesaurus*, and even *The American Century Cookbook*; perhaps the American Century baseball cap or cologne is not far behind. With one or two exceptions, the authors celebrate the unipolar pre-eminence and comprehensive economic advantage that the United States now enjoys. Surveys of public opinion show that most people agree: the American wave appears to be surging just as the year 2000 beckons. Unemployment and inflation are both at twenty-year lows, sending economists (who say you can't get lows for both at the same time) back to the drawing board. The stock market roars past the magic 10,000 mark, and the monster federal budget deficit of a decade ago miraculously metamorphoses into a surplus that may soon reach upwards of $1 trillion. Meanwhile President William Jefferson Clinton, not long after a humiliating impeachment, is rated in 1999 as the best of all postwar presidents in conducting foreign policy (a dizzying ascent from eighth place in 1994), according to a nationwide poll by the Chicago Council on Foreign Relations. This surprising result might also, of course, bespeak inattention: when asked to name the two or three most important foreign policy issues facing the US, fully 21 per cent of the public couldn't think of one (they answered 'don't know'), and a mere seven per cent thought foreign policy issues were important to the nation.[2] But who cares, when all is for the best in the best of all possible worlds?

If this intoxicating optimism is commonplace today, it would have seemed demented just a few short years ago: back then, the scholars and popular pundits who are supposed to know the occult science of international affairs were full of dread about American decline and Japanese and German advance. The American century looked like an unaccountably short one.

This prematurely-reported demise was surrounded in the public and the academic sphere by a great deal of nonsense. Today it is disconcerting to recall the towering influence of work by 'declinists' like Paul Kennedy (*The Rise and Fall of the Great Powers*), Robert Keohane (*After Hegemony*), Thomas McCormick (*America's Half-Century*), and Clyde Prestowitz (*Trading Places*); and it is positively embarrassing to

---

[1] Mindy and Norman Cantor, *The American Century* (New York: HarperCollins, 1998); Harold Evans, *The American Century* (New York: Knopf, 1998); Studs Terkel, *My American Century* (New York: Simon & Schuster, 1998); David Traxel. *1898: The Birth of the American Century* (New York: Knopf, 1998); Donald W. White, *The American Century* (New Haven, CT: Yale University Press, 1996); Olivier Zunz, *Why the American Century?* (University of Chicago Press, 1998).

[2] John E. Reilly (ed.), *American Public Opinion and US Foreign Policy 1999* (Chicago Council on Foreign Relations, 1999), pp. 8, 37.

read recent accounts like Samuel Huntington's *Clash of Civilizations* and Donald White's *The American Century* that still seem to assume an America on the road to ruin.[3] These authors cover the American political spectrum: Huntington identifies himself with conservative politics, Keohane and White with moderate (or neo-) liberalism, Prestowitz with neoconservatism and a new American nationalism, and McCormick with a liberal/left position long identified with the work of historian William Appleman Williams.

The 'key question' of Keohane's book, for example, was 'how international cooperation can be maintained among the advanced capitalist states in the absence of American hegemony.'[4] Samuel Huntington had a realpolitik conception of hegemony that mistook maturity for decline: 'European globalism is no more, and American hegemony is receding, if only because it is no longer needed to protect the United States against a Cold War Soviet threat.'[5] This presumed conclusion to American preeminence was also metaphorical, a vehicle for the passions: Huntington wrapped the end of the Cold War into a coming 'clash of civilizations', through a nostalgic reprise of 1950s modernization theory and a disillusioned lament on the passing of the Eastern establishment and its Anglo-Saxon counterparts in Europe, thus yielding a plea for a renewed Atlanticism (precisely at a time when American trade with Asia towers over Atlantic exchange). From a very different perspective Thomas McCormick, in an otherwise fine book on the postwar period, deployed an understanding of hegemony that propelled him toward a final chapter of deep pessimism: 'American hegemony was dead', he wrote, but that decline might also 'be ushering in frightening developments that would make Lenin a prophet twice in this century'.[6]

Paul Kennedy's book was the most careful and thoughtful in this genre, examining the American position in the world in the light of earlier declining empires and focusing on infirmity in the basic sinews of economic vitality—particularly waning productivity growth in the American economy, which fell from 2.4 per cent growth in 1965–72 to 1.6 per cent in 1972–77, thence to a mere 0.2 per cent in 1977–82. The decline of heavy industrial manufacturing in the 1970s and 80s, much of it in rust-belt factories, did not at the time seem to be matched by a corresponding growth in high-tech or leading edge industries: Kennedy thought 'efficiency measures' would not close the gap with low-wage newly industrializing countries in basic manufacturing, and that the US was falling behind in one leading edge industry after another (he pointed out that the American trade surplus in high-tech goods plunged from \$27 bn in 1980 to a mere \$4 bn in 1985). The US had become a debtor nation *'in the space of a few years'* (his italics), the federal deficit was at an

---

[3] Samuel Huntington, *The Clash of Civilizations and the Remaking of World Order* (New York, 1996); Paul M. Kennedy, *The Rise and Fall of the Great Powers: Economic Change and Military Conflict from 1500 to 2000* (New York, 1989); Robert Keohane, *After Hegemony: Cooperation and Discord in the World Political Economy* (Princeton, 1984); Clyde V. Prestowitz, Jr., *Trading Places: How We Are Giving Our Future to Japan and How to Reclaim It* (New York, 1993). Historian Donald White may have been first on the *fin-de-siècle* scene with his 1996 book (*ibid.*), but still managed some resoundingly bad timing—the subtitle was 'The Rise and Decline of the United States as a World Power'.

[4] Keohane, *After Hegemony*, p. 43.

[5] Huntington, 'The West: Unique, not Universal', *Foreign Affairs*, 75 (November/December 1996), pp. 28–46. See idem., *The Clash of Civilizations*.

[6] McCormick, *America's Half-Century*, pp. 240–41.

all-time high, and estimates were that the national debt might be $13 trillion in year 2000 (or 14 times the level in 1980).[7] Around the same time Harry Figge, a corporate executive, wrote a best-seller (*Bankrupcy 1995*) claiming that public debt would consume the US within a decade.

The end of the Cold War also prompted a spate of melodramatic literature seeking to find in this evidently cataclysmic event a portent of historical closure—a solipsistic genre which we might label 'the end of the Cold War and me'. This tendency was perhaps most pronounced in John Lukacs' fatuously self-important 1993 book entitled *The End of the Twentieth Century and the End of the Modern Age*, but he was by no means alone. The most celebrated account, Francis Fukuyama's *The End of History*, was unarguably different: Fukuyama did view the end of the Cold War as a millennial transition, but few would have imagined doing so through a reprise of the thought of Georg W. F. Hegel—and perhaps least of all the great philosopher himself, who would roll in his grave to see his dialectic grinding to a halt in the valhalla of George Bush and Bill Clinton's philistine United States. Hegel gave us history with a purpose, with a telos, with a capital H, an unfolding with a beginning, a middle and an end: behold, all the past as prehistory, as mere prelude to the manifest world-historical spirit of the present age. Fukuyama's argument had an unquestionable ingenuity, taking the thinker perhaps most alien to the pragmatic and unphilosophical American soul, Hegel, and using his thought to proclaim something quintessentially American: that the pot of gold at the end of History's rainbow is free market liberalism. History just happened to culminate in the reigning orthodoxy of our era, the neoliberalism of Thatcher and Reagan.

Others thought a pretender to the hegemonic throne waited in the wings, as the real victor in the Cold War. In his influential book *Trading Places*, published ten years ago, Clyde Prestowitz thought Japan was ahead of the US in nearly every important industry, and argued that Japan was verging on hegemonic predominance in the world economy.[8] But now it is difficult to find any American who takes Japan seriously. In 1990 63 per cent of foreign policy elites fretted about competition from Japan; that fell to 21 per cent in 1994 and a mere 14 per cent in 1998.[9] Still, many influential writers continue to argue that even if America's decline is not as bad as thought a decade ago, it still lacks the capacity for coherent global leadership. Least of all would it occur to foreign policy 'professionals' to rank Bill Clinton higher than Harry Truman or Richard Nixon—but then they seem to be curiously out of synch with the public on many counts.

Before the war in Kosovo, in a lead article in *The New York Times* titled 'Who's in charge here?' Barbara Crossette lamented Washington's retreat from foreign policy leadership (especially collective leadership at the UN)—just at the time when 'Washington's consistent leadership is needed most'. 'In the last year of the century', she wrote in January 1999, 'the newer, saner world order confidently anticipated when Communism collapsed a decade ago is nowhere to be seen.'[10] This perception

[7] Kennedy, *Rise and Fall*, pp. 434–35, 525–35.
[8] Prestowitz, preface to *Trading Places*.
[9] Reilly (ed.), *American Public Opinion*, p. 5.
[10] Crossette, 'The World Expected Peace. It Found a New Brutality', *The New York Times*, 24 Jan., 1999.

owed something to the alarms and diversions of the Lewinsky debauch and a President understandably preoccupied with impeachment. But many others, like Samuel Huntington, have been consistent Cassandras throughout the 1990s: recently he again argued for civilizational conflict as the dominant force in the post-Cold War world, and expressed doubt as to whether the United States has 'the domestic political base' necessary for it really to lead a unipolar world (he found a 1997 poll showing that only 13 per cent of the American people said they preferred a preeminent role for the US).[11] Another Harvard analyst of international affairs, Stanley Hoffman, argued that even if American power is preponderant today, 'a world that is more fluid, in which we remain "No. 1" but without the ability to control it, is unsettling'. In his view 'a dominant state must also have the will to use [power], and this is conspicuously lacking in the United States today'.[12]

I couldn't disagree more with these authors. They were wrong about American decline, and they are wrong about American global leadership today—which prevailed in Kosovo while managing to keep eighteen other NATO nations in tenuous but effective coalition. But it isn't easy to say *why* they were wrong. Many arguments and predictions look bad from the hindsight of a decade, including some of my own; furthermore there was no lack of facts and events testifying to American decline, just as the inability of the US to get its way in places like Iraq or North Korea remains palpable today. I believe they were wrong not because of the evidence they brought to bear, but because of a flawed understanding of America's position and role in the world in the first place.

For one thing, American pundits confuse a comprehensive and in many ways unparalleled hegemony with omnipotence, with America's ability to get its way on every issue: there is no such power in the world, and there never was. They compare the presumed bipolar stability of the Cold War (or what some have called 'the long peace') with an overwrought image of 1990s global disorder. Yet only a superficial account of the Cold War could overlook the decades marked by an astonishing combination of American omnipotence and inability to render the world tractable. During the height of American power we couldn't win the Korean War but instead were fought to a standstill by Chinese and Korean peasant armies. We redoubled our efforts only to lose in Vietnam, and we couldn't control many other outcomes—in the Suez crisis in 1956, the Cuban revolution, the fiasco of the Bay of Pigs, the Nicaraguan revolution, and catastrophes like the blasting to death of 250 Marines in Beirut in 1983. People forget how unruly the Cold War world was and the degree to which its passing in the late 1980s also closed the chapter on a host of regional contests, some of the them civil wars and some superpower proxy conflicts (in Angola, Afghanistan, Nicaragua, Cambodia, the horn of Africa, to name a few).

The most dangerous period in the past fifty years was precisely when the American century was at high tide—in the 1960s. Then the Soviet Union imagined itself to be overtaking the United States (a contributing cause of the Cuban missile crisis), China went nuclear, and anti-colonial revolutions that had won or were winning power throughout the Third World gave a towering influence to a variety of Third World leaders (Mao, Ho Chi Minh, Kim Il Sung, Patrice Lumumba, Castro, Quadaffi) that would be unimaginable today. Now such people are gone or stuck in a

---

[11] Samuel P. Huntington, 'The Lonely Superpower', *Foreign Affairs* 78:2 (1999), pp. 39–40.
[12] Stanley Hoffman, *World Disorders* (Rowman & Littlefield, 1998), pp. 105, 155.

time warp, along with all the significant alternatives to American power. Then, we had the will to use our power but often enough, not the wisdom; today we may sometimes lack the will to deploy American force, but there is wisdom in that as well—Americans can't solve all the problems of the world: we never could, and we never will. Furthermore if we ask the question, for what contemporary problem is the use of military power the solution, few cases come to mind beyond blunting the worst excesses of a barbarian like Slobodan Milosevic.

Perhaps former UN chief Boutrous Boutrous-Ghali put his finger on the deepest truth about US foreign policy: 'Like in Roman times', he said, the Americans 'have no diplomacy; you don't need diplomacy if you are so powerful'.[13] The United States has such comprehensive advantage in the world that it can occupy itself for a full year with the Monica Lewinsky scandal, a year punctuated by the disastrous collapse of several of the world's important economies (South Korea, Thailand, Indonesia, Russia) and followed by a major new war, and nothing happens except that the American economic lead lengthens. The stock market went up again in 1998 against most predictions and in spite of the global financial crisis, which included a very expensive implosion of the Russian economy in August; it expanded all through the war in Kosovo. Economic growth in the last quarter of 1998 was so robust (6.1 per cent) that in GNP terms it created a Spain overnight; it dropped to a mere four per cent in early 1999, creating another South Korea.[14]

Let me try to isolate five elements that I think account for the American ascendancy, each of which has little to do with preponderant military strength (even though the US has that, too): and these are mass consumption and mass culture, the advantages of a continent—an unappreciated aspect of American technological prowess—and the peculiarities of both American liberalism and the global hegemony that results from it.

I shop, therefore I am

A curious incongruity in our halcyon era is the American savings rate: it hit exactly zero in early 1999, as consumption outran savings for the first time, and continued going south. Meanwhile in Japan the savings rate remains high, as always, but bank interest rates are just above zero for preferred customers, and in March the government handed out free coupons worth about $160 in hopes that consumers would go out and spend them. If the Japanese couldn't sell in the vast American market (like just about every other exporter), their economy would expire. What gives? Basically the Japanese do not get it: capitalism is about spending, not about saving and the US pioneered incomparable ways to spend money not yesterday, but eighty years ago. The 'Roaring 20s' were not just an era of flappers and the Charleston, but years of pioneering innovation when Americans first sampled the seductive possibilities of mass consumption and mass culture that the rest of the world now absorbs as part of its own lifestyle: automobiles, radios, Hollywood films, professional sports,

---

[13] Quoted in *The New York Times*, Nov. 20, 1998, p. A7.
[14] That is, the US GNP of $8.1 trillion (see *CIA Factbook* below) multiplied by 6.1 per cent=Spain's GNP of about $520 bn.

'consumer durables' like refrigerators. At that time American industry perfected both mass production and the means to digest the same goods—*en masse*.

That decade capped an amazingly quick American rise to world pre-eminence: the US had 29 per cent of global industrial production in the 1880s, 36 per cent by 1913 (compared to Britain's 14 per cent), and 42 per cent in 1929—the highest percentage ever, save for the abnormal period just after World War II when all the advanced industrial economies had suffered extensive war damage, except for the unscathed United States—which temporarily held half of all global production.[15] This period witnessed the fruition of assembly-line mass production, as is well known, with Henry Ford's Model T symbolizing both the capacity to turn out automobiles like cookies, and the high $5-a-day wage that enabled Ford's workers to purchase them. Less appreciated was the pioneering combination of salesmanship, mass advertising, and easy credit that General Motors used to compete with Ford and to saturate the American market with automobiles (from 1920 to 1929 the *per capita* auto ownership rate went from 1 in 13 people to 1 in 5, a level not reached by other industrial countries until the 1960s).[16]

Alfred Sloan of GM found a way to splash lots of DuPont paint on to cars (DuPont owned GM at the time), adding colour and style in place of the always-black Model Ts, and parleying graduated brand-names into a national ritual in which Americans climbed the greasy pole by moving from a blue Chevrolet to a green Pontiac, a two-toned Oldsmobile, a big Buick, and finally a black Cadillac that symbolized ultimate status arrival. Hollywood recapitulated the American dream in film, with LA policemen pulling up in black-and-white Chevrolets, and movie stars like Valentino stepping out of alabaster Cadillacs. Sloan also inaugurated the autumnal sacrament of unveiling the next year's new models; buying one was the best way to instantly devalue your neighbour's car: 'used'. The General Motors Acceptance Corporation made the purchase easy by stringing monthly car payments out over several years. And so Americans moved from savers to spenders, strung out on credit unlike any people in the world—but loving it.[17] To be an American is to be maxed out: from 1989 to 1995 average credit-card balances swelled by 135 per cent, but among the poorest 20 per cent of the population, by a whopping 400 per cent.[18]

A Russian immigrant named David Sarnoff, a self-taught engineer working in wireless communications for the Navy, had the vision of a radio in every home; in the 1920s RCA emerged under his leadership, and American firms paid for the free radio programmes by advertising their wares—in every home. Seventy years later another government invention called the Internet, also plastered with advertising, would invade the household. Historian Olivier Zunz, whose book is a useful contribution amid the current *American Century* hailstorm, reminds us that as early as 1914 Walter Lippmann linked democracy to 'the right to purchase consumers' goods at low prices;'[19] Zunz highlights a pragmatic American coalition of business, science

---

[15] W. W. Rostow, *The World Economy* (University of Texas Press, 1978), pp. 52–3.
[16] Emma Rothschild, *Paradise Lost: The Decline of the Auto-Industrial Age* (Vintage Books, 1974), pp. 26–30. The British did not reach the 1929 US rate until 1966, according to data in Rothschild.
[17] Ibid., pp. 39, 82.
[18] Dough Henwood, 'The Nation Indicators', *The Nation*, 19 July, 1999, p. 12.
[19] Lippmann, *Drift and Mastery: An Attempt to Diagnose the Current Unrest* (University of Wisconsin Press rev. edn., 1985), p. 56; quoted in Zunz, *Why the American Century?* (University of Chicago Press, 1998).

and government yielding a huge variety of applied technology oriented toward mass consumption and commercialism, in the 1920s and after—'an array of original achievements in science and industry' that led to 'a concurrent and deliberate reorganization of society.'[20]

In this eruption of mass culture the middle class was the ideal and the normal, average individual—the building block (if many Americans were far from middle class status, they all aspired to it). A vast expansion of higher education, most obvious in the huge land-grant universities still unrivalled by any other country even today, was essential to the creation of a broad middle class and remains a great American advantage.

The pleasures of Austrian economics

It might appear that John Maynard Keynes was the intellectual architect of American-style mass consumption, with his emphasis on demand-led economics and deficit spending by the government to put money in people's pockets. But it was Austrian thinker Joseph Schumpeter who best understood the extraordinary growth spurt of the 1920s. Schumpeter, who taught for years at Harvard, was among other things a theorist of business cycles of all kinds and understood this new burst of wealth to be a combination of new technologies (the assembly line), cheap credit (like GMAC), and cheap energy (petroleum, gushing into the market as American firms developed California and Texas wells) combining to produce a 'leading sector' or flagship industry: automobiles. He placed special weight on innovators and entrepreneurs (like Ford and Sloan), and thought that bank-created money (otherwise called credit) was the element that merged magically (or at least inexplicably) with innovation, ceaselessly to create entirely new industries and—like the auto—entirely new ways of life. Schumpeter focused on structural changes in the economy, qualitative changes that conventional economists—with their emphasis on incremental quantitative change and equilibrium models—have trouble explaining.[21] His ideas also caused trouble for Keynes' theory: American deficit spending reached its height under Roosevelt's New Deal (at about five per cent of GNP), yet it was World War II that finally pulled the US out of the depression; deficit spending reached an all-time high of six per cent of GNP in the Reagan era—precisely the period of ostensible American stagnation and decline.

Now think about our era: for the past several years economists, not least among them Federal Reserve Chairman Alan Greenspan, have been trying to figure out how the American economy can grow so fast with effective full employment, and yet not create inflation. The conventional explanation would look for gains in labour productivity, but (at least until recently) the data did not show gains sufficient to account for this phenomenon. Chairman Greenspan has frequently speculated, therefore, that something new must be happening—perhaps the efficiencies of the

---

[20] Zunz, *American Century*, p. xi.

[21] Joseph A. Schumpeter, *The Theory of Economic Development*, trans. Redvers Opie (New Brunswick, NJ: Transaction Books, 1983), pp. xix, 61–66; see also his often impenetrable tome called *Business Cycles: A Theoretical, Historical and Statistical Analysis of the Capitalist Process*, abridged edn. (New York, Porcupine Press, 1989), first published in 1934.

information age could not be captured by conventional data-gathering, or they would show up in the future. Lo and behold, productivity gains began climbing again in 1996; productivity rose 2.2 per cent in 1998, but manufacturing had a 4.3 per cent rise for the year, and an astounding 5.6 per cent jump in the fourth quarter of 1998.[22]

Were Schumpeter alive, he would say that we have a new leading sector technology (the microchip); cheap energy (petroleum costs less today than it did in the 1950s); a unique combination of the two in that the silicon chip requires raw material inputs that are no more than three per cent of its cost (compared to 40 per cent for automobiles[23]) and the energy to run them is so miniscule that computers can be turned on all the time; the information courses through fibre optic cables, which can transmit 20 times as many messages as copper telephone wire, yet require five per cent of the energy to produce as compared to copper; and finally that credit and wealth creation has been so dizzying (American credit card consumption driving the domestic and world economy in the 1990s; Internet stock offerings jumping 500 per cent in one day) that entire cities seem to be transformed almost overnight—like San Jose, for example, now undergoing a growth spurt worthy of LA's in the 1920s, and suddenly the third largest exporting city in the US. At least one author from the mid-1980s did not mistake temporary difficulties for irremediable American decline; Peter Drucker saw all this coming fifteen years ago. He also thought that Schumpeter, and not Keynes or Friedman, was the thinker who best explained it all: indeed, he thought Schumpeter's ideas would shape our time and the next several decades.[24]

The sign of a good brand

According to Drucker it was not men of ideology, or even intellect, but men of vision who built the American century. If we retrieve the 17 February 1941 issue of *Life* that carried Henry Luce's original essay entitled 'The American Century', we find not much intellect but a heavy dose of ideology—which he called vision, and not just any vision: 'the American vision'. Like Alfred Sloan, Luce was a great sales-man; *The American Century* was a wonderful logo for this eternal optimist to merchandise the American dream, even if his ideas didn't go beyond vexation about creeping 'national socialism' in America (read New Deal), the bankruptcy of isolationists who still could not grasp why Americans should fight and die for 'dear old Danzig or dear old Dong Dang', and the recommendation that the consumptive paradise that had arisen in the 1920s ('the abundant life', as Luce called it), is or should be available 'for all mankind' once they wake up to 'America's vision'. This programme, of course, should not march forward just with an overflow of consumer durables, but under the banner of American idealism: 'It must be a sharing with all peoples of our Bill of Rights, our Declaration of Independence, our Constitution,

---

[22] *The New York Times*, 10 Feb., 1999, p. C3; 27 March, 1999, p. B3.

[23] Peter F. Drucker, *The Frontiers of Management: Where Tomorrow's Decisions are Being Shaped Today* (New York: Plume Books reprint, 1999), p. 27.

[24] All information in this paragraph from Drucker, *ibid.*, pp. 27–28, and Drucker, 'Modern Prophets: Schumpter or Keynes', 1983, reprinted in *ibid.*, pp. 104–115.

our magnificent industrial products, our technical skills. It must be an internationalism of the people, by the people and for the people'.

Amid much frothy rhetoric like this ('We must undertake now to be the Good Samaritan of the entire world', etc.), Luce held out to underdeveloped peoples the chance to escape their problems by becoming American—an absurd proposition in 1941. But he put his finger on a truth—one that keeps people from all corners of the world immigrating to this country. Even in remote Tibet people seek consumer (or couch-potato) heaven: take 'Darchi', a middle-aged peasant who, as he harvested barley near his mud-brick village, told an American reporter that he didn't really care about independence from China: 'I want to buy a television, and then sit back and drink barley beer and watch TV'.[25] Or as Luce put it, 'Once we cease to distract ourselves with lifeless arguments about isolationism, we shall be amazed to discover that there is already an immense American internationalism. American jazz, Hollywood movies, American slang, American machines and patented products, are in fact the only things that every community in the world, from Zanzibar to Hamburg, recognizes in common'. Jean Baudrillard once wrote that the American flag itself was the 'trademark of a good brand;'[26] Henry Luce recognized that in 1941.

We can take a Communist country like North Korea as the antithesis of the American Century (just as it seems to be the Pentagon's *bete-noire* today)—the vanguard of the anti-imperial, anti-American rejectionist front. I first visited that country in 1981, when its industrial strategy had not yet run aground (*per capita* income was then about the same as the South's according to the CIA) and its go-it-alone policies of self-reliance and isolation from the world economy still seemed a plausible path of development to many people in the Third World. As soon as we arrived at the hotel, set on a picturesque riverbank full of weeping willows in the middle of P'yongyang, my omnipresent guides wanted to finger and cluck over my Asahi Pentax 'Spotmatic' camera (then fifteen years old); they were well aware of Boeing aircraft, the dominant industry in the city where I then lived, and asked me how many passengers a 747 jumbo could hold and how long it took to fly across the continent—and exchanged amazed glances when I told them 400 people and four hours. They were fascinated by the Hollywood movies they had managed to see, like their current leader, Kim Jong Il—who is said to possess 10,000 films and to love *Gone with the Wind*. With this experience I grasped the truth of Baudrillard's observation: 'Whatever happens, and whatever one thinks of the arrogance of the dollar or the multinationals, it is this culture which, the world over, fascinates those very people who suffer most at its hands, and it does so through the deep, insane conviction that it has made all their dreams come true.'[27]

If Henry Luce both understood and epitomized this 'insane conviction', the world's peoples did not provide much evidence of a thirst for the American way in 1941 or, for that matter, during 30 years of anti-imperial wars after World War II. Henry Luce's concern, however, was not with 'worlds' but with directions: toward Europe, or away from it. He preferred the latter as the most prominent of the 'Asia-firsters' (dear-old-Dong-Dang again). But his Asia was a place to be led by whites

---

[25] *The New York Times*, Sept. 22, 1990.
[26] Jean Baudrillard, *America* (New York, 1989), p. 95.
[27] Baudrillard, *America*, p. 77.

and ultimately to be dissolved not in anti-imperial revolt, but in the solvent of Americanism. The preferred direction of American expansionists like Luce was westward toward the Pacific, symbolized by the nineteenth-century imagery of pioneers, manifest destiny, and the ever-receding frontier.

At the same time another influential body of opinion, the *Council on Foreign Relations* in New York, was moving away from Europe—but in a different sense. Germany dominated continental Europe in 1941, with Britain blocking its way to the rest of the world. The council therefore envisioned 'a great residual area potentially available to us and upon the basis of which American foreign policy may be framed'. Later termed 'the Grand Area', this space became the council's metaphor for American expansion into various corners of the globe theretofore off limits, especially the British, French and Dutch colonies but also China and Japan, a vast expanse now undermined or made 'open' by the effects of the ongoing European war.

This was not simply a reflection of the council's accustomed Atlanticism, but a Pacific strategy aimed at expansion into a domain marred only by ongoing Japanese aggression. One month before the appearance of Luce's essay the council issued 'American Far Eastern Policy', which recommended all-out aid to China to keep Japan pinned down on the continent, and the embargo of war materials to Japan— policies that Franklin Roosevelt implemented within months.[28] Obviously the Grand Area included what later came to be called the Third World: but what should be the mechanism of American operation within this global realm? Did the Council propose to colonize it like Burma or Indochina, to police it, or to Americanize it *à la* Henry Luce? The answer is that the Grand Area was the world economy and it was to be open for trade, not necessarily human uplift, and the mechanisms of operation would be those later established at Bretton Woods. The American who, in my view, did the most to bring this about had already sketched this future when the European war began, almost two years earlier.

Henry Luce was a publisher, and a most successful one. But his world view was narrow, particularly in its either/or attitude to Europe and Asia. The true captains of the American Century were those who thought in both/and terms: Europe and Asia, the open door and partnership with imperial Britain, intervention in both Latin America and Europe,[29] a world economy with no ultimate limit. Dean Acheson embodied the fullness of American ambition and expressed it concisely in a speech delivered shortly after Germany invaded Poland, entitled 'An American Attitude Toward Foreign Affairs', a text truly pregnant with ideas that built the American Century. As he later put it in reflecting back on this speech, he had really sought at the time to 'begin work on a new postwar world system'.[30]

---

[28] Council on Foreign Relations, aide-memoire E-B26, 'American Far Eastern Policy', 15 January 1941, cited in Laurence H. Shoup and William Minter, *Imperial Brain Trust: The Council on Foreign Relations and United States Foreign Policy* (New York, 1977), pp. 129–36.

[29] Time has not dimmed the impact of a stunning phone conversation between John J. McCloy and Henry Stimson in May 1945: McCloy remarked that 'we ought to have our cake and eat it too; that we ought to be free to operate under this regional arrangement in South America, at the same time intervene promptly in Europe. . .', to which Stimson replied, 'I think that it's not asking too much to have our little region over here which never bothered anybody'. I first read this colloquy in Gabriel Kolko, *The Politics of War* (New York, 1968), pp. 470–71.

[30] Dean Acheson, 'An American Attitude Toward Foreign Affairs', 28 November 1939, in *Morning and Noon* (Boston, 1965), pp. 267–75; see also Acheson's reflections on the speech, pp. 216–17. I am indebted to Heajeong Lee for bringing this text to my attention.

'Our vital interests', Acheson said in this speech delivered at Yale, 'do not permit us to be indifferent to the outcome' of the wars in Europe and Asia; nor was it possible for Americans to remain isolated from them—unless they wished a kind of eternal 'internment on this continent' (only an Anglophile like Acheson would liken North America to a concentration camp). He located the causes of the war and the global depression that preceded it in 'the failure of some mechanisms of the Nineteenth Century world economy' that had led to 'this break-up of the world into exclusive areas for armed exploitation administered along oriental [*sic*] lines'. In its time, 'the economic and political system of the Nineteenth Century . . . produced an amazing increase in the production of wealth', but for many years it had been in an 'obvious process of decline'. Reconstruction of the foundations of peace would require new mechanisms: ways to make capital available for industrial production, the removal of tariffs, 'a broader market for goods made under decent standards', 'a stable international monetary system', and the removal of 'exclusive or preferential trade arrangements'. The world economy was his main emphasis, but in good Achesonian realpolitik fashion he also called for the immediate creation of 'a navy and air force adequate to secure us in both oceans simultaneously and with striking power sufficient to reach to the other side of each of them'.

Dean Acheson later had the opportunity to implement these ideas, first at Bretton Woods, then with the Marshall Plan and the Truman Doctrine, and finally with NSC-68; he was a realist, of course, but unlike others (say, Henry Kissinger) his long Wall Street career had educated him in the logic of the grand area—the world economy. He thus became the person who comes closest to being the singular architect of American strategy from 1944 to 1953. A short few years after he gave this prescient speech and Henry Luce claimed the century for Americans, the United States accounted for half of the industrial production of all the world, emerging from the war as the single unscathed and emboldened superpower—thus making both men look like visionaries. Yet by the turn of the last century the United States was the most productive industrial economy in the world, and everyone knew this by the early 1920s as American firms pioneered mass production and consumption and its banks became the effective centre of global commerce. But it had a laughably small military, and neither the political will nor the domestic political base for global hegemony. The years from 1914 to 1941 were thus not part of an American century, but years of hegemonic interregnum in which England could no longer lead and the United States was not yet ready to do so. The German invasion of Poland changed all that, culminating in the Pearl Harbor attack, which finally committed the United States to global leadership at a time when economic collapse, global war, and the resultant chaos required the construction of the new world system that Acheson envisioned in 1939. Moreover, If Henry Luce's Asia-firstism reflected the time-honoured American idea of a remove into an uncivilized wilderness, Acheson's ambition to secure 'both oceans simultaneously' reflected his precocious comprehension of the enormous advantages deriving from America's bi-coastal position.

Massive fog grips Europe; continent isolated

So read a London newspaper headline during the heyday of the empire on which the sun never set. The global leader whom the United States replaced had the same curiosity as the one that was going to replace it in the dawning 21st century: England and Japan both occupy small islands, set just far enough away from the mainland to breed a solipsistic sense of ineffable superiority. Once the United States was also called an 'island country', sheltered by two great oceans; and it was still so when it pioneered mass consumption and mass culture in the 1920s. The continuing incompletion of the continental market, however, gave us isolationism instead of global hegemony: the US is the only great power that for more than a century was entirely self-sufficient unto itself and therefore invulnerable to external dependencies, and the only one with vast reaches yet to be filled up with people and enterprise (save perhaps for Russia's frigid and still undeveloped frontier in Siberia).

The American position in the world owes much to being the first hegemonic power to inhabit an immense land mass: not an island empire like England or Pacific Century-pretender Japan, but a continent open at both ends to vast potential markets. The US is the only industrial country with long Atlantic and Pacific coasts, making it simultaneously an Atlantic and a Pacific power; the historic dominance of Atlanticists (Henry Kissinger, Samuel Huntington and Stanley Hoffman are contemporary examples), gazing upon a Europe whose civilization gave birth to our own, averts our eyes from this fact. Indeed, the continental divide still makes a New Yorker uncomfortable in Los Angeles (and *vice-versa*).

The transcontinental railroad symbolized the completion of the national territory—by the 1860s America was a linked continental empire. But distant connections to isolated Western towns and farms, Pony Express mail service, and peripheral mudflats like the Los Angeles of the late 19th century, do not a national market make. Instead for fifty years (roughly from 1890 to 1940) Americans peopled and filled in the national territory, at the same time that the US became the leading industrial power in the world. There was but a brief lunge toward formal empire, with the Spanish-American War and the colonizing of the Philippines at the turn of the century, and the limited American participation in World War I; the dominant tendency was expansion to the coast and exploitation of a vast and relatively new market.

The isolationism of the interwar period cannot be understood apart from a political economy founded on protection of the home market and conscious unconcern with the rest of the world. One of Henry Ford's publicists, Samuel Crowther, summed up this homeward-bound dynamic in a book called *America Self-Contained*.[31] The American nationalist was always made to seem 'the boorish provincial' instead of the patriot, while free traders lowered tariffs and let foreigners 'cavort without an admission fee in the largest market in the world'. He thought the US should make its isolation more complete, 'shape our own destinies', instead of doing a lot of 'sordid international shop-keeping' in that 'old system of world economy'. December 7, 1941 was the last day when anyone took Crowther seriously (when I checked his book out of a large university library, the last reader had done so in 1949). 1941 was thus a pregnant year in more than one respect; it marked the beginning of the full industrialization of the far West, which in the postwar period grew apace with a rapidly-developing Pacific Rim—an imperfectly appreciated aspect of American global power.

---

[31] Samuel Crowther, *American Self-Contained* (New York: Doubleday, Doran, 1933).

Franklin D. Roosevelt's New Deal signalled the direct involvement of the federal government in the industrial development of the far West. The New Deal was instrumental in building massive infrastructures (like the Grand Coulee Dam), in the management of western lands and the immense water works necessary to till them (through the Soil Conservation Service and other means) and under federal government auspices and emergency conditions, in subsidizing heavy industries connected to the war effort.[32] Southern California's rapidly-emerging aircraft business was completely dependent on government contracts; defence industries ran three shifts during the war, with airplanes accounting for 34 per cent of all production. Washington also subsidized all kinds of social overhead in the area: the railroads, the highways, the airlines, and the water needed for a vast commercialization and suburbanization. Firms like Lockheed (whose Santa Monica plant was the largest firm and employer in the 1940s), failed several times before the war but flourished thereafter, until the Cold War ended and defence contracts began drying up (in 1996 Disney spent $45m to turn Lockheed's Stealth aircraft design facility, long known as 'the skunkworks', into an animation studio).[33]

If Los Angeles symbolized the prowess of America's West coast at mid-century, at the end of it the symbolic city is Seattle. I lived in Seattle for ten years, beginning in 1977. Coming from New York, it struck me as an isolated and insulated backwater: an Omaha that happened to be situated on the Pacific Coast; the city fathers seemed unaware of the opportunities beckoning from across this great ocean. The city was just then emerging from the 'Boeing bust' of the early 1970s, when severe job cuts caused an even more severe recession; the joke was to ask the last person leaving Seattle to turn out the lights.

A decade later Microsoft had replaced Boeing as the flagship industry of Seattle, a world-class monopoly every bit as important to the American position in the world as John D. Rockefeller's Standard Oil a century earlier. City fathers funded an enormous new dock sprouting hundreds of container-ship cranes helping to make of Seattle a major American exporting city, and nearly foamed at the mouth to deepen the burgeoning Pacific Rim trade. The state's Congressional delegation had become the leading pillar of free-trade legislation. Boeing had long backlogs of 747s on order—from China. The city was so dynamic and expansive that when I read the 'declinist' literature of the 1980s I kept asking myself, 'what about Seattle?'

In other words, the advantage of a continental economy is that things can be falling apart in one region (the rustbelt in the 1980s) and coming together in another (America's Pacific Rim). Today Los Angeles and Seattle are enormously dynamic, polyglot Pacific Rim cities of extraordinary multiethnic and multicultural diversity, wired-up centres of the revolution in communications, entertainment ('grunge' rock, one of Seattle's exports we could have done without), and Internet commerce (recently I sent three books to a colleague in Beijing with a few mouse clicks on Seattle-based Amazon.com's website).

---

[32] John Walton, *Western Times and Water Wars: State, Culture and Rebellion in California* (University of California Press, 1992), pp. 233–5.
[33] *Weekly Variety*, 18 March, 1996, p. 123.

Hegemony means never having to say you're sorry

In 1985 American and Japanese negotiators met at the Plaza Hotel in New York to hammer out an agreement on driving down the value of the dollar in relation to the undervalued yen, the latter having been a cornerstone of Japanese exports. By the time they were done the dollar's value had dropped from 250 yen to 180—a massive devaluation that enabled the US to rebuild its own export position. An observant Frenchman, Jean-Claude Derian, saw in this episode an exercise of America's hegemonic birthright: by using the privileged position of the dollar as 'the corner-stone of the world monetary system', Washington had forced the rest of the world 'to share the cost of reestablishing the US balance of trade'.

What is hegemony? After a recent lecture a student asked me why it was so difficult in this country to have a reasoned discussion about this phenomenon; the minute you use the word, someone accuses you of being a Marxist. Recently postmodern scholar Judith Butler tried to explain her views in a *New York Times* editorial: hegemony, she explained , is when something is so powerful that you have no conscious awareness of it.[34] Roland Barthes believed that a potent surreptitious mastery came from that which could not be named; that is also where Rumpelstiltskin got his power. By refusing the name 'hegemony', we also refuse a debate about what it is, and what it means for the American people. The result, in my opinion, is that hegemony is least understood in its own point of origin—the United States.

When Dean Acheson spoke at Yale in 1939, the US had a laughably small military, and neither the political will nor the domestic political base for global hegemony: the Army had 185,000 men and an annual budget of $500m. The German invasion of Poland changed all that, culminating in the Pearl Harbor attack, which finally committed the United States to global leadership at a time when economic collapse, global war, and the resultant chaos required the construction of the new world system that Acheson envisioned. A few years later the Army numbered more than one million, the Air Force and the Navy were almost as large, the defence budget was over $100 bn, and the US had 1.5 million soldiers, airmen and sailors stationed in 119 countries.[35]

The moment when the baton of world leadership finally and definitively passed from London to Washington came on 21 February 1947, when a British Embassy official informed Acheson that England could not give Greece and Turkey $250m in military and economic aid. Two days later Acheson walked off to lunch with a friend, remarking that 'there are only two powers in the world now', the United States and the Soviet Union.[36] Acheson did not mean that an era of bipolarity had dawned, although he meant that as well; he meant something much deeper—the substitution of American for British leadership. As he later put it privately, when America grasped for world leadership amid the regression of the British empire, it was for the first time in the position of a person who, 'on the death of a parent,

---

[34] Op-Ed Page, *The New York Times*, 20 March, 1999.
[35] Stephen E. Ambrose, *Rise to Globalism* (New York: Penguin 1983), p. 13.
[36] Thomas J. McCormick, *America's Half-Century: United States Foreign Policy in the Cold War* (Baltimore, 1989), p. 72.

hears in a new way the roaring of the cataract'.[37] Acheson's problem was to be pregnant with an idea that he could not articulate, lest Harry Truman lose the next election (for example, by announcing that the United States had now replaced England as the power with all the burdens-of-last-resort in the world system).

To put it differently, the internationalist forces in American politics lacked a strong domestic base, particularly in Congress, which held many former isolationists. George Kennan provided the solution to this dilemma with an elegant metaphor: *containment*. Imagine, for an America to march outward and inherit Britain's role, and you mark it up for the defence. Imagine, a doctrine defining hegemony by what it opposes, obviating the necessity to explain to the American people what it is, and what its consequences will be for them. It is only today, after the fall of the Berlin Wall and the collapse of the Soviet Union, that Americans can see this obscured, underlying system that keeps going in spite of the disappearance of its ostensible *raison d'etre*—the Soviet Union and its many allies.

A central aspect of the containment project was to revive the industrial production of just-defeated German and Japan, to knit together a productive coalition that would revive both countries, keep communism at bay, get them off the American dole, rejuvenate middle classes, and thereby extend American-style mass consumption to our allies. As Japan and West Germany were posted as industrial workshops, cheap energy from the Middle East fuelled their recovery and also created markets for American goods. In September 1947 the Truman administration ruled that huge deals involving Anglo-Iranian, Gulf, and Shell did not violate anti-trust laws, and thus, in Daniel Yergin's words, 'the mechanisms, capital and marketing systems were in place to move vast quantities of Middle Eastern oil into the European market,' and to move Europe off coal and onto oil.[38] Germans drove off in their Volkswagens, Italians in their Fiats, Frenchmen in their Renaults, and Japanese in their Toyotas—into a consumer paradise that recapitulated America's leap forward in the 1920s.

A liberal hegemony?

We still haven't figured out a good name for the postwar American 'grand area', now approximating the globe itself. Is it an empire? If so, where are the exclusively-controlled territories that would approximate colonial India? Has it been neoimperial, exploiting the economies of its members as if they were colonies? How then did Japan or Korea develop so rapidly? This system has not created onerous or inescapable dependencies, and it has not dominated its constituent members. It has established boundaries of inclusion, but it has not necessarily punished exit, if that exit is to a middle ground of neutrality or irrelevance. This order has been a hegemonic one, and it has had—and must have—a hegemonic leader. But hegemony is most effective when it is indirect, inclusive, plural, heterogeneous, and con-

[37] Acheson's notes to himself in preparation for Congressional testimony in August 1950, in *Foreign Relations of the United States* (1950), v. 1, pp. 393 5.

[38] Kai Bird, *The Chairman: John J. McCloy and the Making of the American Establishment* (Simon & Schuster, 1992), pp. 143, 178; Daniel Yergin, *The Prize: The Epic Quest for Oil, Money and Power* (Simon & Schuster, 1991), pp. 422–4.

sensual—less a form of domination than a form of legitimate global leadership. It is hegemonic and liberal at the same time—but how? How did the new system emerge? Was it just a matter of letting Dean Acheson and the other 'wise men' loose?

In retrospect, the construction of the postwar world order looks relatively simple: Bretton Woods in 1944, containment and the Marshall Plan in 1947, NSC-68 and general rearmament in 1950—a mere five years to bring about another '*belle époque*'. The order was to be a liberal one, but in 1945 hardly anyone knew what that meant, since the world had been so illiberal for so long. It might mean a Wilsonian quest to make *this* brave new world safe for democracy, once and for all. It might mean the creed of the Anglophile internationalists, like wartime Secretary of State Cordell Hull, that free trade would create the greatest good for the greatest number, form the preconditions for representative democracy on a world scale, and thereby yield peace among nations. It might mean an extension of Franklin Roosevelt's New Deal to the world, as a kind of regulated 'open door'. It might even be the libertarianism of Senator Robert Taft, the patron saint of Midwestern Republicanism, with its emphasis on the fullest extension of the market, minimal government, and fiscal austerity—even with regard to military spending. Whichever understanding of liberalism one might choose, the question still would remain of how to implement a liberal order in a world that had never experienced one.

All of these definitions are inadequate to grasp the sinews of American power and influence—just like the unexamined triumphalist liberalism that swept the American scene after 1989. In his recent book called *The Liberal Moment*,[39] political scientist Robert Latham argues that the liberal ascendancy of the 1940s involved a beguiling, seductive, spreading, even contagious liberal hegemony, constructed through 'the permeation of values and understandings throughout the global system'. It was also a complex and problematic episode in the history of a modern practice that had defined as liberal an England that had a sharply inegalitarian class society, a highly restricted franchise (even after the reform act of 1867, only 30 per cent of the adult population could vote), and an empire—one that had included not just a host of disenfranchised colonial populations, but through its trading relations, cotton production by millions of slaves or sharecroppers in the American South. The liberal state would include a United States that in 1945 was a democracy for the adult white population and an apartheid-like southern autocracy for the black population. And during the Cold War, a liberal world order led by the United States included Trujillo's Dominican Republic, Tito's Yugoslavia, Suharto's Indonesia, Park Chung Hee's South Korea, and Mobutu's Zaire.

A dictatorship like Trujillo's was obviously not liberal—indeed he was one of the most venal tyrants of this century—but its partial incorporation into the American-organized world order (long connoted as the 'free world') was a commonplace aspect of a plural and diverse system. Trujillo's partial inclusion reflected an essential element of liberal hegemony: the demarcation of boundaries, of limits to the realm, most often expressed negatively. The best thing one could say about Trujillo was that he was not a Communist, and Washington would only support his overthrow if it were assured that the Dominican Republic would not go Communist as a result.

---

[39] Robert Latham, *The Liberal Moment: Modernity, Security, and the Making of the Postwar International Order* (New York: Columbia University Press, 1997).

In other words liberal hegemony was (and is) a complex, heterogeneous historical system that cannot be categorized simply as market driven or democratically governed. But there is still something distinct about the American-built liberal order: it cannot be reduced to a mere capitalist modernity, a sly cloak for empire, or a libertarian empyrean where firms interact in the market and free individuals construct a civil society. Liberalism may have transformed states and markets in important ways, but to stop with that (say, representative democracy as a liberal political form) would ignore the international dimension of liberal modernity: it is closely associated with open international exchange. But there is also the logic of individual rights, representative government, and collective self-determination. Then there is the historical recognition that so much of this was brand spanking new in the 1940s: most of those practices associated with liberalism—free trade, basic civil and political rights, universal suffrage, and national self-determination—can only be dated from the mid-nineteenth century as doctrine and (limited) practice, and only achieved global dominion after 1945. That states could be liberal but not democratic was a commonplace before that time.

One of the great strengths of liberalism is an *accretion of norms* over time coming from demands that liberalism fulfill the promises by which the liberal doctrine itself is defined: by writing its ideals, liberalism inspires a future call to action; by declaring its principles, it calls forth a commitment. An example characteristic of our time would be the now common but historically unprecedented experience of 'humanitarian interventions'. As this article was being prepared, NATO warplanes pounded Serbian targets in hopes of stopping the fighting and the ethnic slaughter of Albanians in Kosovo. By the time I had finished it, the war was over and NATO won a clear victory—in spite of any number of expert warnings to the contrary. Often derided by 'realists' like Henry Kissinger as an idealism or Wilsonianism equating the conduct of foreign policy 'with choices between good and evil',[40] or by Michael Mandelbaum's dictum that intervention in defence of liberal values equals 'foreign policy as social work',[41] this new phenomenon also is an outcome of the mutability (and therefore the attractiveness) of liberalism.

The list of attempted humanitarian interventions is long, and the successes are comparatively few; because the problems are both ubiquitous and intractable and yet all of them are covered by global media like CNN, the perception of a world out of control is widespread. The late Judith Shklar' wrote that a 'liberalism of fear' called forth demands to protect individuals from cruelty and oppression in remote locations,[42] ones that many Americans have never heard of—Rwanda, Somalia, Zaire, Bosnia, Kosovo, Sri Lanka, Sudan, Haiti, and Nagorno-Karabakh; wars in Chechnya and Eritrea; Hutus and Tutsis slaughtering each other in Rwanda—few of these places were heard of during the Cold War. UN peacekeepers have been active in Angola, Mozambique, El Salvador, Nicaragua, and Cambodia; the UN is currently involved in sixteen peacekeeping missions around the world. Many are much more successful than generally recognized: who would have thought that even

---

[40] Henry Kissinger, *Years of Renewal* (New York: Simon & Schuster, 1999), p. 33.

[41] Michael Mandelbaum, 'Foreign Policy as Social Work', *Foreign Affairs*, 75:1 (1996), pp. 16–32. Edwin Feulner, president of the Heritage Foundation, called humanitarian interventions 'feel-good foreign policy'. See 'What Are America's Vital Interests?', *Washington Post*, 6 Feb., 1996.

[42] Judith Shklar, 'The Liberalism of Fear', in Nancy Rosenblum (ed.), *Liberalism and the Moral Life* (HUP 1989), pp. 21–38.

Khmer Rouge leaders like Ta Mok, an architect of the genocide in Cambodia, would not only be defeated, but scheduled for war crimes trials? The next prominent figure in the same dock may well be Slobodan Milosevic.

Woodrow Wilson's clarion call of self-determination for small nations became in the 1990s a micronationalism yielding a host of micronations. But this has also been much less troubled than often thought, or than one would have predicted: Czechoslovakia split in two without serious conflict; former Soviet Central Asia was supposed to erupt as it divided into several nations, but hasn't; and even the breakup of Yugoslavia, which detonated wars over Bosnia and Kosovo, did not do so when Slovenia and Macedonia broke off in 1991–92. The Northern Ireland conflict appears to have been put to rest. Many of these conflicts were settled precisely *because* the big powers chose not to extend their lines of influence and interest to the respective sides of the conflict (something especially true of the Balkans), but also because of a new willingness to participate in collective security operations and to risk the credibility of the United States or the European Community to achieve peaceful settlements.[43]

An old and forgotten book by a disgraced President, Herbert Hoover, illustrates the extraordinary bipartisan hold that liberal idealism has on the American people—even in 1958, when Hoover published his book, and when the cloud of the depression still hung over his head—he was thought to epitomize a discredited conservatism based on the presumed virtues of the self-regulating market. Yet his book—*The Ordeal of Woodrow Wilson*—is full of praise for this Democratic President's valiant attempt to transform old-world politics at the Versailles peace conference in 1919, and for his achievements in spite of the opposition of Clemenceau and other leaders: Wilson came to Paris and saved the League of Nations, helped to found the International Labor Organization and the Permanent Court of International Justice at the Hague, and fostered the beginnings of colonial independence and self-determination through the League's mandate system.[44]

It would have been impossible for another 'idealist', President Jimmy Carter, to have promoted human rights in the 1970s without the success of the civil rights movement in the 1960s, just as the Reagan administration could not have promoted global democratization in the mid-1980s without the previous extension of democratic rights in the US (and the quiet abandonment of its 'Kirkpatrick doctrine', which led to Reagan's coddling of the vicious Argentine junta, Chilean dictator Pinochet, Korea's Chun Doo Hwan and other authoritarian leaders, on the grounds that they weren't as bad as Communists)[45]. One could not have imagined the other big powers allowing German unification in 1989 without West Germany's post-1945 history as the most self-conscious exemplar of liberal values in Europe; it would be impossible to imagine the election of long-term dissident Kim Dae Jung in Korea in the midst of a devastating economic crisis in December 1997, without the decades-long struggle for civil and labour rights in that country. Even something mundane like the cashiering of most members of the International Olympic Committee or the

[43] On the US role in Northern Ireland see Michael Cox, 'The War That Came in From the Cold: Clinton and the Irish Question', *World Policy Journal*, 16:1, (1999), pp. 59–67.

[44] Herbert Hoover, *The Ordeal of Woodrow Wilson* (New York: McGraw-Hill Book Company, 1958), p. 262.

[45] This is documented in William I. Robinson, *Promoting Polyarchy: Globalization, US Intervention, and Hegemony* (New York: Cambridge University Press, 1996), pp. 91–2, 121–5.

firing of the members of the European Commission in March 1999 (in both cases for corruption) exemplifies the enhanced scrutiny of all international organs. A globalized world system founded on the unprecedented 'transparency' afforded by global media, also makes it very difficult to run a command economy today—meaning economies that are predatory and don't play by the rules—which explains much of Japan's predicament in the past few years.

This same liberal order encompassed a vast global militarization (eventually encompassing millions of American troops stationed in hundreds of bases in 35 countries, a blue ocean Navy, and an Air Force that was for decades the key carrier of nuclear weapons—i.e., the full expression of the two-ocean 'striking force' Acheson called for in 1939), a phenomenon often treated as an unfortunate result of the bipolar confrontation. I have called this structure an archipelago of empire: advisory groups, military bases, and transnational military and even economic planning (through the Agency for International Development, the IMF and the World Bank).[46] The acid test of the American kind of liberal hegemony will come if and when this archipelago is dismantled; today it still holds the post-World War II settlement in place, and denies us the opportunity to see if the pacifist norms inculcated in Japan, or the liberal norms of Germany, will survive the removal of US troops and a return to full security autonomy.

So, military power was of course important in constructing a liberal order, then and now: the postwar system took shape through positive policy and through the establishment of distinct outer limits, the transgression of which was rare or even inconceivable, provoking immediate crisis—the orientation of West Berlin toward the Soviet bloc, for example. But the typical experience of this hegemony was a mundane, benign and mostly unremarked daily life of subtle constraint, in which the United States kept allied states on defence, resource, and, for many years, financial dependencies. This penetration of allied nations was clearest in the front line states like Japan, West Germany, and South Korea, which were (and remain today) semi-sovereign states that rely on American defence; it was conceived by people like Kennan as an indirect, outer-limit control on the worst outcome, namely, orientation to the other side.[47]

In sum, this liberal form of hegemony is potent, and it has a message: in the 1940s it crushed one form of statist empire and in the 1980s, another. Today it is eroding if not erasing the last formidable alternative system, the Japan-Korea model of state-directed neomercantilism (one undermined and made vulnerable by its inclusion in the postwar regional order). What is the message? The capitalist market, the open door, pluralist democracy, and self-determination. If this last element was often honoured in the breach by Washington, it nonetheless has been a potent political and cultural ideal in the American arsenal since Woodrow Wilson first articulated his famous '14 Points'. Today this heterogenous mix of Wilson and Trujillo, Roosevelt and Batista, Bill Clinton and Jesse Helms, seems to have no rival on the horizon that could possibly hope to take its measure.

---

[46] Cumings, 'Global Realm With No Limit, Global Realm With No Name', *Radical History Review* (Spring 1993).

[47] Cumings, *Origins of the Korean War, II: The Roaring of the Cataract, 1947–1950* (Princeton University Press, 1990), pp. 57–8.

The making and remaking of American hegemony

Most analysts focus far too much attention on the doctrine underlying America's military archipelago, namely, containment. George Kennan's strategy did have the qualities, as Robert Latham writes, 'of flexibility, openness and universality'.[48] It's just that internationalist doctrines were more flexible, more open, and more universal. Kennan famously located five global nodes of advanced industrial production and declared that we had four and Moscow had one and containment meant keeping things that way. But his theoretical presuppositions were based in a turn-of-the-century *realpolitik* that had little to offer policymakers on the burgeoning crisis of the colonies, and little to offer on the puzzling predicament of how to restart the engines of the allied industrial economies, still at an impasse as late as 1950. Kennan was self-conscious enough to realize that what we call 'Cold War policy' meant something much deeper in the 1940s—'*politics* on a world scale'.[49] But he was not the architect of the new order: he was the engineer of the regional positions of strength that sustained the postwar order. The closest approximation to a single architect was Acheson, and the Secretary of State stopped listening to Kennan in 1949: Why?

Kennan has been famously unhappy with the implementation of his containment doctrine, during and after the Truman period, but in 1994 he was also less sure of what the end of the Cold War meant than most analysts:

I viewed [containment] as primarily a diplomatic and political task, though not wholly without military implications. I considered that if and when we had succeeded in persuading the Soviet leadership that the continuation of the[ir] expansionist pressures . . . would be, in many respects, to their disadvantage, then the moment would have come for serious talks with them about the future of Europe. But when, some three years later [1950], this moment had arrived—when we had made our point with the Marshall Plan, with . . . the Berlin blockade and other measures—when the lesson I wanted to see us convey to Moscow had been successfully conveyed, then it was one of the great disappointments of my life to discover that neither our Government nor our Western European allies had any interest in entering into such discussions at all. What they and the others wanted from Moscow, with respect to the future of Europe, was essentially 'unconditional surrender'. They were prepared to wait for it. And this was the beginning of the 40 years of Cold War.[50]

What does this mean? How can we interpret this rendering of Cold War history? When American defence spending is scaled throughout the period of the Cold War, there is a curious upward blip that most Americans have never noticed: in real FY 1996 dollars, defence spending hit \$500 bn—almost double what it is now—just once: during the Korean War. It never got above \$400 bn during the Vietnam War, and its next crest was at \$425 bn during the Reagan buildup, or 6.5 per cent of GDP

---

[48] Latham, *Liberal Moment*, p. 143.
[49] Kennan's italics, in Latham, p. 147.
[50] *New York Times*, Op-Ed Page, 14 March 1994. Kennan added, 'Those of my opponents of that day who have survived [read Paul Nitze] would say, I am sure, 'You see. We were right. The collapse of the Soviet Union amounted to the unconditional surrender we envisaged. . . . And we paid nothing for it.' To which I should have to reply: 'But we did pay a great deal for it. We paid with 40 years of enormous and otherwise unnecessary military expenditure'.

in 1986. Since the Cold War ended, defence spending has dropped to about $265 bn, or less than four per cent of GDP.[51]

The estrangement between Acheson and Kennan holds the key to unlocking the rapidly unfolding events from the autumn of 1949 (the detonation of the first Soviet atomic bomb and the victory of the Chinese revolution) to the winter of 1950 (Sino-American war, defeat in northern Korea, and the quadrupling of defence spending).[52] The war in Korea was the lever ('Korea came along and saved us', in Acheson's famous words) through which Washington finally found a reliable method that would pay the bills for cold and hot wars on a global scale. It also committed American leaders to containment for the long term, rather than to 'liberation' or rollback.

For Acheson, however, the struggle with Communism was but one part, and the secondary part, of a project to revive the world economy from the devastation of the global depression and World War II—just as he had originally suggested in 1939. At first the problem seemed to be solved with the Bretton Woods mechanisms elaborated in 1944, but when by 1947 these had not worked to revive the advanced industrial economies, along came the Marshall Plan for Europe and the 'reverse course' in Japan that removed controls on its heavy industries. When by 1950 the allied economies were still not growing sufficiently, NSC-68 (a document mostly written by Paul Nitze but guided by the thinking of Acheson) hit upon military Keynesianism (or deficit spending on defence) as a device that finally floated economic boats and primed pumps not so much at home, but in Japan and Western Europe.[53]

The Korean War, seen by the North Koreans as a war of national liberation in the face of American attempts to re-stitch South Korea's economic linkages with Japan, turned into the crisis that built the American national security state and pushed through the money to pay for it: the vast procurements for this war constituted a 'Marshall Plan' that worked for Western Europe and especially Japan (whose industrial takeoff began in the early 1950s). From June to December 1950 the defence budget quadrupled (from roughly $13 bn to $56 bn in 1950 dollars), but it did so in the midst of a massive crisis over China's intervention in the Korean peninsula: only with the opening of Sino-American war did Congress finally begin to fund the national security state at the levels to which it has since become accustomed.

This is the least understood element in the crisis of postwar order-making and the long-term, bipartisan consensus on containment. The repositioning of Japan as a major industrial producer in the context of a raging anti-imperial revolution on the Asian mainland, explains much of East and Southeast Asian history for the next three decades (until the Indochina War finally ended in 1975). And here we encounter a human agency the Achesons and the Kennans never imagined: the fierce energy of aroused peoples in the 1940s, collectivities for whom imperialism and a recent feudal past were hated realities, and the promises of the American vision—an utter chimera.

---

[51] US Defense Department numbers, cited in *Boston Sunday Globe*, 11 Feb., 1999, p. B4.

[52] Cumings, *Origins of the Korean War*, vol. 2, pp. 35–61, 408–38.

[53] William Borden, *Pacific Alliance: United States Foreign Economic Policy and Japan's Trade Recovery, 1947–1955* (Madison, 1984), 12–14. Here I also rely on Borden's 'Military Keynesianism in the Early 1950s', a paper presented to my International History Workshop (University of Chicago, 14 February 1994).

The American struggle with successive anti-imperial revolutions—the Korean, the Chinese, and the Vietnamese—is now over, and in today's world, nearly unimaginable. But then each of these conflicts would also have flabbergasted an American statesman, should a mystic have conjured them in a crystal ball in 1945. The Asian orientation of American policy would not have surprised Henry Luce, perhaps, but the cumulative popular resistance to his 'American vision' would have astonished him. Only in the 1970s would he find evidence that East Asia wanted to join the American Century on his terms: actually, on terms rather close to those he enunciated in 1947, as American firms in declining industries like textiles began to move offshore and to organize production in places like South Korea, Taiwan and Malaysia. A new trope signified this extraordinary shift: 'Pacific Rim'. It miraculously appeared and abruptly closed a decades-long debate about a United States at war with Asia from 1941 to 1975.

The Pacific Rim invoked a new-born community that anyone, socialist or not, could join—as long as they began to go capitalist. Here the great victory, accomplished in the two decades since Deng Xiaoping's epochal 1978 reforms, was China: a China increasingly integrated with the world economy, possessing a market of such obsessive concern to American business as to warm the cockles of Henry Luce's heart. As China waxed and Japan waned on American horizons in the 1990s, perhaps the breadth of this American victory can be appreciated in China's beleaguered efforts to polish its application to the WTO, while Washington continues to demand more reform before approving Beijing's entry. The Asian financial crisis beginning in the summer of 1997, of course, put all the hype about the Pacific Rim and the Pacific Century in the shade, making clear the comprehensive breadth of American hegemony as the century draws to a close.

The techno-world and globalization

The grand area has now become the world, as the Communist bloc and the Pacific Rim dissolved into a new configuration: 'Globalization'. For the past few years, as any academic knows, simply including this term in a grant proposal often guarantees success. But this term hides as much as it illuminates; it is often a euphemism for Americanization, just as the 'multinational' corporation began as, and often remains today, an American or Japanese or German corporation operating in other countries (legend has it that IBM originated this euphemism in the 1960s to hide its American base and its virtual global monopoly in computers). Globalization also muffles attention to new circuits of power in the same old places, ones that have grown apace with the upheavals of the microchip.

Why upheavals? Because one settled industry after another has been undone by information age technology. This is most obvious in the quick obsolescence of the hugely-expensive trunk lines, switching stations and home telephone trappings of the big telephone companies. Fibre optics allow twenty times more messages than the old copper wires, as we have seen; digital switches are so capacious that a single smaller country can be handled with one switch; cellular circuits boom throughout the world, and enable a country like China to leapfrog over the cost of putting a wired telephone in every home; satellites beam messages to any point on the globe:

two years ago I was amazed to drive into the Czech Republic from eastern Germany, and to see satellite dishes sprouting from even the poorest homes. The massive deregulation of recent years is both a consequence and a cause of these upheavals, but it has been a key element in freeing up the new technologies.

Hegemony means not having to say you're sorry when massive state investments in the military sphere turn out to have serendipitous benefits for the private sector. Vice-President Al Gore may recently have claimed that he invented the Internet, but in fact it grew out of technologies and software systems pioneered at the Pentagon's Advanced Research Projects Agency. By contrast, Japan's research and development was almost entirely in the private sector. Today it is redundant to argue that Japan is clearly ahead of the US in any cutting-edge technology, and one reason is the one-third of the US federal budget annually going for 'defence'—a euphemism for state-directed research and development.

As early as 1990 Jean-Claude Derian was generally optimistic that the US would retain or regain the global technological lead, because of American prowess in what he calls the 'sheltered culture' of technology: the arena of enormous military-related spending.[54] The US operated in both the sheltered and the exposed (or market) technological culture; Japan, however, has critical weaknesses: Japan has virtually no sheltered culture, a weak scientific tradition, far fewer Nobel prize-winners, and significantly lower absolute levels of research and development expenditure when compared to the US. It is in the 'exposed' technological culture that Japan has done well, where technical acquisition and product innovation rather than discovery of new technologies is the key. Even so, Derian expressed worries about America's technological lead in several areas, like semiconducters, supercomputers, gigaflop processors, high-definition television, and the airbus. By now these deficiencies have been overcome, or no longer matter.

The new information technologies make feasible enormous new networks of power, centralizing control and management in several urban nodes (New York, Los Angeles, London, Tokyo). A key reason for the renaissance of New York City as a financial and cultural capital in the 1990s is its enormous concentration of service industries (accounting, legal, financial especially, advertising, stock markets); services are by far the largest sector in the American economy now (accounting for about 85 per cent of GNP), and yet few appreciate how dominant American firms are in this sector. Susan Strange has shown that the top six accounting firms in the world are all Anglo-American; together they audit fully 494 of the Fortune 500 firms, yielding a combined income of $30 bn a year. Nine of the top fifteen public telephone operators are based in the US, with five more in Europe, and only one in Japan (state-owned Nippon Telephone and Telegraph). Thus North America and Europe accounted for 75 per cent of all telecom revenues in 1993.[55]

As my colleague Saskia Sassen has argued,[56] this process does not weaken national governments and make of our era one in which transnational corporations rule, because only states can legislate the rules of globalization—something evident in the coordination of the US, the UK, and the European Union in legislating the

---

[54] Jean-Claude Derian, *America's Struggle for Leadership in Technology*, trans. Severen Schaeffer (Cambridge: MIT Press, 1990), pp. 5–6, 175, 267.

[55] Susan Strange, *The Retreat of the State: The Diffusion of Power in the World Economy* (Cambridge University Press, 1996), pp. 106, 135.

[56] Saskia Sassen, *Globalization and its Discontents* (New York: New Press, 1998), pp. xii-xiii.

domain and the rules for new internation zones like the EU and NAFTA (united markets for transnational business), thus to support and propel globalization. New arrangements like the World Trade Organization also spring forth to provide a kind of 'governance without government', as political scientist James Rosenau has called it.[57]

American standards of all kinds are the standards of globalization: practices that group under the august category of 'the rule of law' are organizing the globe in their image, through the growth of transnational legal regimes based on Western practices of property rights, contracts, transparency—the highly developed legal framework for the conduct of capitalism, and something on which every global corporation depends. Even the American flag, as a French intellectual observed, is a kind of logo, 'the evidence of a good brand' (a quintessentially Lucean phenomenon).

The champions of the Internet and cyberspace pride themselves on the democratic and egalitarian openness of their transparent electronic sphere: websites spring up overnight, the web has no controlling centre, cyberspace fanatics abhor censorship, and so on. But power also abhors a vacuum. The race will go to the swift here, to those whose economic interests most benefit from instantaneous global connections. Financial services have been quickest to exploit the new communications network, made up of people whose fondest wish is to be bionically capable of everlasting 24-hour workdays, thus to track all the globe's stock markets. Corporations are hierarchical organizations in competitive environments that make transparency anathema; they are opaque, making secret and often unaccountable decisions, with phalanxes of highly-paid lawyers to protect them; meanwhile they demand transparency of everyone else in their environment—especially consumers (who can feel like they have visited a proctologist just by applying for a mortgage), but also entire nations subjected to the prying eyes of the IMF and the World Bank.

This same centralization of power estranges and isolates poorer regions of the world which often lack even the most basic technology of our age, electricity. When President Clinton visited a remote village in Africa in 1998 and urged that the local school connect up to the World Wide Web, he did not appear to notice that the school had no electricity. Using the Web I can find satellite photos of this village, learn the ethnicity of its inhabitants, and count the number of homes with running water. But the villagers cannot see me or the World Bank employees who catalogue such information. And because knowledge is power, they are less free than before the advent of the computer. Instead of homogenizing these Africans, turning them into the Americans they no doubt would like to be (given the alternatives), 'the technological annulment of temporal/spatial distances', in Zygmunt Bauman's words, tends to polarize us and them.[58] A deepening spatial segregation between rich and poor both within countries and in the world as a whole defines our era, and enhances central power just as it peripheralizes those left behind, creating new polarizations of wealth and poverty that have only increased in the past two decades.[59] One of the most striking elements in the recent economic boom in the US is that household income has increased slowly and incrementally while wealth has grown geometrically (especially in stock holdings); household income was basically stagnant from 1975 to

---

[57] Quoted in ibid., p. 98.
[58] Bauman, *Globalization: The Human Consequences* (Columbia University Press, 1998), p. 18.
[59] Ibid., pp. 2–3, 18.

1995, even if it has increased in the past five years.[60] Such a process, of course, yields a massive transfer of wealth from poor and middle classes to the top decile of the population. While some argue that such data proves that American 'decline' continues, it is far better evidence of the power of the owners of capital and expertise. Corporations are mobile while residential communities are not; professionals who are technically competent and well paid move faster than ever, festooned with portable devices to keep them in touch with some centre (portable computers, cell phones, beepers and pagers), while those in nonprofessional jobs, rooted to a place, lose out. The resulting disparities of wealth seem most obvious in a city like New York, where on any given day a pedestrian can observe amazing opulence and well-nigh medieval squalor.

The ubiquitous service sector tends to polarize income between a handful of very high paying positions and a mass of low-paying and often part-time jobs. This creates an enormous problem for the (Keynesian) demand-promotion so essential to maintaining American-style 'shop-'til-you-drop' consumption, because you can't maintain a Lucean middle-class lifestyle on stagnant wages. Much more important, however, is the pressure brought to bear by neoliberal efficiencies on existing social arrangements that were the ubiquitous products of the post-World War 2 settlements in all the industrial countries (the New Deal in the US, the social market in Germany, the cradle-to-the-grave permanent employment and welfare of postwar Japan), which put a floor on poverty and did so much to create huge middle classes. This pressure has now set off a major oppositional movement to neoliberalism and globalization in Western Europe, with intellectuals coming to see the American challenge as a civilizational confrontation, a matter of life and death: how to protect hard-fought gains for the working and middle classes against an untrammelled 'ecumenical gospel' of neoliberalism pioneered by Thatcher and Reagan, but made into his own by the domestic and foreign economic policies of Bill Clinton.[61]

America's contemporary prowess is by no means as popular as the modern liberal doctrine that it did so much to popularize—as editorials like this one from London's centrist *Independent* illustrate:

... the dumb certitude; the contempt for the poor; the facile amiability; the ostentatious religiosity; the callous laws; the love of guns; the Hollywood sensibility; the all-consuming fetish for material success; the showy insubstantiality of its politics; the celebrity junk; the infantile literal-mindedness; and the faith, withal, in America's planetary moral superiority.'[62]

I might be inclined to agree with this critique—I certainly recognize my fellow Americans in it—but so what? The historian in me would point out that the same thing could have been said—and was more than once, by Sinclair Lewis and other writers—back in the Roaring 20s.

---

[60] *The New York Times*, 'How the US Consumer Feels', 4 Jan., 1999, p. C7.

[61] French sociologist Pierre Bourdieu has been most prominent in this regard; he wrote that 'the prophets of neoliberalism and the high priests of the Deutschmark and monetary stability' are promoting 'a sort of universal belief, a new ecumenical gospel'. See Bourdieu, 'A Reasoned Utopia and Economic Fatalism', *New Left Review*, no. 227 (January/February 1998), p. 126.

[62] Cited from the September 1998 *World Press Review*, in James Warren, 'A Rising Chorus of Boos for Uncle Sam', *The Chicago Tribune*, 7 Aug., 1998.

The 'abundant life' and American ascendancy today

Henry Luce's American Century did not begin in 1900, but in 1941. He spoke in the future tense about the creation of 'the first great American century' with the United States as 'the dynamic centre of ever-widening spheres of enterprise'. The last phrase was prophetic: the US remains the driving force and the constantly meta-morphozing core of commercial spheres with axes running east and west and north and south: huge North and South American and Atlantic and Pacific markets. The frontier technology of the past twenty years, symbolized by the microchip, also appears ready to homogenize the world in Luce's image: billions of Third World peoples are now exposed to McDonald's hamburgers and 'Coca-Colonization', as Luce put it in 1950. What can we say about Luce's 'American vision' of uplift for all mankind, articulated so bluntly? Is his hope for global Americanization soon to be realized? I don't think so.

The Third World is dominated by the advanced countries in a way unprecedented since the colonial era, and with most of it outside the loop of the prosperity of recent years, it is therefore the prime source of war, instability, and class conflict—but with no convincing anti-systemic model to follow. All the systemic alternatives to the Grand Area, to the One World of multinational capital, have collapsed: above all the Eastern bloc and the Soviet Union in 1989–91, but also the neomercantile model of East Asian development. But the least noticed collapse of our time is that of the Third World, the site of revolutionary nationalism and anti-imperial wars for three decades after 1945, the self-constituted alternative to both blocs in the Cold War that lasted from Bandung through the Non-Aligned Movement and into the late-1970s demands for a New International Economic Order. Twenty years later we have a collection of failed states running from Zambia to North Korea, an enormous if amorphous population of stateless people from Kosovo to Sudan, and the recurrent television spectacle of millions of people starving to death, from Sudan again to North Korea. The Third World moves not up the developmental ladder, but from statehood to catastrophe.

Today the pot of gold at the end of the developmental rainbow seems everywhere to recede into the future, even for the 'miracle' economies of the Pacific Rim. When the 'Second World' of Communist countries, blocs, and 'iron' and 'bamboo' curtains unexpectedly disappeared a decade ago, so did American indulgence for the neomercantilism of its East Asian allies, which was always a function of the Cold War struggle with their opposites. Since 1993 the 'Clinton Doctrine' has been one of aggressive foreign economic policy designed to promote exports, to open targeted economies to American goods and investment (especially in the service industries that now dominate the American economy and in which it has a barely-challenged global lead), while maintaining the Cold War positions that give Washington a diffuse leverage over its allies like Japan and Germany and that pose a subtle but distinct threat to potential adversaries like China. All this goes on under the neoliberal legitimation of Smithean free markets and Lockean democracy and civil society—that is, Luce's 'American vision'. In this way, apparently autonomous 'Asian tigers', prospering within an indulgent security network for thirty years, find themselves rendered bewildered and dependent by a dimly understood hegemonic mechanism that now places their entire society and economy under global jurisdiction. Today we are left with the daunting reality that among the claimants to comprehensive, advanced industrial status a century ago (England, France, Germany, Italy, the United States, Russia, Japan), there have been no new entrants and only six of the original group remain (with Russia now having an economy smaller than South Korea's).

There is a great exception to this generalization, however, and that is China. Home to one-fifth of the world's population, it has joined the world economy and the developmental race with a vengeance, propelled by double-digit growth rates in the past two decades. Of China's 1.2 billion people, perhaps 300 million are now engrossed in (and indeed obsessed by) Luce's vision of consumer-durable abundance; the well-educated young in cities like Shanghai are fully wired to the Web and fully enthralled by Hollywood mass culture.[63] The world economy centered in the United States is shaking China, and the coming decades will be ones when China— finally—shakes the world. But that is a story for the future.

Conclusion: still the American Century

If England's century began with the Congress of Vienna and ended in 1914, and if America's began in 1941 as Luce thought (and assuming that we get a century like the British did), this means that Americans should only begin to wring their hands and fill themselves with the proper *fin-de-siècle* angst around the year 2040. At the turn of the new century Americans can perhaps revel in the robust middle age of United States' global leadership. Instead of a premature end to the American Century or a coming clash of civilizations, today there appears to be one dominant global civilization, the American, and several atavisms masquerading as civilizational challenges—Islamic fundamentalism, Balkan mayhem, the (not-very) Confucian East, the obsolescing economic nationalism of Japan and South Korea, the declining Chinese Communist grip on a rapidly growing capitalist China, and a Russia that does not clearly appear to have an economy in 1999, let alone a competing civilization. So in this sense, if perhaps only in this sense, Henry Luce was truly a visionary in 1941.

More important, though, were the internationalist presuppositions moulded into the bones of Dean Acheson, Henry Stimson, John Foster Dulles and many others by the collapse of world order in the 1930s. Our 1990s world is the anticipated consequence, the unfolding of an internationalist telos yielding the liberal hegemony that the internationalists envisioned. The boundless global power immanent in the peculiarly American moment of 1945, soon gave way to a global structure based in, and the outgrowth of, the maturing of liberal modernism. Because of the Other— Soviet communism, old-world imperialism, national liberation movements—the boundaries of the system were policed by naval task forces, the nuclear delivery capabilities of air forces, and, above all, the archipelago of American military bases.

---

[63] I document this in *Parallax Visions: Making Sense of American—East Asian Relations at the End of the Century* (Durham, NC: Duke University Press, 1999); see also Thomas Friedman's Op-Ed column, *The New York Times*, March 25, 1999; and Friedman, 'A Manifesto for the Fast World', *The New York Times Magazine*, 28 March, 1999.

But when the Other disappeared, the structure continued in place and, in the 1990s, achieved the full florescence that its planners had imagined in the 1940s.[64] That is, the 'New World Order' that George Bush and many others cast about for after 1989, was both the same old order and the ongoing fulfilment of postwar planning. But the postwar era also embodied a completely unanticipated history that ran through bloody and disastrous wars in Korea and Vietnam, the ongoing reorientation of revolutionary China, and the recent collapse of the Soviet Union—all experiences that would have flabbergasted a statesman seeking to chart the postwar order in 1945, should a clairvoyant have conjured them in a crystal ball.

But that was then and this is now; all that is over and done with. Indeed, we can look back upon even the central mechanism of 1950, the military Keynesianism of NSC-68 that quadrupled defence spending, and see that it was, like the other contingencies, something that did not have to happen. The American archipelago of global bases and the funds necessary to service it have survived the Cold War, but it isn't clear that they will survive the true long peace that we have entered upon since 1989. In the absence of serious alternatives—of any power with the capability to say no and make it stick—the Pentagon's far-flung bases and its hold on one-third of the federal budget may go the way of the USSR, Mao's China and Ho Chi Minh's Vietnam. It is happening already, if only by attrition: as we have seen, defence spending may still be at the Cold War level of $265 bn, but in constant dollars it has fallen from 6.5 per cent of GNP in the mid-1980s to less then four per cent today.

The end of the Cold War precipitated the collapse of the Soviet Union, of course, which was critical to the current American ascendancy. But the way it ended also had a curious and under-appreciated effect on the world system: it finally rectified the disastrous mistakes of the World War I settlement, which detonated a seventy-years' crisis in world politics: the harsh peace for Germany, which bankrupted it and plunged the country into a depression that was fallow ground for Hitler's rise to power;[65] the failure of the US to join the League of Nations, eventually dooming its attempts at collective security in the 1930s; and the 'mistake' of the Bolshevik Revolution, which created an insurgent nation that for seven decades represented 'the anti-system'. Washington and its allies not only rebuilt West Germany after 1945 but enabled the unification of Germany in 1989 (above all by not standing in the way of it), a remarkably soft peace for the aggressor who plunged the world into war in 1939. Then the insurgent Soviet Union removed itself in 1991, along with its European empire. Finally, the allies invigorated the United Nations, by making it fully inclusive of all the great powers in 1945, and an instrument of reasonably effective collective security in the 1990s.

The dramatic events of 1989 and 1991 thus created a world order bereft of insurgent or revanchist great powers bent on righting past wrongs or overturning the system itself (even if plenty of troublesome small nations remain). A certain balance of power holds sway in Europe where three advanced industrial nations of roughly the same size (England, France and Italy, all with GNPs of around $1.25 trillion[66])

---

[64] Cumings, 'The End of the Seventy-Years' Crisis', *World Policy Journal*, 7 (Spring 1991), pp. 195–226.

[65] Hoover, *Ordeal of Woodrow Wilson*, pp. 238–9; Eric Hobsbawm, *The Age of Extremes: A History of the World, 1914–1991* (Vintage Books, 1996), p. 86.

[66] According to the 1999 *CIA Factbook*, available on the Internet, at the beginning of 1998 the GNPs in purchasing power parity were: Italy, $1.24 trillion; United Kingdom, $1.242; France, $1.32; Germany, $1.74; Japan, $3.08; US, $8.1.

constrain the largest power, Germany (which is comparatively not so large, at $1.75 trillion GNP), and all are now enmeshed in the European Union. Japan is much larger (at $3.0 trillion GNP) and might dominate Asia if it had the autonomy to do so, but with the US still providing for its defence, it does not—and in 1999 it continues its decade-long struggle just to find a way to revive its flagging economy. Furthermore, none of these big powers have within them anything like the volatile mix of social forces that brought forward fascism in Germany and Italy, militarism in Japan, or the 1930s popular front in France. In spite of all kinds of predictions to the contrary,[67] unified Germany does not dominate Europe, Japan has not gone nuclear, China discovered the market, France has a world-historical predicament of national identity, and they are all constrained by American power—the only country with global force projection capabilities; the only country whose constituent parts include a state like California, which, if it were a country, would rank just behind Italy in GNP (at nearly $1 trillion).

This, in brief, is the answer to why various 'realists', not to mention Samuel Huntington and Frances Fukuyama, all got it wrong: *realpolitik* does not govern the contemporary actions of the big powers, regional clashes of older civilizations in places like Bosnia mask the burgeoning triumph of modern civilization (to which they are also—and ineffectively—reactive); and the triumph of the liberal programme does not mean 'the end of history' because modern liberalism is itself a heterogeneous, contested, and deeply unfinished business. The post-Cold War order is the outcome, a fulfillment if by a tortuous path, of the plans, hopes, and dreams of the American and Western internationalists who learned the searing lessons of the Depression and the world war that it spawned. The contemporary global financial crisis is another stanza in that same movement, toward the universality of liberal modernist norms and practices. But it may also foretell a new chapter in world history, as the market approaches its full global reach, unfolding in a vacuum of alternatives and therefore testing, perhaps really for the first time, whether the self-regulating market can be the basis for global order—the recipe for a truly long peace, or for a truly unprecedented disaster. A breakdown of the world economy is the biggest systemic threat to world order in our time; it is the singular catastrophe that could revive *all* the apparently vanquished problems. The coming decades will thus test the proposition whether the continuously unfolding movement of liberal world order has a proper claim to universality, or whether it remains merely the partial and limited world view of its original author, the modern middle class, and therefore unavailing to the continuing plight of the world's majority peoples.

---

[67] John Mearsheimer, 'Back to the Future: Instability in Europe After the Cold War', *International Security*, 15:1 (1990), pp. 5–57.

Index

Acheson, Dean   280–1, 284
   and recovery from WW2   291
Adler, Emmanuel   162
annaliste concept   30
APEC regional institution   122, 260, 268
Appadurai, Arjun   55
Aron, Raymond   111, 162, 180, 182
Arrighi, Giovanni   141
ASEAN   101, 146, 268
   regional forum ARF   254
Asia Pacific economic crisis   4, 16, 83–7,
     92, 245
   and Myrdal, Gunnar   246
   and 'Washington consensus'   263

Balkans   49, 103, 177
Bank of International Settlements   70, 121
belle époque   107, 112, 286
Benjamin, Walter   110
Berlin, Isaiah   106
Bolshevik revolution   22, 298
Booth, Ken   163
Brenner, Robert   140
Bretton Woods   67, 250, 257
Brown, Chris   165
Bull, Hedley   99, 161, 218
Burke, Edmund   109
Buzan, Barry   98

Camp David accords   31
Carr, E. H.   161, 162
Castells, Manuel   141
CERDS Rights & Duties charter   226
China   53, 135, 155, 297
Clausewitz, Carl von   13, 162, 180, 182
Cohen, Eliot   177
Cold War   3, 6–11, 21–39, 121, 183, 201–23
Communist Manifesto   134
Congress of Vienna   18, 297
constructivism   23
Cox, Robert   138, 229

'Doctrine of the International Community'
    46
Doyle, Michael   46, 114
de Maistre   109
'democratic peace'   171
Dulles, John Foster   297

Engels, Frederick   134, 141
Enlightenment, the   10, 52, 62, 105–25
   post-Enlightenment   43

European Council   206
European Union   4, 92, 94, 122, 137,
     205–23, 294
   conditons imposed on E. Europe   211
   decision-making problems   213
   enlargement   212–17
   relationship with NATO   219–23
   security issues   202
   trade with E. Europe   212
   'United States of Europe'   208

feminism   11, 118
Fordist production   137, 139, 276
Fukuyama, Francis   3, 5, 8, 42, 45, 50–2,
     91, 97, 114, 156, 158, 273

GATT and East Asia   257
Gellner, Ernest   10, 106, 109, 119
German reunification   298
Gibbon, Edward   167
Gilpin, Robert   250
glasnost   24, 38
Globalization   4, 8, 9, 12, 13, 16, 42, 51,
     55, 59–88, 91–100, 172–4, 292
   and corporate taxation   74–5
   culturally oriented theory   55
   risks inherent in   228
Gorbachev, Mikhail   21, 24, 25, 28, 186
Gramsci, Antonio   139
Gray, John   109
G7, G8   121, 122, 180, 206, 236, 239

Habermas, Jurgen   44, 106, 109, 119, 124,
    147
Havel, Vaclav   14, 43–4, 51, 200
Hegel, Georg W. F.   5, 50, 131–2, 273
historicism   131
Huntington, Samuel   3, 8, 52–3, 96, 103,
    157, 272
   and Atlanticism   282

idealism (in European politics)   205
Ikenberry, John   47–8, 67
IMF   70, 93, 121, 122, 145, 157–8
   and Russia   190, 198
   and Third World   225, 233–5
International legal bodies   100
International organizations (IGOs &
    INGOs)   93–4, 99, 100, 103, 122
Islamic movements   54, 119

James, Alan   99

Japan, economic success   246–9; failure
        273
Johnson Chalmers   81, 248
'juridical sovereignty'   99

Kant, Immanuel   10, 42, 46, 105, 124, 125,
        130, 147
Kennan, George; containment strategy
        290–1
Keohane, Robert   70, 271
Keynes, John Maynard   67–8, 277
Keynesianism   69, 138
Kojeve, Alexandre   5, 51, 131, 156

League of Nations   298
Lenin   41, 116
        Imperialism pamphlet   136
Leninism   22, 25–6
Liberalism   12, 146–7, 153
        liberal idealism   288
        liberal internationalism   45, 51
        'structural liberalism'   147
Liberal democracy   115, 145
        democratic capitalism   11, 145
Linklater, Andrew   132–3
Luce, Henry   17, 269
        and American idealism   278
Lukacs, John   273

Machiavelli, Niccolo   130, 159–60, 162, 182
Mackinder, Sir Halford   173
Mandel, Ernest   137, 140
Marx, Karl   110–11, 117, 127, 141
Marxism   5, 11, 28, 107, 127–44
        as economism   143
        capital as social relation   143
        future of   142–4
Mazower, Mark   109
McCormick, Thomas   271
Mearsheimer, John   3
Mercosur   101, 122
Milosovic, Slobodan   49, 54
Mitchell, Juliet   118
MNCs (multinational co's)   62–3, 77
Morgenthau, Hans   24, 162, 180, 182
multilateralism   14

NAFTA trade association   232
NATO   49, 92, 122, 150–3, 156, 202, 287
        and European enlargement   211–14
        relationship with EU   219–21
neoclassical realism   13, 167
neoliberalism   138–9
neopositivism   37
'New World Order'   12, 46
NIEO (New International Economic Order)
        123, 226

Nietzsche, Friedrich   50
Northern Ireland peace process   6
North–South gap   117

Oakeshott, Michael   109
O'Neill, Onora   148

Pacific Century   16
Pacific Rim   292
perestroika   24
Peters, Ralph   163
postmodernism   10, 118
Prestowitz, Clyde   271
progressivism   51

Rawls, John   147
Realism   10, 11, 22, 90–1, 111, 167
        'modified realist' approach to European
                politics   205
Roemer, John   132
Rorty, Richard   45
Rosecrance, Richard   95, 250
Ruggie, John   155
Russia   13, 14, 45
        liberalization in   190
        privatization in   190, 194

SADC (South African Development
        Corpn.)   101
Sakakiba, Eisuke   8, 51–2
Schmitt, Carl   12, 152–3
Schroeder, Paul   30
Schumpeter, Joseph   277–8
Soviet Union, former USSR   3, 4, 11, 14,
        22–6, 183–200
Strange, Susan   293
Sun Tzu   162, 182

Taiwan – ITRI   78; monetary authority
        82
'Third Way'   45
Third World   15, 225–44
        and capital controls   241
        and CERDS   226
        and corporate accountability   242
        debt burden   237–9
        trade liberalization   239
        transformists and reformists of
                237–44
Thucydides   162, 182

UN   121, 148–53, 287
        Security Council   148
        UNCED   225
        UNDP, UNCTAD   233
Unger, Roberto Mangabeira   155

Wade, Robert   249
Waltz, Kenneth   96
Walzer, Michael   120, 147
Warsaw Pact   32
Weber, Max   110
welfare spending   9, 75–7
westernization   53
Westphalian system   9, 89–104
White, Donald   272
Williamson, John   153

World Bank   70, 121–2, 145, 289
    East Asia Miracle report   256
    and Third World   233–44
    'Washington consensus'   153, 236
World Trade Organization   69, 70, 71, 73,
        93, 94, 157, 158
    and GATT   207
    and Third World   225, 233–4
    and Uruguay Round   234

Yugoslavia   4, 49, 54, 150–3